IRONMAN'S
ULTIMATE BODYBUILDING
ENCYCLOPEDIA

IRONMAN'S

ULTIMATE BODYBUILDING
ENCYCLOPEDIA

IRONMAN MAGAZINE AND PETER SISCO

CB
CONTEMPORARY BOOKS

Library of Congress Cataloging-in-Publication Data

Ironman's ultimate bodybuilding encyclopedia / Ironman magazine and
   Peter Sisco.
            p.   cm. — (Ironman series ; bk.1)
         Includes index.
         ISBN 0-8092-2811-4
         1. Bodybuilding.   2. Physical fitness.   I. Sisco, Peter.
   II. Ironman.   III. Title: Ironman's ultimate bodybuilding
   encyclopedia.   IV. Series.
   GV546.5.I77   1999
   646.7′5—dc21
                                                  99-10352
                                                     CIP

Cover design by Todd Petersen
Cover photograph copyright © Michael Neveux. All rights reserved.
Cover model: Jonathan Lawson
Interior design by Hespenheide Design

Published by Contemporary Books
A division of NTC/Contemporary Publishing Group, Inc.
4255 West Touhy Avenue, Lincolnwood (Chicago), Illinois 60712-1975 U.S.A.
Copyright © 1999 by *Ironman* magazine and Power Factor Publishing, Inc.
All rights reserved. No part of this book may be reproduced, stored in a retrieval
system, or transmitted in any form or by any means, electronic, mechanical,
photocopying, recording, or otherwise, without the prior written permission of
NTC/Contemporary Publishing Group, Inc.
Printed in the United States of America
International Standard Book Number: 0-8092-2811-4

00 01 02 03 04 VL 19 18 17 16 15 14 13 12 11 10 9 8 7 6 5 4 3 2

CONTENTS

FOREWORD

Ironman magazine was founded in 1936 by Peary and Mabel Rader of Alliance, Nebraska. Their first print run of 50 copies was done via a duplicating machine that sat on their dining room table. *Ironman* started out as an educational vehicle to inform and enlighten those people who were interested in weight lifting, bodybuilding, and, eventually, powerlifting.

The focus of *Ironman* magazine during its first 50 years was on all three sports, with emphasis on weight training in general as a life-enhancing activity. *Ironman* has always stressed the health and character-building aspects of weight training and has always been the leader in bringing exercise and nutrition concepts and ideas to those in the training world.

In the early '50s, *Ironman* magazine was the first weight-training publication to show women working out with weights as part of their overall fitness regimen. It even went so far as to show a pregnant woman training with weights and educating readers on the benefits of exercise during pregnancy—thoroughly modern concepts 25 years ahead of its time. In the late '50s and early '60s, *Ironman* magazine was the first to talk about high-quality proteins derived from milk and eggs as well as liquid amino acids. The bimonthly magazine had, by this time, acquired over 30,000 subscribers simply on the strength of its information. The Raders never worked at expanding its circulation. It grew by word of mouth fueled by the general hunger for and *Ironman*'s ability to provide intelligent, timely, and reliable training information.

By the early '80s, the Raders, now in their 70s, had spent nearly 50 years working incredibly long hours to put out a bimonthly publication. The hard work was beginning to take its toll.

I'd been interested in *Ironman* as a business since the mid-'70s and had in fact talked several times with the Raders about purchasing *Ironman*. Eventually, my dream of owning and publishing a bodybuilding magazine was realized, and in August 1986, after 50 years, *Ironman* magazine changed owners. At that time, *Ironman* had a circulation of 30,000 subscribers, no foreign editions, was published bimonthly, and averaged 96 black-and-white pages except for a color cover. Thirteen years later, *Ironman* magazine is published worldwide with an English-language circulation of 225,000 and additional editions in Japanese, Italian, German, Arabic, and Russian.

The books in the *Ironman* series represent the "best of the best" articles from over 60 years of *Ironman* magazine. *Ironman's Ultimate Bodybuilding Encyclopedia*, the first in this series, covers every aspect of bodybuilding physiology, targeting specific bodyparts, training for mass, optimum nutrition, avoiding injuries, and the hard-to-find tricks and secrets from the top champions.

John Balik
Publisher Ironman

ACKNOWLEDGMENTS

I would like to thank the following people who made this book possible:

John Balik, publisher of *Ironman* magazine, had the foresight to see the need for this book and the others in the *Ironman* series. His knowledge of bodybuilding and his sensitivity to the information required by readers has made *Ironman* the best bodybuilding magazine in the world.

Steve Holman, editor in chief of *Ironman*, creates one informative, insightful issue of the magazine after another, and his own articles in this book show ample evidence of his innovation and encyclopedic knowledge of the iron game.

Mike Neveux is the premier bodybuilding photographer in the world. His photos in this book and in every issue of *Ironman* magazine have inspired and motivated countless bodybuilders around the world by capturing the intensity, power, and magnificence of these great athletes.

A special thanks to Terry Bratcher, art director of *Ironman*, who did an enormous amount of work in the preparation of this book by wading through *Ironman*'s immense archive of articles and photographs in order to help bring you the "best of the best."

Finally, I would like to thank all the writers who contributed to this book. These writers have an incalculable collective knowledge of the sport of bodybuilding. This book represents the distilled knowledge of hundreds of man-years of study in every aspect and nuance of the iron game. Between the covers of this book are wisdom and experience that would cost a small fortune to obtain from one-on-one training with these writers. Sadly, some are no longer with us to be able to share their vast insights, making their advice in these pages all the more valuable. It is the thought, effort, and writing of these individuals that make this book and *Ironman* magazine great.

Pete Sisco
Editor

Arnold Schwarzenegger.

Chapter 1

BODYBUILDING FUNDAMENTALS

Bodybuilding is much more than just a competitive sport or a personal interest. It is an activity that pays enormous dividends over an entire lifetime. It is a lifelong activity that actually increases your life expectancy, self-esteem, overall health, and ability to enjoy the physical rigors of a productive life.

The information in this book is the cream skimmed from Ironman *magazine's 60-plus years of reporting on every aspect of bodybuilding. Whether you are a beginner or a future Mr. Olympia, the comprehensive information in these pages has been culled from the most knowledgeable people in the sport who, collectively, have performed millions of workouts and studied every aspect of bodybuilding in order to learn what works best.*

To understand modern bodybuilding's origins, let's first pay homage to its beginning in Venice, California. Listen to Patricia Larsen's account of the early years on "Muscle Beach."

MUSCLE BEACH Patricia Larsen

The *look* is in Venice: the massive arms, the strong legs, the clothes. Arnold's in Venice.

Lou's in Venice. World is in Venice. Gold's is in Venice. You could disappear for a time into the private world of some of the big-screen people and of the more well-known personalities on the contest circuit. There's no mistake about this. It's an attraction for our kind as much as Disneyland is for families and the Sunset Strip is for those who go for more nocturnal pleasures. Take some time at the original Gold's and work out side by side with the contest guys and gals—some with names you recall, others who simply bring about a nod of searching recognition. Catch the day right in World Gym, a couple of blocks away, and you could be seduced into one of the best training sessions of your life merely because of the headliner who's pumping reps across the floor.

Too heady? There is a lot of hype. But at the same time, there are also dozens of regular health disciples with the look in Venice. The phenomena? That's what's not new. What's happening now in Venice is brought to you courtesy of a voracious media starving to provide another fix of fast-forward living. But it's not new.

Steve Reeves.

Arnold takes a break during a chest workout at Muscle Beach.

There was a larger concentration of muscleheads in a smaller space of beach front nearby right after World War II and continuing until the '60s. People found their way there by word of mouth. The early magazines started talking about it, and even more ironmen checked it out. "It" was Muscle Beach, Santa Monica, U.S.A.

A portion of Venice Beach (about two and one-half miles south of Santa Monica) has been officially dedicated as "Muscle Beach." The Los Angeles Parks and Recreation Department backed a ceremony and a contest for men and women. But don't expect a repeat soon—or ever—of what was happening next to the Santa Monica Pier from about 1945 to 1958.

There are some who recall that Muscle Beach really started out as "mussel" beach because of the area's abundant marine life. Something was happening there with the Marines all right—and the sailors, other GIs, and younger guys—and it had nothing to do with seafood.

Joe Gold: "The hotels were used as housing centers for the military at that time. There were a lot of people who passed through the area during the war, men with the Army, Navy, Marine Corps. And for the couple of weeks they'd be at the beach, their units would train 'em. You could see hundreds of men doing calisthenics all up the beach from the Pier." Everybody who passed through during the war, Gold says, came back.

Gold, who was born and raised in East Los Angeles, moved to the beach just for the love of it as soon as he was old enough. The Army "got him" in 1942. He was stationed in Wilmington (near Long Beach), but would return to Santa Monica every chance he got. And then, ironically, Gold was assigned to a military watch right on the Santa Monica Pier.

The actual "founding" of Muscle Beach is an enigma. According to Santa Monica city records, a workout platform was built on the beach in the '30s as a WPA (Work Projects Administration) "time-killer." Some old-timers recall that a lot of transients were around with nothing to do, and the platform provided both work and a recreation facility. Subsequently, the area was adopted by the Santa Monica City Recreation Department. Joe recalls there were gymnastic bars, high rings, and the like, but that everybody around donated money to buy the weights themselves.

Armand Tanny was enrolled at the University of Rochester in New York. "I was accepted for a pre-med program at UCLA," Tanny says. "I left the East never expecting to see another barbell. I was coming down from UCLA (in West Los Angeles) to the beach around nine o'clock one evening. There was a heat wave and I heard this familiar clatter. I came around the corner and there it was: Muscle Beach. And it was packed."

Zabo Koszewski, who came to Muscle Beach via Camden, New Jersey, remembers that the men would put on muscle shows to raise money to provide more equipment for the platform area. There was nothing "official" about this impromptu "dedication" of Muscle Beach. The moniker, thought up by who knows who, wasn't only a spot on the globe, but a way of life. It gave an identity to hundreds of men who make up the history of bodybuilding; men such as the Mr. Americas: Hugo LaBra, John Farbotnik, George Eifferman, Richard DuBois, Steve Reeves, Larry Scott. Zabo chalked up his share of titles, including Mr. California. Seymour Koenig, Mr. California. Jack LaLanne. Weightlifting champions Marvin Eder, Issac Berger, Chuck Arens, Dave Shepherd. And the "greats"

would visit—John Grimek, Paul Anderson. All this activity, in a 200-square-yard area, attracted tens of thousands of people.

Seymour Koenig: "It was like a little Vatican. You could see nothing but a sea of people. We wanted to be there. We just wanted to be doing it. We wanted to be in the winner's circle."

Photographer Art Zeller came in from New York in 1955. "I was straight into bodybuilding. I liked bodybuilding from day one. I started bodybuilding when I saw a picture of Grimek on the cover of *Strength & Health* magazine. It cost 15 cents, I remember. I read

Arnold back at it.

it and said I want to look like that. Imagine being 21 or 22 and living on the beach. Most of the guys were extras in the movies, and the idea was to work just enough and as little as possible. The thought of coming to Muscle Beach and being there with that group, in the sun and working out with weights, was a dream come true. We worshiped strength. You knew what it meant to lift."

"We were the bodybuilders in the movies," Seymour notes. "That's how we made our living. There was camaraderie, and nobody was trying to get ahead of anybody. If someone got a job [at the studios] you'd put in another guy's name and everybody got the word."

"No one wanted to work," Gold says. "We were all there together at the time. We were enjoying ourselves."

They didn't want to work?

"Eight hours a day he'd be at it." [Joe Gold talking about Zabo Koszewski.] "Zabo'd warm up with three or four thousand sit-ups and ten thousand leg raises. That was only the warm-up."

"The training ideas would come from experimentation," Koszewski says. "We worked fast. There were no methods."

The weights were always heavy, according to Koenig. "I would do 10 sets of heavy presses, 10 sets of heavy cleans; then I would go into snatches, then there were 8 or 10 sets of heavy squats. Only after that would I go into the bodybuilding movements, you know, the triceps and biceps and pecs and lats."

"We worked out three hours nonstop, seven days a week," Gold says. "We took some grueling workouts."

Zeller's training partner for a time was Marvin Eder. "I worked out with him, and whatever I did, he doubled it. His average workout was 10 sets of wide-arm chins with 200 pounds hanging on him. He'd do parallel-bar dips with two guys—300 pounds easy—hanging on him. It was unheard of. I won a contest at Muscle Beach—I did one chin with 200 pounds. I did one dip with 300 pounds. He [Eder] did 10 sets of 10 with that weight. When he came out to the beach, he electrified the place. He was something special. People remembered him for years to come."

"I think I spent half my time doing incidental tricks," Tanny remembers, "athletic feats like backward somersaults, tumbling, inverted iron crosses on the rings, and all kinds of things. We all excelled just to prove we were good at anything, not only bodybuilding. I won a thousand dollars once."

"Let's put it this way," Zeller says. "Bodybuilding for us was a tremendous amount of fun. It was a way of life. Contests were incidental."

"I can't believe today," Koszewski observes, "that if you're in one contest you wouldn't be ready for another contest two weeks later, because it's all drugs now . . . once you were in shape then, that was it."

Koenig points out that besides weight training for several hours, there was also some running. "But it was very casual," Koenig says. "Perhaps some sprints, and you'd hit the surf a couple of times a day and then go back to working out and throw in some chins and dips . . . like an encore."

Robby Robinson.

Acrobats came from all over the world, circus performers, ice skaters, flying adagio artists, human pyramid balancers, dancers, everyone in show business. "They'd all come to Muscle Beach because it was outside and they could get a real workout," Gold says. "It was a spontaneous, tremendous, free attraction; and we, the local people, would practice and train with them. You'd train on the beach for a number of years, and it would be very difficult to go back indoors again. There was always a visiting entourage of wrestlers, those cavaliers of come-on. The game was tug-of-war. Hans Steinke, Jim Londos, Bill Markus. They'd tug the hell out of you," Gold says. "You'd put your head down real close to the chest and it was a real workout with these guys tugging at you."

One of the ultimate strength tests involved a small, portable parallel-bar platform that was only about two feet high and perhaps four feet wide. It was simply four six-by-six boards nailed in a rectangle shape with pipes attached for hand-balancing. Balancing came second, however, to its "plow" function. The test was to push the equipment through the soft sand

from the workout platform to the water's edge and push it back. "It was real low to the ground," Gold explains, "and your thighs would pump up to unbelievable proportions—if you made it, that is. A man could throw up pushing the plow."

Joe Gold: "Basically, as we got older, we all became successful at whatever we did. It wasn't a 'wasted' youth at all."

Art Zeller: "We were young and we didn't worry about the future, because we knew we'd always have time to work and get serious later. It was a Camelot."

Seymour Koenig: "There was this camaraderie. We were friends, we worked out together, and each one worked out as hard as he could, all the time."

Armand Tanny: "It was a phase. Bodybuilding was already on its way. It was a remarkable haven."

Zabo Koszewski: "My friend and I took off on a vacation [1950]. We were driving. Went to Florida and got to Los Angeles. I saw Muscle Beach and thought, well, I'll just stay here."

Bradley J. Steiner provides some excellent fundamental advice for all bodybuilders. Even experienced lifters would do well to consider his words on flexibility of training methods. Understand the fundamentals and, as Steiner says, trust yourself.

TRUST YOURSELF Bradley J. Steiner

There's an ancient saying that goes, *You cannot step twice into the same river.* Change seems to be an integral aspect of everything in this world. The human body, for example, renews itself cyclically; no one is ever the same person he or she was yesterday.

Training should reflect the fact that we change from day to day. Ideally, each workout should be tailored to precisely what we are at the time of the workout. By becoming sensitive and alert to exactly what your body and mind need on any given training day and by coming as close as possible to providing that, you will achieve a wonderful style of personal training.

Obviously, beginners need a planned, scheduled, carefully mapped-out routine until they've built a solid foundation of muscle and strength. Beginners don't know themselves

Ronnie Coleman.

Cory Everson.

very well, in the training sense, and need a structured program to make progress.

Once you've put on muscle and eliminated weak links in both physique and strength—usually after working out for 6 to 18 months—you can start using a more individualized training plan. At that point, you can start tailoring each workout so it specifically matches where you are that day. You need to truly experience your workouts, rather than just go through them mechanically.

I've discovered that many trainees are, in essence, reluctant to trust themselves. They gladly hand over a lot of cash to personal trainers (who can rarely, if ever, do for their clients half of what they claim) in order to get workouts tailored to the clients' individual readiness to work out. A really good trainer (and there are some) can sense what his or her clients require in general. The clients themselves, if they would make the effort, could almost always determine what they require.

Trust yourself. If you've been training in a systematic and disciplined way for a year, you can be your own trainer—and you'll be more effective than anyone you can hire for the job.

SET YOUR GOALS

The first step in getting the most from each workout is to know what you're trying to achieve and to think of the workout as a step toward that objective. Be realistic about your goals. Don't try to imitate someone else's training. Look at yourself as the unique individual you are.

SELECT A GOOD ROUTINE

Your routine should consist of what you know and feel will work best for you. While you should choose exercises from the basic movements, that's not as restrictive as it may seem. For example, you can do power cleans on a day when your customary deadlifts appear more onerous than enticing. Just make sure that power cleans work well for you. If they don't, try another basic movement that does—

"The Myth," Sergio Oliva.

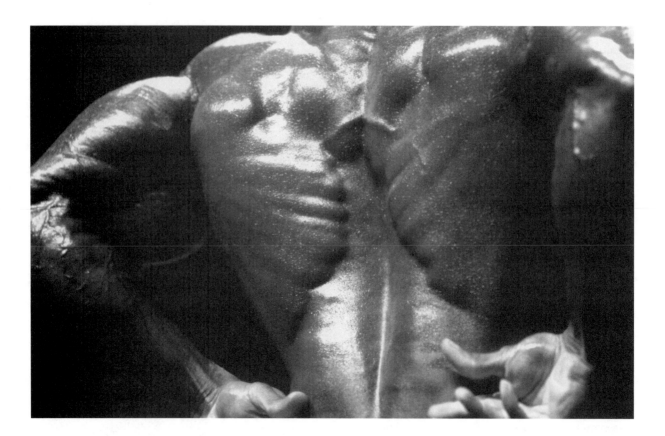

maybe stiff-legged deadlifts, high pulls, or good mornings. Maybe your body will respond well to the great but currently almost unheard of barbell teetotum exercise. If so, go for it.

Personally, I've always favored total-body workouts. I believe they produce the best results. If splitting your routine works better for you, do that. You are the expert on your body.

TRAIN FLEXIBLY

Don't approach a workout with the idea that you're going to do such-and-such in this-or-that way, regardless of how you feel. Your workout should be just what your mind and body need at that time. I've seen many trainees miss workouts because they couldn't train on a given day the way they expected to be able to train. That's crazy. Adjust the day's workout. Doing a different workout doesn't mean failure, and it's certainly better than no workout at all.

A lot of people may feel uneasy with this idea. You may fear that you won't work hard enough. Based on my experience, I predict that you'll train harder overall—but you'll do it on days when you're ready for it. On days when you have less energy or power, you'll modify your efforts. You'll go with the flow. You won't become a shirker, however. That I can guarantee.

How can I guarantee it? Because your body will be receiving what it needs when it needs it, you'll build greater strength and better condition. That, in turn, will result in a greater capacity for training. With more strength and the enthusiasm that comes from success, you'll happily push harder for increasingly greater progress.

Each workout should be a live experience of working with yourself. You'll discover progress that will amaze you. Try it. As the immortal John Grimek once wrote, you ought always to strive to enjoy your training. Anyone who knew him knew that Grimek had training know-how. Believe in yourself. Have confidence in yourself. Once you've built a foundation, use what you've learned to train sensibly and individually for the rest of your life.

Richard Winett, Ph.D., who specializes in training information for "masters" (over 40 years of age), has a blueprint for gaining muscular bodyweight that applies equally to younger bodybuilders.

BLUEPRINT FOR GAINING MUSCLE
Richard Winett, Ph.D.

Virtually all athletes, including bodybuilders, are most interested in reducing bodyfat and becoming leaner to improve appearance and performance. In fact, the most letters and calls I've ever received from any of the *Ironman* columns I've done were sparked by the ones on bodyfat reduction. Those responses support my contention about the importance of a sleek appearance.

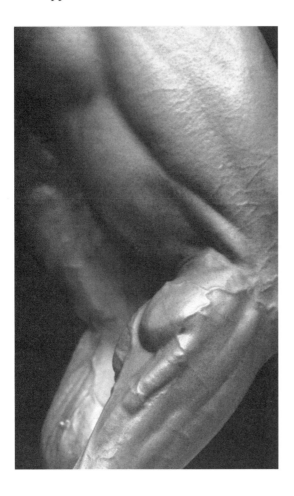

But let's face reality. We're all interested in building muscle. We all realize the importance of reducing bodyfat and becoming fit. But there's supposed to be a part two—muscle building. This discussion is devoted to my recent personal experiences in trying to do what, until lately, many experts thought was not possible—add muscular bodyweight in the middle years after many, many years of hard training.

First, let's define the phrase *gaining muscular bodyweight.* By this, I mean adding weight when most of the gain is muscle mass; that is, you gain weight; but your percentage of body fat remains virtually the same. Within reason, anyone can gain weight; but unless they follow a carefully thought-out plan, most people will not gain weight that is 80 to 95 percent muscle mass.

In addition, after you've trained for a long time (for example, more than seven years) and are reasonably muscular, it's difficult to add muscular bodyweight. Indeed, as I suggested at the start of this article, until recently most experts thought that at best, masters could just fight to hold on to what muscular bodyweight they already had.

Here are some guidelines for gaining muscular bodyweight as a mature athlete:

1. Start the process of gaining muscular bodyweight only after you are already very lean and muscular (for you) at a lower bodyweight. In other words, start at a point at which you're satisfied with your muscularity.
2. Plan for very small gains in bodyweight over a relatively extended period of time. For example, set as a goal gaining one to two pounds of lean mass per month.
3. In order to gain one to two pounds per month, you need to consume only 3,500 to 7,000 extra calories a month. That's right—you only have to eat about 120 to 240 additional calories per day.
4. To make sure you're on track, however, monitor your calories for 10 days prior to starting your weight-gain effort—

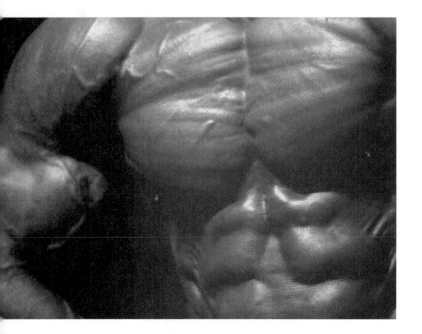

just as you would if you were beginning a weight-loss diet. You'll want to have a very good estimate of how many calories it takes per day, on average, to maintain your bodyweight at your present level of activity.

5. Continue to keep track of your calories each day during your weight-gain program. Simply add 120 to 240 calories per day to the average you calculated for the 10-day period prior to starting the program, and you'll know exactly how much you should be eating.

6. Keep your diet very low in fat, high in complex carbohydrates, and moderate in protein. Guideline percentages would be 10 to 15 percent of calories from fat, 65 to 80 percent of calories from carbohydrates, and 10 to 25 percent of calories from protein. For a simpler approach, try 10 percent from fat, 20 percent from protein, and 70 percent from carbohydrates. An even simpler approach—if your fat intake is low and you're eating a good, well-rounded diet with plenty of fruits, vegetables, and grains—is to get a good estimate every day of your total calories before you start, and add a small amount of food to your diet.

7. Since you only need to eat an additional 120 to 240 calories per day, your added food can easily be a few pieces of fruit, or bread, or an extra serving of cereal, rice, or pasta. There's no need to take any special supplements.

8. Be consistent. Always try to reach your calorie goal for the day. If you fall short on one day, try eating a little extra food over the next day or two to compensate for the shortfall.

9. If the weight gain is going to be converted into muscular bodyweight, you must train very hard. If you slack off on your workouts, you won't add muscle mass. Likewise, if you overtrain, you won't add muscle mass.

10. The best training prescription for gaining muscle is to concentrate on getting stronger. Even so, you should follow a periodization program that features different repetition ranges, sets, and intensity. Since you want to avoid incurring overtraining injuries while you're becoming stronger, your specific prescription involves very short, higher-intensity routines.

11. Continue with your aerobic training. Reducing your aerobics makes gaining weight easier, and you'll burn fewer calories; but you'll also lose fitness and possibly add more fat than muscle through your weight-gain program.

Continue to gain weight for as long as you remain muscular. Once you begin to lose your muscular appearance, it's time to stop gaining. In fact, you may want to lose one to two pounds to regain your muscularity.

For most people, however, it's more appropriate to gain muscular weight during a several-month period of very close dietary monitoring and hard training. Once you've added the lean muscle, your goal for the next several months becomes maintaining your weight gain and muscular appearance. If you feel you can still put on more muscular weight, repeat the process three to six months later. In other words, you want to gain and maintain, and then gain and maintain some more.

Joe Mullen has some excellent advice on how to get rapid results. Here are some important points on setting goals, understanding the role of genetics, recordkeeping, and getting maximum results with minimum effort.

SET THE STAGE FOR RAPID RESULTS Joe Mullen

Beginning bodybuilders are often faced with the same problem as astronomers: creating order out of chaos.

Back when I was a novice bodybuilder, things were a lot simpler. Bodybuilding advice could be found only in two or three monthly bodybuilding magazines.

There were fewer champions, fewer opinions, fewer associations, and more camaraderie. Now everyone has a secret method, a point of view, a muscle-building product, a mail-order course, and/or a clothing line.

Understandably, beginning muscle builders can become confused by the sheer volume of contradictory information available. Yet designing a training program is quite simple, once common sense is applied to the problem.

The components of a properly designed beginner's program (in fact, the components apply to all programs) are as follows:

- Defining goals
- Assessing your present state of health
- Analyzing your genetics
- Training specifically
- Acquiring useful knowledge
- Getting maximal results from minimal exercise
- Keeping accurate records

DEFINING GOALS

A *goal* can be defined as a rational, preplanned result. They can be short-term, say one to three months; or long-term, say one year or more. It's important that goals be realistic. Nothing is more self-defeating than expecting too much too soon. *Any* progress toward your goals is progress. As long as you progress steadily, you will eventually reach your goal. Patience is the most important virtue in weight training.

The complexities of the human body are such that any statements about "what to expect" are pure guesswork based on the so-called average person—whatever that means. Each of us is unique. Our genetics and body chemistries vary from slightly to dramatically when compared to each other. Our activity levels are different, as are our lifestyles. So specific goal expectations will be achieved sooner in some cases and later in others. But they will be achieved.

ASSESSING YOUR PRESENT STATE OF HEALTH

Exercise can be dangerous. In fact, exercise can kill you. That's why it is recommended that one talk with her or his physician before undertaking an exercise program—especially if it is to be of a high-intensity nature.

These are dangerous words. What is high-intensity for one could be low-intensity for another. For a person recovering from a heart attack, the act of walking can be high-intensity. But it can have little conditioning effect on someone in reasonable shape. Don't guess about your health; have a thorough physical examination before you undertake a fitness program.

ANALYZING YOUR GENETICS

Genetics, more than any other factor, determines your ability to reach personal goals. Genetics in the bodybuilding sense refers to the following:

- Bony framework—the length, width, and circumference of bones
- Origin and insertion of muscles (length)
- Cross-sectional muscle diameter (width)
- Neuromuscular innervation (governs the action potential of muscle contraction)
- Digestion
- Assimilation (the chemical use of muscle-building nutrients)

Mike Christian.

Of these factors, only digestion and assimilation can be controlled. You can, however, take advantage of the others, which all relate to how you look in the mirror.

Take advantage of your genetics by bringing your body into muscular balance with corresponding strength balance between similar muscle groups. Traditionally, bodybuilders do not use this approach. Instead, they exercise the total body, emphasizing the genetically gifted areas. The net effect is imbalance, both visually and in the strength relationships of muscle groups to each other.

Muscle imbalance can be the cause of distress, ranging from lower-back problems to "round shoulders." Strength imbalances such as overdeveloped chest muscles and under-developed upper-back muscles can create the round-shouldered appearance. Like a great sculptor, always keep an eye on proportion and sculpt balance into your physique.

TRAINING SPECIFICALLY

You must decide which bodyparts play a paramount role in your goals—then specialize. If bodybuilding is your goal, then all body segments must be considered and balanced. If it's improvements in sports you're seeking—soccer, for example—design a program to concentrate on the muscles involved. Obviously, there is no reason to build big biceps to enhance soccer playing. Train specific to your goals.

ACQUIRING USEFUL KNOWLEDGE

Acquiring useful knowledge is a difficult task for a beginner. There are many sources of information, and it will take a while to separate the good, the bad, and the ugly. One of the best places to find legitimate information is in a local medical library. Many hospitals have excellent medical-information centers that are of great benefit, and most of their information is unbiased.

Shawn Ray.

GETTING MAXIMAL RESULTS FROM MINIMAL EXERCISE

Logically, any exercise beyond the minimum required to stimulate results is wasted time and effort. Too much exercise can overtax the recuperative ability of the muscles and, in effect, prevent rapid progress.

Here are six excellent basic exercises that together make a good routine.

Squat, machine squat, or leg press
Bench press
Pulldown to front or chin
Military press
Upright row
Parallel-bar dip

THE EXERCISES

If you are just beginning bodybuilding, the routine listed above will be a perfect starting point. Here is a description of each exercise:

Squat

Take a loaded bar off a rack and onto your shoulders. Take two steps back away from the rack and position your feet about shoulder-width apart with feet angled slightly outward. Squat down until the thighs are parallel to the floor, then drive back up to the start position. Be sure to look straight ahead throughout the movement to prevent the back from arching or rounding, and never bounce out of the bottom position.

Bench press

Recline on a flat bench and take a loaded bar off the rack with a slightly wider than shoulder-width grip. Unlock your arms and slowly lower the bar to mid-chest level, keeping the elbows out away from your body to maximize pectoral action. Without a pause, ram the bar back to arm's length while keeping your hips down.

Pulldown

Grab the pulldown bar with a slightly wider than shoulder-width grip. While arching your low back, pull the bar down to mid-chest level; elbows should be back behind the torso in the contracted (bottom) position. Hold this contracted position for two seconds, then return to the stretch position.

Lee Haney.

As few as six exercises in your workouts can produce maximum results. Select exercises that are multijoint movements (sometimes called *compound movements*). These movements involve muscle contraction around more than one segment.

As an example, close-grip pulldowns and parallel-bar dips are multijoint movements, and they involve more than one muscle group. Barbell curls and triceps extensions are examples of single-joint movements, contracting fewer total muscle groups than the multijoint movements.

So, for a beginner to stimulate mass body growth (upper-body, lower-body, or both), basic multijoint exercises are best.

Squat—start position.

Ronnie Coleman.

Squat—finish position.

Machine, or hack, squat—start position.

Machine, or hack, squat—finish position.

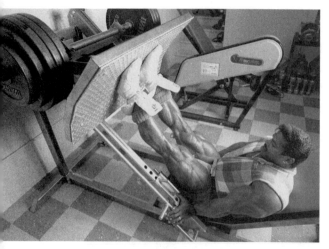

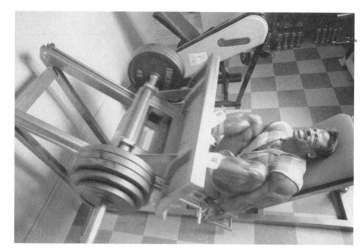

Leg press—start position.   Aaron Baker.   Leg press—finish position.

Arnold checking his leg development with Ken Waller.

Military press

Either take a loaded bar off a rack, or clean it to shoulder level. From this position, drive the bar overhead while keeping your torso as perpendicular as possible. Lower to the upper chest and repeat.

Upright row

Grab a barbell with a shoulder-width grip. Stand erect and pull the bar to chin level. Lower to the arms-extended position and repeat.

Dip

Get up on some parallel bars with arms locked. From here, lower slowly until your upper arms break parallel, then ram yourself back up to the arms-locked position. Try to keep your elbows angled slightly away from the body throughout the exercise. Also, if

Ronnie Coleman.

Bench press—start position.

Bench press—finish position.

Undergrip pulldown to front—start position.
Jean-Pierre Fux.

Undergrip pulldown to front—finish position.

Wide-grip chin—start position.   Henrik Thamasian.

Wide-grip chin—finish position.

you're too weak to do eight dips, do as many as possible, then do negatives; simply put a bench behind you so that you can lift yourself into the arms-locked position with your legs. Then, from the top, lower slowly (about six seconds) to the bottom and repeat.

While most of these exercises can be done with barbells, I'd advise using machines because of the increased safety and adjustability. Also, the production of force in one direction produces a counterforce in the opposite direction, and exercise performed on machines

Arnold performs the military press on a Smith machine.

Upright row—start position.　　　B. J. Quinn.

Upright row—finish position.

can allow the transference of the counterforce to be supported by the pads rather than the body.

Proper body support and positioning will enhance overall training, reduce potential injuries, and allow maximum poundages to be used safely and securely.

Speed of movement

Speed of movement during exercise is one of the most misunderstood components of exercise. The most common mistake is to move too quickly. Men, in particular, equate potential progress with the amount of weight being hoisted. The so-called cheating method, which is touted by some bodybuilders, is a waste of time. While it is claimed that this method will allow the muscles to use more weight than they normally would, the effect is just the opposite.

Attempting to curl more weight by bending slightly forward and then backward while swinging the weight throughout the motion will not make the upper-arm muscles work harder. Using the lower-back muscles to increase the momentum (speed of movement) while reducing the muscle contraction input is counterproductive. Muscles can either lift the weight or not. Throwing weight is a great ego trip, if that's your goal, but there is a difference between a strict curl using the arm muscles and an underhand power clean using just about everything except the arm muscles.

Proper muscle contraction involvement requires strict adherence to style of performance. Proper style mandates a controlled speed of movement.

Dip—start position.   Justin Brooks.

Dip—finish position.

Mike Mentzer.

Johnny Moya and Robert Russo.

The exercises listed in this article are most productive when performed with a four-second lifting and a four-second lowering count. This speed of movement ensures proper style, reduces the amount of cheating, eliminates potential injuries, ensures excellent muscle contraction, and focuses on proper weight use.

Sets and reps: The numbers game

How many sets and reps are required? Chances are, nobody really knows. Results have been achieved using varying sets and reps. Beginners should limit their sets to no more than two. Take one set to warm up your mind and body, and work to failure on the second set.

There is no magic number of reps that can guarantee results. Each of us is different in that a certain number of reps is enjoyable to do and other amounts are not enjoyable. Our minds are attuned to certain numbers that "feel good" to perform. Because muscles perform better when warm, several reps will be required to warm the muscle to enhance its performance and help prevent injury.

Beyond the warm-up, it may not matter at which point you reach muscular failure. So, depending on your mind-set, pick a number that you like.

Let's say, on average, it takes 4 to 6 reps to warm the muscle (depending on your age) and a few more to reach temporary failure. Therefore, 8 reps can be used as our minimum-rep guideline.

Next, you must select a number of reps that can be considered your maximum-rep cutoff. A maximum-rep cutoff is used to gauge progress and to signal you to increase resistance. If, for example, you are using 8 reps as your minimum, then you can stay with a certain resistance until you perform several reps above the minimum—anywhere from 2 to 4 more—within a set.

Arnold Schwarzenegger.

If 10 reps is as high as you enjoy going, that's fine. If you prefer to work up to 15 reps, so be it. After all, exercise is supposed to be enjoyable. The important thing is to do as many reps (in good style) as possible. If you reach or exceed the maximum-rep cutoff you set for yourself, that's the signal to increase the resistance slightly before you do that exercise again.

When you do increase resistance, do it in very small increments. Small increments will allow you to match or exceed your previous attempt at each exercise.

To accurately measure your progress, multiply the amount of weight you are using by the amount of reps you performed. Each time you do this, the total arrived at should increase. Large increases in resistance will decrease your total effort dramatically.

KEEPING ACCURATE RECORDS

Accurate recordkeeping is essential to bodybuilding progress. You should log the obvious things like sets and reps, but you should also jot down "start time" and "finish time." If you are decreasing the time factor, that's a good signal. If your workouts keep taking longer, that's a signal that you are wasting valuable time.

Bodybuilding can be an enjoyable and rewarding pastime. All you need to do is let common sense prevail. Remember, you are a unique individual; design your workouts accordingly.

Chapter 2

BODYBUILDING PHYSIOLOGY

Most serious bodybuilders are also armchair physiologists. This is born from a need to understand the entire muscle-growth process and how it is linked to genetics, bone structure, hormone secretion, and other related elements.

This chapter gives you an invaluable overview of the elements of physiology you need to be aware of in order to keep your growth on track and your expectations realistic. For example, here Bradley J. Steiner shows you the relationship between your bone structure and your bodybuilding potential.

YOUR BONE STRUCTURE AND YOUR POTENTIAL   Bradley J. Steiner

Not everyone can achieve championship status as a lifter or bodybuilder. The limitations faced by people in their quest for strength and development are to a certain extent the result of heredity, whatever the advertisements for programs, courses, and routines may claim. Now, I'm not being negative or pessimistic about this—I'm being realistic and honest. If you pay attention to what I'm saying, I just may save you tons of grief.

As I've often said, anyone can develop greater strength by working out regularly and realistically. That doesn't mean, however, you'll automatically be transformed into a Hercules. Hardly. Among the factors that influence just how big and strong and well-built you can become is the matter of bone structure. There are essentially three major physical types: ecto-morph, mesomorph, and endomorph. In simple English, that translates to small-boned, medium-boned, and heavy-boned people.

Most people are not exclusively one type. Rather, they are predominantly ecto-, meso-, or endomorphs with some characteristics of the other types. The prevailing type determines developmental potential. The late, great Paul Anderson is an example of an extreme endomorph. Model Kate Moss is probably a good representative of an ectomorph.

Obviously, the person who has a very heavy-boned structure is most likely to excel in competitive powerlifting. Someone like the magnificent Dr. Terry Todd is a clear example of what someone born with a heavy structure can do when he trains well and with discipline.

It is, however, absolutely impossible for someone with a light frame—no matter what diet, training, or formula he or she follows—to achieve similar development.

On the other hand, the extreme endomorph will have a problem if he or she wants to achieve great bodybuilding results rather than powerlifting attainments. The endomorph really can't develop the pleasing athletic proportions of the ideal mesomorphic trainee. I'd categorize someone like Reg Park as predominantly mesomorphic with endomorphic tendencies, which accounts for his unbelievable physical development (real, not steroid induced) coupled with a matchless physique. Park was a powerhouse extraordinaire, as well as a well-built lifter.

Most who excel in bodybuilding are mesomorphs. Nature has given these people naturally good proportions. They are easy gainers. They generally take to any athletic activity, but if they take up weight training, their photos usually grace the covers of magazines. That

doesn't mean they don't train hard. Without hard and long training, even an extremely blessed mesomorph will not achieve extraordinary development.

Now we come to the ectomorph—the small-boned trainee. Since I am one, I tend to be especially interested in that group. To my knowledge, the only ectomorph who ever won a major bodybuilding contest and whose strength was really impressive was Jules Bacon. You can't remember how long ago he was Mr. America? My point exactly. Given today's standards, I don't believe we'll ever see another small-boned lifter or bodybuilder reach the top in competition.

If you're truly small-boned, no training program or diet will alter the fact. Don't be deceived by the advertisers that claim their products or courses "build a champion." Frankly, I've never been too upset about my status as a hard gainer. I love weight training passionately, and I've been at it since 1963. I want to encourage anyone of my "type" to go

Joe Spinello is an example of a meso-endomorph.

Dave Palumbo.

Aaron Baker.

for it. Don't be concerned with the results; just develop yourself.

As an ectomorph, I've had to discover the best ways for a small-boned person to train. Here are some tips:

- Don't use extended, complex workouts.
- Focus on brief, hard, heavy training.
- Use the basic exercises.
- Get enough sleep and rest between workouts.
- Follow a balanced, nutritious diet, including the proper supplements.
- Concentrate only on your unique capacity to respond to training. Don't waste time following programs concocted for totally different people.

As you begin to achieve the maximum development your heredity will allow, you'll be overjoyed. Health, well-being, self-confidence, and improved performance capacity for whatever you do are rewards above and beyond sheer power and muscle size. Those are important lifetime goals, and they're yours if you train properly.

Author Jerry Brainum gives bodybuilders a crash course in endocrinology in this article.

HORMONE WARS Jerry Brainum

While you may not be aware of it, a struggle for biochemical domination is occurring within you. The victor of this war ultimately determines whether you make muscular gains or lose muscle and even get fat. The two combating armies are collectively called *anabolic* and *catabolic* hormones. The most familiar of them from a bodybuilding perspective are testosterone (anabolic), growth hormone (anabolic), insulin (anabolic), and cortisol (catabolic).

Anabolic refers to the metabolic building processes. The actions of anabolic hormones involve either an increase in muscle protein synthesis or a decreased breakdown of muscle

Henrik Thamasian and Shelby Cole.

protein. Increased breakdown of muscle is the chief characteristic of catabolic reactions. You would think that since cortisol, the body's primary catabolic hormone, is so outnumbered by the anabolic forces, it would be more or less an ineffectual player in the hormonal battle between anabolic and catabolic reactions, but that isn't the case.

Since cortisol, a product of the adrenal gland cortex, is a primary stress hormone, it's activated by any type of stress the higher brain centers that govern its release perceive. Since stress is ubiquitous, the body is constantly secreting cortisol, with peaks in the early-morning hours and a low during the initial stages of deep sleep.

While cortisol has gotten a bad reputation among bodybuilders due to its potent catabolic activity and tendency to promote body-fat accretion, it's also essential to life. During stress reactions, it's the first line of defense in (among other functions) maintaining energy levels and blood pressure. While such reactions can be lifesaving under certain circumstances, the results are hardly desirable when you're resting or after you exercise. They include muscle loss, mineral excretion, sodium retention, and other enemies of the bodybuilding process.

For natural bodybuilders, meaning people who eschew all forms of pharmaceutical bodybuilding assistance, controlling cortisol is vital for muscle gains. Note the use of the word *controlling*. You don't want to totally eliminate cortisol activity in your body, as that would be a life-threatening condition.

The key is to control the catabolic reactions induced by cortisol while emphasizing the anabolic processes that promote increased muscle growth. You do that by upping your body's production of the endogenous anabolic hormones mentioned previously by both following a sensible training program and using certain specific nutritional substances and diet techniques.

Let's get one thing straight, however. No natural food or supplement can match the power of drugs such as anabolic steroids. Such steroids promote muscle gains through two primary mechanisms:

1. Increased muscle protein synthesis
2. Decreased catabolic reactions in muscle

The first mechanism involves a genetic alteration of certain protein-synthesizing enzymes that simply can't be duplicated by any known food supplement; however, the second process, *anticatabolism*, can be manipulated without drugs.

Research concerning the mechanisms of anabolic steroids shows that most of their effects come from their anticatabolic activity. The upgraded protein synthesis is relatively ephemeral, lasting only a few weeks at best. After that it's all anticatabolic, as the steroids somehow counteract the actions of cortisol in muscle.

Exactly how they accomplish this anticatabolic activity is still subject to debate. While

Craig Licker.

some people say that steroids block cellular cortisol receptors in a manner similar to the way another drug, Nolvadex, blocks estrogen cell receptors, that doesn't add up. For one thing, muscle tissue contains at least 50 times more cortisol receptors than androgen receptors, the receptors anabolic steroids interact with. A more plausible explanation is that such steroids can interfere with cortisol activity in muscle, most likely at the gene level.

HOW CORTISOL BREAKS DOWN MUSCLE

Understanding cortisol's catabolic activity in muscle provides some insight into the way certain food supplements may help spare muscle by inhibiting it. Cortisol is known to reduce body protein stores in all tissues except for the liver. It does that through several mechanisms, including a reduction in the synthesis of cellular RNA, which is essential for protein synthesis. Since anabolic steroids promote muscle

protein synthesis by increasing RNA, cortisol has exactly the opposite effect.

Cortisol mobilizes amino acids from muscle for transport to the liver, where they undergo a process called *gluconeogenesis* that results in increased glucose production. While this is vital for a rapid source of energy during severe stress, it also results in muscle breakdown. Insulin opposes cortisol in the action, but high-stress activity promotes cortisol domination over insulin.

Recent studies show that consuming carbohydrates and protein immediately following a workout both increases insulin release and potently blunts cortisol. The dosage of carbs required for this effect is 1 gram per kilogram (2.2 pounds) of bodyweight taken immediately after training and again one hour later. In addition, including at least 50 grams of protein helps maximize insulin release.

Cortisol appears to promote the synthesis of a protein-degrading substance called *ubiquitin* that rapidly breaks down muscle. Interestingly, a drug called Clenbuterol that's

Craig Licker.

B. J. Quinn.

favored by some bodybuilders may work by inhibiting ubiquitin synthesis in muscle, thereby exerting an anticatabolic effect. Other hormones, such as growth hormone and insulin-like growth factor 1 (IGF-1), appear to inhibit the ubiquitin system as well.

Cortisol also works by stimulating the exit of the amino acid glutamine from muscle. When that occurs, rapid muscle catabolism follows. Several studies show that taking supplemental glutamine may block much of the catabolic effect of cortisol in muscle. The problem is, many of the studies that show anticatabolic effect of glutamine used intravenous solutions containing a stable dipeptide—up to 40 grams of glutamine in a complex with another amino acid, alanine.

If you attempted to take that quantity of glutamine orally, most of it would not reach your blood or muscle. Intestinal cells, which are replaced about every three days as they slough off during the process of food movement through the digestive organs, use glutamine as fuel. When you take it orally, about 85

percent of the dose goes to the intestinal cells. Even if it were somehow to survive the intestinal hijacking, the liver has enzymes just waiting to degrade the rest of it.

Nevertheless, a study conducted about two years ago showed that as little as two grams of oral glutamine significantly increased growth hormone release. That alone would give you an anticatabolic effect, since growth hormone opposes the actions of cortisol in muscle. In fact, studies indicate that decreasing cortisol release in the body results in an upgraded growth hormone response.

Some preliminary studies show that vitamin C may also inhibit the catabolic actions of cortisol; however, the evidence is not particularly impressive. More likely, substances like

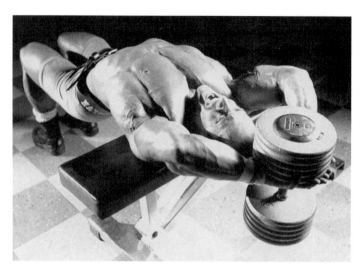

Dave Palumbo.

branched-chain amino acids and even dietary fat are the nutritional cortisol inhibitors.

A new study reported at the 1997 meeting of the American College of Sports Medicine found that one of the branched-chain amino acids (BCAAS), leucine, successfully reduced the catabolic effects of cortisol in rat muscle without affecting muscle glutamine levels. That's interesting, because past studies showed that BCAAS work by either increasing muscle glutamine synthesis or preventing its release under the influence of cortisol.

Another study, reported at the Experimental Biology 97 meeting in New Orleans, examined the effects of dietary fats on plasma hormones in runners. The study compared three levels of fat composition in the diets of the runners: 17 percent, 32 percent, and 42 percent. The results showed that the 32 percent fat diet significantly reduced cortisol levels in the runners compared to the 17 percent fat diet. Under the 42 percent (high-fat) diet, cortisol levels increased only marginally. The diet lowest in fat produced the highest cortisol levels.

The authors of this study suggest that higher-fat diets may help eliminate some of the excess cortisol release through an upgraded prostaglandin synthesis. Prostaglandins are hormonelike substances made from dietary fat that, among other actions, influence hormonal secretions. They were recently publicized by the best-selling diet book *Enter the Zone* by Barry Sears.

Another possible explanation for the way a high-fat diet dilutes cortisol involves increased testosterone production. Testosterone has an inverse relationship to cortisol; that is, when testosterone is elevated in the blood, cortisol is depressed, and vice versa. When testosterone is elevated, anabolic muscle reactions occur.

Natural bodybuilders seeking to benefit from the anticatabolic effects of testosterone without using synthetic versions, such as anabolic steroids, often resort to purported testosterone precursors. These over-the-counter products fall into a gray area of legality due to the Food Supplement Act of 1994. Consequently, they are freely available and legal, at least for now.

One example of a reputed testosterone precursor is the adrenal hormone DHEA, which is produced in the pathway that begins with cholesterol and results in testosterone. That could be a problem, however, as DHEA, in some instances, may take divergent pathways, winding up as either an undesirable by-product of testosterone metabolism called dihydrotestosterone (DHT) or, even worse (for

Danny Hester.

Michael Ashley.

Albert Beckles.

males), estrogen. Dht is linked to male pattern baldness, prostate enlargement, and acne; while estrogen, in males, leads to gynecomastia (development of breasts), increased fat deposition under the skin, and water retention.

Those over 40 will probably get the most benefit from dhea. At that point in people's lives, dhea synthesis generally undergoes a precipitous drop, in which case conservative doses of 50 milligrams a day may take the desirable testosterone pathway by converting to the immediate precursor to testosterone, androstenedione.

Recently, androstenedione itself became available as an oral supplement. Some studies show that a liver enzyme can convert androstenedione directly into testosterone, which can increase plasma testosterone levels up to 300 percent over baseline for about two hours; however, it can also be converted by another enzyme, aromatase, into estrogen. In addition, no one has figured out how long an oral supplement of androstenedione continues to remain effective—assuming that it is effective for testosterone-raising purposes.

Still another over-the-counter hormone that has been suggested as a cortisol blocker is melatonin, a hormone synthesized in the pineal gland of the brain from the amino acid

Arnold Schwarzenegger.

tryptophan. While melatonin is undoubtedly an effective soporific (meaning it puts you to sleep), several studies show it has a negligible effect on cortisol release.

Tribestan is a trade name for an herbal-derived supplement imported from Bulgaria. Virtually all the studies on this enigmatic substance were done in the former Eastern-bloc countries and India, so, until recently, it was ignored in Western countries. Tribestan allegedly works by increasing the response of luteinizing hormone in the pituitary gland, which controls testosterone synthesis in the Leydig cells of the testes. The main problem with Tribestan is getting it and getting it at a good price.

Of the available cortisol-inhibiting supplements, the most controversial is a fatlike substance called phosphatidylserine (ps). Ps is found naturally in the body, where it's incorporated into cell membranes. Studies show that it increases cognition, or brain function, in older people and may preserve optimal brain function in younger people. As for its effect on cortisol, two published studies show it blunts acth release by the pituitary gland. That would decrease cortisol because acth

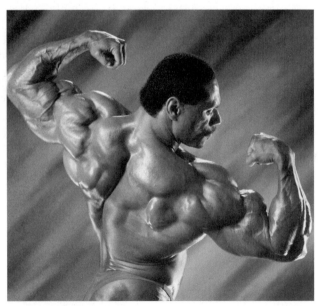

Mike Christian.

travels in the blood to the adrenal glands, where it dictates cortisol release.

The apparent effective dosage of PS for this purpose is 800 milligrams a day. Since the average single pill dose of PS is 100 milligrams, that would entail taking a minimal eight capsules a day. In contrast, the effective dose for so-called smart drug (improved mental function) purposes is only 300 milligrams a day. The controversy over PS involves the dearth of studies attesting to its cortisol-blocking actions and the source of the substance itself.

Many of the studies showing the efficacy of PS used a form derived from bovine (cow) sources, including the two exercise studies that indicated a decreased cortisol response. Unfortunately, bovine-derived sources strike fear in many people because of an association with the so-called mad cow disease, which is usually fatal. While there is absolutely no evidence linking bovine-derived supplements with the onset of that disease, most of the PS sold today is derived from soybeans.

Some people, especially those at companies that still sell the bovine variety, say soy-derived PS is different due to its slightly varied fatty acid configuration. Animal studies show, however, that the soy version is just as effective as the bovine version in terms of brain-boosting activity. The real question is, Does PS actually have any anticatabolic effects in hard-training natural bodybuilders?

A study that's looking at this question is now under way at California State University, Chico. The results may show once and for all whether PS does have value for those interested in promoting bodybuilding progress in a safe, effective, and natural manner.

Eliot Jordan's comprehensive article shows the connection between insulin and muscle building and the role of growth hormone.

THE INSULIN–MUSCLE MASS CONNECTION   Eliot Jordan

Some people refer to insulin as the most anabolic hormone of them all, which includes testosterone, growth hormone, and insulin-like growth factor 1 (IGF-1). To many people, however, insulin is primarily associated with two types of diabetes. Type-1, also called insulin-dependent diabetes mellitus, is characterized by a failure to secrete insulin in response to insulin-provoking nutrients, such as carbohydrates. Type-2, or non–insulin-dependent diabetes, is associated with either a failure to secrete enough insulin or a decrease of insulin cell receptors.

Since the symptoms for both types of diabetes include elevated blood glucose levels, or

Russ Testo.

Mike Christian.

hyperglycemia, insulin is most associated with carbohydrate metabolism. Insulin, however, is an all-purpose storage hormone that not only promotes storage of carbohydrates as glycogen, but also plays an integral role in bodyfat accretion and muscle protein synthesis.

The latter effect is the subject of debate in scientific circles. Some researchers say that insulin exerts merely a permissive effect on muscle cell protein synthesis, while others believe it's anticatabolic in that it appears to prevent excessive breakdown of muscle protein. Still another popular hypothesis is that insulin directly stimulates muscle protein synthesis, an anabolic action.

Much of the confusion regarding how insulin affects muscle is based on variously designed studies. Just as anabolic steroids work better if supplied with an anabolic stimulus in the form of exercise, the same thing appears to be the case with insulin. In other

words, just taking insulin will not promote muscular growth unless accompanied by a certain type of exercise. The type of exercise required is weight training.

A study published in a 1996 issue of the *American Journal of Physiology* underscores this notion. The study involved rats placed on a weight-training protocol as compared with sedentary rats. The purpose of the study was to find out how insulin affected muscle protein synthesis and to clear up some of the confusion regarding the hormone's role as either a protein synthesis promoter or an anticatabolic substance.

As expected, giving insulin to nonexercising rats didn't affect muscle protein synthesis in any way. Nor did giving it to aerobic-exercising rats provide any anabolic stimulus. Providing insulin to weight-training rats, however, did promote increased muscle protein synthesis—but only in the exercised muscles. The researchers point out that past studies showing only an anticatabolic effect of insulin on muscle were incomplete because they involved either sedentary or aerobic-exercising rats. Apparently, there has to be a minimum level of muscle contractile activity that can be produced only by resistance exercise (such as weight training) for insulin to promote muscle protein synthesis.

The study also examined the effects of insulin on both fast-twitch and slow-twitch muscle fibers. Slow-twitch fibers are most associated with endurance exercise, while fast-twitch fibers are those involved in anaerobic exercise, such as bodybuilding. Fast-twitch fibers are far more prone to muscular growth than the slow-twitch variety.

The study showed that insulin is absolutely required for muscle protein synthesis in fast-twitch fibers, but isn't a necessity for slow-twitch fibers. This most likely relates to the greater protein synthesis occurring in the fast-twitch fibers. Thus, insulin works hand-in-hand with resistance exercise to promote increased muscular growth.

I recall talking with Tim Belknap, the 1981 Mr. America, who has been a type-1 diabetic since he was 13. He told me that shortly after he began taking insulin to control his diabetes, he started bodybuilding and quickly gained 30 pounds of pure muscle. He attributes his rapid initial muscle gains to the insulin, but is quick to advise nondiabetic bodybuilders against

using insulin for muscle-building purposes because of likely side effects.

Belknap is referring to the possible side effects of indiscriminate insulin use. Since insulin rapidly decreases blood glucose levels, it can produce a state of *hypoglycemia* (low blood sugar) potent enough to put you in a coma. That's especially true if you're also on a restricted-carbohydrate diet.

On the other hand, the anabolic trio of insulin, growth hormone, and anabolic

Dorian Yates.

Bertil Fox.

steroids is considered by some to be the reason for the 250-plus behemoths you currently see competing in professional bodybuilding. Having conferred with many of these competitors, however, I can tell you that there's no standard insulin regimen; the doses and even the type of insulin are determined by either guesswork or trial-and-error experimentation.

Several bodybuilders have nearly become comatose because of insulin use. In most cases this occurred just before a contest, when the insulin was injected as a means of increasing muscle glycogen storage. The supposed purpose of this technique is a kind of high-tech carboloading that makes the muscle appear fuller at the contest. Insulin helps with this because it turns on the rate-limiting enzyme for muscle glycogen synthesis, glycogen synthatase. Unfortunately, several of insulin's physiological properties make this technique very tricky.

You must know precisely how to balance insulin use with carbohydrate intake. As noted earlier, taking large amounts of insulin without concurrently taking in carbohydrates is a ticket to Comaville. Another problem is that insulin stimulates water and sodium retention, which is exactly what bodybuilders seeking that ripped appearance don't want. Insulin also promotes bodyfat accretion—a look that's definitely out in bodybuilding contests.

Perhaps the most prudent way to deal with insulin is through natural means. You can potentiate insulin's effects with no fear of side effects by increasing your intake of the trace mineral chromium. Since the body absorbs only about 5 to 10 percent of oral chromium, you can take 200 to 600 micrograms a day in divided doses with no fear of detrimental effects. Vanadyl sulfate exerts an independent insulin-like action, particularly in regard to muscle glycogen storage; however, its effects on protein synthesis are still subject to debate.

Taking a combination protein and carbohydrate drink right after training boosts insulin output 37 percent higher than consuming carbohydrates alone. While some advise actually drinking this combo during a workout, the advantages are few, while the possible side effects (such as bloating) are likely to occur. A postworkout drink containing about 50 grams of protein and 50 to 100 grams of carbohydrate should do the trick in providing the needed insulin anabolic effect after a workout.

Vince Taylor.

Lee Haney.

GROWTH HORMONE RELEASE DURING EXERCISE IS LINKED TO INTENSITY LEVEL

A new study just published in *Medicine and Science in Sports and Exercise* (29:669–676; 1997) looks at the short-term effects of exercise on growth hormone (GH) release. Previous studies showed that effective growth hormone release during exercise depends on a number of factors, including exercise intensity and duration, the amount of muscle mass trained, and the existing level of fitness. Diet also plays a role, with research showing that high levels of sugar or fat in the blood during exercise blunt GH release.

While scientists have charted the acute responses of GH release and exercise, the chronic effects of exercise on GH secretion are less well known. Assuming that exercise of a certain level of intensity does elicit a GH response, the question becomes, Does the increased hormone release remain constant with continued exercise stimulus, or does it wane over time?

To find the answer, researchers studied the GH responses to 20 minutes of high-intensity exercise in six untrained men, testing them after three and six weeks of training. An important aspect of the training is that the subjects used a constant load, not attempting to increase resistance during the course of the study.

The results showed that following an initial high level at the start of the training period, the GH release was tapering off after just three weeks. That finding agrees with past studies, in which experienced subjects had a decrease in GH release after regular exercise.

Basically, the body adapts to a certain level of exercise intensity, and if you don't attempt to increase your intensity, responses such as

Shawn Ray.

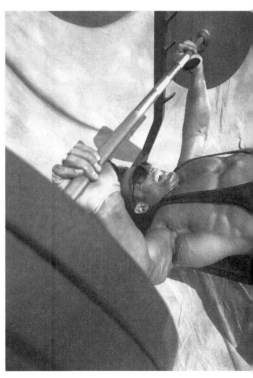

Alex Sicignano.

Growth hormone (GH) release is linked to training intensity. Mike Mentzer.

upgraded GH release gradually dissipate. Specifically, your exercise must make inroads into what scientists refer to as the *lactate threshold*, meaning the precise level of exercise intensity that results in an increased lactic acid release.

The authors of the study suggest that with exercise experience—at the same level of intensity—GH secretion is either reduced or is degraded more rapidly. Other studies show that it takes at least 10 minutes of high-intensity exercise—enough to cause a pronounced muscle-burning sensation—to elicit a significant GH response.

The lesson of the study is familiar to most bodybuilders: To make consistent gains, you have to up the level of intensity. That often involves factors such as increased poundages, shorter rests between sets, more- or less-

frequent training sessions, or an outright change in exercises—in short, anything that will push the envelope of training intensity. If you don't push the envelope, you set yourself up to fall into a training rut.

HORMONE RESPONSES TO SINGLE-SET AND MULTI-SET EXERCISES

Advocates of the high-intensity training system say that for maximal muscle gains, you must do the least amount of work necessary to get the job done. The idea is that you have a finite recovery ability, and the less you tax it, the faster you'll grow.

While many bodybuilders have embraced the tenets of this system, whose high priests include Nautilus inventor Arthur Jones and former Mr. Universe Mike Mentzer, others resist the notion that you can get any benefit from weight training with only one performed-to-failure set. Some people feel that doing only one set of an exercise just isn't enough to promote maximum gains, except perhaps for beginners.

Bodybuilders who have consistently over-trained—which is to say, the majority—are often pleasantly surprised to find that they start making gains again when they switch to a high-intensity, low-volume routine. In most cases, however, the rapid gaining period associated with the switch is short-lived. It's hard

Justin Brooks.

Joe Spinello.

to say why this happens. It may be due to a
subtle decrease in perceived intensity level; if
you're doing only one set, you have to give it
your all, and anything less is an exercise in
self-deception.

There may, however, be other reasons that
bodybuilders prefer doing a higher-volume
style of training. Many have discovered that
they make more consistent gains on a multi-
set routine, which may have something to do
with the differences in anabolic hormone
secretion between low-volume and higher-
volume routines.

This notion is highlighted by a new study
published in the *Canadian Journal of Applied
Physiology* (22:244–255; 1997). The study
involved eight "recreationally trained" (a
euphemism for not-hardcore) bodybuilders
who used either a one-set-per-exercise or a
three-sets-per-exercise weight-training program. The exercises in the two programs were
identical; the only difference was the volume.
The study also involved a crossover design,
which means that after being randomly
assigned to either the one- or three-set program, the men rested for a week and then
switched programs.

The researchers took blood measurements
of various hormones, including growth hormone, testosterone, and cortisol, both before

and at several intervals after the exercise sessions. The results of the tests clearly showed
that using the higher-set routine resulted in a
greater secretion and sustenance of all anabolic hormones measured, as well as the catabolic hormone cortisol.

One explanation for the increased hormonal flow induced by the three-set training
was that it led to higher blood lactic acid levels, which in turn promoted a release of GH
from the pituitary gland.

As for testosterone release, the one-set
routine led to a negligible output compared to
the three-set routine. So, from the standpoint
of anabolic hormones, it appears that a higher
volume of exercise offers clear advantages over

Shelby Cole.

Henrik Thamasian and Shelby Cole.

the typical high-intensity one-set-to-failure routine. Even so, a closer look at the study confounds those results. Both routines involved a 10-rep protocol, so the men doing the one-set routine didn't train to complete muscular failure. Training to failure is considered a vital aspect of the high-intensity system; in fact, people like Jones warn that unless you train to utter failure, you aren't using maximum intensity.

In other words, the men doing one set were just doing one normal set. What would happen if they did that same set to complete muscular failure, which means the number of reps is inconsequential? That's a topic for future studies. In the meantime, if you're looking to make muscular gains, you're probably still better off doing one hard to-the-bone set than three unfocused, low-intensity sets.

This magnificent article by William A. Sands, Ph.D., simply and accurately describes what goes on in your muscles during a workout. The information in this article is so valuable, it should be stenciled on all gym equipment!

HOW DO MUSCLES GET BIGGER?

William A. Sands, Ph.D.

One of the really amazing things about living tissues is their ability to adapt to training stress. This adaptation is the basis on which all athletic training is built. In bodybuilding, it's what makes muscles bigger. Tissues, especially muscles, usually have several means of responding to stress. Muscle tends to adapt in fairly predictable directions, but less predictable magnitudes.

When you begin a training program, the first type of adaptation that occurs in the neuromuscular system is "learning." Although strength performance increases rather quickly as a result of training, almost all of the adaptation in the early stages is neural. The body learns to call upon more muscles for a given movement. This is called *intermuscular coordination.* Unfortunately, it requires very little in the way of hypertrophy; that is, the muscles don't get bigger. They simply learn to produce more tension.

The second training effect on muscle is called *intramuscular coordination*, which means that the individual motor units within the muscle become better synchronized—again, this is mostly learning—and the muscle is able to produce more force. Intramuscular coordination doesn't result in much hypertrophy, either, in the sense that the muscle doesn't get bigger. Instead, it just gets better at using what it already has. The small amount of hypertrophy that does take place usually results in a consolidation of the internal structure of the muscle first, rather than an increase in its outward appearance, or size.

In short, the early stages of strength training result in increased strength performance by neural mechanisms. In fact, neural mechanisms are dominant during the first 8 to 12 weeks of any new workout program. As the training progresses, hypertrophy gradually replaces neural adaptation mechanisms, but it takes 8 to 10 weeks for the muscles to start getting bigger. Even so, the first stages of hypertrophy cause internal changes in the muscle without much visible increase.

If you think about it, it's a smart way to design a neuromuscular system. The body has

René Endara.

Aaron Baker.

no way of knowing whether the increased muscular stress will last for long. It's metabolically expensive to build new muscle. Building muscles requires access to good nutrition, which our ancestors may not have had in abundant supply. Therefore, it seems particularly smart to be able to adapt to new performance demands without having to take on the burden of making new muscle tissue. If we continue the increased training demands beyond 8 to 12 weeks and thus exhaust the body's ability to use neural mechanisms, however, the body must resort to enhancing the muscle structure itself and associated tissues. Finally, we get significant hypertrophy.

The above information has important implications for your training. First, in evaluating any training program's ability to produce significant growth, you must continue to use it for at least 8 to 12 weeks. Second, while you may experience remarkable changes in

strength performance in the early stages of a workout program, they are usually due to what I call the honeymoon period, when the body adapts mostly by learning to handle the new training stress. Third, even when hypertrophy begins, it's usually focused on consolidating the existing muscle tissue—for example, removing fat or increasing connective tissue.

Once you're out of the neural adaptation period, changes in the external appearance of muscles and in strength performance are mostly due to the significant hypertrophy that occurs. The question then becomes, What causes this hypertrophy?

Muscle is a mixture of several tissues and several different types of muscle cells. Hypertrophy is believed to involve several factors, including an increase in the cross-sectional area of a muscle, an increase in the size of individual muscle fibers, and an increase in the so-called associated tissues in a muscle, such as connective tissue. The question of whether you can actually increase the number of muscle fibers—known as *hyperplasia*—is still fairly controversial. Although researchers have demonstrated hyperplasia in some limited circumstances, the general consensus is that it doesn't occur in adults.

Hypertrophy, on the other hand, occurs in two basic forms, *sarcoplasmic* and *myofibrillar*. The type of hypertrophy you achieve depends largely on the type of training stimulus you use. Sarcoplasmic hypertrophy refers to an increase in sarcoplasm, which is basically the gunk that surrounds the contractile units, or myofibrils, in the muscle cell.

The sarcoplasm is where most of the metabolism of strength activities takes place, an important factor for strength athletes because increasing the amount of glycogen (muscle sugar), enzymes (controlling chemicals), buffers (chemicals used to deal with excess acidity), and so forth in the muscle cell supports strength activities and results in increased muscle size. It's an increase that's sort of based on supporting material within the muscle cell, however. Strength training and high-intensity anaerobic training, such as some types of interval and circuit training, tend to encourage sarcoplasmic hypertrophy.

Myofibrillar hypertrophy, then, involves the actual contractile units. The myofibril is a subunit of the muscle cell, in which the machinery of tension is housed. Strength training causes the myofibrils to increase in both size and number. The myofibrils are composed of several different proteins and respond to strength training stimuli by increasing in thickness and in number within the muscle cell. The different types of proteins inside the myofibrils help scientists know what type of cell they're looking at: type I, or slow-twitch; or one of the four type-II, or fast-twitch. It's the nerve supplying the muscle, however, that actually determines the type of muscle cell. Interestingly, all of the various fiber types are capable of hypertrophy, but the type-IIb fibers are the most capable of getting larger. The most effective type of exercise for training those fibers is heavy weights used for sets of 8 to 12 reps.

The bottom line, though, is that you should include a variety of training methods—different sets, reps, and weight stimuli—so that all the available muscle cells can contribute to enlarging the overall appearance of the muscle. Training at only one type of intensity will result in restricting hypertrophy to only a few types of motor units and their associated fiber types.

In general, it takes time and patience to build bigger muscles. Because the early strength development you experience when you begin a training program may not be related to a stable increase in muscle size, you should be particularly cautious of interpreting such miraculous strength increases. With all training programs the question is, Will these improvements in strength actually lead to stable improvements in hypertrophy? Most studies on strength training don't last long enough or include a sufficient number of subjects to answer it. With bodybuilders, however, scientists have the opportunity to study adaptations over time—which could contribute enormously to the development of sound and serious methods of enhancing strength and appearance.

Aaron Baker.

Dave Palumbo.

Chapter 3

SHOULDER TRAINING

Broad shoulders is a metaphorical term for many positive characteristics: strength, power, character, and dependability, to name a few.

Broad shoulders and well-developed traps are two bodyparts that are immediately noticeable from across a room or from the far end of the beach, even when the person is wearing clothing that conceals the rest of his physique. Small wonder that bodybuilders pay so much attention to training this area of the body.

In this chapter, we examine several proven approaches to shoulder training. First, professional wrestler, strongman, and ultimate hardcore bodybuilder and author Don Ross gives us his secret "Compound Shoulder Blast."

COMPOUND SHOULDER BLAST
Don Ross
Here it is: the formula for thick, ripped, balanced deltoid development. It's not an easy program; in fact, it's probably the hardest deltoid routine ever invented.

Since results are in direct proportion to the effort applied, brave through two months

of this program, and you'll have incredible shoulder development.

Most size programs focus on medial (middle) deltoid exercises, including presses, laterals, and upright rows. While these are great foundation builders, they do little to affect the anterior (front) and posterior (rear) deltoid heads. Need proof? Check out a local physique show, or look around the gym. You'll notice that most bodybuilders lack balanced deltoids. The tie-in between the pecs and delts (front head) is missing, and there is little in the way of rear delt development. These delts have a hemispheric look when viewed from the side. Balanced delts, like those of the top Mr. and Ms. Olympia contenders, have comparable development of all heads.

The deltoids have three major functions (excluding rotation, which we work with lat, chest, and rib cage exercises). These functions are:

- Raising the arms from your sides to an overhead position, as in the side dumbbell lateral

Ronnie Coleman.

- Raising the arms in front of you to an overhead position, as in the straight-arm front raise
- Bringing your arms out to the sides and back from a position straight out in front of you, as in the bent-over flye

All shoulder exercises, including presses, upright rows, and bent-over, elbows-out rows, are variations of these movements. For balanced development, the muscles must be worked with each function the deltoid performs. The Compound Shoulder Blast incorporates all the deltoid functions.

The look we are striving for is that of deep, vascular, striated, carved-out-of-rock definition and separation between the heads. To achieve this while providing maximum growth-building intensity, we will use low reps and continuous movement. This means no rest between sets. Instead, we will blast nonstop, alternating exercises and shifting the tension from one muscle area to another throughout the program. Your medial delts rest as you train your anterior delts, and your anterior delts rest as you train posterior delts. The trick is to do this while keeping the poundage respectable enough to stimulate the deep muscle fibers.

A compound set is similar to a giant set, in which you do a cycle of several different exercises for one set each, then repeat the cycle. The main difference between a compound set and a giant set is that the compound set is several exercises done as one without putting the weight down. (A giant set can be several exercises done with different equipment in the same cyclic manner.) With each compound set cycle, you descend in poundage.

Begin this program with two cycles. Then progressively increase to four. I've done as many as six during the final weeks before an exhibition or photo shoot. The Compound Shoulder Blast is done entirely with dumbbells. You will use the same weight throughout a cycle. In the beginning, you may have to put the dumbbells down for a few breaths, but your first goal is to go through each cycle without putting down the weight.

Progressively decrease your rest periods between cycles, resting only as long as necessary. Once you get those rests down to 10 seconds, you've mastered the routine! Shortening your rest periods is a method of increasing intensity similar to increasing poundage. Don't increase the weight on these exercises until you've mastered the short rests. Once you've accomplished this, strive to use heavier dumbbells whenever possible.

EXERCISES

1. **Front raise.** Start with a pair of dumbbells at arm's length in front of you, all four ends on your front thighs, palms toward you. Keep your arms slightly bent. Raise the dumbbells up in front of you to eye level. Lower slowly. Do as many reps as possible. Use a weight you can do 8 to 10 reps with.

2. **Standing lateral.** Move the dumbbells to the sides of your thighs to begin. Keeping your elbows slightly unlocked, raise the dumbbells out to your sides. Keep your palms down and your thumbs from coming up. Raise the weights to eye level and lower slowly. Do these until you can't complete any more reps.

3. **L-lateral.** Now bend your arms in an L-shape, hands parallel with elbows. Continue your side laterals to failure; 3 to 5 additional reps should be possible in "L-lateral" style. Do as many as possible.

4. **Upright row.** Continue the set with upright rows, bringing your elbows high and the dumbbells to chest level. Let the dumbbells move away from each other as you bring your elbows to shoulder level. This movement brings your elbows out to the sides more than standard barbell upright rows, working the delt at the attachment near your trapezius. The change makes this unique row more of a delt movement than a trap exercise.

5. **Overhead press.** When you can't do any more upright dumbbell rows, swing the weights to your shoulders (with your palms facing forward) and press them overhead. Keep your elbows out to your sides during these dumbbell presses. Continue until the weights won't go up.

6. **Bent-over flye.** Bend over at the waist until your upper body is parallel to the floor. (If you have low-back problems, brace your head on a stool, table, or high bench.) Start with the dumbbells touching, palms toward each other. Raise the weights out to your sides,

Dumbbell front raise.   Sonny Schmidt.

Standing lateral raise.   Shawn Ray.

Shawn Ray.

Andreas Munzer.

keeping your elbows slightly unlocked. Do as many bent-over flyes as possible.

Take a 10-second rest (or as short as possible), then repeat the cycle. Always take a full 10 seconds between cycles to allow the muscles to rid themselves of lactic acid buildup.

I developed the Compound Shoulder Blast while training for a string of guest-posing appearances in 1983 and '84. It evolved from another deltoid dumbbell program in which I began with upright dumbbell rows and then worked down in weight until I arrived at a poundage I could do laterals with. From there,

I moved to L-laterals, then bent-over flyes. The next step was to formulate an exercise incorporating all the deltoid movements. The results were so spectacular and the routine so intense that I always went back to it—and still do. It never fails to blast my shoulders to new levels of development.

The late Kay Baxter (who possessed perhaps the all-time greatest shoulder development among women) learned the routine from me and also made outstanding gains. We both used it to train competitive bodybuilders with equal success. Everyone who has used it has to admit that it's the toughest deltoid routine imaginable. Some ego-trippers get psyched out by the limits in poundage when they first start—but remember, it's the intensity, not the weight, that counts. You'll get much more from this than from push-pressing a heavy weight overhead or swinging up big dumbbells in cheat-lateral fashion.

If you have the heart and the guts of a true champion, give the Compound Shoulder Blast a try. In six weeks, your shoulders will look like cannonballs.

Steve Holman, editor of Ironman *magazine, is one of the most knowledgeable people in the world on the subject of bodybuilding. He has put his encyclopedic knowledge of bodybuilding to use developing the Positions of Flexion (*POF*) system of training. Here, Steve provides us with his complete* POF *workout for devastating delts that is guaranteed to slap on size.*

DEVASTATING DELTS   Steve Holman

Cannonballs. The twin planets. Olympian orbs. No matter how you refer to your shoulders, one thing is certain: with a power-packed pair of delts, you'll feel as though you can practically command the universe. There's something about wide, round shoulders that gives the bodybuilder a mighty and powerful demeanor. Can you imagine Shawn Ray, Mike Christian, or Gary Strydom strutting around without their devastating deltoid development? Not a pretty picture. When a bodybuilder is lacking in the delt department, he or she looks slump-shouldered, narrow, and just plain destitute. Fortunately, a little muscle goes a long way when it comes to delts. All it takes is a small amount of additional mass in each lateral (side) head to boost a bodybuilder's torso from mediocre to heroically Herculean. Why, then, are there so many bodybuilders with shriveled shrimp shoulders instead of cannonballs crowning their clavicles? It could be an epidemic of bad genetics, but more often than not we can attribute the problem to overtraining.

OVERTRAINING: THE DELT DESTROYER

The lateral head of the deltoid is a rather small muscle—even smaller than the biceps. It is located in such an important spot, however, that it often is bombarded with inordinate amounts of work in a desperate attempt to build greater width and roundness. In the case of a small muscle group like the lateral delt head, this additional work usually means stagnation or even a loss of mass; the muscle simply can't recover and grow, so it stays in a constant state of catch-up and often breaks down instead of building up. To prevent this overtrained state from occurring, you must make your delt work efficient and precise—efficient in that it should utilize the least amount of work necessary to stimulate maximum growth, and precise in that it should primarily stress the important lateral head.

If you have knowledge of anatomy, you may be asking, "But what about the other two delt heads?" While it's true that the deltoid is made up of three heads—anterior (front), lateral (side), and posterior (rear)—it's also true that the front and rear heads receive so much work from other exercises that they rarely need direct stimulation. For example, any type of press or curl works the anterior head to a degree, while rows and chins work the posterior head. Remember, too, that no muscle is an island. With their close interrelationship, the three delt heads are somewhat dependent on each other—when one head works, they all work to a degree. For example, any lateral head exercise—such as

Ronnie Coleman.

lateral raises—will indirectly work the other two heads.

The lateral head doesn't receive nearly as much stimulation from other exercises as the front and rear heads, so you must blast it with cruise missile precision if you want it to attain dramatic density and fullness. One of the best ways to construct and chisel this awe-inspiring development is with the Positions of Flexion (POF) training strategy.

PRECISION TRAINING WITH POF

Most bodybuilders' delt training has about as much accuracy as an Iraqi Scud missile; it's a shotgun approach that's haphazard and fraught with trial and error. In order to blast all the angles, the average bodybuilder attempts to use every shoulder exercise in the book, which more often than not causes an overtrained, overdrained state that limits rather than promotes massive development. The Positions of Flexion strategy is a much more sane and logical method of acquiring startling shoulder size.

The POF training approach states that each major muscle group has three, and only three, positions (or angles) that need to be worked in order to achieve the most complete development possible: midrange, stretch, and contracted. By choosing one exercise for each of the three positions, you train the muscle without waste. Let's take the lateral deltoid and dissect it into its three positions.

- Midrange: Overhead pressing movements
- Stretch: Bottom of a one-arm incline lateral raise, or one-arm cable lateral raise (arm across the front of the torso)
- Contracted: Top position of an upright row (upper arm out to the side and angled slightly upward)

When you understand these positions, training the deltoids in a precise, efficient manner is simply a matter of devising a routine that forces the delts into the growth zone every workout without disrupting your recovery ability.

POF midrange exercise.   Art Dilkes.

POF contracted exercise.   B. J. Quinn.

Getting into position for POF stretch exercise.
Joe Spinello.

EXERCISES

Behind-the-neck press

Take a loaded barbell off a rack onto your shoulders as if you were about to do squats. Sit on a bench, plant your feet on the floor, and press the barbell overhead. Lower the bar to the back of your neck below ear level and repeat. *Tip*: Don't pause at the bottom. Also, for a searing delt burn, try a set without locking out on any of the reps. Alternate exercises: standing barbell press, seated dumbbell press.

One-arm incline lateral raise

Sit sideways on an incline bench, leaning one shoulder against the bench while you work your other shoulder with a one-arm lateral raise. The incline allows the lateral delt to get a full stretch in the bottom position. *Tip*: Keep the dumbbell parallel to the floor at all times. Alternate exercise: one-arm cable lateral raise. (*Note*: If you use the one-arm cable lateral raise as an alternate, do not bring your arm all the way up to the parallel position. This requires you to use less weight, and the lower end of the movement—the stretch—doesn't receive enough resistance.)

Wide-grip upright row

Use a slightly wider than shoulder-width grip on these. While standing upright with the barbell hanging at arm's length, pull the bar up to the chest. Keep it close to your body. Stop at mid-chest level, lower slowly, and repeat. If this exercise hurts your wrists or shoulders, use dumbbells for less joint restriction. *Tip*: Try using a lighter weight once in a while and raising the bar to your nose instead of stopping at your chest. Alternate exercises: dumbbell upright row, dumbbell lateral raise.

THE ROUTINES

If you're an advanced bodybuilder, you'll have developed enough recovery ability to handle more sets than the beginner or intermediate,

Vince Taylor.

Upright row.

but you still won't be able to overdo it without suffering the inevitable consequences of overtraining. Remember, the lateral head is a small muscle and doesn't require all that much work to get it growing. Here is an excellent advanced delt routine that works each lateral position with efficiency and precision. (Note: M = midrange, S = stretch, and C = contracted.)

Advanced POF Delt Routine
Behind-the-neck press (M):
    3–4 sets × 8–12 reps
One-arm incline lateral raise (S):
    2–3 sets × 8–12 reps
Wide-grip upright row (C):
    2–3 sets × 8–12 reps

At the top end you'll be doing 10 sets, which is probably more than enough lateral delt work for most advanced bodybuilders. If you're still in the intermediate stage, you won't be able to handle this workload, and your delt routine might look something like this:

Intermediate POF Delt Routine
Behind-the-neck press:
    2–3 sets × 8–12 reps
One-arm incline lateral raise:
    2 sets × 8–12 reps
Wide-grip upright row:
    1–2 sets × 8–12 reps

This routine provides 7 sets at the top end and 5 at the bottom. If you work all of your sets with fierce, gut-busting intensity, this program (or a variant of it) will max out your delt development in record time.

Beginners will no doubt overtrain in a matter of days with POF and should therefore stick to a more basic strategy. Here's a good beginning deltoid routine:

Beginning Delt Routine
Barbell military press:
    2 sets of 8 to 10 reps
Wide-grip upright row:
    1 set of 8 to 10 reps

Behind-the-neck press.

One-arm incline lateral raise.   James Demelo.

If you're past the beginning bodybuilding stage and you're interested in developing a pair of devastating, dynamite delts—or Olympian orbs, if you prefer—give POF a try. Its precision, efficiency, and shocking effectiveness will turn your shoulders into boulders in no time flat.

One thing to look out for in all shoulder training is the all-too-common rotator cuff injury. Jerry Robinson provides a look at how to train this muscle the right way—by getting your position straight.

ROTATOR CUFF TRAINING
Jerry Robinson

If you haven't experienced it yet, you probably will at some point in your training career: shoulder pain. It could be a dull ache that never seems to go away completely, or a sharp stab when you're doing upright rows or behind-the-neck presses.

Wide-grip upright row.

The shoulder is a complex joint, capable of performing many movements over a broad range of motion. Four small muscles known as the *rotator cuff* assist during all of these move-

Mike Mentzer.

Justin Brooks.

Strengthening the cuff muscles decreases the risk of injury and is an essential element in rehabilitating the muscles once you've trashed them. Because the shoulder is capable of such a variety of movements, however, you can perform rotator cuff strengthening exercises in many positions. But which position is best?

WHAT THEY SAY IN THE LAB

To find out, researchers measured the strength of 12 subjects while they were performing the two movements that serve as the basis for most cuff exercises: internal and external shoulder rotation. These evaluations were done using Cybex isokinetic resistance machines, which are ideal for measuring strength because they force the target muscle to work against maximum resistance at every point throughout the movement. That's in

ments. Unfortunately, the typical training routine doesn't adequately condition the rotator cuff muscles, so almost everyone who trains hard injures the cuff at one time or another, experiencing the symptoms just described.

In fact, everyone—whether he or she trains or not—experiences some rotator cuff degeneration by about age 40.

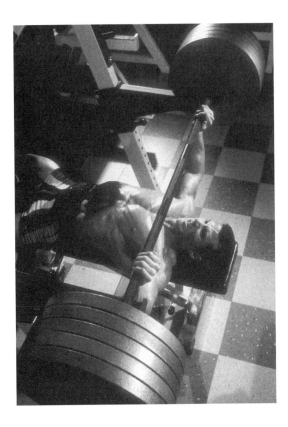

The greatest torque values for internal rotation were achieved in position 1, with the upper arm hanging straight down. The greatest torque values for external rotation were achieved in position 2, with the upper arm pointing straight ahead. These findings suggest that the best orientation for working the internal rotators is different from the best orientation for working the external rotators. As you might guess, the most efficient way to exercise the internal rotators is with your upper arm hanging straight down. This is the anatomically most "natural" position, in which the internal rotator muscles are acting most directly against resistance. Similarly, the most efficient way to exercise the external rotators is with the upper arm pointing straight ahead.

HOW TO MAKE WHAT THEY SAY IN THE LAB PRACTICAL

So, what do you do with this information?

First, if you lift consistently and want to add rotator cuff work to your routine, build on the recommendation for external rotation exercises only. Here's why. External rotation is motivated by two small cuff muscles, the teres minor and infraspinatus. Internal rotation, the opposing action, is motivated by a medium-size cuff muscle, the subscapularis, and also by three large non-cuff muscle groups—the lats, pecs, and teres major.

Given the lengths to which we all go to train our lats, pecs, and teres majors, the so-called balance between the external and internal rotators is a bit like a tug-of-war, with a child on one side and Arnold, Lou Ferrigno, and Lee Haney on the other. Not a pretty picture. The gross imbalance sets the stage for external-rotator injury. The bottom line for most strength athletes is, the internal rotators get sufficient attention, but the external rotators don't. So you should concentrate on training the external rotators.

Second, from a purely mechanical perspective, the external rotator training position endorsed in the study looks to elicit the best

contrast to most weight-lifting equipment, such as dumbbells and barbells, which are isotonic. With isotonic devices, the resistance remains constant throughout the movement; consequently, the weight is often too heavy where the muscle is weakest and too light where it is strongest.

The researchers tested internal and external rotation in three positions:

- **Position 1.** Subject standing up, upper arm hanging straight down, with the axis of internal and external rotation parallel to the axis of the body.
- **Position 2.** Subject sitting, upper arm parallel to the floor and pointing straight ahead, with the axis of rotation along a line going straight out from the body.
- **Position 3.** Subject lying on his or her back, upper arm parallel to the floor and pointing straight out to the side, with the axis of rotation along an imaginary line passing through both shoulders.

results. When you throw a little anatomy into the picture, however, things change. It turns out that this position is exactly the one used to test for what's known as impingement syndrome, which involves certain structures in the shoulder pressing, or impinging, on other structures, causing inflammation and severe pain.

To render the position usable for training, you have to make two small modifications:

- The angle formed by your upper arm opening out from your chest must be slightly greater than 90 degrees.
- The angle formed by the underside of your arm and your torso must be slightly less than 90 degrees.

With those modifications made, the position becomes optimum for training the external rotators.

Try the following exercise, based on this ideal position:

Hold a light dumbbell (20 pounds or less) in your right hand and rest your right triceps on the top of a freestanding incline bench. Your right elbow should be bent at a 90-degree angle. Your body should be at a diagonal to the bench. The angle at your armpit should be slightly less than 90 degrees. If necessary, bend your knees to adjust your height relative to the support to achieve this angle.

Maintaining the right angle and holding the elbow steady, lower the dumbbell until your forearm is just below parallel to the floor. If necessary, you can place the back of your left hand under your right elbow to make the position more comfortable.

Still maintaining the right angle, slowly raise the weight back to the starting position. Resist the tendency to jerk the weight as you reach the bottom of the movement, and begin lifting it up again. Jerking puts potentially injurious stress on the external rotators.

Repeat for 2 sets of 6 to 8 reps with each arm. The best schedule for external rotator work is to do it twice per week at the end of an upper-body workout and follow it with a rest day.

Never work the cuff before working your upper body, or you play Russian roulette with those four small, all-important muscles.

Arnold Schwarzenegger is considered by many to be the greatest bodybuilder of all time. When he was building his legendary physique, his friend Gene Mozée was right alongside him taking notes and photos. Gene's articles give every detail not just of how Arnold trained, but also how he thought about training . . . and winning. His Ironman *articles provide invaluable information on how to train and think like a champion.*

ARNOLD'S TRAP TRAINING
Arnold Schwarzenegger, as told to Gene Mozée

In my early bodybuilding years, I rarely worked my traps. I assumed that these muscles received enough work from bent-over rows, lateral raises, and presses. I was fooling myself. It was only when I began competing against Sergio Oliva and saw his huge traps that I realized how much larger mine could and should be to round out my development for that massive upper-body appearance. I stopped regarding the traps as a minor muscle group, and I decided to insert some specialized trap exercises into my routines in order to develop these muscles to their limit.

Shrug.

Dumbbell shrug.

When specializing on your traps, always keep in mind that you should never allow them to dwarf the deltoids. Traps that are too big in proportion to the delts will make your shoulders appear narrower. Huge traps give the upper body a rugged, powerful, and massive appearance, but if the deltoids are under par, the result is a grotesque round-shouldered look. I've seen some powerlifters who had pear-shaped upper bodies because they did heavy deadlifting and little delt work. Strive for a perfect delt–trap balance at all times.

Because about half the traps are ordinarily not in view (unless you have facing mirrors that enable you to see them from the back) and because the upper-front portion is not as showy as, say, the biceps or pecs, many bodybuilders slide into trap deficiency. For the competitive bodybuilder, no muscle can be considered minor. Every weak link is a glaring deficiency. What you *can't* see can hurt you!

TRI-SET TRAP PROGRAM

Before I start blasting my traps, I work my deltoids. This warms up the entire shoulder girdle and delivers massive quantities of blood to the area for a total flush-pump.

Because I find it necessary to spend a great deal more time developing my deltoids—to bring them up to my arms and chest—I do the following routine twice a week but only during the last 60 days before a contest. During the rest of the year, I do nothing special for my traps.

Barbell shrug

This exercise builds size and adds power to the entire shoulder girdle. I use a wide grip and try to raise my deltoids as high as possible on each shrugging motion. I use 275 pounds and

do 1 set of 8 reps, rest 30 seconds or less, and then move on to the next exercise in the tri-set routine.

Upright row

This great exercise builds up both the traps and the delts. I use around 175 pounds with my hands spaced about 10 inches apart. I pull the bar up to my neck, then lower it slowly back to the starting position. I do 8 reps, pause for about 30 seconds, and move on to the final exercise in the tri-set.

Dumbbell shrug

This exercise reigns supreme for concentrated trap blasting. I hold a 120-pound dumbbell in each hand and try to touch my ears with my deltoids. At the highest point of the shrug, I force my delts backward as far as I can to fully

Behind-the-neck press.

contract my traps and upper-back muscles. I keep going until I've blasted out 8 to 10 burning, aching reps. I now take a full one-minute rest before doing a second tri-set. I do a total of four tri-set cycles.

After completing my trap program, I like to remove my shirt and observe how much more powerful and massive my delts and traps appear. I pose and contract the traps from several angles in front of a mirror for three to five minutes. This accentuates the contour of the traps and improves definition. It also gives me greater trap control, which is a real asset in competition.

Heavy deadlifts, cleans, high pulls, and heavy pressing movements are good mass builders for traps; however, the specialization routine that I use builds tremendous shape and definition, as well as size. This program works for me because I don't need a lot of trap work. The tri-set routine helps me train harder and faster, and it gives me that great growth pump that I need.

Seated dumbbell press.   Art Dilkes.

One-arm cable lateral.   Greg Kovacs.

TRAINING TIPS

1. Work your traps after delts, while the blood is already in the shoulder area.

2. If your traps are especially weak, train them three times a week.
3. Perform the exercises at a moderately slow speed, feeling the tension from beginning to end as you fully contract your traps on each rep.
4. Never rush through your trap exercises. Tri-setting lets you complete the routine quickly, but you should perform each repetition properly.
5. On the last rep or two of the final set, you can use a slight cheat to get the weight up without decreasing the poundage.
6. Beginners can usually get all the trap work they need by doing deadlifts with a shrug at the end of each rep.
7. Intermediates can superset any two of the exercises in my tri-set routine for 3 or 4 sets of 8 to 10 reps.
8. Specialize on your traps only until they're on par with your delts. Don't let your traps overwhelm your delts.

Don Long.

9. Do all the exercises correctly. If you're not sure how to perform them, ask a more advanced trainee for help.
10. If you haven't been doing any trap work, start with only two tri-sets during the first two weeks, add a third after six trap workouts, and then add a fourth after another six trap workouts.

Well-developed, shapely traps connect the neck, shoulders, and back into a massive, symmetrical muscle display that caps the top of the torso. Traps cannot be measured in pounds and inches, but only in the look of envy and amazement on your training buddies' faces. Start working your traps now, and in a few months your entire torso will improve dramatically.

ARNOLD'S DYNAMITE DELTOIDS
Arnold Schwarzenegger, as told to Gene Mozée

Deep, broad shoulders featuring well-developed deltoids are a symbol of strength and power. In fact, any physique, regardless of size or shape, that lacks full deltoid development loses much of its impressiveness.

Although powerful shoulders are vitally important in almost all sports, most athletes don't have the kind of deltoid development that one might expect. Gymnasts and champion weightlifters and bodybuilders stand above all others in displaying the finest deltoids.

Any enthusiastic bodybuilder who trains diligently can, with intelligent specialization, create outstanding shoulders. The more fully these muscles are developed, the broader the shoulders will be.

Mohamed Makkawy.

Anyone who wants to increase his or her shoulder width, particularly after bone growth has ceased (in the early to mid 20s), can still do it by developing thicker, rounder delts. One-half to one inch on each shoulder—which you can build with proper specialization—can make a tremendous difference, changing your appearance from ordinary to super.

The importance of shoulder superiority was proven to me when I stood between Dave Draper and Reg Park at a Mr. Universe contest. Both of these great bodybuilders were in fantastic condition, and both are of a height comparable to mine. When they handed me the victor's trophy, I was thankful I had worked my deltoids so hard in preparation for this competition; my improved width and thickness—from both front and back—enabled me to surpass those great superstars. I believe that much of my bodybuilding success has been due to intensive deltoid training.

The deltoid is a unique muscle because it has three distinct sections: the anterior (front) head, the lateral (side) head, and the posterior (rear) head. It is the lateral head that gives width to your shoulders. The anterior head gives depth to the upper body when in profile, and the posterior head fills out the uppermost

regions of the outside of the back. To build truly massive deltoids, you must develop all three areas equally. The anterior head gets more work than the other two because most chest exercises also hit this section. The lateral and posterior heads must be isolated with more concentrated movements to achieve full development.

When I began training, I relied mostly on pressing movements for my delts. I was stuck on dumbbell presses and behind-the-neck presses for six years. After coming to America and watching all of the top bodybuilding stars train, I added many new and different exercises to my deltoid routines. My shoulder caps became rounder, thicker, and more defined.

Great deltoids enhance your whole physique, no matter what angle they're viewed from. With a good set of delts, the competitive bodybuilder is able to hit many more poses and appear much more impressive when standing relaxed. Even on the beach, nothing looks better than a body that has good delts, abdominals, and calves. These three bodyparts exemplify everything that is athletic and aesthetic in a physique.

Before describing the exact exercises and routines that I used to build my deltoids, I'd like to discuss bone structure. Individuals who have straight clavicles, like Steve Reeves, Frank Zane, and Don Howorth, definitely appear to have an advantage when standing relaxed, but their lack of trapezius development is a weakness. Sergio Oliva and I have more sloping collar bones, but we have greater trap development than the aforementioned bodybuilders—and more powerful and massive shoulders.

Just as you should avoid the all-delts, no-traps look, you should also steer clear of huge traps and poor delts. The key is balance, with both delts and traps symmetrically developed to complement each other.

As did most of my bodybuilding peers, I graduated from the school of trial and error. I would try an exercise, and if it didn't produce the desired results, I dumped it. The productive movements that brought new improvement became mainstays of my workouts. The following exercises have produced the best results for me, and I believe they will prove equally helpful to you.

MY FAVORITE DELT EXERCISES

For warm-up, I like standing circle presses. Grasp a light barbell with a medium-wide grip and press it from your chest over the top of your head to the back of your neck. Lower it only halfway on each side of your head. It really heats up the delts and eliminates any possibility of injury from the heavy delt routine that follows. Do one set of 30 to 50 reps.

Special dumbbell press

Clean a pair of heavy dumbbells to your chest. Turn your palms toward each other and then rotate them forward as you press the weight three-quarters of the way to lockout position. This keeps continuous tension on the delts. Lower the dumbbells to the starting position—palms facing each other—and repeat.

Once you complete 6 tough reps, grab a lighter set of dumbbells and do another 6 reps. Continue to do descending sets without rest. I keep going until I complete 5 sets, and I like to end this giant set with a set of bent-over laterals, 8 to 10 reps. I repeat this entire procedure five times.

Lying rear-deltoid raise

Lie on your side on an abdominal board that's set on about the second rung. Hold on to the foot strap with your inner hand and grab a dumbbell with your other hand. Raise the dumbbell across your body until the rear deltoid is fully contracted. Lower and repeat for 12 strict, concentrated reps. Go from one arm to the other without pausing. I do 5 sets.

Cable side lateral

Standing sideways next to a cable crossover apparatus, grab the low cable handle with your

Behind-the-neck press.   Don Long.

Dumbbell shrug.

outer hand. Raise your arm out to the side as high as possible until the outer head of the delt is thoroughly peaked. You'll get a continuous tension that's impossible to achieve with a dumbbell. Bend your arm just slightly to take the stress off the elbow and put it all on the lateral head. Go from one arm to the other without resting. I do 5 sets of 12 reps.

Alternate dumbbell front raise

You can use a slight cheating motion on these. With almost straight arms and your palms facing back, raise one dumbbell to about the three-quarters position overhead. Then, as you lower it, raise the other dumbbell. Continue in

this alternate fashion for 12 reps per arm. This really flushes the delts, particularly the front area. I do 3 sets.

Usually, at the end of my delt routine I grab a pair of 65-pound dumbbells and do one-third lateral movements to keep the delts fully pumped and under continuous tension. I perform these partial side raises until my shoulders burn and ache all the way down to the deepest fibers of the muscles.

This routine is designed to give me a continuous, relentless pump from start to finish. Only the most advanced competitive bodybuilders should attempt this supershock program, and even then I would suggest it be scaled down to prevent overtraining and

Barbell shrug.   Terry Mitsos.

burnout. Remember, it took me many years to be able to grow from such a severe program.

OTHER PRODUCTIVE DELT EXERCISES

I have used many deltoid movements over the years. Here are some of my other favorites.

Behind-the-neck press

There are two ways to perform this terrific exercise. One is to use the strictest style with a full lockout. The other—the one I prefer—is a half-movement where you push the bar just above your head and then lower it. You can do this exercise sitting with your back braced or on a Smith machine, which I like because it prevents cheating and directs the effort more fully toward the front delt. The best grip is where the forearms are perpendicular to the floor. To avoid injuries, don't lower the bar too far.

Front press

This exercise hits the upper pecs, the area just below your clavicles, along with the delts. Here, again, I like to use the Smith machine because I can drop it low on my chest, which places both the front delts and upper pecs under greater tension before I push upward.

Dumbbell press

You can do this movement sitting or standing. The dumbbells can be lowered as far as you like, or pressed as high as you want. I used to press them to full lockout in my early years, but now I prefer half- or three-quarter movements to maintain continuous tension on my delts and to make them work harder.

Shawn Ray.

Standing lateral raise

Take a dumbbell in each hand and raise them to shoulder height, your upper body leaning slightly forward and your arms barely bent. The weight must start from a dead stop. Lower the dumbbells slowly. Try to elevate the backs of the dumbbells so that they are higher than the fronts.

One-arm bent-over cable lateral

I prefer to do these one arm at a time because I can pull the cable farther back and get a nice, full range of motion. Step into a cable crossover machine, grab a low handle with the opposite hand, and bend forward at the waist so that your upper body is parallel to the floor. Alternate arms for 12 reps each without stopping. This is pure rear delt all the way.

Bent-over dumbbell lateral

This is the exercise that I use with my giant-set dumbbell presses. Grab a dumbbell in each hand and bend forward at the waist until your torso is parallel to the ground. Raise the weights up and out with your arms straight until they're level with your ears. Don't swing the weights up. Lower them slowly while keeping your back parallel to the floor throughout the exercise. Forcibly contract your rear delt heads in the top position for a second or two.

TRAINING TIPS

1. Beginners should use a simple approach —one set of one exercise for each of the three delt heads, as in the following routine:

Front barbell press   1 × 10
Dumbbell lateral raise   1 × 10
Bent-over dumbbell lateral 1 × 10

2. After three months, add a second set of each exercise.

3. During my first years of training, when I was looking for bodyweight, I did 6 to 8 reps, and I trained deltoids three times a week, as I do now. Now I train for shape, density, and cuts, so I use higher reps—about 10 to 15 on most delt exercises.

4. One of the most effective ways to blast the delts is with a superset routine such as this one:

Superset 1

Front press   3–5 × 10
Standing lateral raise   3–5 × 10

Superset 2

Behind-the-neck press   3–5 × 10
Bent-over dumbbell lateral 3–5 × 10–15

5. Advanced bodybuilders should never do more than 25 sets total for the deltoids.

6. Always warm up your delts to avoid injury, especially before performing heavy presses.

7. When you're training for muscle mass, always try to increase the weight rather than the reps. The heavy sets hit the deepest muscle fibers and stimulate more growth.

The deltoids can take plenty of hard work. They grow best with nonstop bombardment from all angles. I'm sure that if you follow my training advice, your deltoids will soon take on a new, improved look with more size, shape, and muscularity. Remember, maximum effort produces maximum gains.

Bruce Patterson.

Chapter 4

CHEST TRAINING

Here are some of the most comprehensive chest training tips, routines, tricks, and secrets taken from the pages of Ironman. *We begin with Ron Harris's routine to "wreck your pecs." Ron offers excellent heavy compound movements and secrets to getting the most out of them.*

WRECK YOUR PECS Ron Harris

Along with the infamous walk—that elbows-out swagger that some lifters employ to demonstrate how huge they are—one of the most popular moves among bodybuilders is the "puff," a trick male animals use to appear larger to potential enemies and mates. Leaning back, they ruffle their feathers or fill their lungs to simulate a larger, more imposing upper body. We do it to simulate a bigger chest. It's understandable why we do it—we all dream of having a giant chest like that of Arnold, Lee Haney, or Bertil Fox.

With proper training, you won't need to do the puff to make your chest look bigger. Here's how to get the thick slabs of pec meat that command respect and freak out spectators at contests, the beach, or even the gym.

PEC-WRECKING EXERCISES

Incline Press

Everyone calls the flat-bench press the king of upper-body exercises. It's certainly a great movement, but a king? No way. The gyms are filled with guys pressing tons of weight on the bench, but only a few have great chests. Many have droopy, bottom-heavy pecs. For a full, square set of pecs with thickness from collarbone to breastbone, you should give priority to inclines.

You need the right type of bench for this movement. Some incline benches are set at 45 degrees, which is far too extreme an angle for working the upper chest. If you have access to an adjustable bench that goes down to about 30 degrees, use it. Otherwise, put a box or block under one end of a flat bench to simulate this angle. Anything higher, and you'll be doing shoulder presses.

Because your shoulders always want to take over when you're pushing, you have to hold them back and down so your chest can do the work. You should feel a distinct pumping

Incline press—start position.   David Liberman.

Incline press—finish position.

and cramping in your chest, not in your shoulders, when you do any type of bench press.

Either dumbbells or barbells are great for inclines. Dumbbells let you bring the bells together at the top of the rep for a more powerful contraction. With a strong mind–muscle connection, however, you can get this type of searing pump with a barbell also. Machines may make it easier to focus on the muscle, but I believe that free weights are the best way to go for building mass.

Bench press

Since the bench press, when performed properly, is a true mass bonanza for all the pushing muscles of the upper body, it should be your first exercise at every other chest workout, alternating with inclines. The most common mistakes I see on this movement include using too wide a grip, relying too much on spotters, arching the back, and bouncing the bar off the chest. All of these errors come from trying to use too much weight. I ask people, "Would you rather use these dangerous tricks and get more weight up, or do it right and have a bigger chest?" They usually sulk and say, "Aw, leave me alone. I do it my way." So I pat them on their little baby chests, smile, and walk away.

Here's the correct way to do it. Position your hands far enough apart that your fore-

Bench press—start position.

Bench press—finish position.

arms are perpendicular to the ground as you lift. Slowly lower the bar until it touches your lower chest. Don't bounce, but instead pause for a split second to take away any momentum, and then drive the bar up to the top and squeeze your pecs hard. Don't lock out your elbows, or you're asking for an injury. Besides, if you lock your pectoral muscles, your arms won't be able to lock out.

You can also use dumbbells on this movement, as they let you bring the weights together. Pick one or the other movement, however, because they're essentially the same exercise.

Machine flye

I'm going to be a heretic here and make a statement that most of you will find incredible: I believe dumbbell flyes are absolutely useless. Looking at them in terms of gravity, there's no resistance at the top or bottom of the movement. What's worse, some people turn it into a dumbbell press with bent elbows. For once, machines win hands down.

My favorite is the flye machine that doubles as a rear delt machine, where your arms are out in a bear hug position rather than bent with your hands pointing at the ceiling. Not only is it safer on the shoulder joints than the standard pec deck, but it allows you a much greater range of motion.

The best way to do these is to keep your back pinned to the support and slowly squeeze your arms together until your pecs are fully contracted. At the contraction point, really squeeze your chest hard. Taking your fingers off the handles and pushing with the heels of your hand seems to facilitate a more natural movement and greater pump. If you're very flexible in your shoulder girdle, you'll be able to get a much better stretch by letting your arms travel farther back. If you don't have access to this type of machine or want a change every once in a while, use a cable crossover for this exercise.

As for the pullover, I never did believe there was any merit to that exercise, and I was recently pleased to learn that Dorian Yates shares this opinion.

Machine flye—start position.   Michael Ashley.

Machine flye—midpoint position.

TIPS FOR WRECKING PECS

1. Use a full range of motion. A big mistake many people make when doing incline or flat-bench presses is to use an incomplete range of motion, missing either the top or bottom range. For best results, you must go all

Ronnie Coleman.

the way up and all the way down. If anyone tells you that the top range is all delts and triceps, you can be sure that he or she doesn't know how to do the exercise correctly.

2. Press with your pecs, not with your arms. My big Filipino buddy Edwin has huge, coconut delts that rival Paul Dillett's, with giant 20-inch arms to match. Although he can easily press 405 for reps on both the flat and incline press, his chest is shallow and underdeveloped. Nowadays he does his presses correctly and is playing a frustrating game of catch-up with his chest.

Get your shoulders down and back and experiment with a light weight until you find out how to press with your chest, not your shoulders and arms.

3. Forget the weight. While you should always train as heavily as possible and increase the weight as often as you can, make sure you perform these exercises using good form. Heaving a lot of weight may make you feel

macho when you're with your buddies, but it will keep you from building the best chest you can.

4. Stretch and flex after every set. Until about four years ago, I never had many striations on my chest. Then I read John Parrillo's articles advocating fascial stretching and posing after each set, and I started incorporating this technique. After every set of presses, grab a pair of light dumbbells and get into the bottom position of a dumbbell flye on a flat or incline bench. Hold for 10 seconds, trying to go lower on every rep. (If you're trying this for the first time, use a very light weight and don't stretch too far.) This stretches the pecs tremendously. When you're finished with the stretch, get up and flex your pecs into a most-muscular pose. The pump is unbelievable. Four years of using this technique have given me all the veins and striations in my chest that I could ever want.

5. Achieve peak contraction. This is one training principle that turns the average rep into a growth-producing blitz. Rather than simply moving the weight up and down, actively squeeze it hard for a second at the contraction. This magnifies the pump—as well as the soreness you feel the next day.

6. Use pre-exhaustion. If you just can't feel presses in your chest, try doing them immediately after heavy machine flyes. If you don't feel your chest after that, check your pulse—you might be dead.

Next, Jerry Brainum shows us how to develop a 50-inch chest by looking at the techniques used by the men who did it.

HOW TO DEVELOP A 50-INCH CHEST Jerry Brainum

A great chest is the hallmark of every bodybuilding champion. Look at Lee Haney's chest; the awesome one simply dwarfs every other bodybuilder in this area. When you see Lee in person, his pectorals look like thick slabs of concrete, albeit sculptured concrete. What would Arnold Schwarzenegger have been without the massive chest development that pro-

Dumbbell flye.

pelled him to a record seven Mr. Olympia titles?

These men didn't start out with massive chests. They trained with persistence and high motivation. Great genetics also played a decisive role. While you may not build a chest comparable to Lee's or Arnold's, anyone can improve his or her present state of development in this area. What it takes is hard work combined with proper training techniques.

When speaking about the chest, bodybuilders usually refer to the pectoral muscles and the rib cage. Rib cage development is somewhat limited; that is, the younger you begin to exercise, the greater the size increase. This is because after age 21, bone endings fuse, and you are stuck with what you have. After the bones fuse, however, you can still give the illusion of a deeper chest by developing your serratus muscles. These are the fingerlike muscles that project along the sides of the chest. Since the function of these muscles is to lift the chest, pullover exercises of various types

strongly affect the serratus. This, in turn, serves to lift up the chest, producing the illusion of deeper chest development.

Perhaps the most outstanding example of super serratus development is former three-time Mr. Olympia Frank Zane. One of Frank's trademark poses consisted of a stomach vacuum with his hands behind his head. This pose readily displayed Frank's incomparable serratus muscles in bold relief. It made him look even more muscular than he really was (not that he wasn't muscular!).

Having observed Zane train regularly in the original Gold's Gym in Venice, California, I can tell you that he was a great believer in the single dumbbell pullover. He never failed to do this exercise as part of his chest routine. He usually did the exercise while lying across a high flat bench. Keeping his elbows slightly bent to relieve strain on the joint, Zane lowered the weight just past his head in a smooth, slow manner. If you wish to emulate Zane's prodigious serratus development, try his style of pullovers for about 4 sets of 15 repetitions, or 2 sets if you are a beginner. Pullovers work better if you use moderate weight with higher reps (10 reps or more).

Although the pectoral muscles participate in a variety of actions in moving the arms in various positions and helping to stabilize the shoulders, the basic function of this muscle is bringing the arms across the chest in a hugging motion. Two types of exercises strongly affect the pectorals: presses and flyes.

Chest pressing movements involve various kinds of bench presses. You can use either a flat, incline, or decline bench, or combine all three in one workout. Each exercise focuses on a different area of the pectorals. The flat-bench press works the central, meaty area of the pecs; incline work concentrates on the upper part; decline on the lower.

Presses are compound exercises because they also work other muscles besides the pecs, including the triceps and shoulders. Because of the large muscle mass used in presses, greater poundages can be used compared to more isolated chest exercises such as flyes. The experience of most bodybuilders clearly shows that the best results in chest development come from combining presses and flyes.

The venerable flat-bench press has fallen into disfavor in the past few years. Many bodybuilders say it's an overrated exercise; that it works the shoulders and triceps more than the pecs; that it's dangerous. The bench press can be dangerous if you use too much weight or sloppy form. But even if you're careful with form and you warm up, you still may be subject to a serious pec tear while doing bench presses if you use anabolic steroids.

Recent research with lab animals shows that steroids weaken muscle-tendon attachments, making it easier to incur a serious injury, such as a pectoral tear.

Some people believe that steroids make muscles too strong for their tendon attachments, and this, too, could be a factor in injuries. Although pec tears rarely happen in sports, the increased incidence of this injury is in direct proportion to the upsurge in steroid usage. What it adds up to is that doing heavy bench presses using steroids is a risk factor for

pec tears. I've seen this happen too often to believe otherwise.

Besides the danger of injury, however, are bench presses an overrated exercise for pec development? Quite the contrary. Because of the simplicity of the bench press, it's a suitable exercise for both beginning and advanced bodybuilders of both sexes. But you must use good form. This means warming up with a weight light enough to do 15 to 20 reps, followed by progressively heavier sets. Experts suggest various grips, but for pec development a medium, or shoulder-width, grip is best. Too narrow a grip concentrates on the triceps; a grip that's too wide places excessive strain on both the wrist and shoulder joints. It's best to experiment with grips to find what feels natural to you. Because of varying bone structures and muscle attachments, everybody's best grip spacing will be different.

Those who feel that flat-bench presses do little for pecs often substitute incline presses. This exercise is done with either a barbell or dumbbells (as are flat presses), although some favor the dumbbell version because of the greater stretch potential. The more you pre-stretch a muscle, the greater the contraction (due to a tighter lineup of muscle fibers induced by the stretch).

Bodybuilders often arch their backs, especially during incline presses, to use more weight. This technique turns the incline press into a sloppy type of flat press. Better to use less weight and good form. Supertrainer Vince Gironda suggests bringing the bar (if you use a barbell) to the neck for greater muscle development. If you prefer dumbbells, says Vince, keep the palms facing each other (as in a flye exercise); otherwise 75 percent of the work is on front deltoids.

Another important aspect of incline presses is the angle of the bench. The higher the incline, the more the exercise focus shifts to the deltoid. A slight incline (30 to 45 degrees) is best. This also pertains to incline flyes.

Decline presses aren't done very often these days, but they're a good exercise. Where you lower the bar determines which area of the pec is affected. For instance, if you lower the bar to your neck, the concentration will be on your upper pecs; lower it to the low chest, and you hit the lower-pec portion. You don't need a steep angle, unless you get off on the feeling of blood rushing to your head (also known as "Mussolini presses"). As in other pressing exercises, either a barbell or a pair of dumbbells is suitable.

Jason Arntz.

Paul DeMayo.

At this point you probably feel like you need a lift. Fine. Let's go flying.

Similar to press exercises, flyes can be done in either a flat, incline, or decline position. While some people refer to press exercises as compound movements (for reasons discussed earlier), flyes are more isolated movements. This isn't strictly true, in that you don't really isolate the pecs while doing flyes—although you do more closely mimic the primary pec action of crossing the arms over the chest. Because of this, flyes have a more potent muscle shaping action as compared to press exercises.

With incline flyes, it's best to lower the dumbbells in line with your head. When Arnold Schwarzenegger did these, he stopped just short of touching the dumbbells at the top

Justin Brooks.

Flavio Baccianini.

Shelby Cole.

position of the exercise to keep constant tension on his pecs. Don't go too low—stop when your pecs feel stretched. Lowering the weight too far strains both the pecs and shoulders. When doing flyes, be careful not to bend your arms too much, or the exercise turns into a

dumbbell bench press. Perform all flyes in an arc motion for best results. Picture your arms as mere conduits; let your pecs do the work.

The lower pecs rarely are a problem for most bodybuilders, but if you wish to focus on this area, decline flyes are excellent. Be careful, however; too much decline pec work may give your pecs a bottom-heavy appearance. This type of flye produces better results if you do higher reps (12 or more).

Most bodybuilding champions use cable crossovers as a finishing exercise at the end of their pec routines. Heavy weight isn't necessary on this movement; it's purely a shaping exercise. To influence varied pec areas, you can cross your hands in different positions—that is, over the face, across the chest, and so on. Varying body position also changes exercise focus. The more you bend, the more the shoulders come into play, while standing erect adds lat involvement. High reps are best here, as well. I've seen top champions average 20 reps per set in this exercise.

As in cable crossovers, pec deck machines place primary concentration on the inner-pec area. To minimize injury potential, make sure your arms are in an approximately 90-degree angle (perpendicular) to your torso. It's also important to resist the exercise both ways: as you contract the muscle and as you return to the starting position. Use a slow, smooth motion; and, as in flyes, don't risk injury by overstretching the pecs. You don't need heavy weight here, either. This exercise is good because the horizontal position involves the entire pectoral muscle, both upper and lower areas.

Although dips aren't a flye movement, they work the same area (lower pecs) as decline flyes. For pec concentration, lean forward as you dip; doing these with your body erect focuses on the triceps. Forget this exercise if you have a shoulder injury, unless you like deep pain.

Bodybuilding author Greg Zulak shows how to overcome a defiant chest by using special techniques that will induce complete chest development for the "upper-pectorally challenged."

COMPLETE CHEST DEVELOPMENT FOR THE UPPER-PECTORALLY CHALLENGED Greg Zulak

In the eyes of the law we may all be equal, but once you take up bodybuilding, it soon becomes obvious that we're not all equal in our response to exercise and our genetic potential for building muscle. To paraphrase George Orwell's dictum in his famous satire on communism, *Animal Farm*, we are all equal, but some are more equal than others.

When they passed out the bodybuilding genetics, some of us got the gold mine, while others got the shaft. Consequently, one person can gain more mass and muscle in six months than another can gain in two years. To make matters even more confusing, despite the fact that all of a person's muscles are attached to the same body, we all have certain muscle groups that we make fast and easy gains on and others on which we make slow, if any, progress. Even the champs have their weak

Henrik Thamasian.

bodyparts that don't respond as well as the rest of their body.

Arnold Schwarzenegger, for example, could never get his thighs to match his massive torso. Sergio Oliva's biceps, while huge, never had real peaks. Lee Haney also had problems with his biceps, while Robby Robinson lacks calves. Johnny Fuller has high lats, and Vince Taylor lacks upper pecs. And so it goes. There are very few bodybuilders whose physiques are so complete that they don't have any poor muscle groups.

For me it's been especially difficult to build my pecs. This has always frustrated the hell out of me, because I just have to look at a weight and my delts grow. They grow when I do curls, for goodness' sake!

My lats also respond well and grow fast. But my pecs, especially my upper pecs, have always developed slowly. I have to blast my chest just to get a bit of response, and what muscle I get seems to be in the lower sections, so I've always been envious of guys who have pecs that jut out from their necklines.

Mohamed Makkawy.

On the other hand, I know guys who can do set after set of presses and laterals and can't get a pump in their delts, but can do a few sets of bench presses and blow their pecs up like balloons. That's the way it is. Nobody says that life is fair. What I've discovered is that if you have a structure that's not conducive to building thick, full pecs, particularly in the upper portions of the pectoralis major, you have to resort to special methods to get your muscles to respond. The number-one requirement for getting your pecs to grow is very high-intensity training. Certain intensity techniques, including pre-exhaustion, supersets, tri-sets, and drop sets, are very effective with chest training, especially when straight sets fail to work.

Another way to increase tension and workload when you're doing dips and barbell chest exercises is to hold the weight in an unorthodox way.

TECHNIQUES FOR PROBLEM PECS

The trouble with traditional chest training is that it's hard to isolate your pectorals on compound exercises like the bench press. The bench press is the second-most-popular exercise, after curls, in gyms everywhere. But let's face it—some people's structures just aren't suited to flat-bench pressing. For those folks, it's a better idea to perform bench presses to the neck. It also helps to bring your legs up and cross them over your body, which forces you to hold your back flat and keeps you from arching or cheating. If you keep your elbows wide and pulled back in line with your shoulders and lower the bar slowly to your neck, you should realize more development in your upper pecs, which will improve your overall chest shape and help you avoid that unsightly hollow in the upper chest that's so common among bodybuilders.

Here's a tip from Larry Scott, the first Mr. Olympia, that makes bench pressing to the neck even more effective. Twist your hands as you hold the bar so it runs diagonally across

Craig Licker.

your palms, not straight on. Your thumbs should be under the bar, with your little fingers on top and the forefingers of each hand on the front side of the bar and almost pointing at each other.

The first thing that happens when you hold the bar with a diagonal grip is that your elbows go high and wide. That's good because the more you twist your hands, the higher and wider your elbows go, and this position greatly increases the stretch to your upper pecs. Larry recommends that you consciously keep your elbows high and wide throughout the full range of motion. If you do the exercise this way, you'll get 100 percent more stretch in your upper pecs than you were getting before. If, as you perform your reps, you begin to feel the stretch lessening, you've allowed your elbows to come forward and drop. Keep them high and wide at all times, and your upper pecs will burn like crazy.

When doing bench presses to the neck, make sure you don't quite lock out at the top.

Instead, stop an inch or so short of lockout to keep constant tension on your pecs, but don't get into the bad habit of only doing half-reps. In the quest for constant tension, a lot of lifters start off doing three-quarter reps, which is permissible. But then they usually gradually shorten the range of motion to the point where the bar moves only 8 to 10 inches at most, and they're doing half-reps, if that. This causes the pecs to miss out on quite a bit of work. Constant tension is great, but try to maintain it over the largest range of motion you can, not the shortest.

Bench presses to the neck performed Scott-style are even more concentrated and effective when you use the Smith machine,

Mohamed Makkawy.

Robert Russo and Johnny Moya.

because you don't have to worry about balancing the bar. All you have to do is press and focus on making those pecs pump and burn. Form is more important than sheer weight, so it's better to use moderately heavy poundages than super-heavy weights, which encourage cheating and poor form.

By the way, turning the bar so it runs diagonally across your palms works great on incline presses as well, especially when you do them on the Smith machine. If you find it

Joe DeAngelis.

difficult to make your upper pecs work hard on this movement, try doing it this way. Believe me, your upper chest will ignite.

The same diagonal grip also works with dips. The wide-grip dip, sometimes known as the Gironda dip (after famed training expert Vince Gironda) calls for you to invert your hands, or turn them inward so that your palms face out and the knuckles of your hands point at each other, not forward or outward. This forces your elbows to move out wide and puts all the pressure on your pecs. The Gironda dip is best done with the V-dip bars, which are 34 inches wide. If it hurts your wrists to dip when using this technique, try taking a wider grip on the bars. The wider you go, the less it hurts your wrists and the more stress it places on the lower and outer sections of your pecs.

Dipping this way builds the outer and lower pecs. Regular dips performed with your elbows back primarily build front delts, triceps, and lower pecs.

ALIGN YOUR BODY CORRECTLY

Whether you're doing bench presses, incline presses, or flyes, make sure that you align your body before you begin so your pecs get the mechanical advantage, not your delts or triceps. Many people are what training expert John Parrillo calls "delt bench pressers" because they flatten their chests at the top of

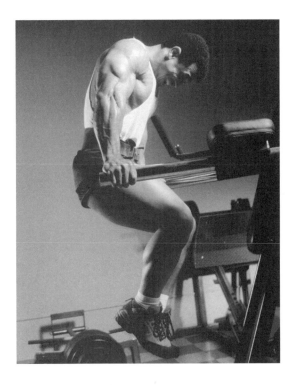

Take the bar from the rack and roll your shoulders under your body. Feel as though you're pushing your rear delts down toward your waist, and keep pushing them down hard throughout the set. Never let up. At the same time, arch your sternum (chest bone) up. As the weight goes up, push through with your pecs, not your delts. Keep your shoulders down and back.

In addition, move the bar in an arc, not straight up and down. The arc allows you to contract your pecs hard at the top. I suggest that you practice with light weights until you get the motion down pat.

Use the same delts-pushing-down, chest-pushing-up position on flyes so you keep your delts out of the movement as much as you can and your pecs are the primary movers.

One final tip for when you're doing dumbbell presses or flyes. You'll get a harder pec contraction if you turn your elbows in at the very top. In other words, in the fully contracted position, touch your elbows together, not the dumbbells.

THE PRE-EXHAUSTION PRINCIPLE AND YOUR CHEST

The technique of pre-exhaustion was invented by my friend and mentor Bob Kennedy, who announced to the world in a 1968 *Ironman* article that performing lateral raises before presses had enabled him to work his delts much harder than normal. Arthur Jones of Nautilus fame later expanded the pre-exhaust principle to include flyes before bench presses for pecs, leg extensions before leg presses for thighs, and pullovers before pulldowns for lats. In effect, performing any isolation movement for a specific muscle before a compound movement for the same muscle pre-exhausts the target and permits you to train it with greater intensity.

The idea behind the pre-exhaust principle is simple. You can work a particular muscle structure much harder than would otherwise be possible if you eliminate the weak links that prevail in all basic compound movements (exercises that involve two or more muscle

the movement and push the bar up using delt strength, not pec strength. To change this and become a pec bench presser, you have to set up your pectoral girdle before you begin the first rep to put the tension on the right muscles.

Dave Palumbo.

groups). Since this is a chest article, let's use chest exercises as an example.

The problem with popular compound chest exercises, such as bench presses, incline presses, and dips, is that you hit muscular failure when the weakest of the involved muscles, the triceps, can no longer perform. Since this occurs long before you work your chest muscles to any significant degree, your triceps grow well but your pecs typically become underdeveloped.

By performing an isolation exercise—such as flyes or pec deck flyes—before a compound chest exercise—like bench presses, incline presses, or dips—you can pre-tire, or pre-exhaust, the chest muscles and correct this problem. By the time you begin the compound movement, your pecs are already tired and exhausted, but your triceps are still fresh and strong. Then, when you hit failure on the compound exercise, it's because your pecs have given out, not your triceps.

Here are two ways to use the pre-exhaust principle for chest training: You can do standard pre-exhaust supersets, taking little rest

between exercises, or you can do modified pre-exhausts, performing 3 to 5 sets of the isolation movement before you begin the compound movement. In our example, that means 3 to 5 sets of flyes before you begin your benches or inclines. Either method is effective, and both can be used to good advantage. Here are some sample routines.

Upper-Chest Pre-exhaust
Superset Workout

Pec deck flye	$4 \times 8–12$
Smith machine incline	
press (diagonal grip)	$3 \times 8–12$,
	1×25
Incline flye	$3 \times 10–12$,
	1×25
Cross-bench pullover	$2–3 \times 12–15$

Upper-Chest Modified
Pre-exhaust Workout

Incline flye	$4 \times 6–12$,
	$1 \times 20–25$
Pec deck flye	$3 \times 8–12$

Smith machine incline press (diagonal grip)	3 × 6–10, 1 × 20–25
Flat-bench dumbbell press	3 × 6–10, 1 × 20–25
Cross-bench pullover	2–3 × 15

Modified Pre-exhaust Overall Chest Shaper

Pec deck flye	3 × 10–12
Incline flye	3 × 8–12
Bench press to the neck (diagonal grip)	3 × 6–10
Incline dumbbell press	3 × 8–10
Cross-bench pullover	2–3 × 15–20

BUILDING PECS WITH SUPERSETS AND TRI-SETS

Although you're performing supersets when you do standard pre-exhausts, they're not regular supersets, because you perform the isolation movement first, before the compound movement. By supersetting flyes after bench presses, or incline flyes after incline dumbbell presses, however, you can greatly increase the training intensity on your pecs and force a lot of blood into the muscles. Furthermore, by doing tri-sets in a special way, you can incorporate the benefits of both pre-exhausts and supersets into one set. For example, here's one of my favorite combinations for the pecs:

> Pec deck flye
> Smith machine incline press (diagonal grip)
> Incline dumbbell flye

This works well because these three chest exercises don't work the muscles in the same way. Larry Scott often tri-sets incline dumbbell presses and incline dumbbell flyes, but many guys are going to have a problem with that mix because the incline dumbbell presses and incline barbell presses both work the triceps

heavily. By the time you finish the barbell presses, your triceps are fried. In the tri-set just listed, however, your arms remain fresh because the triceps are used only on one exercise, the incline press.

Sometimes I do bench presses to the neck before the tri-set and finish with a few rounds of cross-bench pullovers. This enables me to use a heavy–light system and really give my pecs a good workout. Try it sometime, and you'll know what I mean.

Here's the complete routine:

Tri-Set Overall Pec Pounder

Bench press to the neck (diagonal grip)	3 × 10, 8, 6
Pec deck flye	3–4 × 10–12
Smith machine incline press (diagonal grip)	3–4 × 6–10
Incline dumbbell flye	3–4 × 10–12
Cross-bench dumbbell pullovers	3 × 15

If you don't feel your pecs on this one, you'd better check your pulse.

Another of my favorite combinations for chest is incline dumbbell flyes after incline dumbbell presses. I like to do this superset after 4 or 5 sets of bench presses to the neck, a routine that pumps up the upper pecs. Because they are small muscles, it's very difficult to get much lactic acid buildup in the upper pecs, and it's also hard to get and maintain a pump. Even so, this superset blasts the area and fills in that hollow at the top of the chest.

To stress your upper pecs even more and get fuller development, adjust the angle of the bench after each superset, going from a low incline of 20 to 25 degrees up to 70 degrees.

Here's the complete routine:

Superset Upper-Pec Pounder

Bench press to the neck	4 × 10, 8, 6

Superset

Incline dumbbell press	4–6 × 8–12
Incline dumbbell flye	4–6 × 8–12
Cross-bench pullover	3 × 15

If you lack inner pecs, finish with some cable crossovers or pec deck flyes, and if you need more lower-pec development, add some dips. Three sets of each should do the trick.

The following variation incorporates both pre-exhaust and regular supersets:

Combination-Superset Upper-Pec Sizzler

Superset

Peck deck flye	3–4 × 10–12
Smith machine incline press (diagonal grip)	3–4 × 8–15

Superset

Incline dumbbell press (varied angles)	3 × 8–12, 1 × 20–25
Incline dumbbell flye	3 × 8–12, 1 × 20–25

Joe DeAngelis.

THE BEAUTY OF DUMBBELL WORK

Because you can lower dumbbells below the level of your torso on flyes and presses, you can give your pecs more stretch than they get when you use a barbell. A basic rule of exercise physiology states that the more a muscle is stretched at the beginning of a rep, the harder it can contract at the finish. This adds up to greater muscle stimulation and growth. I can't emphasize enough the importance of getting a good stretch on all your chest exercises.

Dumbbells also give you greater pec isolation. When you use them, your pecs do more work, which is why many people who get unimpressive results with barbell bench presses and inclines often do much better with dumbbell bench and incline presses. If you've been performing lots of barbell chest movements and have little to show for it, switch to an all-dumbbell routine for a while.

The techniques used with the following workout are the same as those required for the previously listed routines. In this case, begin

with flat-bench dumbbell presses, starting light and pyramiding up in weight on each set as you would with a barbell. Do 4 or 5 sets, decreasing your reps from 12 to 15 down to a hard 6, then drop the poundage and pump out 20 to 25 reps on the last set.

The next step is to perform 6 supersets of incline dumbbell presses followed by incline dumbbell flyes, adjusting the angle of the bench every 2 sets. Do 2 sets at 25 degrees, 2 at

40 to 45 degrees, and 2 at 60 to 65 degrees. On the last set, reduce the weight and do 20 to 25 reps of each exercise, really burning out your pecs.

Finish with 3 sets of cross-bench dumbbell pullovers, at 15 to 20 reps per set supersetted with 3 sets of Gironda dips, on which you do as many reps as you can get. Arch your chest hard and stretch those pecs on each rep by taking as big a breath as possible on the pullovers. On the dips, lower as far as you can for maximum stretch, and keep those elbows wide.

Here's the complete routine:

Dumbbell Chest Chiseler
Flat-bench dumbbell press   4–5 × 12–15,
10, 8, 6,
1 × 20–25

Mike Quinn.

Superset
Incline dumbbell
    press (varied angles)   4 × 8–12,
1 × 15–20
Incline dumbbell
    flye (varied angles)   4 × 8–12,
1 × 15–20

Superset
Cross-bench
    dumbbell pullover   3 × 15–20
Gironda dip   3 sets to failure

For variety, do the incline flyes before the incline presses in pre-exhaust style at every other workout. This will shock the muscles and keep you growing.

Here's an all-dumbbell superset routine that hits every section of the pecs hard. Less-experienced trainees can do 3 supersets of each combination instead of 4.

Dumbbell Superset Strategy
Superset
Incline dumbbell press   4 × 8–10
Incline dumbbell flye   4 × 8–12

Superset
Flat-bench dumbbell press   4 × 6–10
Flat-bench dumbbell flye   4 × 8–12

Superset

30-degree decline dumbbell press	4 × 8–10
30-degree decline dumbbell flye	4 × 8–10
Cross-bench dumbbell pullover	3 × 15

Reverse the order of the exercises in each superset at every other workout and do them in pre-exhaust style. If your pecs aren't pumped like balloons after you complete this workout, you're definitely loafing and not serious about developing your chest. You should be drenched in sweat, and your pecs should be on fire after this torture.

If you weren't blessed with the structure and insertions for building big pecs, you'll have to earn them the old-fashioned way—through hard, intense work. Train at extremely high intensity, aim for a good pump and a hot burn in the target muscles (which indicate lactic acid buildup), and go for a maximum stretch on every rep. Use constant tension when you can, but over the largest range of motion possible.

If you give some of these routines a fair try, your pecs will improve greatly. Let me know how you make out.

Next we get the benefit of Gene Mozée's first-hand, detailed account of exactly how "The Oak" built his 58-inch chest.

CREATING A CAVERNOUS CHEST
Arnold Schwarzenegger, as told to Gene Mozée

I've never been a big believer in the "great bone structure, great potential" theory. Ideal bone structure is definitely an advantage, but it's not the most important factor in developing a great physique. Most bodybuilding champions had to overcome great adversity to reach their pinnacles of success. I believe that building a great physique is 90 percent perspiration and 10 percent potential, or good bone structure. In my own case, I certainly conveyed no image of a future bodybuilding champion when I began training. Not only was I thin, but my chest was very shallow and flat. No one would have ever guessed that I had a 58-inch chest and a 500-pound bench press in my future based on my potential—or lack of it. Hard work and an intense desire to succeed can overcome almost any obstacle.

Right from the beginning, I was always greatly impressed with Reg Park's fantastic physique. I was as tall as he was, and I set my

Ronnie Coleman.

the side. Some guys who look great from the front because they have good pecs seem to disappear from the side because they lack deep rib cages. Their chests and waists look about the same thickness.

Fully expanding the rib cage is one essential factor in developing an impressive chest, particularly in the early training stages, since the rib box is the foundation on which you build your whole torso. To develop the chest, back, and shoulders to their ultimate capacity, you have to fully expand your rib cage. Chest expansion results from a combination of breath-stimulating and chest-stretching movements. Heavy leg work—particularly squats—helps induce deep breathing and elevates the ribs upward and outward. I recommend that you do a light set of dumbbell pullovers immediately after every set of squats to fully stretch your rib cage and expand your chest. In addition, you should do pullovers with your chest workouts, as I'll explain later.

If you have a very flat chest and lack depth, it will take at least a year to enlarge your rib box. If an individual concentrates only on the pecs in the beginning, his chest size will be limited. So right from the first workout, I suggest that bodybuilders include pullovers.

The pectorals are much easier to develop; but the bigger the foundation on which they sit, the greater the development and impressiveness they will achieve. The pecs should be worked from all angles. Basic exercises like bench presses, incline presses, decline presses, and parallel-bar dips are heavy movements that pack muscle on your chest. Flyes, pulley crossovers, and pec deck flyes are more effective for shaping and striating your pecs than for building muscle mass.

Complete pec development results from working all four regions of the muscle: upper, lower, outside, and inside. The following exercises are the ones that I have found build size, shape, and muscularity most effectively. After describing how and why each exercise is performed, I will show you how to use it in your workout program at all levels of training experience.

goals to build a Mr. Universe body that would someday equal or surpass his. Park's body was fully developed and symmetrical, but I would say without a doubt that he had the greatest chest development in the world at that time. He had massive, perfectly developed pecs and a huge rib cage. When he stood relaxed, his chest looked twice as thick as his waist from

Joe Spinello.

BENCH PRESS

For years, the one chest exercise I used was the basic bench press. It's the key exercise for building a massive chest. It works the whole pectoral mass, as well as the shoulders, lats, and triceps. It also induces heavy breathing, which encourages rib cage expansion. I use a medium-wide grip, with my hands about 8 to 10 inches beyond shoulder width on each side. I inhale deeply as I lower the bar to the highest part of my chest just above my nipples, and then I exhale as I ram the weight back to the top. I always begin with a light weight for a warm-up set of 20 to 30 reps to get the blood into the area and loosen me up. I then add weight on each succeeding set and do 8 reps on each until I reach a limit set, usually around 405 for 6 reps. I rest about two minutes between sets. I do at least 6, and sometimes 10, sets.

INCLINE BARBELL PRESS

This movement is unsurpassed as a builder of the pectoralis minor, or upper pec. Some people prefer to do these with dumbbells, but I like the barbell version better. Using the same grip as in the bench press, I inhale as I lower the bar just below my collarbones, and exhale forcibly on the way up. I like 5 sets of 8 to 12 reps. Again, I add weight on each set. The whole chest area, from the collarbones to the point where the pectorals attach at the bottom of the chest, is now flushed with blood.

FLAT-BENCH FLYE

This is a great exercise for shaping the outer sections of the pecs, and when you do it correctly, it also opens up your rib box and deepens your chest. Start by holding two dumbbells at arm's length over your chest while lying on a flat bench. Inhale deeply as you lower the dumbbells with your arms slightly bent. Lower the weights as far down as possible, until they almost touch the floor. Exhale as you return them to the starting position, and forcibly squeeze your pecs at the top so that the inner attachments also get some benefit. I do 5 sets of 10 reps.

PARALLEL-BAR DIP

This exercise flushes the whole pectoral area and is particularly great for building the lower pec, giving you that impressive deep muscular ridge that separates the pecs from the abdominals. These will give your chest that carved-in-marble look. I use an 80-pound dumbbell for 5 sets of 8 reps, and superset them with flat-bench flyes. I inhale deeply as I go all the way down for a full stretch, then exhale as I push back to the top. By the time I finish the fifth superset, my pecs are so engorged with blood that I feel as if they're going to burst through my skin.

STIFF-ARM PULLOVER

I finish off by thoroughly stretching the entire structural area of the chest to its fullest capacity. This exercise can enlarge your structure by raising, thickening, and deepening your rib cage and all of its cartilage, ligaments, and attachments. It's important to do this one correctly, or you won't get the full growth stimulation it delivers. Lie across a sturdy flat bench and grasp a medium-weight dumbbell with both hands flat against the top inside plate. Starting with the weight at arm's length at a position above your chest, inhale deeply as you lower it slowly behind your head with your arms straight until your chest is stretched to

the limit. It's very important that as you lower the weight, you make sure that your hips also go down and remain down throughout the movement. Exhale as you pull the weight back to the starting position. I do 5 sets of 15 to 20 reps with a 30-second rest between sets. I walk around the gym and take very deep breaths and force my chest to remain at maximum expansion until I return to the bench for my next set. The ache in the sternum this movement produces will astound you—it pulls your chest apart and forces it into new growth. (A word of caution: If you feel any shoulder discomfort, you're lowering the weight too far, and an injury may result. This can happen if you try to use too much weight.)

TRAINING TIPS

- I train my chest three days a week, on the same days I train my back.
- Before a contest, I add pulley crossovers, which I sometimes superset with pullovers, and do 5 sets of 12 to 15 reps.
- Always concentrate all of your mental energy on the task at hand. Don't let anything distract you. Talk *after* the workout, never during it.
- Always push yourself by fighting for those last 2 or 3 reps, but use good exercise form at all times.
- Always be aware of the way you breathe. Inhale as deeply as you can on all chest exercises, and hold your chest high at all times. Don't ever slump or slouch. Good posture is an asset for enlarging your chest.
- Beginners should use an all-around basic program that includes bench presses and pullovers. After 6 months, add more chest work as follows:

Bench press	4 × 8–10
Flat-bench flye	3 × 10
Dip	2 × 8–10
Pullover	3 × 15

After you have been training for 9 to 12 months, set up the program as follows:

Bench press	5×8
Incline press	3×10
Flat-bench flye	3×10
Dip	$3 \times 8–10$
Pullover	4×15

Advanced trainees can use my program as follows:

Bench press	$6 \times 20–30, 15,$ $10, 6, 6, 5$
Incline press	$5 \times 12, 10,$ $8, 8, 8$

Superset

Flat-bench flye	5×10
Dip	5×8
Pullover	$5 \times 15–20$

These are the most productive chest exercises I have ever used. I have at times done more sets of certain movements, and I have forced out higher reps to bring out maximum definition before a contest. Anyone can get great results by doing these exercises the way I recommend.

Ronnie Coleman.

Chapter 5

BACK TRAINING

Proper back training is often ignored by beginning bodybuilders for the simple reason that the back isn't easy to look at—out of sight, out of mind. But the muscles of the back make an enormous contribution to the overall thickness of the upper body. No physique is complete without the thick musculature of the back, enhancing the shoulders and chest and exaggerating the taper down to the waist.

First, Judd Biasiotto, Ph.D., shows us why the deadlift is the "get-huge movement."

THE GET-HUGE MOVEMENT
Judd Biasiotto, Ph.D.

I'm convinced that it was one sadistic person who invented the deadlift. It's far and away the most gut-wrenching of the three powerlifts. (Let's face it, they don't call it the deadlift for nothing.) I remember that when I started in the sport, my coach told me that the deadlift separates the men from the boys. I believe I tested out as a fetus the first time around.

This lift is a killer—no doubt about it. Not only do you need powerful legs and an iron-strong back to be a good deadlifter, but you also need heart—and I do mean a lot of it. I've seen guys with wills of tempered steel broken by this exercise. It's a nasty lift, and you have to be an ironman to use it in your training.

As tough as the deadlift is to perform, it's one of the most beneficial exercises you can do. It can give you the quintessential combination of unbelievable mass, power, and symmetry. Rep for rep, no exercise does it better. Some athletes say that the deadlift is primarily a lift for the lower back, while others say it's a power movement for the legs. The truth is, it works every major muscle group in your body—the legs, buttocks, lower back, stomach, upper back, arms, and neck. Even the muscles in your forehead and temples get involved.

Arnold Schwarzenegger has said that if he had to point to one thing that was responsible for his success in life, it would be the deadlift. Okay, he didn't actually say that, but he did say that when it comes to developing total-body thickness, there's no better exercise. Mr. Olympias Franco Columbo, Dorian Yates, and

Deadlift—start position.   Art Dilkes.

Deadlift—finish position.

Lee Haney have made similar statements. In short, if you want thickness and power, the deadlift is the way to go.

BASIC RULES

There are a number of things you need to know about deadlifting before you incorporate the movement into your training. First, of course, you need to get a pair of those cute little wrist bands that Nike sells. The other rules for deadlift survival are as follows.

1. **Develop good form.** The deadlift is one exercise that requires picture-perfect form. One mistake and you could be singing soprano for the rest of your life—so take your time. Before you do a single rep, understand exactly how the lift should be performed, and don't start your first set until you've mastered it. This will not only help you get maximum development from your deadlifts, but it will also keep you from ripping your spine out of your lower back.

2. **Train smart.** Warm up before you start working out—and stretch out before and after each exercise. This will increase your development and decrease your chance of injury. The most common cause of injury is lack of flexibility. When training, increase your workload and intensity gradually. If you've never deadlifted before, it's probably a good idea to use light resistance until you get your form down pat. Take your time. Remember, you're trying to develop your body, not destroy it.

3. **Don't kill yourself.** This is a primary rule of weight training. Believe me, if you're not careful, the deadlift can kill you—or at least injure you seriously. When your body says no, don't say go. Or, in the profound words of *Hee Haw*'s Dr. Archie Campbell, "If you do something and it hurts, don't do it."

   Pain is a warning signal that something's wrong. If you experience pain while deadlifting, stop—and don't start

Chris Duffy.

again until the pain is gone. Whatever you do, don't try to work through an injury. The deadlift is a great exercise, but it can be dangerous—so it requires your full attention. Lifting is supposed to be a lifelong activity, not a life-threatening one.

In light of all of these guidelines, make sure you give the deadlift a fair chance. It can make the difference between your being good and being great, so give it time.

PERFORMING THE DEADLIFT

Although the deadlift is a real butt buster, it's an extremely simple movement to perform, so simple that your little sister could do it—provided that your little sister is Lenda Murray. You just have to pay attention to form.

As you may already be aware, there are two methods of deadlifting: the conventional

method and the sumo method. If you're using this movement strictly for bodybuilding, I suggest you stick with the conventional method. If you're considering wearing the red, white, and blue at next year's World Deadlift Championships, however, you might want to consider the sumo method. In general, if you're long-waisted and you have long arms and a strong back, you should use the conventional method. Conversely, if you have superstrong hips and legs and are short and short-waisted, you may want to give the sumo method a try.

Sumo-style is also the best method of deadlifting if you don't have a bionic back. The sumo method is a leg lift, not a back lift, so you pull the weight with your legs, not with your back.

On a sumo-style deadlift, your hands are inside your legs. Most lifters position their hands so they're half on and half off the knurling. The closer your hands are, the less distance you have to pull the weight. On the other hand, the closer your hands, the less control of the bar you have. What's more, if your hands are positioned entirely off the knurling, you'll probably have difficulty gripping the bar. It's also a good idea to use a one-hand-over-and-one-hand-under grip, which cuts down on the bar's torque.

Michelle Sorensen.

lift is breaking inertia—getting the weight off the ground. Generally, once you get past this point, the lift is yours, especially if you've kept your hips down.

That's something you want to concentrate on. When the weight gets heavy, many lifters have a tendency to raise their hips and drop their back forward. Not only is it nearly impossible to pull the weight from that position, it's extremely dangerous. Remember that this is a leg lift, not a back lift.

There's one last point: when pulling the weight, keep the bar close to your body. The farther the weight is from your body, the less leverage you have—and, consequently, the harder the lift. I've heard that for every inch the weight moves out in front of the body, you can add 40 pounds of resistance to the bar. I'm not sure the arithmetic is accurate, but the concept certainly is.

Now let's look at the conventional performance style. As I said, this is the method I generally recommend for bodybuilding, and if you're tall and have long arms and a strong back, it's definitely the deadlift for you. The legs play a big part in this style as well.

As with the sumo method, you use an over-under grip to cut down on the torque. In

As with the squat, foot spacing is an individual matter. Some universal rules apply, however: You point your toes slightly outward, lock your thighs in a just-above-parallel-to-the-ground position, and keep your back tight, straight, and upright, with your head straight and facing forward. The hardest part of this

Justin Brooks.

the conventional method, however, you position your hands outside your legs to cut down on the distance over which you must pull the bar. As with the sumo method, your toes are pointed slightly out, your thighs are locked in a just-above-parallel position, your back is straight, and your head is positioned straight forward. A common problem occurs when the thighs are too high at the start. This may cause some real trouble when the lift gets beyond the knees—like ripping your lower back in half.

When you're in the correct position, pull the bar with a fluid motion. Don't try to jerk the weight from the floor. Remember that the back and thighs work together throughout the lift. Consequently, the two bodyparts should lock out together at the top. It's also a good idea to drive your head backward as you lift the bar. Everything tends to follow your head. By driving your head back, you force your shoulders back and your chest up—and force your hips to stay down as well.

So there you have it—the deadlift in a nutshell. As I said, it's a simple skill. Be careful, however. It's a simple lift that can make or break you.

Shawn Ray.

Shawn Ray has one of the most aesthetic physiques of all time. The symmetry in his back is near perfection. Kevin Neilsen tells us how Shawn built his champion back.

SHAWN RAY'S CHAMPION BACK TRAINING Kevin Neilsen

Shawn Ray hasn't been in this gym for a while, so when he swings open the door and stands there, framed by the blinding summer sunlight outside, sweaty pros and wide-eyed gym grunts alike stop in midset. They know what's coming.

They've seen it before, though not often. Shawn likes to make the rounds. It keeps him fresh, he says. Consistent inconsistency is the paradox that balances his life. His gyms, his exercises, even his wardrobe are the perpetual shell game he plays on his psyche to keep it on its toes—and on a nonplussed public trying in vain to unravel his secrets. What those present can predict, though, is that they are about to witness a workout intense enough to incinerate the gym.

Shawn trains hard. His celebrity glitters, which misleads many into thinking he's more show than heave-ho—but the best pros know he's on the bleeding edge of pain and

Cable row—start position.

Cable row—finish position.

poundage. For that reason more than any other, Shawn trains alone. Too many have been sorely chagrined after asking if they could work in.

After years of watching the Shawn Ray saga unfold, one uncovers a pattern. The details are in flux, but the order that guides them is carved in stone. It's always the same four-on/one-off program, and always the same sequence of bodyparts: chest and triceps on day 1, legs on day 2, back and biceps on day 3, and shoulders on day 4. Today must be day 3, because Shawn eyes the chinning bar first, then orients himself to the rest of the back equipment in the gym. He puts down his bag, rummages around in its depths, and pulls out some lifting straps. These are his sole accessories.

Surely, one reason Ray continues to improve every year is that he wants no part of his body inhibited by weight belts or knee wraps. The results of this objective have become his trademark: Shawn Ray has no flaws. No bodybuilder is more balanced in muscularity; none is more symmetrical.

In this respect, even his training philosophy could be described as holistic. When he works his back, he looks in the mirror to watch the stress travel all the way from his

Achilles tendons upward over his calves and hamstrings, through his hips, spinal erectors, lats, rhomboids, and traps, even up to his neck. That, to Shawn Ray, constitutes one repetition, and it stands to reason that a belt would only short-circuit the route.

Out of this philosophy comes his recent eye-popping improvement in thickness and density. Only three years ago, Shawn was legitimately criticized for his weak back. Not only was he in the shadows during posedowns because of his insufficient lat spread, but he also wasn't displaying the layered look of a Dorian Yates or a Flex Wheeler. That was a good lesson for Shawn, and the next time we saw him in the gym, his approach to back training had changed.

It was obvious to everyone in the gym that Shawn was piling on more coal, stirring the fires to a new intensity, stretching harder on extensions and squeezing tighter on contractions. This explains why he needs straps: Shawn doesn't want one precious rep to slip from his grasp before the muscles have been drained of their final twitch of life.

Warriors who have fallen in his wake can attest to the demands he makes on himself. Never is there a down set. Always the weights are pyramided heavier, harder, stricter. Never is his rep goal less than specific. It's not 8 or 10, but whichever number is his goal for the day. If it's 10, he finds a way to do 10 on every set. If it's 8, he always gets 8.

Every time Shawn trains his back, he changes the exercise mix, hitting every imaginable movement over the course of a season but remaining faithful to his proven mass builders: heavy, basic free-weight exercises. Among other things, he knows that only free weights can produce his patented depth and fullness.

The one element that doesn't change is his warm-up. On back day, it's always chins. These aren't counted as an exercise, but neither are they trivialized as just a bit of fluff to get the circulation going. Quite the contrary, Shawn stretches his arms wide, uses an overhand grip, cinches up his lifting straps, crosses his ankles, tightens his body into position, and grinds out 13 repetitions, slowing his pace as he goes to make it more difficult.

It's obvious that Shawn is intellectually as well as emotionally involved in each repetition. His goal is not merely to reach the bar, but also to allow his muscles to savor the journey. From bottom to top, he distributes the work equally to every muscle in his back, consciously contracting one, then another, adroitly shifting the workload back and forth, step by step up the ladder of his back. If he feels his repetitions are too slow to finish all 12 at that pace, he quickens it; if he's going too fast, he decelerates.

Four sets of chins, and he's ready for his first exercise. This time it's seated cable rows. Shawn hooks up a close-grip V-handle, stacks the weight, and once again cinches up his straps. There's no warm-up set—just metered, steady, squeezing repetitions as he stretches forward until his scapulae seem to rotate right over his shoulders, and then flexes them back to where they started. Every fiber is brought into play along the way until the muscle reaches absolute contraction.

Bent-over barbell row.

Deadlift.

Shawn goes for 10 reps, gets them, and then adds more weight in the hope of bringing them down to 8. This time he puts even more into the movement and adds some power to the contraction. His erectors and Christmas tree pop and squirm, tightening, and with an audible moan he hauls on the cable like a swamp dredge. He gets 10 reps again, so he adds even more weight. Once more he puts everything into it, but does not miss a muscle anywhere along the way as he squeezes out 8 full repetitions.

Still more weight, more strain, and the movement on his fourth set is the strictest of all. His reps are flawless, massive, isolated yet explosive; extending to the outer limits of his reach, then driving backward into the contraction. He gets 8 reps. Barely.

Now come bent-over barbell rows. Shawn uses a wider-than-normal grip and a narrow stance. Again, he tightens his straps, then smoothly reps out 10 tight rows, pulling the bar into his solar plexus rather than his navel. Here, he seems to concentrate on his lat spread and thickness. He begins with a working man's weight and raises the angle of his body more to accommodate the poundage than to isolate the muscle, but it works. Every rep flays out

his lats and turns his erectors to steel. His back seems to double in thickness, stacking muscle upon muscle.

Again, he pyramids the weights on 4 sets, all to failure, all for 8 reps.

Next, he straddles the T-bar. His stance and grip are the same as he used for the barbell rows, but this time he pulls with his body at an obtuse angle into his gut. As Shawn rows, he rocks through a small arc, sending his lats into full spread from high under his delts all the way to his waist; and, as always, there's that joint-ripping stretch, that crushing contraction. Every set increases in poundage as he works his way through 4 strict sets of 8 to 10.

Just when we think it's all over, Shawn inhales deeply, glares into the lifting room, and marches boldly into no-man's-land. Our jaws drop as he loads a barbell with plates and eyes it in preparation for the most vicious back exercise known—the deadlift.

Rather than use the conventional over-and-under grip, Shawn grabs the bar with both hands over, no doubt to distribute the stress symmetrically over his back. All the more reason for straps. His form is not that of a classic powerlifter. He tries to get all the bodybuilding benefits he can out of his deads. Instead of an explosion at the start, he feeds in the power smoothly so it covers his back evenly. Then, instead of thrusting forward with his hips, he lifts with his back. Predictably, he does 4 sets of 8 to 10 reps, not one of them for the faint of heart.

For now it's over, and he may not use this particular mosaic of exercises again for a year. Lost and forgotten as it may become among his myriad permutations of back workouts, however, it will have left its mark of incremental thickness and width. It was only one workout, but it works. Shawn Ray makes sure everything works.

Shawn Ray's Blistering Back Blitz du Jour

Chins	4 × 12
Seated cable row	4 × 8–10
Bent-over barbell row	4 × 8–10
T-bar row	4 × 8–10
Deadlift	4 × 8–10

David Prokop talked to Jean-Pierre Fux to learn how he has created perhaps the most awe-inspiring back in bodybuilding today. Notice that he uses lower repetitions but very heavy weights—a recurring theme, as you'll see, in the training of top champions known for enormous strength.

JEAN-PIERRE FUX'S BACK TRAINING David Prokop

Commenting on the awesome back of the 28-year-old Fux (pronounced *fooks*), a writer-photographer said, "I'm not planning to go to the Olympia, but if I was guaranteed that they would do a callout to compare the backs of three men—Dorian Yates, Nassar El Sonbaty, and Jean-Pierre Fux—I think I'd change my mind. I mean, that alone would be worth the price of the plane fare and the admission to the show."

It's easy to understand such sentiments when you see the back development of the 6′½″, 270-pound muscle phenomenon. When was the last time you saw lats heading off at a right angle from the waist? Or traps that look as if they belong to somebody from another planet?

Jean-Pierre says that he built that back—and the rest of his awe-inspiring physique—with a sound, consistent training program that features short but intense workouts, usually with very heavy weights, and a tremendous amount of variety. In fact, he never does the same back workout twice.

As quiet, mild-mannered Jean-Pierre explains to us in his native Swiss German (with his training partner Daniel Scherrer translating), "I think the body falls asleep when it knows from one workout to the next what it has to do. For example, if Monday is your chest day and you always go in and do two or three sets of bench presses to start the workout, always with the same number of reps, the body gets used to it and your improvement stops. In our approach, we may do a chest workout a certain way one week, but the next time we come in we may change the exercises or the order of exercises, change the number of reps, or change the angle of the

Jean-Pierre Fux.

exercise or the width of the grip, so it's a whole new situation for the body. We try to surprise the body every time."

Jean-Pierre's back day is Thursday. On Monday, he normally trains quads and calves, and on Tuesday he works hamstrings, chest, and front delts. Wednesday is a rest day. Thursday he trains back, traps, and rear delts.

Friday is another rest day. Saturday he works calves again and then trains his biceps and triceps. Sunday is yet another rest day, which means he takes three rest days a week. That's a testament to the intensity of his workouts.

"Only with more intensity can you bring your body up from one level to the next," he says. "You have to overload the muscle more and more, and that you can do with short workouts and more intensity, not working longer. You have to work harder, not longer."

For his back, Jean-Pierre normally does three to four exercises, totaling about seven sets, and then does one exercise for traps, usually one or two sets. "A lot of rowing exercises. Sometimes with a barbell. Also, we use different grips—sometimes wide for outer lats, sometimes narrow. Different angles—like sometimes we stand almost upright and pull to the stomach. Other times we're more bent over and pull the barbell to the chest. Sometimes we do this with a palms-up grip, and sometimes with palms down. So barbell rows are a big part of our chest training.

"We also do pulldowns on a cable machine, also with different grips. We choose whatever grips we feel will work the weaker parts of our back. Whichever grip we feel is best for that part of the back, that's the grip we use.

"Another exercise we use is one-arm rowing with a dumbbell. Also seated rows on a rowing machine, again with different grips. And we may do other exercises for the back, such as T-bar rows.

"So we'll usually pick 2 or 3 exercises from this group. If it's 2, we'll do 3 sets apiece. And if it's 3, we'll do 2 sets each. So that's a total of 6 sets, not including warm-up.

"Normally at the end of our back routine we do deadlifts, because by then the whole area is really warmed up, and it's better if you go really heavy then. During the off-season we go very, very heavy in this exercise, sometimes 1 rep. But during the precontest phase we'll do 6 to 10 reps with a lighter weight."

Jean-Pierre's back training, therefore, consists of 2 or 3 rowing or pulldown exercises for 2 or 3 sets apiece, for a total of 6 sets, fol-

One-arm dumbbell row.

Cable pulldown.

Behind-the-neck pulldown.

lowed by 1 set of deadlifts. The rep range is between 6 and 12, sometimes up to a maximum of 15, and on the deadlift his rep range is 1 to 10.

Jean-Pierre says he sticks to a lower rep range because he has a chronic inflammation in his right forearm, and it particularly bothers him if he does higher reps in pulling-type exercises. Surprisingly enough, it doesn't bother him when he does heavy deadlifting. Impressive as his back is, he feels it would be even better if it weren't for the problem with his forearm, because he could probably do more reps and use more weight.

He's also aware, though, that the problem could be a blessing in disguise. "I think I focus more on doing the work with the back and not with the arms," he says. "One of the big mistakes you see people making in working their backs is they pull a lot with the arms and use body motion, rather than just using the back muscles. I think that's why—especially on an amateur level—you hardly ever see a really

great back. So I think this forearm problem could actually be a good thing for me because I have to focus more on just using the back, and that's why I think my back got really big."

After completing his back workout with the deadlifts—normally 1 heavy set after 2 or 3 light warm-up sets—he immediately works his traps. Typically, he does just one kind of

Chin.   Flex Wheeler.

shrug—with a barbell, with dumbbells, or on a machine. Despite the awesome appearance of his traps, he does only 2 or 3 sets.

"We need not do a lot of work for traps, because we train them right after deadlifting, where the traps are very involved," Jean-Pierre says. "That's why we do just 1 exercise, 2 or 3 sets, sometimes 6 to 12 reps, sometimes between 15 and 25." Incidentally, no one in Switzerland can deadlift as much poundage—750—as Jean-Pierre.

Of course, high-intensity training maintained month after month year-round will result in overtraining or burnout. In order to let his body recuperate, Jean-Pierre trains 12 weeks on a heavy cycle, followed by a 3- to 4-week period when he does a whole-body routine three times a week, one exercise per bodypart, with more reps and lighter weights. Then he starts in again with another 12-week heavy phase.

"It's very important to look at the back as different parts and then do movements that work those different parts," he says. "It's possible that some parts of your back will grow very well, so it's not good if you only use the exercises and grips that work those strong parts and you neglect the weak parts. You have to work the parts that need the most work. Of course, you have to recognize what those parts are. That's one of the problems. I think if people had eyes in the back of their heads, there would be a lot more good backs in this sport. Bodybuilders always stand in front of the mirror, posing, and they see their chest and biceps, not their back. I use a second mirror at home to really check what part of my back needs the most work," he concludes. "And because my back is really thick on the inside, or central area, I hardly ever use narrow grips. I try to work the outer part of my back, so most of the grips I choose are wide."

Bodybuilding author Jerry Brainum talked to then–Mr. Olympia Lee Haney to see firsthand how he developed the number-one back in the world of bodybuilding. Haney gives no-nonsense advice garnered from years in the gym.

LEE HANEY'S OLYMPIAN BACK TRAINING   Jerry Brainum

In order to appear "scientific," many bodybuilding articles begin by comprehensively listing precise anatomical and kinesiological relationships among particular muscle groups. These articles are often written by training theorists or armchair philosophers. While these authors usually possess impeccable academic credentials, they often don't even train themselves!

My bodybuilding education has been more practical; you might say that I am an honor graduate of the "school of hard knocks," at which trial and error was the prevailing curriculum. My classroom has been in the gym. And while they say that education never ends, I believe I've earned my Ph.D. in bodybuilding by virtue of the dissertations I have presented at the last three Olympia contests. Just call me Professor Haney. In today's class, we will be discussing Back Training I

Lee Haney.

tions—upper back, middle back, and lower back. When viewed in this manner, it becomes immediately evident that total back development requires a variety of exercises to hit the back from several angles in order to involve all the muscles.

In my own case, favorable genetics caused my back to respond rapidly to exercise. My early back routines revolved around exercises such as lat pulldowns, T-bar rows, and bent-over barbell rows. I attempted to use as heavy a weight as I could for these exercises, and they eventually formed the foundation for my present back development. As a matter of fact, I still stick with these same basic exercises (with a few more added over the years), and I truly believe that they should form the core of anyone's back routine.

One secret for total back development is the use of strict and proper form in your back exercises. Exercises such as bent-over barbell rows or T-bar rows can be devastatingly dangerous to your lower back if you cheat or throw the weight. The proper way to perform these or any other exercise is in a slow, controlled manner. It's a good idea to visualize your arms as merely "hooks" when performing your back exercises; this technique encourages you to pull with your back rather than your arms. The use of this mental visualization technique will improve your back training enormously.

and II. Get out your notebooks, students—the lecture is about to begin.

THE FORMULA FOR A GREAT BACK

I've always admired the back development of Robby Robinson and Roy Callender. Both of these men were noted for backs that were not just wide, but massively thick in both the upper and lower areas—in short, they possessed complete back development.

I've seen countless bodybuilders who looked like Olympia material from a frontal view, but when they turned around to show their backs . . . well, let's just say that their lack of full back development was glaringly apparent.

Because the back is such a large muscle group, it is probably best to view it in sec-

Aaron Baker.

I believe it's also very important to perform full-range movements for the back. This means pulling the weight (if you are doing rows) all the way up and then lowering slowly for a full stretch in the muscle.

THE BEST BACK EXERCISES

As this is being written, I am in my precontest training phase before the Olympia, which is comprised of three workouts a day. I start this final phase eight weeks before the contest, and find it useful because it allows me to make maximum use of the limited energy stores that I have as a direct result of strict precontest dieting.

I come to the gym in the morning and do only back training; my afternoon session consists of abdominals and cycling (aerobics); my final session for the day, done in the evening,

is a shoulder routine. With this in mind, here is exactly how I am currently training my back in preparation for the Mr. Olympia contest.

Lat pulldowns

Every few workouts, I'll warm up my back by doing a few sets of chins, but I don't do this on a regular basis. The reason is that proper technique in the chinning exercise is very difficult if you weigh 260 pounds like I do. What does the proper technique consist of? In the finish position, your back should be arched, and the chin bar should touch your lower-sternum (chest) area. Attempting to perform chins in this manner tends to irritate my shoulder and arm tendons, so I prefer to do lat pulldowns instead. In this exercise, I usually perform 5 sets of 10 to 12 reps, making sure to fully stretch and squeeze the muscle throughout the movement. I prefer pulldowns to the

T-bar row—start position.   Ronnie Coleman.   T-bar row—finish position.

front, but I'll frequently substitute behind-the-neck pulldowns for them. Both variations hit the back at slightly different angles.

T-bar row

This is a power movement, especially effective for thickening the middle-back area. You must be very careful to use proper form in this exercise; it's easy to incur a serious lower-back injury if your form gets too sloppy. Keep your legs bent to help relieve some of the stress on the lower back, and, most important, keep your back flat and slightly arched. If you do this exercise in the usual "banana-back" position favored by many bodybuilders, sooner or later you'll severely strain your lower-back area. I like to do 5 sets of 10 to 12 reps here.

Bent-over barbell row

I usually do either these or T-bar rows, but prior to a contest, I'll frequently do both. I feel that this is the very best exercise for thickening the entire back. I like to get a full stretch in this exercise by doing it while standing on a block. Again, proper form in this exercise is absolutely essential, in terms of both development and prevention of injuries. This means no jerking or heaving the weight! Do only 5 sets of 10 to 12 reps.

Low-pulley seated cable row

In this exercise, I'll use either a V-bar handle or a straight bar; as I get closer to the Olympia, I'll use the straight bar exclusively because it allows me to squeeze, contract, and fully involve all the smaller muscles of the upper back more effectively. I use a close grip and pull the bar into my stomach area, while at the same time arching my back and lifting my chest in the contracted position. This lifting and squeezing method works all the smaller muscles of the upper back, such as the upper traps, and all those little muscles that assist the lats in their pulling and add so much detail in certain back poses. Five sets of 10 to 12 reps is the norm for me in this exercise.

Bent-over barbell row—start position.

Bent-over barbell row—finish position.

Low-pulley seated cable row—start position.

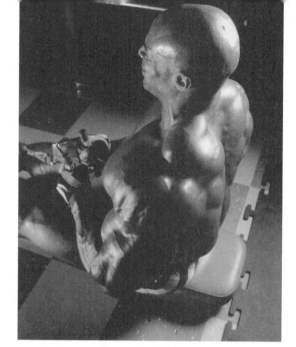

Low-pulley seated cable row—finish position.

One-arm dumbbell row—start position. Greg Kovacs.

One-arm dumbbell row—finish position.

One-arm dumbbell row

Many people seem surprised when I tell them that I use only 70 to 75 pounds in this exercise. The secret lies in the technique. Those people you see in gyms all around the country heaving up 150-pound dumbbells are getting a great workout—for their biceps and rear delts—but very little stimulation is being applied to the back.

When properly performed, this exercise is great for both stretching out the lats and carving out impressive upper-back detail at the same time. I've also found it to be excellent for muscle control stimulation in poses such as the front lat spread, which is one of my "trademark" poses.

One of the advantages of the one-arm dumbbell row is its ability to protect the lower-back area. If you do the exercise like I do, with your knee braced on a bench, all the stress is taken off your lower-back area, thus preventing possibly serious lower-back injuries. A possible disadvantage is the fact that in most people, one arm tends to be stronger than the other. In order to offset this problem, you must take care to do an equal number of reps for both arms. It's also important in this exercise to use a full-range movement. In practical terms, this would mean that in the contracted position, the dumbbell should be just opposite your head.

My friendly kinesiologists tell me that the contracted position of the lat involves the upper arm going slightly past the torso in rowing exercises. They also point out that bringing up the dumbbells higher greatly increases the involvement of the smaller upper-back muscles that work in tandem with the lats in the rowing movement.

That is the current routine I am using in preparation for the "showdown in Sweden." My year-round back routine consists of pulldowns, T-bar rows, and cable rows done for a total of 10 to 12 sets. As you can see, I'm a firm believer in sticking with the basic exercises for the back—no fancy frills for me. I'm only interested in exercises that produce definite results. I don't have time to fool around at this stage of the game!

For lower-back work, I prefer to do stiff-legged deadlifts, but I usually do them as part of my thigh routine, right after leg curls. For traps, I like to do barbell shrugs with the weight held behind my body for 4 or 5 sets of 12 to 15 reps. I've found from experience that the traps are worked more directly in this position, although I admit it takes a bit of getting used to. By the way, I also perform a type of upright row, also done behind my back, for traps.

BLAST THE BACK Arnold Schwarzenegger, as told to Gene Mozée

I really enjoyed training my back because it responds better than any other muscle group. It may not appear that this is so to the beginning bodybuilder, because the back isn't as visible as the arms or chest. The neophyte's first awareness of the back muscles begins when he or she sees that much-desired V-shaped torso emerging, but beginners always focus their attention on the front view—and, therefore, on the lats—with little thought of developing the total back.

I was fortunate when I began training because I had a great role model in Reg Park. His massive back was wide and thick, and it bulged with rippling muscle tissue all the way from his trapezius at the top to his spinal erector muscles at the bottom. His fabulous back was the hallmark of his Mr. Universe physique. When I first saw pictures of Park's back, I resolved that someday I would surpass what he had accomplished. I've always believed in trying to be the best and having a goal that may seem impossible to anyone else. My close friend and training partner thought I was totally nuts.

"You could never have a back like that, no matter how long and hard you train," he said. I didn't care for that statement at all. The word *never* was like a challenge to me to prove that my know-it-all friend was wrong. My desire for a great back formed the core of much of my training from that day forward. I read

everything about bodybuilding that was available. I studied how all the champions trained, their favorite exercises, sets and reps, and specific routines for each muscle group. I adopted many of these ideas and training techniques, and they helped form the basis of my future bodybuilding training.

One of the most important things I learned early in my bodybuilding career was the value of rowing movements for the back. *Rowing* is an all-encompassing word. It can designate many different exercises that are done on a variety of equipment. The motion of rowing affects mainly the back, and variations of the movement strike different areas of the back—lower, upper, center, and outer. It's important to know which exercises do what and where.

Working the back muscles fully involves three basic angles of attention—bent-over rowing movements, overhead pulling movements,

T-bar row.

and horizontal pulling movements. Chinning exercises, which are great back builders, are a sort of reverse rowing motion in which you pull your body toward the bar instead of pulling the weight toward your body.

My favorite rowing motion is the one in which you stand on a block, take a wide grip on a barbell, and pull the bar to your waist. This works the center of the back and, to a lesser extent, the lats and teres major. You get the most benefit from this movement when you lower the bar to your toes, which gives you a full stretch.

The pulling motion to the waist should be slow and deliberate. I emphasize pulling the bar to the waist, not the chest, because when you pull to your abdomen, your elbows move back, and this motion involves the mid-back muscles. Too many bodybuilders show a muscular deficiency in the heavy, cablelike muscles on each side of the upper spine.

I have a unique way of doing this exercise that ensures variation. I start out using as wide a grip as I can, and with every succeeding set I narrow my grip on each side by the width of one hand. I keep doing this until my thumbs are touching. This way I develop my outside lats and center back.

I also like to do this exercise with an underhand, shoulder-width grip every so often. I learned this one from Reg Park, and it really blasts the lower lats.

Another of my favorite bent-over rowing movements is the T-bar row. The equipment amounts to a bar that is pivoted to the floor on one end, with the plates on the opposite end. You face away from the pivoted end, straddle the bar, bend over, and grip it near the plates. From this bent-over position, you pull the unattached, loaded end of the bar up until the plates barely touch your chest. Because your grip is so narrow, you can't draw your elbows back as far as you can on regular barbell rows. This is, nevertheless, a superb outer- and lower-lat developer at the mid-back level. I prefer to do this movement while standing on a block so that I can fully extend and stretch my back muscles on each rep as I lower the bar to my toes. Very little balance is involved because the bar is fastened at one end, and you're better able to concentrate all of your attention and power on the motion itself.

Most gyms have a special floor attachment and handle for T-bar rows. If yours doesn't, grip the bar with your right hand closer to the plates on the first set, then switch, putting your left hand closer for the second set, and so on. Keep your back flat, not humped, throughout the exercise. I add weight on each successive set.

The seated cable row is another sensational back exercise. Be sure that the pulley is set at the same level at which you are sitting, or lower. You can do this movement with either a narrow or wide grip. The wide grip will affect the center-back area, while the narrow grip works the outside and lower lats. I prefer the narrow grip, because I get a fantastic stretch when I extend my arms all the way out.

Seated cable row.

Again, balance remains minimum because you're sitting down with your feet braced. You can pull comfortably all the way to your waist, and you can handle plenty of weight. While I normally perform 10 to 12 reps on all rowing movements, I have gone as high as 20—but that's usually before a contest or a special posing exhibition.

You can also do the seated cable row with a split cable and individual hand grips. Whereas the single-grip, two-handed handle or a straight bar stops at the chest, the twin handles allow you to pull your elbows back beyond the line of your body. This lets you stimulate your back in an entirely different manner.

Another excellent back developer is the one-arm bent-over dumbbell row. This exercise enjoys great popularity among those who have back problems. If you support yourself on a bench with your free arm, you take the stress off your lower back. Draw the weight up alongside your waist so that you can raise your elbow higher than your waist. The muscles that travel up and down along the sides of the spine get lots of work. I refer to this area as the center back. The movement is a good lat shaper as well, and adds sweep to the outer-lat area.

Always use a full range of motion on this one—all the way up to waist level, with your elbow high, and all the way down to a full stretched position on each rep. Cramp and contract your back muscles at the top, and then lower the weight slowly. Alternate the right and left arms with little or no rest between sets.

The aforementioned exercises constitute the basic rowing movements. There are other variations, but these are my personal favorites. In general, I do 5 sets of 10 to 12 reps on all rowing exercises. I perform the first set with a lighter poundage as a warm-up, and then I add weight on each succeeding set.

Although rowing movements comprise the nucleus of my back training, I also employ other exercises for total development. I recommend choosing a good exercise for each of the four back areas. One should take care of the width of the lats, the second should involve the lower lats, the third should hit the upper

and central back, and the fourth should work the lower back.

For lat width, I do either wide-grip chins or wide-grip lat pulldowns. For the lower lats, I do chins or lat pulldowns with a narrow grip. For the upper- and middle-back areas, the best exercises are wide-grip bent-over barbell rows for the central parts and T-bar rows for thickness and the outsides of the lats. Both of these exercises will hit your lower back to some degree, but if you need more

work, you might include hyperextensions or good mornings.

The deadlift is also a great lower-back exercise. I used it often when I trained with Franco Columbo. We deadlifted once or twice a week, never for more than 3 sets, adding weight on each set. For example, we'd do 400 pounds on the first set, 500 pounds on the second set, and 600 pounds on the third set. We did this right after our rowing workout. The deadlift really gave our backs a massive look, and I think it accounted for the deep cuts and striations across our lower backs.

EXERCISE DESCRIPTIONS

Here are instructions for how to perform my other favorite back exercises:

Wide-grip behind-the-neck chin

This is a fantastic exercise for adding width to your back. Take a very wide grip and do a warm-up set of 15 slow, strict chins with no jerking, then add weight for your next set. I attach a 25-pound plate to my waist for my first set after my warm-up, and then I add a 10-pound plate on each succeeding set and strive for 10 to 12 reps with about one minute's rest between sets. If on the fifth set I am unable to get 10 full reps, I do as many as I can and then finish with some half- and quarter-chins.

Triangle-grip chin

You hang a special triangle handle over the chin-up bar for this exercise, which really works the lower lats and the serratus anterior muscles of the chest. I like to feel my scapulae (shoulder blades) spread at the bottom of each rep, and after that I pull myself up to the mid-abdominal area, not the chest. This really works the lower-back origins of the lats. If you don't have access to the triangle handle, substitute close-grip front pulldowns on a pull-down machine.

Medium-grip bent-over row

This is a little different from the wide-grip version I described earlier. Use a hand spacing that's only slightly wider than your shoulders, and bend at your waist until your torso is parallel to the floor. Keep your elbows out wide, hold your back flat, and pull the bar to your solar plexus instead of your waist or chest. This movement really works the upper- and outer-back areas, particularly the teres major muscles. It also works the rear deltoid heads.

Lat pulldown

Take a wide grip on the bar and pull it down behind your head until it touches the base of your neck. As you pull down, put your chin on your chest. Allow the bar to rise up slowly while you lift your head slightly and let your arms fully straighten to get a complete stretch. As usual, I do 10 to 12 reps per set and add weight on each one. This is one of the best exercises for the upper lats.

Straight-arm dumbbell pullover

Do this exercise on a flat bench. Take a dumbbell and lie across the bench while holding the weight at arm's length above your chest. As you inhale, lower the weight slowly behind your head, keeping your arms straight. Exhale forcibly as you return the weight to the point above your chest. This is a good movement for deepening the rib cage, and it also develops the serratus and lower-pec areas. I like to use slightly higher reps on this one—usually around 15.

TRAINING TIPS

1. Train your back two or three days per week, on the same day that you train your chest.
2. Beginners should use a basic three-days-per-week, full-body routine with bent-over barbell rows and stiff-legged deadlifts as the primary back movements. After a few months of training, add wide-grip pulldowns or substitute them for bent-over rows.
3. After you have been training steadily for 9 to 12 months, you might try the following back program:

Wide-grip behind-the-neck chin	3×8–10
T-bar row	3×10
One-arm dumbbell row	3×10

4. Intermediate to early-advanced bodybuilders can do four exercises for the back, as follows:

Wide-grip behind-the-neck chin 4 × 10
Bent-over barbell row 4 × 10
T-bar row 3 × 10
Straight-arm pullover 3 × 15

5. Advanced bodybuilders can handle a tougher workout, as follows:

Wide-grip	
behind-the-neck chin	4 × 10–12
T-bar row	4 × 10–12
Bent-over barbell row	4 × 10–12
Close-grip chin	4 × 10–12
Seated cable row	4 × 10–12

6. Here is one of my all-time-favorite back programs. I used it when I was training for the Mr. Olympia. It's a chest-and-back-superset workout, and it's so severe that I used it only during the last two months before a contest.

Superset 1
Barbell bench press
Wide-grip behind-the-neck chin

Superset 2
Incline barbell press
T-bar row

Superset 3
Dumbbell flye
Medium-grip barbell row

Superset 4
Parallel-bar dip
Narrow-grip chin
Straight-arm pullover

The chest-and-back superset workout saves time, provides a great growth pump, and helps carve deep cuts into both muscle groups. I do 5 sets of 10 to 12 reps on all of the back exercises except pullovers, on which I do 5 sets of 15 reps.

I've used many combinations of the aforementioned exercises in my back-training programs. The exercises that have been the most beneficial to me are those discussed above. You can create your own back program once you find the movements that work best for you. Give my suggestions a try and watch your back grow to new levels of width and thickness.

Arnold Schwarzenegger.

Larry Scott.

Chapter 6

ARM TRAINING

Arms: the ultimate bodypart. Probably 90 percent of young men who start lifting weights do so because they want bigger, more powerful arms. Strong arms are the linchpin of almost all other training exercises. Your back, for example, will never grow maximally if your arms are too weak to perform deadlifts or pulldowns.

This chapter is positively loaded with the best arm training routines from Arnold Schwarzenegger, Larry Scott, and Mike Mentzer. If someone has better biceps than Larry Scott or better triceps than Mike Mentzer, I've certainly never seen them.

This chapter covers biceps, triceps, and forearm training.

ARNOLD'S ULTIMATE BICEPS

Arnold Schwarzenegger, as told to Gene Mozée

I found out many years ago that there is more to peaking the biceps than just curling. It won't do much good to increase the number of sets and the frequency of your biceps work.

That approach will likely result in disappointment and overtraining.

If you have been trying for ages without success to improve your biceps peak, my biceps program is just what you need to break through to greater impressiveness and achieve the whole package—size, shape, peak, and cuts. The following routine has worked well for everyone I've seen use it correctly. All of the guys in the gym I trained at in Munich before I came to the United States used my curling techniques, and they developed that egg-shaped biceps formation. (We called it egg-shaped because a superpeaked biceps resembles an egg standing on end.)

I remember when I was in Chicago several years ago and had the occasion to train with my rival, Sergio Oliva. After following Sergio's routine—20 sets of various barbell curls—I grabbed a pair of dumbbells and did 3 sets of alternate dumbbell curls. Sergio asked why I used the bells after such a heavy biceps routine, and I told him I

Dumbbell curl.

needed them to fully pump my biceps. Barbell movements build great mass, but you can't work the biceps completely unless you use dumbbells.

The biceps attaches to the shoulder joint and to the elbow joint on the forearm. It can do three things: flex the shoulder when raising the arm forward, as when doing a front raise with a dumbbell; flex the elbow, as in a regular curl; and turn the palm faceup when the elbow is in the bent position (this is called *supination*). For building ultimate peak, the rotating, or supinating, aspect of the biceps muscle is the most important. You can only do this rotating motion with dumbbells. No amount of barbell curls ever produced the same intense contraction and resulting soreness that I got from rotating my palms upward and outward as far as I could at the top part of the curling motion.

I am not a big fan of the preacher bench. It's too restricting for my taste. I think it puts too much strain on the elbows, as well. Also, I don't think pulley curls build mass and peak the way dumbbells do, and I could never stand most curling machines because they are so restrictive.

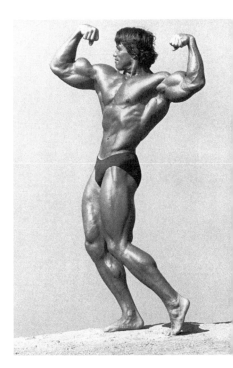

Bodybuilders generally start a curl with their wrists straight, and as they raise the weight, they bend their wrists toward their shoulders for better leverage. They essentially eliminate gravity and diminish resistance with this technique. Sure, they can handle more weight, but the biceps share the load with the forearms, and the final part of the curl is nullified as far as a peak contraction is concerned. I never curl that way. As I curl, I let my hand lag so that the weight of the dumbbell settles more toward my fingers, and I keep my wrist in this extended position throughout the curling motion. This makes the arm a longer lever and sustains maximum resistance. Combined with supination, it forms the basis of my biceps peak program. Here are the exercises I use:

Isolation incline curl

While on an incline bench, hold the dumbbells so that your wrists are in the extended position, with your knuckles dropping back toward your forearms. Hold your elbows close to your sides, but keep the dumbbells 8 to 10 inches away from your sides. This focuses the stress on the outer heads of your biceps. Curl the dumbbells as high as possible with your wrists locked in the extended position. Forcibly tense the biceps at the top of the curl, and continue to force supination of the hands by rotating them until the little finger is higher than the thumb on each hand. You must feel intense pain with each rep. Do 5 sets of 10 reps with as much weight as you can handle in the strictest form.

Alternate supinating curl

Hold a pair of dumbbells in the standing position, with the backs of your hands facing forward. Curl one dumbbell at a time, and when you start curling, rotate the hand so that the palm faces upward about halfway through the motion. Two inches from the top of the curl, twist your hand so that the little finger is higher than your thumb, and forcibly tense

Concentration curl.

your biceps. The pain of contraction will be incredible. Lower the dumbbell in the exact manner that you curled it, and repeat with the other arm. Do 10 reps with each arm, alternating after each rep. Do 5 sets with a one-minute rest between sets.

Supinating concentration curl

Almost everyone does this exercise incorrectly. Try it my way, and watch your biceps take on new bulges! Grasp a dumbbell with your right hand, stand with your feet apart, and bend forward until your back is parallel to the floor. Support yourself with your left hand on your left knee. Once again, start with the back of your hand facing forward, and rotate your palm upward as you curl the weight to your deltoid—not your chest. Add the final extra twist and flexion at the top as in the previous exercise. Keep your mind totally focused on the biceps, and try to peak it to the fullest on each rep. After 10 reps, switch to the left hand. Do a total of 5 sets for each arm. Remember, curl to the deltoid on each rep.

TRAINING TIPS

1. Use this program three times a week, with at least one day's rest between biceps workouts.

2. Do all of your biceps exercises together for a maximum flushing and pumping effect. After you finish your biceps work, do triceps and forearms. I like to do all my arm training on the same day that I work my delts—shoulders first, then arms.

3. Concentrate. Focus your full attention on each repetition. Don't look at anything else except your biceps, and don't think of anything else except your biceps. Visualize them getting more peaked and chiseled with each rep.

4. Totally contract the biceps by tensing them during the last two inches on the way up. Lower the weight all the way down to a dead stop on each rep for a full stretch before doing the next rep.

5. Do all peaking exercises moderately slowly so that the biceps feel the tension every inch of the way up and down.

6. Don't cheat. Strict form is essential. Let your biceps do all of the work. Keep forcing the biceps to work harder by increasing the weight whenever possible.

7. Less-advanced bodybuilders should do only 3 sets of each movement.

I like total silence when I curl. My mind is inside my biceps; I want no distractions. When I'm doing bench presses, anybody can make noise, but when I do biceps, I want total quiet so that I can focus every last measure of concentration on forcing my biceps to peak and split to the maximum.

If you want greater peak, deeper separation, and more chiseled cuts, give my program a try. It won't happen overnight; it could take about a year to reshape and peak your biceps, but you'll see good improvement after a couple of months. Everyone who needs biceps

Dumbbell curl.

Standing barbell curl.

improvement can benefit from these training techniques. Use them exactly as I described, and soon you, too, can have more massive, peaked biceps.

Mr. Loaded Guns himself, Larry Scott, developed his biceps to their absolute genetic limit. In this fabulous article by David Prokop, you'll see how the best biceps in the business nearly went unrealized until Larry found a routine that caused his arm growth to take off. Larry had the genetic potential to develop the best arms in the bodybuilding world, but years of incorrect training left them unexceptional—until he discovered what worked for him!

LARRY SCOTT'S CLASSIC BICEPS ROUTINE David Prokop

Imagine a baseball player today having the opportunity to step back in time to talk to Babe

Larry Scott.

Ruth. Imagine him hearing the Babe say, "All right, kid, I'm gonna tell ya exactly how I hit 60 homers in 1927." As a bodybuilder, you've got a comparable opportunity here, because '60s superstar Larry Scott was to biceps what Babe Ruth was to home runs—the master!

Scott, who won the first two Mr. Olympia contests in 1965 and 1966, started bodybuilding about 10 years earlier as a high school student in Pocatello, Idaho. (Although Larry came to prominence in California, and in bodybuilding circles was considered as much a part of that state as the Beach Boys, he was actually born and raised in Idaho.) Oddly enough, what initially got him interested in bodybuilding was a muscle magazine he found at the Pocatello city dump.

"It had a picture on the cover of a bodybuilder named George Pain flexing his triceps," Scott recalled, "and there was an article inside on training triceps. I didn't know anything about exercising, but I saw that picture of George Pain, and I thought, 'Golly, this guy looks incredible!'"

At the time, Larry had reached his full height of 5′8″, but he weighed only 120 pounds—not exactly a Herculean physique. In fact, he weighed less than almost all of the boys in his school. So he took the magazine home and started doing triceps exercises. Since he didn't have a barbell, he used an old tractor axle instead. He performed mostly barbell kickbacks (although in his case you'd have to call them axle kickbacks) and supine triceps presses.

"This was between my junior and senior years in high school," Larry related. "I worked only triceps the whole summer. I just wanted to see if I could get any size. I didn't really have a lot of faith that I would grow and that my body would change."

When he returned to school in the fall, Scott started working out at the YMCA and began training his biceps as well, using the following routine:

Beginner Routine*

Standing barbell curl	3 × 10
One-arm dumbbell	
concentration curl	3 × 10
Zottman dumbbell curl	3 × 10

* This workout was part of a whole-body routine in which Larry would do 1 set of each exercise, then go through the entire sequence two more times.

Larry Scott.

"I didn't know what I was doing," Larry admitted.

"There was a fellow at the YMCA who was a former boxer, and he gave us advice on how to train. He told us we should go through the whole body three times, so we did. What did we know at that age? We went through the whole body, one set per exercise, and then we'd do it again, and then a third time. It was exhausting, and it was a terrible workout! But that's what I was doing right at first."

The standing barbell curls, one-arm dumbbell concentration curls, and Zottman dumbbell curls were followed by three triceps movements—supine triceps presses with a straight bar, dumbbell kickbacks, and barbell kickbacks. In each case he did a single set of 8 reps, then moved on to the next exercise. Recalling this primitive training method, Larry said, "What I did for my beginning routine wouldn't be what I would recommend for a beginner now."

Despite the obvious shortcomings of his approach, Scott's progress was such that he placed second in the Best-Built Senior contest at his high school. This wasn't a bodybuilding contest per se, but a loose form of competition in which students cast ballots for the guy they thought had the best physique.

After graduating from high school, Larry moved to Los Angeles to attend an electronics college, but returned to Idaho after only six months. While he was in L.A., however, he trained at Bert Goodrich's Gym in Hollywood.

Larry Scott and Freddy Ortiz outside Vince Gironda's gym.

Although the gym is long gone, Larry still remembers getting some invaluable training tips there from Lou Degni, a bodybuilder who, he said, "had an incredible physique and was way ahead of his time." It was while he was training in Hollywood, after he had been using the beginner routine about a year and a half, that Scott formulated the following intermediate regimen:

Intermediate Routine
Standing barbell curl	3 × 6–8
Bent-over dumbbell concentration curl	3 × 6–8
Standing dumbbell curl	3 × 6–8

By this time, Larry had switched to doing 3 sets of each exercise, gradually increasing the weight with each set, before moving on to the next bodypart. That's the approach he was fol-lowing when he returned to Idaho—until the day the legendary Steve Reeves visited the gym where Scott and his bodybuilding buddies were training.

"We found that training the whole body in each workout while trying to increase the weight with each set wasn't very effective," Larry related, "so we asked Steve what he thought about what we were doing.

"'That's crazy!' he said. 'You should change your way of training and start using a down-the-rack training system.' He didn't tell us which exercises to do, but he told us how to do them. He said, 'Do a set with 100 pounds; decrease the weight and do a set with 90 pounds; decrease it again and do it with 80 pounds . . .' And so we started training in a down-the-rack fashion, but we still continued to train the entire body each workout."

During this intermediate phase of his training, Scott was doing 9 sets for biceps and 9 for triceps at each workout. The triceps exercises were barbell kickbacks, one-arm dumbbell kickbacks, and supine triceps presses. Although he was no longer going from exercise to exercise with every set, he was still training his entire body at each workout. Remember, however, that this was the late '50s, and the split system of training we take for granted now hadn't been introduced yet.

"We didn't know anything about a split routine," Larry said. "By the way, speaking parenthetically, that came out of Salt Lake City from a fellow by the name of Dave Fitzen, who split the body in half, training half the body one day, the other half the next day. That occurred right around 1960. A lot of people take credit for that, but he was the one who came out with that split concept. And a number of us from Idaho and Utah brought it out to California. It was quite a novel way to train the muscles more intensely and give them time to recuperate. It was a new concept. Nobody had ever thought of that before. We had always trained the whole body in one day, and it was exhausting!"

After about a year and a half on this intermediate routine, during which time Scott still emphasized triceps training much more

Mike Mentzer on the preacher bench.

The Scott bench.

Dave Palumbo.

than biceps work ("I'd go through the biceps training, but I'd really put my everything into the triceps"), he won the Mr. Idaho title. Larry now weighed about 155 pounds, and his arms measured about 15¼ inches. Then he moved to Los Angeles and started the meteoric buildup that resulted in his becoming the

greatest bodybuilder in the world—and produced those beautifully peaked, 20-plus-inch arms that connoisseurs of the sport talk about to this day.

Despite the heavy emphasis on triceps training in his beginner and intermediate days, Scott was to learn something rather ironic when he returned to Los Angeles—specifically, that his biceps were the more impressive bodypart!

"I happened to go into a club in North Hollywood, and there was a fellow in there by the name of Reid Flippen," he explained. "He was from Utah, and I was from Idaho, so we had a little bit in common, I guess. And he said, 'Your arms look pretty good; let me see them.' So I flexed my triceps. He said, 'Your triceps isn't your best part; it's your biceps.' So I thought, 'Oh, no!,' thinking of the attention I had focused on the triceps. Up to that point, I had never even liked biceps work. But I guess the genetic shape [of the biceps] was what he was referring to. So then I started working more on biceps."

Every serious student of bodybuilding history knows, of course, that during his heyday, Larry Scott trained at Vince's Gym in Studio City, which is in Los Angeles's San Fernando Valley, and that he became so identified with arm development and training that two new terms were added to the lexicon of the sport—"Scott curls" (which were actually preacher curls) and the "Scott bench" (which, again, was a preacher bench, albeit a bench of rather unique design).

The following is the arm routine that enabled Larry Scott to go from 15¼- to almost 21-inch arms in just a few years—and earned him an honored spot among the all-time greats of the sport:

Advanced Routine
Preacher bench dumbbell curl
    6 reps, 4 burns
Wide-grip preacher bench barbell curl
    6 reps, 4 burns
Reverse-grip curl with EZ-curl bar
    6 reps, 4 burns
Series repeated five times

"I was introduced to the preacher bench by Vince [Gironda]," Larry continued. "I really worked hard on the preacher bench, taking advantage of the low connection I had on the biceps. So I got really involved in that, and my arms really started to grow.

"For one thing, my training was much better. Vince had a lot of unique, well-designed equipment. I started to make good progress."

"Good progress" is the understatement of the century. After Larry had been training at Vince's Gym for about a year, he placed third in the Mr. Los Angeles contest—a significant step up for him, considering the higher quality of competition he faced in California. (Remember, only a year earlier he had weighed 155 pounds at a height of 5′8″.) And that was just the beginning.

"About two months after the L.A. contest, I met Rheo Blair, a nutritionist. I started taking his protein powder—the first time I'd taken protein—and I put on 8 pounds in just two months, which was unheard of for me. It

Larry Scott.

was just really incredible! That protein must have been exactly what my body needed.

"I put on 8 pounds of muscle! I mean, 8 pounds would have normally taken me about two years. To put it on in two months was just amazing!

"A year later, I won Mr. California, which was a total surprise to me and to everyone else," he continued. "So I was really excited about my training and my progress. I kept training harder and harder, but my biceps routine stayed pretty much the same. Just the intensity changed.

"I was doing a set of dumbbell curls on the preacher bench. Then, with no rest, I would do a set of wide-grip barbell curls on the bench and then a set of reverse-grip EZ-curl bars—again, with no rest. I would do 5 series of these 3 exercises, resting only long enough between series so my training partner could do his.

"So I was doing five series of 3 sets, and on each exercise I would do 6 repetitions with 4 burns at the end of each set. Burns, of course, are small quarter-movements either at the top or the bottom of the exercise. I'd do them at the top until I got a little bored with it, and then I'd do them at the bottom.

"That routine really got my arms to grow. That was a very effective program. As a matter of fact, to this day I've not found anything that effective for building biceps."

Were the burns the key to this routine? Was that the magic that was at work, or was it something else? "Well, I think the thing that worked so well was, first, I had—genetically—a low connection on the biceps. And the preacher bench works low biceps. And then there was the intensity of this type of work-out—it's extremely painful! That series I just mentioned is very, very painful, but it just blows the arms up like nothing I've ever

seen—if the preacher bench is designed correctly.

"Most of the benches you see have a flat face, and they don't work. People who hear me talk about arm training go out and try that on a regular preacher bench, and they say, 'Ah, he must have been a genetic freak because that doesn't work for me at all.' That's because they have a lousy bench.

"As a matter of fact, I remember Arnold saying to me, 'I don't know how you ever made any progress on a preacher bench.' And I went in to shoot some photos on the preacher bench at the gym in Venice where he was training, and I thought, 'God, no wonder he says that. This is terrible!'

"The correct design of the bench is that it has to have a face that's convex rather than flat. In other words, the face should bulge out in the middle. Most preacher benches are flat because they're easier to manufacture that way. But the bench has to have a convex face. And the area at the top where you place your armpits has to be rounded and well padded, because you're going to be bearing down real hard on that bench when you're doing the curls. Most benches have a sharp ridge on top, and it hurts your armpits.

"Most preacher benches are also designed with the post set back, and when the exercise really gets difficult, you hit that post with your groin, so you can't really get into it hard. The post should be offset toward the front. Manufacturers also make the face of the preacher bench too long, so the dumbbells hit the face of the bench at the bottom. What you want is a bench that has a short face, bulging out in the middle and rounded on both sides, and also rounded and padded where your armpits are, with the post placed toward the front so your groin won't be pressing up against it. If you get all those little features on it, it's a great piece of equipment!"

In fact, Scott said that the design of the bench is so important that nowadays when he's on the road and does biceps work on a regular, flat-faced preacher bench, he loses arm size! "Then, when I get back on the right equipment again, my arms come back up. So

the normal preacher benches that you see won't give you the results that you want. I mean, you can make better progress doing incline dumbbell curls than you can doing curls on the normal preacher bench, but you get a good preacher bench and, boy, you can build some arms!"

With single-minded determination, going through a four-pound tin of protein powder every eight days and drinking some two and a half gallons of milk a day, Larry actually built up to a peak bodyweight of 212 pounds in '65 and '66. His best competitive weight, when he was Mr. Olympia, was about 205. As for those arms, he said, "My arms got so big, they were hard to carry around. My traps just got exhausted carrying them. I used to tuck my thumbs into my belt loops just to give my traps a rest."

It's significant to note that during those glory days of the '60s, Larry Scott's biceps routine remained the same—right down to the order of the exercises, and even how he did each exercise. The routine was like a magic formula he had discovered, and he wasn't about to tamper with it.

"I had a particular style for each of the different curls," he explained. "The dumbbell curls were done 'loose' style. I didn't care how I got 'em up; I just wanted to get them up any way I could. Then the barbell curls were done with very strict form. I would get my armpits way down on the bench, and I would make sure that my form was totally strict. As a matter of fact, the magic to that whole combination is the barbell curl. You do the exercise with very strict form, your body over the bench—you don't help the arms at all with even a little bit of leaning back—and that's what really gives you the tremendous growth.

"Then you finish off, when your arms are just about to die, with reverse-grip EZ-bar curls, and that works the brachioradialis and hits the low biceps. The biceps is exhausted at that point, but the brachioradialis isn't.

"And it's also a curling muscle, so you can use that muscle to help you put extra work into the low biceps. It really gives you a great pump. In other words, the pattern to this rou-

tine was to do the dumbbell curls with as much weight as possible to basically tire the biceps, then place maximum concentrated stress on the biceps by doing the barbell curls in a very strict fashion, and, finally, when the arms were all but dead, do still another exercise that worked a part of the biceps—the brachioradialis—that still had some life left." Clearly, it's a routine that reflects a touch of genius.

"And it never worked as well if I split those exercises up or changed the order of the exercises," Scott said. "That combination had a magic quality to it."

Incidentally, during this advanced phase of his training, Larry worked biceps twice a week, following, of course, a split routine. He always trained arms, shoulders, and neck together. In his beginner days, he trained his arms three times a week, and during the intermediate phase he worked them four times a week.

"By the way," he continued, "that bench that Vince had, we've improved it in several respects; so it's an even better piece of equipment now. You know, after doing curls on that thing for 20 years or more as I've done, you've got to be pretty dumb not to figure out some ways to make it better."

Looking back over the evolution of his biceps training, Larry said he wouldn't change a thing about his advanced routine. The beginning and intermediate routines are quite another matter, however.

"They were terrible," Scott admitted. "I would never recommend that anyone use those. I would recommend that a beginner or an intermediate do it totally differently. A beginner doesn't know yet what is right or wrong, so he has to just have blind faith as he's trying different exercises. I'd suggest he change exercises at least every week, because the changing stress provides much better growth, and it rejuvenates the ligaments and tendons so you don't get injured all the time.

"I'd make sure I did only 6 repetitions—6 is a better figure for growth than 8 or 10. I would also do the burns—I think the burns are wonderful to add some extra stress to it. I would do probably no more than 9 sets per bodypart, increasing the intensity. I would also vary the way I trained. Instead of just doing down-the-rack workouts, I'd do down-the-rack, I'd do straight sets, I'd do supersets. I'd change that system of training a lot. I wouldn't do the same thing over and over again. And, of course, I'd follow a split routine rather than training the whole body in each workout, as I had been doing."

Larry made one final point about biceps training, and it's really important to anyone who wants to build Mr. Olympia–quality arms: "When I got to the advanced stage of my training in the '60s," he said, "I began to realize that I couldn't go up to the heavier weights unless I began to work and strengthen my forearms. So I started to train the forearms real hard so that I could get the wrist curled at the bottom of the movement on the preacher bench. Because when you're doing biceps curls and you're way down on the bench, you can't get the bar up unless you get your wrists

curled, and you can't get the wrists curled unless you have the forearm strength. So I started working forearms very hard, and I noted that as I worked forearms harder, I could use heavier weights in the biceps exercises. Consequently, it was the forearms that were the key to building bigger biceps."

T. C. Luoma's insight into triceps training provides you with all the fundamental information you'll need to understand how to get your arms growing. He includes complete programs for the beginner, intermediate, and advanced trainee.

THREE HEADS ARE BETTER THAN ONE T. C. Luoma

Most people take up bodybuilding because they want to put some size on their arms. Consequently, they gravitate to biceps exercises rather than triceps movements. It's the triceps that gives the arm most of its mass, however, particularly when the arm is relaxed. Because the triceps is bigger than the biceps, it stands to reason that it requires more of a workload than does the two-headed muscle that occupies the other half of your shirtsleeve.

The beginning and intermediate routines in the following program stress proper form used in a logical arrangement of exercises. The advanced routine assumes that you've already learned proper form and focuses on improving weak points and offering specific techniques to shock your triceps into new growth.

BEGINNER TRICEPS TRAINING

Start out right—with your elbows stiff. Here's a technique to practice in the privacy of your own home that will get you ready for your first triceps workout.

Face the mirror and, with your arms hanging straight down, place your elbows next to your torso. Take a deep breath and . . . don't do anything. That's right, don't move your elbows.

I'm kidding, of course, about this being a real technique, but you get the point. Most people throw their elbows around more during a triceps workout than an NBA center does while he's coming down with a rebound. If you can remember to keep your elbows stationary, then you're most of the way there in terms of learning good form.

One of the best all-around triceps movements is the pushdown, which is done on a lat pulldown machine. Find an attachment that allows you to assume a palms-down, thumbs-in grip (a bar that is straight or only slightly angled). This kind of grip works the inner head of the triceps. To put more emphasis on the outer head, use a rope attachment, which allows you to work with a palms-together, thumbs-up grip. Together, these two variations will help you achieve complete development; however, at this stage, you want to alternate the two grips at consecutive workouts.

To do pushdowns correctly, stand facing the bar and place your hands on it about nine inches apart. Lean forward slightly so that you'll be able to achieve a full contraction at the bottom without hitting your thighs. Then, without letting your elbows stray, push the bar down all the way. At the bottom of the movement, contract the muscle and pause for a count of one or two before slowly allowing the bar to return to the starting position.

Remember to use your triceps only. This is not an ab exercise, so don't crunch your torso down; and it's not a lat movement, so don't power the bar down with your back. Controlled cheating is permissible when you become an advanced bodybuilder, but for the time being, stick with the basics.

Although you'll eventually figure out what rep range works best for you, try 3 sets of 15 to start. A good barometer of how you're doing is if you feel a slight pump or burn in your triceps. If it doesn't feel right, try a few more reps. It sometimes take a couple of workouts to fall into the groove.

Lying triceps extensions are often the most difficult triceps movement because the form can be tough to master, but they are worth it because they work the entire muscle. Take a barbell or EZ-curl bar and lie flat on your back on a bench. With the arms fully extended and your elbows locked, find your starting point by moving the bar so that it's in the same plane as

Pushdown.   Robert Russo and Johnny Moya.

your eyeballs. Once you've got it there, slide it a couple of inches toward the top of your head so that your arms are at a slight angle to the ground—you want the tension to remain on your triceps during the entire movement, even at the resting point, instead of on the bones and joints of your arms and shoulders.

Lying triceps extension—start position.
Steve Cuevas.

Lying triceps extension—finish position.

That's your starting point: mentally freeze your elbows there. Now bend them, lowering the bar with your lower arms until it's just past the top of your head and your triceps are fully stretched. With your elbows still frozen at the same spot, raise the bar until they're locked again; mentally contract the muscle, pause for a count of one or two, and then repeat. Make sure that the movement is slow and controlled. As with the previous exercise, 3 sets of 15 reps is a good place to begin.

Here's how the beginning triceps workout shapes up:

Pushdown	3 × 15*
Lying triceps extension	3 × 15

* Alternate palms-up and palms-down variations at consecutive triceps workouts.

How often should you train? Once a week is better than nothing, twice is better than once, and three times is usually better than twice. Any more than that, and you're pushing it. If you train consistently two or three times a week, you should be ready for the intermediate routine in about four to six months.

INTERMEDIATE TRICEPS TRAINING

Since the two exercises just described—pushdowns and lying triceps extensions—form the backbone of most triceps routines, I recommend that you continue doing them. It's time to start doing every movement to failure, however, and it's also time to add another exercise as well as an occasional forced rep and superset. One good combination is working in some kickbacks with your pushdowns. After you do a set of pushdowns, pick up a pair of appropriately light dumbbells and do some kickbacks. You don't want to do this superset on all three sets of pushdowns; once or twice per workout is plenty. The trick of mentally freezing your elbow in space works for this move-

One-arm reverse pushdown—start position.
Dave Palumbo.

One-arm reverse pushdown—finish position.

ment, too. When the dumbbell is fully extended, your upper arm should be approximately parallel to your torso. In the correct position, if you were to release the dumbbell at the point of peak contraction, the weight would not go flying across the gym and hit some poor geek in the melon—it would fall straight down. So don't use body English or momentum to fling the weight back. Kick it back slowly, using your elbow like a hinge; contract for a count of two; and then lower it.

For added intensity, try doing the kickbacks with both arms. Although you usually see people doing kickbacks one arm at a time, there's no reason why you can't bend over and work both arms together until you reach failure.

There's another effective superset that you can perform after your lying triceps extensions. Do as many extensions as possible, and then proceed immediately to a set of close-grip bench presses with the same weight. You

might think that the weight you use for extensions is pathetically light for close-grip benches, but you should be so tired from the extensions that the close-grips will feel twice as heavy.

To do the close-grip presses, position your hands about five or six inches apart on the bar and perform a standard bench press, keeping your elbows tucked in as you bench the weight. Contract your triceps and lower the bar until it lightly touches your chest. Continue until you reach failure. Again, superset the close-grip benches with your lying triceps extensions on at least one set at each triceps workout.

The third addition that I recommend for intermediate trainees is dips, a great movement that contributes to the overall mass of the triceps. I suggest, however, that you do only one set of one rep. Doesn't sound like much? Well, try it this way: With your upper body perpendicular to the ground (leaning in

One-arm cable overhead extension—start position.

One-arm cable overhead extension—finish position.

Dumbbell kickback—start position.

Dumbbell kickback—finish position.

works the chest more) and your elbows tucked in close to your body, lower yourself as slowly as possible, even if it takes 60 seconds. Once you hit rock bottom, push yourself up again in the same manner, taking as long as you can. That's it—you're done.

At this point, your growing triceps routine lays out as follows:

Pushdown 3×15^{1}

Superset with
Kickback $1–2 \times 15$
Lying triceps extension 3×15^{2}

Superset with
Close-grip bench press $1–2 \times 15^{2}$
Dip 1×15

[1] Alternate palms-up and palms-down variations at consecutive triceps workouts.
[2] Or to failure.

Dip. Bruce Patterson.

There will come a day, most likely after you've been training for a year or two, when you just won't be satisfied with your work level, or you'll notice that your triceps have hit a plateau. When that happens, it's time to move on to an advanced routine.

FOR THE ADVANCED BODYBUILDER—HITTING ALL THE ANGLES

As with any advanced routine, your ultimate goal with your triceps training is to work the muscle beyond the pain barrier. That means forced reps, supersets, and giant sets until your triceps glow like painful cysts. It's also time to assess your weak points and correct them. For instance, if the exercises you've been doing have worked for your upper triceps but not the lower portions, some partial reps may well prod the deficient area into growth.

Just about any of the exercises just discussed will target the lower triceps if you only work through the lower range of motion. When doing pushdowns, for example, only let the bar come up one-half to three-fourths of the way before you push it down again.

If your inner triceps have failed to respond to your satisfaction, try subjecting them to some one-arm cable extensions. By assuming a thumbs-in grip and twisting your wrist until the thumb points down, you put emphasis on the inner triceps.

Aside from intensity and overcoming weak areas, the key to an advanced routine lies in using every combination of angles and exercises possible to constantly stimulate new and previously unexplored muscle fibers. What used to be just a set of pushdowns now becomes a test of will—you go to failure on the pushdowns to work the outer triceps; immediately drop the weight and go to failure using a reverse grip to hit the inner triceps; and then pick up the lower cable, gripping the rubber ball on the end, and do some cable kickbacks to work the outer, upper triceps.

Either before or after this giant set (remember, the key is to do everything differently all the time), do some dips between two benches. Instead of just using your bodyweight for resistance, pile as many 35- or 45-pound plates on your lap as possible and crank out your reps. As you reach failure, have a partner pull off the top plate and then keep on going. Continue in this manner until you're just using your bodyweight and you can't do another rep.

There's no end to the angles and techniques you can come up with. Just about any combination is a good one if you consistently hit different angles and you consistently feel a pump or burn after your workout. Although some people get by with as little as 9 total sets, others find that they need up to twice that number. By the time you reach the advanced level, you'll know what works best for you.

Once again, David Prokop interviewed a top champion in order to glean all the crucial information on how to train a specific bodypart.

Mike Mentzer was the first bodybuilder in history to garner a perfect score in a bodybuilding competition. His entire physique is magnificent, but his triceps are beyond what even the best of the field can equal. Here is how he built them.

MIKE MENTZER'S HEAVY-DUTY TRICEPS WORKOUT David Prokop

Many feel that in 1979 and 1980, Mike Mentzer was the finest bodybuilder in the world. The Pennsylvania native finished a close second to Frank Zane in the '79 Mr. Olympia, although he outweighed Zane by 30 pounds and was more defined. Then in 1980, when Arnold Schwarzenegger came out of retirement to recapture the Olympia crown in a highly controversial decision, Mentzer was inexplicably placed fifth, even though he looked better than he had the previous year and was considered by most to be at least equally favored to win.

Mike—who, as a protest against what he considered corrupt judging, never competed in another bodybuilding contest after that '80 Olympia—was perhaps just as well known for his training concepts as he was for his titles. Given the quality of his physique, that's definitely saying something!

Mike's high-intensity training program, aptly named Heavy Duty, was essentially based on the exercise philosophy of Arthur Jones, the developer of Nautilus machines. According to Jones, the key to maximum muscle gains is to train very intensely—doing only the sets that are minimally necessary to stimulate muscle growth and spacing workouts sufficiently so that the body has time to recuperate. In other words, train harder, train shorter, train less frequently.

It was a message that left an indelible impression on Mentzer, who was only 24 when he met Jones at the '71 Mr. America contest. Mike would subsequently bring the concept to tremendous popularity in the sport—through his own bodybuilding accomplishments, which also included the '78 Mr. Universe title earned with the first and only perfect score in history; through the accomplishments of his brother Ray, who won the '79 Mr. America using the Heavy Duty system; and through his popular

Mike Mentzer.

Heavy Duty magazine column, his mail-order business, and his seminars.

Due to the impact that the Heavy Duty concept had on the sport during that period, it's probably safe to say that if Mike Mentzer wasn't the best bodybuilder in the world in '79 and '80, he certainly was the most popular. The fact that he and Ray were the only brothers ever to become Mr. America simply added to the Mentzer mystique.

Mike started working out at the age of 12. His early inspiration was the great Bill Pearl, a four-time Mr. Universe winner.

"The guy who kept me going, the image that kept me going, the goal that I wanted to attain was that of looking like Bill Pearl,"

Mentzer said. "I even got my hair cut like him at one point, getting a flattop. I was especially inspired by his huge triceps, particularly when his arms were hanging down at his sides. I spent more hours than I care to admit at this point just mindlessly gazing at Bill Pearl's arms in muscle magazines."

Indeed, the day would come when Mentzer's triceps development actually rivaled that of his boyhood idol. Mike was renowned for both his triceps and calf development; but even so, he feels that there's no doubt as to which was better.

"Yeah, I had good calves," he said, "but when I was in my best condition, my triceps were my best bodypart."

Mike trained for a couple of years on his own with a barbell set his father had bought him, but his formal introduction to weight training came when he was 14 or 15 and his father introduced him to John Myers, a local powerlifter who had been working out for 10 to 15 years. As he said, "John Myers took me under his wing and taught me how to power-lift and train heavy."

They worked out three days a week with another weightlifter, Russell Hertzog, who was a regional champion in Olympic lifting and had a well-equipped home gym in his garage.

"Russell Hertzog taught me the essentials of Olympic lifting," Mentzer recalled. "And that, combined with John Myers's thrust in the area of powerlifting, gave me a good all-around base in strength training. I learned how to squat, bench press, and deadlift, and also how to do the military press, snatch, and clean and jerk. All of those things at a relatively early age helped to develop the basis of my physique."

Mike was a kid working out with two adult weightlifters, and he naturally relied on them for training guidance.

Triceps pushdown—start position.

Triceps pushdown—finish position.

"I didn't have a clear-cut, explicit philosophy of my own at the time," he said. "I followed what was printed in the magazines, primarily the *York* magazine, which is what these guys were doing. I was influenced largely by them."

Here's the triceps routine Mike followed during the time he trained with Myers and Hertzog:

Beginning Routine
French presses
(lying or standing)   2 × 6–8

"When I first started working out with John Myers, I was training primarily as a powerlifter, doing 3, 4, sometimes 5 sets per bodypart with basic exercises—squats, bench presses, behind-the-neck presses, curls, and French presses," Mentzer recalled. "Most of the training information was obtained from the

York magazine, which was advocating much fewer sets than Weider was at the time, and I made great progress. By the time I was 15, I was squatting 500 for 2 reps, bench pressing around 360, and had developed a very muscular physique.

"The one direct triceps movement that John Myers had me do was one of his favorites—French presses, both lying and standing varieties, no more than a couple of sets with fairly heavy weight done in strict form. Also, I was doing heavy bench presses for my chest, and, of course, bench presses also work the triceps. Guys who are great bench pressers and overhead pressers usually have well-developed triceps.

"And this is an important point, too, in understanding why today I limit my students to only 1 or 2 sets for triceps. I have them do bench presses and dips for their pecs before they train triceps, and those are both very direct triceps exercises."

As he said, Mike made great progress while training on the power-oriented program with Myers and Hertzog. In time, however, he went off on his own and started training at the Lancaster, Pennsylvania YMCA, which was about 12 miles from his hometown. He was exposed to many more people and a lot of diverse training ideas, and those ideas took him off-track.

"When I started training on my own, I took a turn in the wrong direction. I started doing many more sets. That was a mistake. My progress slowed down, and at times halted. Now I understand that progress should never halt. If a bodybuilder is training with sufficient intensity and is not overtraining, there should be an adaptive response—every time! When a person goes out in the hot August sun to get a suntan and doesn't overexpose himself, he doesn't have to go home at night and pray to God that he wakes up with a suntan. There's an adaptive response every time. It's automatic.

"The same principle applies to exercise—and this doesn't just apply to Mike Mentzer. These are universal, objective principles of productive exercise. When the intensity of the training stimulus is sufficiently high and you don't overtrain or train too frequently, there will always be an adaptive response; specifically, you'll get bigger and stronger."

What Mike started doing for triceps at the Lancaster YMCA was what he called "the magic four."

"I did 4 sets of 3, 4, 5, sometimes even 6 exercises," he said. "Why 4 sets? I don't know. Probably because Arnold [Schwarzenegger] and Franco [Columbo] did it."

Here's a typical triceps workout from that period:

Intermediate Routine

Lying French presses	4 × 8–12
Standing French presses	4 × 8–12
Dips	4 × 8–12
Triceps pressdowns	4 × 8–12
Triceps kickbacks	4 × 8–12
Total sets: 12 to 24*	

* Four sets each of 3 to 5 exercises.

"I tried everything," Mike said. "I didn't understand the nature of full-range exercise at the time. I uncritically and blindly accepted all of the doctrines and ideas printed in the magazines because I didn't know how to critically analyze anything. I assumed that if it was printed, it had to be valid. I didn't know how to discriminate, but now I do. I've learned how to critically analyze not just philosophical and political ideas, but training ideas. And I have no doubt—I say it unequivocally, and I can prove it to anybody open to a rational argument—that Heavy Duty high-intensity training is the only proper way to train for maximum muscle gains."

It was while Mike was still using the high-volume approach that he entered the '71 Mr. America contest—which was held, coincidentally, in York, Pennsylvania. Mentzer finished tenth behind Casey Viator, who was the first teenager to become Mr. America. Mike was quick to add that prior to this contest, his bodybuilding improvements had come to a virtual halt.

"I was making no further progress," he revealed. "I was doing up to 40 sets for my pecs, for instance, and I was making no progress, becoming very disenchanted and discouraged."

It was at that show that Viator introduced Mike to Jones, a meeting that completely revolutionized Mentzer's philosophy toward training. What Jones explained to Mike is how muscle growth occurs; one could call it the science of muscle growth.

"The volume or the duration of your training is not the most important aspect," Mentzer explained. "As a matter of fact, the duration of your training is always a negative—whether you train for a long period or a short period. Whenever you train at all, you're making inroads into your recovery ability. That's always a negative.

"The most important aspect of the workout is the intensity, which, properly defined, refers to the percentage of momentary effort you're generating. If you understand the nature of high-intensity physical training, you also know that the higher the intensity of the effort, the less the duration has to be—not just that it should be, but it has to be. When you're training as hard as you can, it's not that you shouldn't train long, although you shouldn't—again, because of the factor of limited recovery ability—but you can't train hard and long for the same reason that nobody sprints for a mile! When you're running as hard as you possibly can, no holds barred, you cannot run more than 400 meters, which is why there is no 800-meter sprint. After 400 meters, it becomes a middle-distance run.

"If, in fact, it was the volume of training that built muscle, the logic would have to proceed like this: if it were the amount of training

that was responsible for an individual getting bigger and stronger, then as he got bigger and stronger, he would have to keep training longer and longer to keep getting bigger and stronger. That's impossible because the human body possesses a limited recovery ability.

"Arthur Jones explained to me very clearly, very logically, what the science of exercise is really about. I embraced it immediately and started using high-intensity training principles. And my physique really started taking off."

Mike switched to the following triceps routine, based on his newfound philosophy, immediately after meeting Jones. It's the routine he used until he retired from competitive bodybuilding.

Advanced Routine

Superset

Nautilus triceps extension	2 × 6–8
Weighted dip	2 × 6–8

Total sets: 4

"I would do the Nautilus triceps extensions to failure, 6 to 8 reps, and follow that immediately—with no rest—with 1 set of heavy dips, again 6 to 8 reps. Actually, I would do two cycles, or supersets," Mentzer said. "If I made one mistake in my training—and I did make more—it's that despite being the archadvocate of lesser training, I was doing too much. If I were to go back into contest training today, I wouldn't do more than one—or at the most two—sets per bodypart."

In making the switch to high-intensity training, Mike cut back not only on the length of his workouts, but also on the frequency of training. As he put it, "I quit training six days a week for up to three hours a day. Instead, I started training 30 to 45 minutes a day three days a week. And within a short period of time after I started doing that, I won the Mr. America contest."

As Mentzer's career progressed and he became an Olympia contender, he found it advantageous to cut back on the frequency of his workouts even more. He eventually settled on an every-other-day split in which he trained half of his body on Monday, and instead of covering the other half on Tuesday, he took Tuesday off and did the second installment on Wednesday.

"Why adhere so blindly to a seven-day schedule just because we have, for matters of convenience, adopted the Gregorian calendar?" he asked. "The body's physiological processes aren't mediated by tradition. That's crap! Let's use our minds, perceive what our bodies are doing; so I did that. And then a short time after that, there were periods where, using the same reasoning, I was still tired on Wednesday from Monday's workout, so I waited till Thursday to work out."

Mike also challenges the compulsion many bodybuilders feel to train the muscle from every angle to get complete and maximum development. This is essentially another way of saying that it's important to do a large variety of exercises, and Mentzer, as you might imagine, doesn't agree.

"I don't even think it's a valid issue," he said. "Number one, no one's ever defined what they mean by 'training the muscle at different angles.' From how many angles can you train the biceps and triceps? Hanging upside-down by your feet? Doing exercises on an incline board at an infinite number of angles? What the hell does that mean, training a muscle at different angles? It's a layman's attempt—a poor attempt—at making something sound scientific when it's not.

"What is important—and this is the issue—is that weight-training exercise is about movement against resistance. Where there's no resistance, there's no exercise. A muscle has to move through its fullest range of motion against resistance.

"What I think bodybuilders mean when they talk about training the muscle at different angles is that they sense in certain exercises that the resistance drops off at a different point than it does in some other exercises. And what they want to accomplish by doing more than one or two exercises is to provide resistance at those points in the range of motion where the first exercise didn't provide it. That's really all it is, I think. With conventional free-weight exercises there really is no way to provide equal resistance through the entire range of motion. The only way to do it is with a Nautilus machine. The Nautilus cam was designed to provide resistance equally at all points in the range of motion. So that ceases to be a problem."

Triceps mass makes up two thirds of upper-arm size.

In terms of triceps training, the fact that the triceps has three heads would, in itself, seem to imply that it takes a variety of exercises to fully develop the muscle. Or does Mike feel that you can develop all three heads just by using, say, one or two exercises?

"You can if you're providing resistance through the full range of motion and the muscle is performing all its functions. In fact, why do an exercise if it's not going to work all three heads?" he says. "Dips, which I call squats for the upper body, work all three heads of the triceps. So does the Nautilus triceps machine. Triceps pushdowns on a lat machine come close to working all three heads equally—because the exercise involves the multiple functions of the triceps, which are to extend the forearm and then bring the whole arm back and into the body. With pushdowns you have that, and even more so with dips."

So despite the fact that the triceps has three heads, Mike stands firm that the best way to train it is to do one exercise—or at most two. His preferences are the Nautilus triceps machine and dips. Mentzer suggests that if you don't have access to Nautilus equipment or just want a little more variety, you should do triceps pushdowns and dips, but he cautioned that if you want to get the full benefits of the Heavy Duty methods he teaches, never do more than two exercises for triceps.

"I came to realize," he said, "that the issue of overtraining is the most crucial one facing most bodybuilders. And it comes down to this: If a bodybuilder performs one set more than the least amount required to stimulate an optimal increase in size and strength, he will not gain optimally; he may even halt progress entirely.

"And don't train too frequently. In most cases, that means not more than three times out of every seven to nine days. All of my clients are training, at the most, three days a week, and they're all making great progress."

Ironman *has always featured the greatest articles on the subject of old-time strongmen and other forefathers of bodybuilding. This article* by Randall J. Strossen, Ph.D., *is a fine example of the tremendous knowledge of training that comes from these "men who knew how to get a grip."*

CAPTAINS OF CRUSH
Randall J. Strossen, Ph.D.

The mark of a strongman is his grip, so it's no accident that some of the most memorable stories in strength history involve feats of hand strength. While discussions of grip strength naturally lead to tales of old-timers, there are some modern-day strongmen who bear watching. Let's meet four of them.

One of the most visible of the modern grip men is Gary "the Gripper" Stich, who specializes on the standard grip machine and is the world's best performer in this event. At 5'9½" and about 200 pounds, Gary holds the current right- and left-handed world records on the grip machine, with 310 pounds and 260 pounds, respectively—a far cry from the 50 or so pounds you're likely to see loaded on one of these machines in your local gym. Be forewarned, though, that the grip machine can be a relatively poor test of pure hand strength, because skilled practitioners can essentially perform a seated one-hand shrug that passes for a feat of hand strength.

Even though Gary is best known for his grip-machine world record, he performs another exhibition of grip strength that actually seems more impressive: holding an Ironman Super Gripper in front of his chest, he can close it in its toughest position using only his two thumbs. Rumor has it that the Stich household doesn't need a bottle opener.

While he's not strictly a grip man, Steve Sadicario, a.k.a. "the Mighty Stefan," is a professional strongman in the old-time tradition who must also be counted among those who have unusual strength from the elbow to the fingertips. The compactly built 5'6", 190-pound Mighty Stefan performs a variety of classic strongman feats in the tradition of the Mighty Atom and Slim-the-Hammerman. The Mighty Atom originally inspired Steve to be a professional strongman, and Slim-the-Hammerman personally instructed Steve when he was first starting out.

A good number of Sadicario's feats involve primarily the hands and wrists. For example, bending 60-penny nails and tearing a deck of cards in half are staples in his routine, and his most impressive feat is breaking a piece of number-8 jack chain in his bare hands.

Lest you dismiss these accomplishments, however, remember that no one in any of the Mighty Stefan's audiences has been able to perform them.

Another professional strongman who excels in a variety of feats of strength, with an emphasis on hand and wrist power, is 6′1″, 250-pound John Brookfield. The mild-mannered Brookfield is a man to consider betting heavily on if there were ever a decathlon of hand and wrist strength movements—especially if endurance, as well as pure strength, were factors. And beyond his impressively versatile skills, John has performed a feat of hand strength that strength historian David P. Willoughby considered to be outright extraordinary: Brookfield can tear a chunk the size of a quarter out of the center of a full deck of cards. Not that this is all John can do with cards. He also tears an entire deck in the box more easily than some people can open their mail, and he has torn two full decks in half at once.

Brookfield got started in the hand-strength area because, while his weight training had allowed him to develop good all-around strength, he felt his grip was lagging. Not only did John set out to correct this situation, but he was determined to develop the world's strongest grip. That was several years ago. Since then, he has moved relentlessly toward his goal.

John's feats include bending 60-penny nails in half in less than a minute, and bending 378 of them in half in less than two hours—both of which are world-record performances. John has also bent two 60-penny nails at once, another bending feat that might well be the best in the world. If the sight of 60-penny nails—6 inches long and ¼ inch in diameter—doesn't impress you, take a look at the 10-by-⅜-inch 100-penny nails John can bend in half anytime. Since he can also bend and break

horseshoes at will, you probably won't be surprised to learn that he can wrist curl more than 300 pounds for reps, even though he doesn't specialize in them. If we had to pick the top all-around performer in feats of hand and wrist strength, John Brookfield would get our nod.

Without a doubt, crushing strength is the most popular and dramatic method for testing grip men. Let's meet the first man named to this elite group, the man who most likely has the strongest grip in the world today—Richard Sorin. From going at it in a competitive handshake to comparing performances on a dynamometer, a man's crushing power is usually taken as the measure of his grip; and while Richard Sorin excels in many feats of hand strength, it's his crushing ability that truly puts the 6′5½″, 270-pounder in a class by himself.

For more than 25 years, the standard measure of crushing strength has been the mega-duty handgrippers made by Warren Tetting, first for Peary Rader and now for IronMind Enterprises, Inc. The number 1 stops nearly everyone who tries it, and even men like Gary Stich and the Mighty Stefan can do only about 10 reps with it.

Closing the number 2 (extra heavy) is in an entirely different league and requires the grip of someone at the level of John Brookfield. And the number 3 (super), to the best of our knowledge at the time of this writing, can be closed only by Richard Sorin. Since the average strength athlete will barely budge the number 3 gripper, it might be easier to appreciate Richard's crushing strength if you know he can do 34 complete, consecutive repetitions with the number 2 gripper, which he can also close using just two fingers.

Those of you who are toiling to close the Ironman Super Gripper with its two springs in the tougher position might get a kick out of knowing that Richard can do that with two fingers. The other day he set up an Ironman Super Gripper with four springs in the toughest position and closed it like it was nothing. As John Brookfield said, "I believe you could search the world over and not find anybody to match Richard's crushing strength."

Even so, crushing is not all Richard can do with his hands. He can, in fact, perform a wide range of feats, but let's concentrate on a certain impossible pinch-gripping feat he can do.

The classic mark of an authentic strongman's pinch grip is the ability to pinch-grip two York 35-pound plates together, smooth sides out. Almost nobody can do this, but Richard Sorin first performed the feat when he was a mere 12 years old. Two giant steps more difficult—and a feat that in all likelihood you will never see anyone do—is the pinch grip with two of the narrow York 45-pound plates that were introduced in 1972.

Yet another two giant steps more difficult is an impossible feat of pinch-gripping: hoisting a pair of the old-style (pre-1972) York 45s. Not only are these plates much wider, but they have very thin rims so that they must be squeezed together that much harder or they will come crashing down. Richard can do a full deadlift with these old 45s and swing his arm back and forth while pinching them. Now, that's incredible.

Feats of hand strength tie the iron game to its colorful past, and they know little bounds in terms of size, shape, gender, or age of their practitioners. So start squeezing. Maybe you'll be the next to join the Captains of Crush.

Thomas A. Seward, Ph.D., gives us a firsthand account of helping a trainee develop his forearms using some of the proven best forearm exercises. Learn how being forewarned can make you forearmed.

FOREWARNED IS FOREARMED
Thomas A. Seward, Ph.D.

Malcolm hadn't been around the gym for more than a year. I heard through the grapevine that he'd joined the Paradise Island Spa, drawn no doubt to the glitter of its

Reverse curl—start position.   Aaron Baker.

Reverse curl—midpoint position.

chrome-plated dumbbells. He might also have been drawn to the provocative bikini babe who graced the Paradise's ad, offering muscles, fitness, eternal youth, and—if your hormones were active and your imagination overactive—herself. So it was with some surprise that I found him standing in front of me as I was placing a pair of dumbbells back on the rack after a set of curls.

"Hi, Tom," he said sheepishly. "How you been?"

It was Malcolm all right, but only the name was the same. Gone were the T-shirt, shorts, and sneakers of a year ago. The new Malcolm was attired in the height of body-building fashion, decked out in fluorescent tights and a Gorilla Gym tank top that hung loosely from his shoulders via two gauzelike strands that left all but his navel and lower back bare. His footwear featured magenta laces with mauve tips, and the top of his head was covered with a red bandanna that pulled his

long locks back and sent them slithering down his back.

"Malcolm, you look . . ." I hesitated, not knowing whether to comment on his outfit or his physique, then decided to go for the latter, "great."

"You really think so?"

It was not a rhetorical question. As the only bodybuilder in town who'd ever won a state or regional contest, I was regularly asked to appraise the physiques of the younger athletes.

"I'm going to enter the local contest again," he said. "What do you think my chances are this time?" His request was so filled with optimism and enthusiasm that I gave in and kissed the rest of my workout good-bye.

"Okay, Malcolm," I said, resigned to it. "Go put on your posing briefs."

Malcolm rushed into the dressing room and was back in a few short minutes. He began pumping himself up with light dumbbells,

Seated dumbbell reverse wrist curl—start position. David Hughes.

Seated dumbbell reverse wrist curl—finish position.

Seated dumbbell wrist curl—start position.

Seated dumbbell wrist curl—finish position.   David Hughes.

and the oil he had hastily slapped on began dripping, splotching the weight room floor. He was definitely bigger than before, and his definition wasn't half bad.

"All right, Malcolm. Strike some poses for me."

He swung around to face the mirror and grimaced out a double-biceps that had his arms quaking with tension. About 10 poses later, I called a halt.

"You can stop now," I told him. "I've seen enough. I'd say you're good with signs of greatness."

"Wow, Tom! You're not kidding me, are you?" he asked almost apologetically.

"Of course not. But I said *signs* of greatness, meaning only that the potential is there."

"Oh," he replied with noticeable irritation.

"To get bigger, you need to pay more attention to the details. You've definitely got some outstanding bodyparts, but I can also see a few weaknesses."

He stared at me blankly.

"You've trained hard and made real progress," I continued. "That's obvious. Now it's time to stand back and evaluate the results. So don't be surprised if my words sound a little harsh. It's for your own good."

"Okay, Tom. You're right," Malcolm conceded. "I want you to tell me where I need to improve."

"Well," I said, "your most conspicuous weakness is in your forearms."

His jaw dropped, and he was speechless.

"I know what you're thinking—nobody pays any attention to forearms. No one poses them. They're just there, right?"

He shrugged.

"Look at it this way," I said. "Having the rest of your body well-developed and in proportion except for your forearms is like having 31 out of 32 teeth in your mouth when you smile."

Malcolm raised his eyebrows.

"All the great bodybuilders of our time, from Grimek through Scott and up to Yates, have known the importance of developing their forearms to the fullest," I continued. "But I daresay you've never done a single forearm exercise in your life."

Now Malcolm began hemming and hawing.

"I'll answer the question for you," I said. "Of course not. And that's why they look so out of place hanging there from those great upper arms of yours. You've got gap-toothed arms."

Malcolm had already resumed his flexing in front of the mirror. He extended one arm after the other, this way and that, manipulat-

Wrist-roll—finish position.

Wrist-roll—start position.   Danny Hester.

ing his wrists in an effort to get his forearms to bulge.

"Your forearms would look all right on a guy with smaller upper arms, but right now you have Popeye arms in reverse."

As I made that last comparison, I could see him droop. I was becoming cruel, and it was time to pick up his spirits.

"You've still got a good three months left before the contest," I said. "With some concentrated effort I believe you can bring your fore-

arms up a bit, maybe even enough to fill in the gap."

"Yeah, that's what I want. But how?"

"I thought you'd never ask," I said, laughing to myself. "The first thing you've got to do is add a forearms workout to your routine. Let's go over the exercises first, and then I'll suggest how to fit them into your program."

Malcolm nodded.

"The muscles of the forearm are activated by the flexion of the fingers and the movement of the wrist," I explained. "That's an important point to remember that will help you understand why I suggest specific ways of doing your forearm exercises. The first of these is wrist curls.

"Go ahead and grab a pair of 30-pound dumbbells and sit on this bench," I instructed. "Put your forearms on your thighs with your hands extending beyond your knees, palms up. Let your hands hang down and allow the dumbbells to roll to your fingertips as you open your hands slightly. Now roll the weights back into your palms, grasping them firmly, and curl your wrists upward as far as they'll go. Do about 12 slow, even reps."

Malcolm did exactly as he was told.

"Exchange those 30s for 20s now and go back to the bench. Place your forearms on

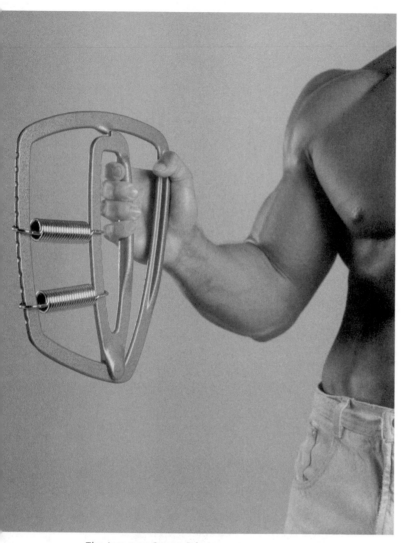

The Ironman Super Gripper.

I took back my work of art, unwound the rope, and attached a 10-pound plate to the other end of the rope. With Malcolm still staring in wonderment, I held the dowel at arm's length with both hands, palms down. Alternating my hands in a wrist action, I rolled the rope onto the dowel, lifting the plate from the floor until it touched the dowel.

"Here," I said, offering him the contraption after I unrolled the rope and lowered the plate back to the floor. "Your turn."

Malcolm took the wrist-roller with the enthusiasm of a child trying out a new toy. He held it out in front of him with his arms parallel to the floor as I had done. The plate rose slowly and steadily as he wound the rope with the brute strength of his forearm muscles. Only after the plate was firmly against the dowel did I speak.

"If you roll your wrists forward and downward to raise the plate, as you just did, you use the underbellies of your forearms. Let the plate back down to the floor now by reversing the action of your wrists."

With some effort, Malcolm followed my instructions again. This time he smiled in relief as the plate touched down.

"Now lift the plate using the same reverse motion you just used to lower it. So you'll be pulling the backs of your hands toward you, alternating sides, in order to raise the weight," I clarified.

He took a deep breath and completed the task.

"I can feel my forearms starting to burn on top. They're really getting pumped up," he said with relish after he lowered the plate by alternating hands in the forward motion.

"I assume you noticed that each time you rolled the weight up with one hand, you had to loosen your grip somewhat on the other hand so you could rotate the dowel. That continual relaxing and gripping of your fingers is an added benefit of the wrist-roll," I remarked.

"Now it's time to tie your forearms into your biceps workout with front curls." I pointed to an empty Olympic bar on the floor nearby and told him to get it. Then I explained how to perform the movement.

your thighs again, but this time hold the dumbbells with your palms facing down. This is called reverse wrist curls. Do about 12 reps."

Malcolm followed my instructions to the letter, and when he finished, he looked up at me in anticipation.

"Now your forearms should be ready for some real work with my pièce de résistance," I said dramatically. I fished my wrist-roller out of my bag and handed it to Malcolm. He looked at it quizzically. It consisted of a 16-inch-long, 1¼-inch-thick wooden dowel with a thin rope wrapped tightly around it. The rope was knotted securely at one end and threaded through a hole I'd drilled in the middle of the dowel.

"Hold the bar with your palms down and your hands at a comfortable width," I said. Now roll your wrists back as far as they'll go and then curl the bar up toward your shoulders, keeping your elbows snugly against the sides of your body."

Malcolm began his front curls.

"You'll feel this kind of curl in your lower biceps and the tops of your forearms," I explained. "It creates a continuous tension in both areas so that they're both strongly affected."

He nodded his head in agreement as he continued to perform rep after strict rep. After about 15 curls, he put the bar down and looked at me with his eyebrows raised high. He was game for more.

"What's next, Tom?"

"That's enough exercises for the moment," I told him. "Get your training journal and a pen, and I'll jot down sets and reps and tell you how to fit them into your arm routine."

Strong forearms aid in all curling movements.

Arnold Schwarzenegger.

He went to his bag and brought out a dog-eared notebook with a pen clipped inside the spiral binding.

"Here's what you should do," I said. "Begin your arm workout with forearms. Attack them full-force when you're fresh so you can get the most out of your effort."

Then I wrote the following in the notebook:

Palms-up wrist curl	2 × 12
Palms-down wrist curl	2 × 12
Forward wrist-roll	2 × failure
Backward wrist-roll	2 × failure
Front curl	4 × 12

"After that you go right into your biceps routine full-force," I elaborated. "You'll probably find that your forearms tire before your biceps, but do the best you can with them. Remember, it's your forearms that you need to build up right now, not your biceps."

This time when I spoke strongly, Malcolm didn't bat an eyelash.

"Since you've never really worked your forearms to any extent, I suggest you begin by using lighter weight than you think you should," I cautioned, "and don't go to failure on the wrist-rolls for a couple of weeks either."

"Gotcha! Thanks a lot, Tom." He smiled and shook my hand. Then he gathered up his gear and left the weight room.

A new guy from North Carolina moved into town that year and blew away the competition at the local contest, but the following year belonged to Malcolm. His physique was complete, forearms and all, and he took the Overall and Most Muscular.

Workout 1: Acclimation (Weeks 1 to 3)
Tri-set
Decline supinated wrist curls ×
    60–70 seconds

Decline pronated wrist curls ×
60–70 seconds
Super Gripper × 60–70 seconds

Perform three tri-sets. Take no rest between exercises, and then rest 90 seconds between tri-sets.

Workout 2: Intensification (Weeks 4 to 6)
Superset
One-arm supinated dumbbell wrist curls
× 30–40 seconds

One-arm pronated dumbbell wrist curls
× 30–40 seconds

Superset
Super Gripper × 4 reps, squeezing for
6 seconds
Super Gripper × 10 reps with continuous
tension

Perform each superset four times. Rest 90 seconds between supersets.

Lee Apperson.

Chapter 7

ABDOMINAL TRAINING

"Washboard" or "six-pack" abs are the finishing touch on a champion physique. This relatively small muscle group reveals itself only when trained to perfection and after all excess bodyfat has been dieted and trained off. Follow the advice in this chapter, and you can't miss.

First, Gene Mozée shows us how Arnold achieved his legendary midsection perfection.

ARNOLD'S MIDSECTION PERFECTION Arnold Schwarzenegger, as told to Gene Mozée

The first thing you see when you look at a well-developed body is the midsection—that's where the eyes are drawn. A fantastically cut midsection adds a tremendous amount of attractiveness to the overall appearance. It makes the whole upper body appear much more muscular from the front, and the entire physique more balanced.

Bodybuilding has always been a constant learning process for me—the longer I continued to compete, the more I learned. That is why I continued to improve year after year, always striving for greater perfection. Every year after the Mr. Olympia contest, I evaluated my strengths and weaknesses. I decided which areas I needed to focus on to make substantial improvements for the coming year, and then I planned my training strategy accordingly. My goal was to always show some new and dramatic improvement at the next contest.

In 1972, after I had won my third straight Mr. Olympia, which took place in Essen, Germany, I realized that I was fortunate to have beaten Serge Nubret and Sergio Oliva. In looking at the pictures from that contest, it was very obvious that I was not as cut as I could have been. My abdominals, in particular, lacked razor sharpness. I knew right away that if I was to defend my title the next year as the world's premier bodybuilder, I would have to improve my abdominals considerably.

For the first time in my life, I began to realize the importance of sculptured abdominals. In the past, even though I had always tried to maintain a small, hard midsection, I

had never placed much importance on the idea of having rippling definition there. Year by year I had been adding more size to my arms, chest, shoulders, back, thighs, and calves, as well as more shape and definition. There was no doubt that I had been neglecting my midsection.

I had always relegated abdominal training to the position of least importance in my workout schedule. The last six weeks before the Mr. Olympia contest was the only time I would do any gut work at all.

The more I thought about improving my midsection, the greater my enthusiasm for the idea became. I began to visualize myself on the posing platform with fabulous abdominals. I thought of all the poses in my routine that I could improve with sliced-up abs, rather than just sucking in my waist for my usual abdominal vacuum. I decided right then and there to begin training this bodypart in January rather than waiting until July, as I had done in the past.

Crunch.   B. J. Quinn.

Hanging leg-up.

Seated twist.

All training, regardless of the sport, requires mental discipline. You have to be motivated to train any muscle group hard. For most bodybuilders, the arms, chest, shoulders, and back are the favorites. The thighs and calves take a little more mental effort, but once you get your head straight and adjust your attitude, leg work becomes enjoyable. The exercises for the waistline, however, are much less exciting. Drudgery and boredom can easily cause trainees to slack off on ab training or neglect it entirely. One notable exception is Zabo Koszewski, who would do 1,000 sit-ups and 1,000 leg raises in a workout. No wonder he was considered to have the world's greatest abdominals when he was competing! Even now, although he is long retired from competition, he still begins every workout with 500 sit-ups and 500 leg raises.

I decided to make a gradual adjustment into abdominal training. At the time, I was also recovering from knee surgery caused by an accident that occurred when a posing platform collapsed during an exhibition in Europe. I thought it was wiser to be careful not to overwork in the beginning. I started with 1 set of 20 reps on each of three exercises.

The first month I trained abdominals three times a week, working up to 3 sets of 20 to 30 reps on each exercise. Starting with the second month, I increased my abdominal routine to four days a week, still doing just 3 sets but increasing the reps to 30 to 40. I wanted maximum concentration on each rep, so I tensed my abdominals. I couldn't do as many reps that way, but my abs worked harder and received more benefit than from less-concentrated reps.

In the past, I would do 100 reps on leg raises, blasting them out as fast as possible. But as soon as I discovered that the quality of each rep was far more important than the quantity of reps, I began to focus on quality reps—and my abdominal definition began to improve rapidly. By performing reps more slowly, I was able to isolate my abdominals more fully by minimizing any assistance provided by the hip flexors, psoas major, and psoas minor, which assist in raising the legs. That's why both sit-ups and leg raises are more effective if your legs are slightly bent at the knees. It also takes the strain off the lower-back area. This forces the rectus abdominis muscles to work harder by lessening any assistance from the hip flexors.

During the third month, I increased the sets to 4, and in the fourth month I moved up to 5 sets of each exercise. This gradual increase in the amount of sets and reps got me into the groove of abdominal training, to the extent that it became almost as enjoyable as working my arms and chest. Week by week I could see my waist getting smaller, tighter, and more muscular.

Seated knee-up.

TRI-SET AB BLITZ

I increased my abdominal training to six days a week for the last two months before the '73 Mr. Olympia contest. I also added a fourth exercise to the routine. Here is the exact training program I used to get deep, rippling cuts in my abs and add to my overall muscularity, which enabled me to win another Mr. Olympia crown.

Crunch

This movement thoroughly works the rectus abdominis muscles with a short-range contraction and isolation of the abs from the navel to the sternum. It is great for burning fat and shrinking the size of the waist. You perform crunches by lying on your back on a bench with your feet propped up so that only a half sit-up is possible. Place your hands behind your head, raise your hips off the bench, and exhale as you do a half sit-up—squeezing, or crunching, your abdominals into the contracted position. Repeat for at least 20 reps, and work up to 40 as you get stronger. Without resting, immediately go right to the next exercise.

Hanging leg-up

This movement not only thoroughly works your abs—particularly the lower region—but it also helps chisel cuts into your serratus and intercostals. While hanging from a chinning bar with a shoulder-width grip, raise your knees up as high as possible—try to touch your chest with them. Lower your legs slowly and repeat for 20 reps. Be sure to exhale as you bring your knees up, and inhale as you lower them. Again, increase the reps to at least 40 as you progress. Without any rest at all, complete this tri-set by going to the third exercise.

Bent-over twist

This exercise hits the external and internal obliques. I do it while bending forward with my torso parallel to the floor, my feet about 24 inches apart, and an empty bar across the back

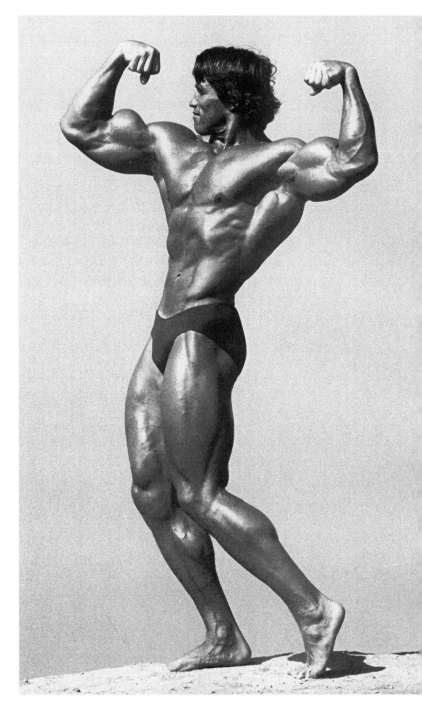

of my shoulders. I bend sideways to the right until the bar touches my left foot; then I bend back past the starting position all the way to the left until the bar touches my right foot. I do this in one continuous motion with no pauses; you should, too. Keep adding reps until you reach 40 or 50.

When I was training for the Mr. Olympia, I did five round-robin sets like this. When I completed a tri-set, I went on to the next with no rest at all. During the final two months of contest preparation, I added the following exercise to make it a quad-set routine.

Roman chair sit-up

Most bodybuilding champions prefer this version of the sit-up to any other. It works the entire abdomen from top to bottom; and if you add a twist alternating from side to side, it works the obliques as well. With your feet secured on the Roman chair—your buttocks should be supported by a bench or stool— lower your upper body until it is parallel to the floor. Then raise back up and fully contract your abs as you complete the sit-up

motion. Remember to exhale as you sit up, and inhale as you go down. Start with 20 reps, and gradually increase to 40 as your waist gets stronger. I inserted this exercise into the routine just before the bent-over twists.

By doing these exercises nonstop in tri-set and quad-set style, I was able to blitz my waist with a maximum-intensity workout in the shortest time possible. I preferred to do this program at the end of my workout, usually during the evening session of my double-split routine.

After completing my midsection workout, I tensed and posed my abdominals, repeatedly flexing them while concentrating on bringing out the definition by attempting to isolate each row of the rectus abdominis group. It's almost like doing sets of 10 reps. After I worked each muscle group, I used isotension contraction movements to etch deeper cuts and add more shape.

Along with the abdominal blitz program, I paid more attention to my diet, especially in the last eight weeks before the contest. I was consuming about 250 to 300 grams of protein and about 60 grams of carbohydrates when

going for more definition. The last 60 days before the contest, I cut down to 200 to 250 grams of protein and 10 grams of carbohydrates a day. I also severely reduced my intake of fats and cut out almost all dairy products.

Getting your abdominals in top shape can make you look 25 to 50 percent more impressive than you would if your waist were out of condition. Now, who could pass up a deal like that? Get started on your abdominal improvement program today. When you see the sensational improvement it can add to your physique, you'll be glad you did.

In this article, Steve Holman shows us how to use his Midsection Machete program to achieve granite abs.

GRANITE ABS Steve Holman

It's no easy task to get those ab peaks and valleys etched like so much carved granite—especially for people who spend loads of time doing conventional leg raises and crunches.

Steve Holman shows his own "granite abs."

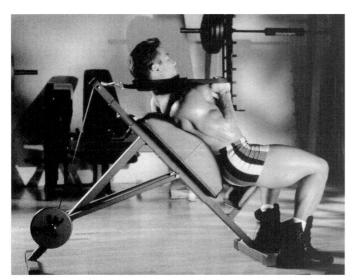

Ab Bench crunch pull—start position. Danny Hester.

Ab Bench crunch pull—finish position.

Unfortunately, these folks are taking the long and winding road. Contrary to popular belief, leg raises and crunches are far from efficient midsection exercises. The fact is, the conventional leg raise—the way most people do it, with momentum and without a hip roll at the end of the rep—works the hip flexor muscles, not the abdominals; and the crunch is really only half an ab exercise, making it a partial, inefficient movement.

Experts have been touting the crunch performed on the floor as the perfect ab-training exercise for about a decade now, but if you think about it, when you do this movement on a flat surface, you're forced to stop it short—when your back is flat—and you miss the back half of the abdominals' range of motion. To get full-range exercise for your abs, you must start your crunches with your back arched 30 degrees to the rear of center.

According to Frederick C. Hatfield, Ph.D., creator of the patented Ab Bench, "The best way to train the abdominals is to first pre-stretch the muscle, then contract it against resistance—which is exactly what the Ab Bench crunch does. This exercise allows you to stretch the rectus abdominis prior to contracting into a crunch position. Full-range movements like this are generally more productive in improving strength, tone, and mass. It has to do with the amount of work being accom-

plished on every set. Full-range crunches are 100 percent more productive than conventional on-the-floor half-range crunches, because the amount of work you're accomplishing is virtually doubled."

Full range of motion is why the Ab Bench crunch pull and cable crunch with low-back support are the ultimate exercises for developing the rectus abdominis, the long muscle on the front of your midsection that runs from your rib cage down to your pelvis. The function of this muscle—and it is only one muscle; the ridges are caused by tendons running across it—is to pull your rib cage toward your pelvis. When you train it, the movement shouldn't start halfway through the range of motion, as it does on a conventional crunch. You want to train the rectus abdominis through its full range, which is why the Ab Bench positions your torso back over the curved pad—so that you pre-stretch your rectus abdominis prior to each ab-contracting crunch. You get maximum results for every ounce of effort and build the rectus abdominis to its full potential with full-range exercise.

The rectus abdominis isn't the only important midsection muscle you can train on this patented piece of equipment, though. Bob Blum and Fred Koch wrote an extensive article on the external obliques in the February 1996 *Ironman* in which they made the astute

Erector crunch.   Danny Hester.

to the front of the pelvis. To work these muscles completely, try Ab Bench twists. Start in the pre-stretch position, but instead of curling your torso straight down, do a twisting crunch movement. Pull forward and diagonally with the right side of your rib cage until your right shoulder is directly over your groin. Focus on trying to crunch the right side of your rib cage down to your navel. Release back to a full stretch and repeat with your left side. (Note: If you don't have an Ab Bench, you can simulate many of the following exercises using cables.)

For a slightly different effect on the rectus abdominis and obliques, try low-ab twists. Sit up as if you were doing the Ab Bench crunch pull, but hold at the point where your torso is almost perpendicular to the floor. From this position, twist and try to crunch the right side of your rib cage down to your navel, then the left. This involves a shorter range of motion than Ab Bench twists, but the exercise allows you to concentrate on squeezing the lower internal obliques and rectus abdominis muscles.

To work the transverse abdominis, the girdlelike muscle that encases your midsection, try side spins. According to Koch and Blum's article "Transverse Abdominis," which appeared in the March 1995 *Ironman*, the transverse abdominis is often considered a breathing muscle—it's the muscle you use to suck in your gut—but it also assists in trunk flexion. Side spins on the Ab Bench train this function with resistance. Sit upright and sideways on the Ab Bench with your left shoulder facing the pad. Grab the straps with the hand that's farthest from the bench. Hold the straps in front of your chest with the straps over or under the other arm—whichever is more comfortable. Turn your torso away from the bench, keeping your back straight and your hips stationary. The range of motion is short, so turn only as far as your natural flexibility allows. Do not jerk or force an exaggerated range of motion.

You can also work another important midsection muscle group on the Ab Bench— the spinal erectors—with erector crunches. Sit on the Ab Bench so that you're facing the bench with your abs against the back pad and

observation that this muscle group takes up more area than the rectus abdominis. That makes it a very important midsection muscle group, especially for the competitive bodybuilder who's after that raked-by-a-bear-claw look on either side of the rectus abdominis. The external obliques insert on either side at the lower rib cage and run around the midsection

Arnie List.

Danny Hester and Tina Jo Bagne.

your pelvis tilted slightly back. Cross your forearms over your chest with an Ab Bench handle in each hand, and anchor them near your shoulders. Contract your spinal erectors as you pull your torso back and arch your lower back. Hold for a count of two at the top of the range of motion. Slowly release and curl forward, keeping tension on your erectors and holding your waist stationary.

This is a much more effective lower-back exercise than the hyperextension because you're in a sitting position bending forward at the waist. In hyperextensions, your glutes are the major players; erector crunches take your glutes out of the movement.

With these five exercises—crunch pulls, twists, low-ab twists, side spins, and erector crunches—you train all of the largest midsection muscles, including the lower back, and you get the added benefit of an almost injury-proof lower back. Here's how Hatfield explains this therapeutic phenomenon:

"For those who have bad backs, it has become axiomatic that ab work is the best therapy for this condition. And for those whose backs are virgin to troublesome herniations, subluxations, and ruptures, it's the best therapy for prevention."

Low-back strengthening. Full-range abdominal exercise for every major midsection muscle group. Pre-stretch. Complete contraction. If you want the type of midsection that's sliced and diced, don't make midsection training an afterthought. Try 2 to 3 sets of these five exercises twice a week on an Ab Bench or with cables. Really hit the muscles hard, just as you do with other major bodyparts like chest or arms, and you'll soon get the delineated results you're after. You'll also quickly realize why the Ab Bench is becoming known as the Midsection Machete.

This comprehensive abdominal training information from Dave Tuttle provides an explanation of what you are trying to achieve when you train your abs. Follow Dave's advice and you will develop phenomenal abs!

PHENOMENAL ABS Dave Tuttle

THE FUNCTION OF THE ABDOMINAL MUSCLES

Abs are easily among the most popular bodyparts, and with good reason. While peaked biceps are certainly desirable, and huge quads a definite plus, there's something about a chiseled midsection that truly makes a physique. Perhaps it's because superior abdominals are so difficult to achieve, or because the eyes are naturally drawn to the center of the body on stage. While judges have been known to overlook deficient calves or lower-back development, competitors rarely, if ever, dominate the stage without dynamite abs. Yet the intense desire for great abdominals is often a bodybuilder's downfall because the myths of the past can bring progress to a dead stop. Let's look at the kinesiology of the abs and see how to design the ideal workout.

There are four muscles in the abdominal region: the rectus abdominis, the external obliques, the internal obliques, and the transversus abdominis. The transversus abdominis is the deepest of the four. Its fibers run horizontally, wrapping around the trunk of the body between the spine and a fibrous membrane beneath the rectus abdominis all the way from the ribs to the hip. The transversus abdominis enables you to pull in your belly, which not only improves your posture but is also essential for most competition poses.

The internal and external obliques work together to accomplish a variety of contraction movements. As the name indicates, the internal obliques lie underneath the externals. The fibers in the internal obliques run in various directions, but generally upward between the iliac crest of the hipbone and the ribs on both sides of the body. The fibers of the external obliques generally run downward between the same points. Both of these muscles assist in compression of the abdomen and flexion of the trunk, the movements involved in the basic sit-up. They also work synergistically to help rotate the trunk. For example, when you rotate your trunk to the right during trunk flexion, you simultaneously contract your right internal oblique and the left external oblique.

The king of ab muscles is the rectus abdominis. This is the muscle on the front of the abdomen, and it's what people generally refer to when they talk about abs. Its surface layer is comprised of four pairs of muscle bundles separated by three horizontal tendinous intersections and the vertical linea alba. Together, these elements create the so-called peaks and valleys of the ab region.

Beneath this layer is a continuous sheet of muscle. The rectus abdominis originates at the pubis, the front portion of the hipbone, and is inserted at the xiphoid process, the bottom of the breastbone, and the cartilage of ribs 5 through 7. The primary function of this muscle is to flex the trunk, although it also assists the other three muscles in compressing the abdomen.

Some athletes believe that the rectus abdominis is divided into upper and lower abs, which leads them to tailor specific routines for the two "bodyparts." In fact, there's no more truth to this notion than there is to the idea that the arm has an upper and lower biceps. Every muscle functions in just one way: by shortening and lengthening. So rather than varying your exercises based on the part of the rectus abdominis they supposedly target, focus on the physiological action at hand. Visualize the entire muscle shortening and lengthening during each and every rep. That will create the most stimulation for your abs and develop them to their maximum potential.

BEGINNER WORKOUT

Crunch	3 × 6–10
Twisting crunch	3 × 6–10

This quick workout introduces you to the demands of ab training. Always start with a warm-up on each exercise using 40 percent of the weight you will lift on your three main sets. This is important, because each exercise works the muscles differently. Try to do at least 6 reps per set, and focus on progressive resistance. When you can do 10 reps with a given weight, increase the weight. This will temporarily lower the number of reps you can do, but over time you'll gain strength and get up to 10 again. Keep repeating this process, and watch as your abs gain incredible mass and definition.

Crunch

Find an isolated area in the gym where you can lie down, preferably on a mat. Lie with your back against the mat, then bend your legs so that your calves are at a 90-degree angle to your hamstrings. Place your hands behind your head or your arms on your chest with your hands on top of each other. (Once your strength improves, you'll hold a weight in your hands in this position.) Now, without twisting, slowly raise your upper body as far as you can, contracting your abs until they're totally crunched together. Hold for a second, then slowly return to the starting position. Do not allow your upper body to drop to the mat: lower it in a controlled movement, and avoid bouncing off the bottom. Repeat for as many repetitions as possible.

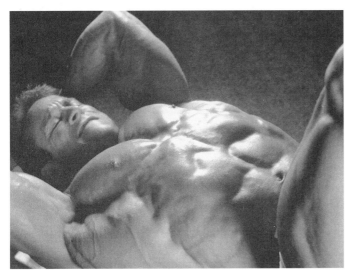

Crunch—start position.   Arnie List.

Crunch—finish position.

Twisting crunch.   B. J. Quinn.

Twisting crunch

This movement is identical to the crunch, except you twist your body as you come up, rotating to the right and then the left on alternate reps. Repeat until you reach the desired number of reps.

INTERMEDIATE WORKOUT

Crunch	3–4 × 6–10
Twisting crunch	3–4 × 6–10
Abdominal cable pulldown	3–4 × 6–10

Abdominal cable pulldown

You can perform this exercise on any cable machine that has an upper cable. Select a rope attachment that has two knots, or a bar with

Abdominal cable pulldown—start position.
Jennifer Goodwin.

Abdominal cable pulldown—finish position.

double straps, and attach it to the machine. Then find a pad to rest your knees on, and position it approximately three feet in front of the machine. Grab the straps or rope with your arms and slowly lower yourself into the kneeling position. Next, bring your arms down so that they rest next to your body and the straps or rope ends are next to your head. Lock into this position, so that the only muscle movement will be in the abdominal region.

Now imagine that there's a tree floating horizontally in front of your knees. Instead of pulling straight down, move outward and then downward as you wrap your abs around the tree. Curve them as you bring the rope or straps to the ground while minimizing leg movement. That will isolate your abdominals to the greatest extent possible. Your elbows should nearly touch the ground at the end of the contraction. Then return to the original position and stretch your abs, making sure you don't move your arms and bring your lats into play for more than stabilizing purposes. Use light weights until you master the movement, then increase the resistance progressively. The abs respond to heavier weight the way any other bodypart does. The bottom line is, you get greater abdominal development.

ADVANCED WORKOUT

Crunch	4 × 6–10
Twisting crunch	4 × 6–10
Abdominal cable pulldown	4 × 6–10
Knee-up	4 × 6–10

Knee-Up

This exercise has a similar effect to the leg raise, but it's safer to perform. During the contracted position of the knee-up, the legs are bent at the knee, which results in less stress on the lower back than occurs with leg raises.

Knee-up—start position.   Arnie List.   Knee-up—finish position.

Begin by hanging from a chin-up bar with your arms a bit more than shoulder-width apart (or use a device called AbOriginals). In either case, start with your legs straight down. Then raise them slowly, bending the knees so that your thighs are parallel to the ground and your calves are at a 90-degree angle to your thighs (that is, perpendicular to the ground). Your knees should be a bit more than a foot away from each other.

Hold the abs briefly in this contracted position, then lower them again to the starting point. Do not use weights on this movement, since that will produce unnecessary back stress. While knee-ups also recruit the hip and thigh muscles to some extent—specifically the rectus femoris, psoas, and iliacus—your abs will feel a real burn when you do them correctly.

DON'T OVERDO A GOOD THING

Don't let your desire for great abs become your downfall. The most common reason that bodybuilders hold themselves back in the midsection department is overtraining. It's not uncommon to see athletes work their abdominals every day or every other day, as though the abdominal muscles would fall apart if they weren't constantly subjected to training stress. Everyone understands that this is absurd when it comes to chest or leg training, so why are abs treated differently? The muscle fiber composition of the abdominals is functionally identical to that of the other skeletal muscles, and you should train them just as you'd train any other bodypart.

It's important to keep things in perspective. Exercise your abdominal muscles once per bodypart cycle. Train them hard, then let them rest. Once they've recuperated, hit them again with total intensity by applying tried-and-true progressive-resistance training principles.

DIET

Bear in mind that you can't burn a lot of calories doing sit-ups, particularly when compared to movements that involve large bodyparts. In fact, since abdominal training, like all weight training, is anaerobic in nature, you can't actually burn fat at all during a weight-training session. While fat will eventually be burned whenever you create a calorie deficit, there are far better ways to melt away that extra midsection baggage than by overtraining your abs.

You can have the greatest abs around, but if they're covered with a layer of bodyfat, no one will see them. Therefore, the last crucial ingredient for exceptional abs is dietary

Mike Mentzer.

B. J. Quinn.

Kevin Hall.

restraint. In order to reduce your bodyfat level, you must create a calorie deficit. Then, once you get your fat percentage to the desired point, you must maintain a balance between your calorie intake and expenditure.

You don't have to live like a monk, however. The secret to long-term dieting is to eat smaller portions of those foods you enjoy. Don't cut out the meals of your dreams. Just eat smaller meals and fill up on salad or other low-calorie foods. That way you'll still get psychological satisfaction from your food while assuring that you're on the path to great abs.

Judd Biasiotto, Ph.D., has a treasure trove of information from his experience as a powerlifter. In this article, he explains the benefits of ab training and how to properly target the abs.

POWER AB TRAINING
Judd Biasiotto, Ph.D.

When I was a competitive powerlifter, I was constantly being reminded that I didn't have a whole lot of muscle mass. I looked more like an 11-year-old stamp collector than a powerlifter,

people said. To add insult to injury, *Powerlifting USA* referred to me a number of times as the weakest strongman in the world—another reference to my shortage of muscularity. I honestly don't believe I looked that bad, but I could understand where the editors were coming from. After all, most of the guys I competed against were either lower primates or examples of modern-day Cro-Magnons. You know the kind: 5' tall, 5' wide, and they eat everything raw, hate their mothers, and have hair on the bottoms of their feet. Well, I'm nothing like that. I'm tall—for my weight class—and I cook my vegetables, love my mother, and shave the bottoms of my feet once a week.

I have to admit that no one who's seen me in person has ever accused me of lifting weights, and I don't exactly look like Eddie Coan or Dorian Yates. Still, at 132 pounds I squatted 603, bench pressed 319, and

Lee Apperson.

deadlifted 551. It might also be noted that I made those lifts after going through major back surgery. So I'm not without muscle, and I certainly have power.

What was the secret to my success? Powerful abdominal muscles.

You may not believe it, but that's a serious answer. The main reason I was able to make such lifts, especially after surgery, was my abdominal strength. I don't want to brag (of course, you know I will), but when I was competing, I'd venture to say I probably had the most powerful abdominal muscles in the world. Prior to my surgery, however, I never worked my midsection. Very few powerlifters did at the time. Even today, it's easier to find a television evangelist who doesn't ask for money than it is to find a powerlifter who routinely works abs.

The fact is, I started working mine out of necessity. After my back surgery, I needed my ab muscles to be as strong as possible to stabilize my back. Initially, I wasn't using any specific program. I just worked my abs every chance I got—between sets, during TV commercials, and at other odd moments. I did sit-ups until my abs screamed for mercy.

It all paid off, because once I really got into my ab work, the slight back pain that remained after the operation disappeared. I also noticed that my deadlifts and squats became easier to perform as my abdominal strength increased. Interestingly, I'd been told numerous times in the past by experts in kinesiology that if I strengthened my abdominals, I'd probably be able to increase the poundages I was lifting on both my squat and deadlift.

In my head, I always knew they were right, but I never had it in my heart to work my abs until after my surgery. Or maybe I just didn't comprehend how significant abdominal strength is in performing the powerlifts.

To make a long story short, once I realized the benefits of having powerful abs, I took a more scientific and systematic approach to developing mine. I read everything I could get my hands on about the subject, and over the years I've accumulated an enormous amount of information and knowledge. I believe I know what works and what doesn't. Here's the scoop.

As I said, few lifters systematically train their abdominal muscles, and the majority of those who do go about it incorrectly. I have to admit, I started out doing it wrong myself. For instance, my initial training program consisted mainly of incline-board sit-ups, straight-leg sit-ups, and Roman chair sit-ups. It sounds like a pretty good program, right? If you whip off a quick 25 reps of any of these exercises, you're going to experience a pretty good burn, and, anatomically, it appears that the abdominals are the primary muscles involved.

Now, it's true that the abs come into play in all three of those exercises, but their contribution to the full range of motion is quite limited. According to Jerry Robinson, author of the Legendary Abs program, "If you lie flat on your back with legs extended, your abs have the capacity to raise your shoulders about 30 degrees off the floor. No further. Any motion above and beyond that is not the work of the abs. Since the straight-leg sit-up calls for about 90 degrees of trunk flexion, two-thirds of the motion is wasted on other muscles."

The same can be said about incline-board sit-ups; and as for Roman chair sit-ups, well, they don't bring the abs into play at all. In short, they're absolutely worthless for developing the abdominals. In fact, Dr. Hugh Studdard, a nationally known kinesiologist from Albany State College in Albany, Georgia, warns against using any abdominal exercise in which the psoas muscles are the prime movers. According to him, the psoas major and the iliacus share a common distal attachment that acts as one muscle at the hip joint. Authorities refer to this attachment as the *iliopsoas.* However you refer to them, the two muscles work together to form a strong hip flexor. Consequently, when you perform straight-leg or Roman chair sit-ups, the iliopsoas becomes the prime mover, thus decreasing the amount of force the abdominals generate.

Believe it or not, there's more bad news about these exercises. Not only are they ineffective at stressing the abdominal muscles, but they're extremely effective at stressing the lumbar region—that is, your lower back. Unfortunately, the stress that those exercises put on your lower back can be debilitating over a period of time, which, as you might imagine, is not such a good thing.

The problem is easy to avoid, however. Just don't do abdominal exercises that involve the psoas muscles.

Arnie List.

Ab Bench.   Alex Marenco.

Before I move on to what you can do to develop awesome abs, a little anatomy lesson is in order. As you're probably aware, skeletal muscles are made up of two different types of muscle fibers. The so-called slow-twitch fibers contract more slowly and have a high capacity for aerobic (meaning *with oxygen*) production of adenosine triphosphate (ATP), the fuel that's used by cells. The fast-twitch fibers contract rapidly and have a higher capacity for anaerobic (*without oxygen*) production of ATP.

Fast-twitch fibers are activated in short-duration, explosive activities such as sprinting or powerlifting, which depend almost entirely on anaerobic metabolism for energy. Slow-twitch fibers are more active during endurance activities, in which energy is generated by aerobic metabolism. Consequently, fast-twitch fibers are best developed with exercises that involve heavy resistance performed for a low range of repetitions, while slow-twitch fibers are best developed with high-rep, low-resistance exercises. Now, here's the kicker, something that a lot of lifters don't understand: Because the muscles of posture—the abdominal erectors—are predominantly made up of slow-twitch fibers and therefore would be more responsive to high repetitions, if you want powerful abs, you should train them with high reps, performing 15 to 25 per set.

That brings me back to Jerry Robinson's Legendary Abs program. Frankly, it's one of the best ab programs on the market, and I recommend it without reservation. One of the major premises of the program is that when you perform exercises in a systematic sequence, they can give you greater benefits than when you perform the same exercises at random. This is what Robinson refers to as synergism: a combination of elements that creates a whole effect that's greater than the sum of the individual effects.

Of course, the question is, How do you know what sequence to use? According to Robinson, the ideal order of a series of exercises is partly defined by a principle called the *interdependency of muscle groups*. It sounds complex, but it's really very simple. Robinson explains it as follows.

Imagine the stomach muscles divided into upper abs and lower abs. The line is usually drawn between the top two and bottom two abdominal lumps. This isn't a technical division, and you won't find it listed in *Gray's Anatomy*, but for the sake of our discussion it exists nonetheless.

The upper abs can in turn be divided into center and outer sections. From now on, we'll use the term upper abs to refer to the center section; the outers we will call by their actual names, the external obliques.

First, consider just the upper (center) abs and the lower abs. They are interdependent in this way:

To work the lower abs, you need to use lower abs and upper abs.

To work the upper abs, you only need to use upper abs.

Notice that the upper abs play a role in the work you do for both areas. As a result, if you tire the upper abs first, their fatigue will limit the amount of lower-ab work you can do. The solution: exercise your lower abs first. That way you can exhaust the lowers completely and then work the uppers to their limit with exercises that concentrate on them.

There you have it: the interdependency of muscle groups. Put that together with the other anatomical factors discussed previously, and you have a solid set of guidelines:

Henrik Thamasian.

1. Avoid exercises that involve the psoas muscles.
2. Use high reps of 15 to 25 with low resistance.
3. Work your lower abs before your upper abs. The only thing that's left is to determine which exercises to use.

The best exercise I've found for the lower abs is hanging leg lifts. You'll need a horizontal bar from which to hang—by your hands, not your

Hanging leg lift.   Mike O'Hearn.

Henrik Thamasian.

neck. Grip the bar so your hands are slightly wider than your shoulders. Try to relax your upper torso as much as possible, but at the same time keep your abs contracted—a neat little trick that's well worth mastering. Your feet should be positioned in front of you; that

is, in front of the vertical plane. Once you're hanging from the bar in this position, bring your knees to your chest. As you raise your knees, rock your pelvis forward. That will help you get maximum ab movement.

After you pump out a 20-rep set of hanging leg lifts, followed by approximately 30 seconds' rest and then a second set of 15 reps, you're ready to give your upper abs a little more attention. The best way to do that is with the Ab Bench. It's by far the best ab machine on the market. If your gym doesn't have one, talk your gym manager into getting one. If you're not a good salesperson, you can buy one for your very own living room. If you can't swing either of those options, you can do pulldown ab crunches, which, if performed properly, are every bit as effective as the Ab Bench crunch pull.

Assuming you have an Ab Bench, you should do 2 sets of 20 and 15 reps with approximately 30 seconds' rest between sets. If you don't have access to this equipment, perform pulldown ab crunches for the same number of sets and reps, as follows.

Mike Quinn.

Use a rope attachment on a cable machine, or, if that's not available, use a lat pulldown attachment and wrap a thick rope around it with the ends hanging down. Kneel in front of the machine facing away from it, grab both ends of the rope, and bring your hands to the top of your head. While in this position, lower your chin to your chest. Crunch over until your elbows touch your knees. Crunch and contract your upper abs for a count of three, then return to the starting position with your back slightly arched. Keep your hands against your head throughout the exercise. The entire program looks like this. Remember to take a 30-second rest after every set.

Hanging leg lift	2 × 20, 15
Ab Bench crunch pull	2 × 20, 15

For best results, work your abs four times a week. As with any exercise, you'll want to increase the resistance as your ability increases.

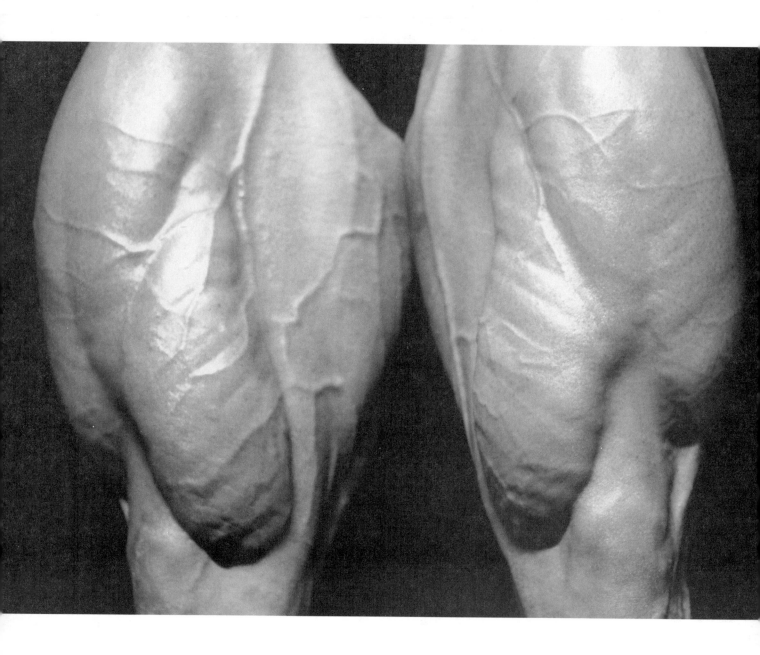

Chapter 8

LEG TRAINING

There is only one way to begin a chapter on leg training: with Mr. Intensity, Tom Platz. In this far-ranging interview with David Prokop, Tom reveals exactly how he developed the most massively impressive legs in the history of bodybuilding. Pay attention, and you'll discover how a guy with "no legs" built them to massive proportions with the aid of long socks!

TOM PLATZ'S AWESOME THIGHS

David Prokop

Tom Platz—stupendous thighs! If you're a serious bodybuilder, you really can't think of one without thinking of the other.

No one else in the history of bodybuilding ever developed a bodypart to rival Tom Platz's thighs at their best. Put it this way: there have been great bodyparts attached to various musclemen over the years—and then there are Tom Platz's thighs. End of discussion.

Tom Platz was and is to thigh development what Babe Ruth was to home runs—the best! No one else even comes close. Still, the 5'7½", 220-pound-in-peak-condition bodybuilder is almost as well known for the unbelievable intensity and focus of his leg training as he is for the leg development itself—training intensity so awesome, it almost seems unreal. Just like those legs.

So perhaps more than anyone else, Tom Platz is bodybuilding's man of absolutes: no one ever took leg development to such a freaky out-of-this-world level; no one ever took leg training to such a twilight zone extreme; no one in bodybuilding is more closely associated with one bodypart. Even so, to regard Tom as all legs and no upper body is to do him a grave injustice—you don't finish third in the Mr. Olympia contest, as he did in 1981, on great legs alone.

The normal assumption one might make, of course, is that anyone who could hit the weights that hard has to be some kind of a wild man who needs to be locked up in a cage between workouts and fed raw meat. The fact is, however, Tom Platz is a well-educated, gentlemanly individual who not only had the guts and drive to boldly go where no one had ever

Tom Platz.

gone before in weight training, but who can also articulate with great clarity and feeling what that journey was like for him.

IM: Tom, to start at the very beginning, when did you first get the idea that you wanted to do weight training? And when did you actually start bodybuilding?

TP: When I was 10 years old, probably closer to 9½, I looked at a muscle magazine and saw that picture of Dave Draper on the beach with Betty Weider on one arm and two girls on each leg and another girl on the other arm. He was holding the Weider Crusher in his hands, and in the background were the waves and the surfboard stuck in the sand.

I looked at that picture, and it was like, "God! I don't believe this." It was an incredible, tranformational moment that changed my life forever. That photo just motivated me and

inspired me and said something to me—about the physicality of California, about lifting weights and having muscles of iron. I was just totally moved by that; it was like becoming a priest, having a calling from God at that young age. That's what I had to do with my life. I knew that at the time. In fact, when I was 11, I was dead set on becoming Mr. Universe. And I knew it was going to happen; I had rehearsed it many, many times in my own mind.

On the facing page of the magazine I remember a picture of Arnold drinking protein out of a blender, and it was almost like his biceps were hanging out when he was doing that. I showed both of those pictures to my dad, and I said, "That's what I want to do for a living." Somehow I expected money to be involved in the sport, although there wasn't at that time. I was assuming there would be business opportunity in bodybuilding, and eventually there was for me many years later.

IM: So you actually started training when?

TP: When I was 9½.

IM: And what was the nature of your training at that time? Did you actually do a full training routine?

TP: When I was 9½, I can remember doing bench presses on the cellar floor after dinner. My father would take my brother and sister and me downstairs to the basement, to the cellar—they have cellars back east—and I would lie on the floor, and he would read the Weider instructional manual to me. My brother and sister were just learning how to count at that time, and they would learn how to count by counting my reps. I remember my elbows would always hit the cement floor, and I couldn't figure out how to do this thing called the bench press. It seemed like such a stupid exercise, and I couldn't figure out why it wasn't working right [laughs]. Later I learned that there was such a thing as a bench you could lie on so your elbows could go below the level of the bench and you could do the exercise properly.

I also did curls. You know, I did just the very, very basics—just learning what the muscles were, learning what the exercises were and how they could be applied, learning the very basics of human movement or kinesiology applied to bodybuilding.

IM: And did you do some work for the legs at that time as well?

TP: No, I never did any leg work back then. I think I tried a couple of sets of squats, but my father wasn't sure how to do squats. And some of the friends I had later on in life up until the age of 15 told me that squats weren't good for you, that they would make your butt big or they were bad for your back.

I also had a back problem when I was a child—I was born with some kind of deformity in my lower back where something wasn't fused together. Squats bothered it, so I didn't squat, but I continued to do upper-body exercises at that time.

IM: I take it your father wasn't really an experienced person with weights or athletics.

TP: No, he wasn't. You know, he was very much a military person, very much a corporate executive, and he wasn't an athlete. But he

was able to lift the entire bar over his head, which was 135 pounds at that time, all the weights that I had, and I was completely mesmerized by that act [laughs].

IM: When did you adopt a more formal training program, and when did you actually start training your legs?

TP: When we moved to Kansas City, I was [pauses], well, I was always big for my age. I was a big kid. I think at age 15 I was like 165 pounds. I was training and I had a big chest, and I always looked like I trained. I drove my motorcycle down to the health spa, and I applied for a position as an instructor. I was very young at that time—in fact, too young to legally be employed. And I think the manager of that particular health spa, which was called the European Health Spa, sensed a great deal of passion and excitement in my voice for the practice of weight training, and he hired me! He hired me at age 15, and I was able to drive my motorcycle down each day to the plaza to work after school, to instruct people.

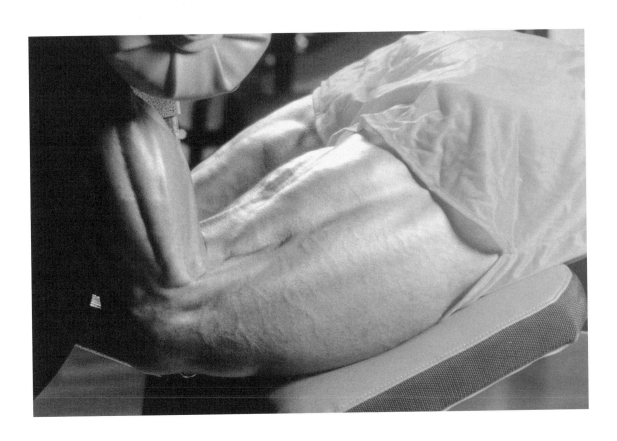

I think the manager probably felt that my excitement and passion for weight training would be a useful tool in obtaining or signing up future members. Which it was! I was really into bodybuilding and excited about it, and I would talk about it to new people coming into the gym. Bodybuilding was a passion of mine, and that excitement translated into gross sales.

I worked there, I think, for a couple of years—from age 15 to 16 or 17. And I just started doing squats because there were a couple of serious lifters there [and] somebody showed me how to do squats. I tried it one day; my first workout was 95 pounds for what felt like a very hard set of 10. I really didn't like the exercise that much. I mean, I sort of just did it to do it. I did 3 sets of 10 eventually just because it was leg day supposedly, and leg day was my 15-minute workout, whereas chest and back and arms were my big days. Legs were trivial. That was my attitude.

IM: So at age 15 you started doing leg work for the first time, and the workout would consist simply of squats?

TP: Yes, 95 pounds—never more than 105 pounds—for sets of 10.

IM: How long did you actually stay with this one-exercise beginner routine?

TP: Well, I trained for about two years like that—just sort of making my leg day an easy day. I think I did some abs that same day and some other things. It was a day I would go into the gym more or less to recuperate and to talk to some of my friends, never really applying the energy necessary to legs that I did to other bodyparts. In fact, I was known in high school as having, you know, twig legs and a huge upper body.

IM: That's rather surprising. Most people who know about your bodybuilding accomplishments might just assume that you started working legs right from the very beginning and your leg development just took off.

TP: No, it was completely the opposite. In fact, a lot of my high school buddies would say to me years later, "Oh, my God, in high school

Tom Platz.

you never had legs. In fact, you were known as having no legs."

It wasn't until we moved to Detroit and I went to a place called Armento's Gym, which is still there, that I really got into leg training. I think I was in the 12th grade, and there were a lot of serious Olympic lifters in that gym.

In Detroit, it seemed everyone worked for the automobile industry. Just like everyone in Los Angeles seems to work for the studios or on films or production of some kind, everyone in Detroit works for GM or Ford [laughs]. And a lot of the people who were working at those car factories were very serious lifters. Norman Schemansky, the famous Olympic weight lifter, used to train at Armento's Gym. A lot of his students, a lot of his training partners were my initial teachers for the squat. And there's another guy from Michigan State, Freddie Lowe, who inspired me to squat. Great Olympic lifter.

When you've been taught how to squat by an Olympic lifter, it's a very serious thing. I mean, the bar real high on your neck. You know, the very strict squat performance—your butt touching the ground. They taught me to develop ankle flexibility, which was a prerequisite to being a great squatter. And I did what they told me. You know, I was a young kid—maybe 165 pounds—and these guys were 240 to 300 pounds. I was like, "Whatever you say, I'll do" [chuckles]. And they showed me how to squat. I think they saw that I had the genetic predisposition for leg strength or leg size. And as they showed me and planned my workouts for me, I gained strength and size very rapidly.

They would actually write my workouts up for me, these Olympic lifters. Especially one guy—his name was Bob Morris—who would really work with me. He would put the weight on the bar for me, him and his partners. They wouldn't let me leave the gym until I adequately squatted and met all their requirements according to proper squatting protocol. Being a 16- or 17-year-old kid, I was very inspired.

So rather than adopting bad form, I adopted perfect form. And since I had the genetic predisposition for squatting ability—a high degree of ankle flexion, low center of gravity, correct muscle attachment sites for the necessary and proper kinesiological function in relation to my anatomical structure—well, they noticed all those things. And they would actually tell me what to do, when, how much to do, how many reps to do, and they were often amazed! Because at the end of the workout, once a week they would say to me, "Well, Tom, now that you did your heavy weights, I want you to do a set of 10 with a lighter weight. Just a warm-down set." So we'd sometimes put 310 or 315 pounds on the bar to warm down with—this is when I'd been squatting for a few years; this wasn't the first day—and rather than

doing 10 reps, I'd do like 25 or 30. And, you know, they were blown away by the reps I could do with heavy weights. They taught me how to squat with very strict form and very true to the Olympic style. They would not allow me to train like a powerlifter or to squat like a powerlifter. Nor did I want to.

IM: For people who aren't familiar with the respective techniques here, what's the difference in style between powerlifting and Olympic squatting?

TP: In powerlifting squatting, the bar is real low on your back, and you use your butt and your lower back almost exclusively. Your legs are just a leverage piece of equipment basically [laughs]. The stress isn't on your legs—well, it is to some degree, but you're using your butt

Dave Palumbo.

and your lower back to push yourself up. And the angle at which you squat is sort of a forward lean rather than an up-and-down angle. The upper body is leaning forward, and your knees stay in front of your toes.

In Olympic squatting, your knees are in front of your toes, the bar is very high on your back, and you go down to the point where your butt is touching the ground or your heels.

Olympic squatting technique is more of a straight up-and-down movement in which the stress is directly on the quadriceps. If you think about it, in bodybuilding you try to make the exercise as hard as you can make it. It's, "How hard can you make each exercise and how productive can you make the muscle response in reference to that?"

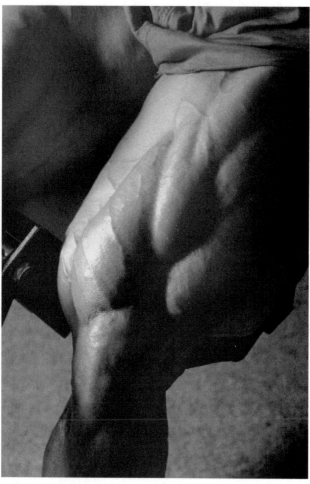

Tom Platz.

In powerlifting, the objective is, "How easy can you make the exercise so that you can lift the most weight?" Powerlifting is not an easy sport, by any means, but the point of it is, "How do you get the most weight up and establish the best possible leverage," whereas in bodybuilding the objective is to make the exercise hard. I liked Olympic lifting for that strict protocol involved. And every Olympic lifter that I knew had great leg development.

In fact, back then bodybuilders never squatted. I first came out to L.A. in '77, and the squat rack at Gold's Gym was way in the back behind all the old equipment. Nobody ever used it. The bodybuilders were all doing leg extensions, hack squats, and lunges.

I came out to Los Angeles, started doing squats, and people were going, "What is he doing? Is he crazy? It makes your waist big. It makes your butt big." But after a while that all died down, and I like to think that I was somewhat instrumental in making the squat a popular exercise to train legs. A lot of the guys joined in with me.

IM: When you lived in Detroit, were you still doing only one exercise?

TP: Well, I would do squats with the Olympic lifters, but I was fascinated by this one bodybuilder whose name was Farrel. That was his first name; I don't even know what his last name was. He trained in the Detroit gym— Armento's Gym—and he was a thin guy, a little thin bodybuilder, but he had tremendous leg separation and shape. More so than the Olympic lifters. Not the same size, not the same denseness and quality of musculature that the Olympic lifters had. But he had tremendous shape and tremendous separation, which I wanted to have in addition to the size of the Olympic lifters.

So I watched him train, and he taught me how to do hack squats—how to put my heels together.

The platform that we had back then was just an itty-bitty platform, and, you know, you had to put your heels close together. But he taught me to put my heels close together and

Tom Platz.

point my feet out like a duck. And his theory was that it would develop the lateral section of your thigh, which it did—and does!

So we did hack squats on both of my squat days back then. I would go, oh, usually about 5 sets. I would generally work up in weight as a warm-up, and then I'd work down.

But this became my second most useful exercise in leg development.

IM: And how long did you stay with that routine?

TP: Well, my late high school days and all through my college days I stayed with that routine. In fact, I even followed that routine up to my competitive years, and I really didn't start doing leg extensions until before a contest.

IM: So squats and hack squats were the combination that laid the foundation for your thigh development.

TP: Absolutely. Beyond any doubt.

IM: Can we get an idea here of the sets and the reps and the kinds of weights you were handling? I take it the weights you were using gradually increased with time.

TP: Well, I can remember training through various weight barriers during the course of the years. I can remember the first time I did 315 for reps in the squat—three plates on each side. It was a big accomplishment. I mean, that's what the big guys did, and I was able to do that for a set of 3 to 4 reps. I was totally mesmerized and excited and passionate about the exercise. It felt perfect—it felt like a piston inside a cylinder. That's the way I sort of visualized myself doing the exercise.

I developed little techniques back then—like wearing high socks. If I wore high socks, I would look shorter in the mirror. And if you're real short, you don't have that far down to go. At least that's what the mind perceives. So I developed these little mental strategies to really train myself to handle heavier and heavier weights. Nobody taught me; I just developed those things on my own.

The Olympic lifters also taught me things like looking up high, looking at an imaginary spot on the wall or the ceiling to allow you to perform perfect squats. And I have my own little things that I worked in there as far as mental training was concerned, but now I'm getting away from the question you asked me.

You wanted to know about reps and sets and the weights I was using. Like I was saying, I hit various barriers at different times. I remember doing 405 for the first time in my career. I remember doing 505 for the first time in my career. And so on. I mean, 505 for 15 reps was a tremendous accomplishment for me.

But back then, during the early days of the intermediate stage of my leg training, 315 for

2 or 3 reps was a normal heavy day for me in the squat. And I would never do more than 10 sets of squats, counting the warm-ups.

Here's the way I set up my leg training. One day would be my heavy day in the squat. That heavy day would consist of anywhere from doubles, 2 reps, up to, say, 6 reps. Maybe as high as 8. Two to 8 reps would be a heavy day, depending upon how I was structuring my training at that particular time—whether I was peaking to handle heavy weights or just training prior to that point.

Then in my other squat workout for the week, I would train for reps. On the rep day I would do 2 sets of reps only. I did that because it felt right at that time. It just felt right for me. In fact, the Olympic lifters had a similar program where they would lift various percentages on different days. And I followed suit according to their protocols and their training strategies.

On the rep day the reps would be somewhat higher, obviously. Usually between 15 and 20.

IM: And you said you did only 2 sets on the rep day?

TP: Only 2 sets. But when I say 2 sets, I'm not counting the 2 or 3 warm-ups. And when I say 10 sets on the heavy day, I'm including the 4 or 5 warm-ups I would do to get up to the heavier weights.

IM: And on the heavy day you would always, I take it, strive to move up to a heavier and heavier weight as time passed.

TP: Each workout I'd add 5 pounds to the bar on each side. I would start low enough in my training cycle so I could add two 5-pound plates to the bar each time. I wanted to add 5 pounds to each side, if I could, every workout on my heavy day. And a lot of times I was able to do that for a prolonged period of time.

IM: And you were also doing hack squats?

TP: Hack squats were done directly after the squat sessions.

IM: What was the sets-and-reps format with the hack squats?

TP: Usually I would warm up a little bit to get up to a heavy weight—maybe five 25s on each side—and then I would work down. It was a very difficult, old-fashioned hack squat machine. It wasn't very smooth at all. In fact, it was usually rusted, and it wouldn't slide very well. One hundred pounds was like 500 pounds [laughs]. I trained in the dungeons in those days, the old-fashioned, YMCA-style dungeons with no windows. And those are the gyms I loved and enjoyed. In fact, I can tell you stories about that, too, but I won't.

Anyway, in the hack squat I'd start out by putting a plate on each side, two plates on each side, three plates on each side. Then I'd put five plates on each side and start my way down.

IM: How many sets would you typically do?

TP: Usually 5 sets, not including the warm-up sets. And the reps would be somewhere between 6 and 8. I'd perhaps work down from maybe 500 pounds to a light weight.

Tom Platz.

IM: Were you doing low reps on the warm-up sets in both squats and hack squats?

TP: I'd push maybe 10 reps, just to warm up.

IM: With something fairly light?

TP: Sure. But progressive enough to allow me to graduate to a heavier set, to a heavier weight the next set.

IM: Why were you working your way down in weight in the hack squats consistently like that?

TP: Well, I've trained all my life on instinct. Fred Hatfield watched me years later and said, "Oh, obviously you're very schooled in the acquisition of muscle and in muscle physiology." And I would say to him, "Fred, I just do what feels right" [laughs]. I was always the kind of bodybuilder who really followed instincts—and my instincts led me to do things that were correct as far as muscle growth was concerned and what was effective specific to my body type and my fiber type.

IM: So this intermediate routine you've just described was what you followed until you started competing in bodybuilding contests?

TP: Yes, I'd say I followed this program for about four or five years—from age 17 to about 21 or 22. I started competing as a powerlifter originally. My first bodybuilding contest was in about 1973, so I actually started competing while I was still doing this intermediate routine. In fact, I stayed with this routine right up till the time I moved to California, in 1977. By that time I had already won the Mr. Michigan title at age 19, finished second in the Teenage Mr. America, and placed high in the Mr. America contest. So I competed in quite a few contests while I was still on this routine, although I didn't compete that often, because I was busy studying for final exams and I was working full-time as well—usually as a gym instructor and selling memberships. Then, after I moved to California, I switched to what you could call my advanced leg routine.

IM: Given the awesome leg development you ultimately achieved, something rather dramatic must have started happening immediately after you got into serious leg work.

Tom Platz.

TP: It became almost a special sport to me—a different sport from bodybuilding. The squat rack became like the altar, where life and death would pass in front of my eyes, and I looked forward to that every squat workout.

IM: So this was really, really tough training you were doing.

TP: Very tough, but I responded very well to very hard training, and I became motivated to train harder because the harder I trained, the more strength and leg development I attained. So it was like, "God, how hard can I train? How much do I want to grow?"

And I became pretty much known for having great leg strength and great leg development. I can remember not winning Best

Legs in the '76 Mr. America, and I was upset. My legs were huge; they were tremendously huge. It's just that they didn't have the cut-up look back then.

It was at that time I decided that I wanted to have both—size, which I already had, and great definition. That's one of the initial reasons why I started doing different types of training and got into more of an advanced strategy.

IM: It must have been a very dramatic, powerful experience for you to see the kind of development you were achieving.

TP: Oh, I was completely inspired by it. I can remember when I would squat, we'd turn the radio off, the whole gym would stop training, and everyone would focus on me squatting.

IM: Wow!

TP: It was like you could hear a pin drop. The Olympic lifters taught me to squat with no music; perfect silence; perfect, total concentration. And when I walked in, the gym would be rolling, people would be making noises and dropping weights. But the moment I went over to the squat rack, everyone would stop and focus on me—encourage me and push me. It was like 15 or 20 guys around the squat rack encouraging you to do your best. It was awesome. And we shared that enthusiasm throughout the gym.

IM: Some people develop very large muscles without necessarily handling the heaviest weights. In your case, though, you not only developed huge thighs, but you could also handle tremendous weights with them.

TP: I think it's because of my training style. My instinct led me to do things that would induce the muscle size acquisition as well as muscle strength acquisition. What I mean by that is that I was able to train both fiber types, red and white, specifically, through instinct.

On the rep day I feel I was training more red fiber, more endurance fiber. And on the heavy day I was training more white fiber— explosive movements for more white fiber. And I feel that they both complemented each other. In fact, that was the basis of my training throughout my entire career, one that I adopted for my upper body as well after some time—one day heavy, one day light. I felt it was important to train that way.

IM: So, in other words, to train one type of fiber you did strength work, and to train another type of fiber you did more endurance work?

TP: Exactly. And when you do endurance work, you develop things like capillary enhancement. Capillaries develop to increase blood flow to the muscle, which makes the muscles larger. Mitochondria enhancement. I've learned there are a lot of beneficial things that take place on a cellular level as a result of higher reps, so higher reps have an important place in a bodybuilder's training.

I think there are three things that determine success in bodybuilding. One is instinct, knowing what to do in the gym based upon what feels right. The other one is education—knowing about nutrition, biomechanics, exercise physiology.

Through education it's possible to learn more about how to make muscles grow, although there are a lot of skinny scientists in the gym who know all about how to make muscles grow, but they don't have big muscle themselves. I'm not devaluing education here; I'm just saying that education combined with instinct is very, very important. And when you add the third factor—genetics—to instinct and education, that equals a champion.

But I think the most important things, beyond genetics and education, are instinct and attitude. You know, an unwillingness to quit, and a need—an absolute need like eating and breathing—to be successful. When you have that need, you can even train totally wrong and eat totally wrong and still become one of the greats eventually if you have the genetics—and you're simply training hard enough to take advantage of your genetics. But that's a topic for a whole other interview.

IM: Thigh training in itself is very, very demanding on the body, particularly if carried to the extreme that you did. Obviously they don't call you Mr. Intensity for nothing. The

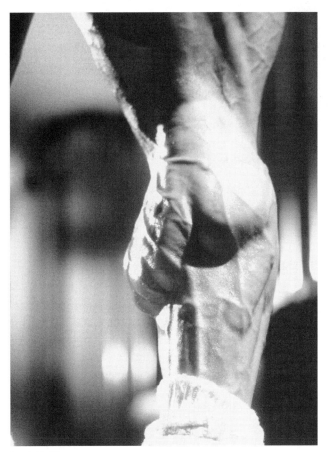

Paul DeMayo.

ability to endure these kinds of workouts—is that something that you had to develop, or is it something that came naturally to you?

TP: Progressively, I was able to endure more and more intensity. But I would begin rehearsing the leg workout days in advance. If I was going to do my rep day on Monday, I would rehearse it every night after the previous Friday, when I did the heavy day. As I had more and more years of experience, I was able to attain higher and higher levels of intensity. And intensity is something you develop over time. It's closely associated with internal passion and desire and need, but you have to work your way up there—like climbing a ladder. You can't jump to the top rung the first day. It takes a little time to get there.

IM: What was the heaviest weight you used on the squat during the intermediate stage of your training?

TP: Let me think back now, because it's been a long time. I would say back then my best would have been about 500 pounds for a double or a triple. Later I was able to do much more—615 for as many as 15 reps.

IM: Considering your thigh development and the weights you were able to handle in your leg workouts, were you possibly the kind of guy who could have been a world champion powerlifter in the squat?

TP: I really think that I'm genetically predisposed [for that]—I'm made to be a powerlifter. I have the personality of a powerlifter. I like to lift heavy, I like to see the bar bend, I like to hear the plates jingle.

I mean, to hear the plates jingle, that deep-throated kind of roar of the old-fashioned 45-pound plates, the big ones—I love it! I used to leave little spaces between the plates so that every rep would jingle in my ears. I mean, I loved that feeling of power.

It's the same thing as my old Corvette, the 283 fuel injection. Firing it up in the morning, going to the gym. Power—it's the feeling, the taste of power and chalk dust or gasoline and sweat. I sort of relate and correlate the cars and bodybuilding. The display of power and torque closely associates with intensity in training.

IM: Everyone who was around bodybuilding in the early '80s knows you were fond of Corvettes. Do you still drive one?

TP: I now drive a Porsche 911 Turbo Carrera. I had Corvettes for many years, as you know. I really have a passion for the big-block engines, but I wanted to experiment with different types of automobiles, and I decided to go with Porsche some time ago. Actually five years ago.

IM: Do you, in fact, have a propensity for driving fast too?

TP: Oh, yeah. I love speed. I love to go fast. I used to go to Germany to do exhibitions all the time. They would pick me up at the airport and let me drive—actually, I'd be imploring them, "Let me drive, let me drive" [laughs]—and I'd get the car we were driving to do about 200 miles an hour down the autobahn. I love speed; I especially love the feeling of tremendous torque. Anything where it's a display of power just excites me.

IM: So you're just a power-oriented guy.

TP: I guess coming from Detroit, yeah [laughs loudly].

IM: The Motor City.

TP: Motor City, there you go. Applied to the body. But getting back to the point I was making earlier, if you look at my genetic structure, I was supposed to be a powerlifter. The sport of Olympic lifting took a lot of technique and skill that I really didn't have the time to develop, because I had other interests at the time, and I wasn't devoted to the study and the skill of Olympic lifting. In any event, if I did what I'm best at, I would be a powerlifter.

[Speaks emphatically] But when I won the Michigan state title in powerlifting, you get a pat on the back and a beer mug—and you go home, okay? "All right, guy, you did a good job!" When I won the Mr. Michigan bodybuilding contest, I mean, Joe Weider was on the phone, I'm getting flown out to the West Coast, articles are being written about me, I'm getting asked to do exhibitions—it's more glamorous and more closely associated with the whole performing/acting situation. I've viewed myself as a performer all my life. I was an athlete and a performer—not to mention being a diplomat for bodybuilding and a businessman as well. But I think I was more and ultimately a performer rather than just a bodybuilder. And that's why I went into bodybuilding rather than powerlifting.

Here's Arnold's "Thigh Blasting for Mass and Muscularity" leg routine.

ARNOLD'S THIGH BLASTING FOR MASS AND MUSCULARITY

Arnold Schwarzenegger, as told to Gene Mozée

It's said that experience is the best teacher and that you learn from your mistakes. This definitely applies to me when it comes to thigh training. I made the same mistake a lot of beginners make—I didn't train legs at all during my first year of bodybuilding. I concentrated on my arms, chest, shoulders, and back, because these muscles were more visible and grew more quickly. I began handling heavier and heavier poundages on bench presses, curls, standing presses, and deadlifts. As my strength improved, my upper body began to assume more massive proportions, but my legs remained thin and weak.

When I finally decided to start training my legs, I naively assumed that it would take only six months for them to match my upper body in development. The sad but true fact was that it took more than six *years* before my legs began to catch up. Live and learn.

While training in my native Austria, I never had the opportunity to use a lot of modern equipment. I never did leg curls until I moved to Munich, Germany, and began training in a fully equipped gym for the first time. My thigh biceps development was nonexistent. I became so desperate to improve my under-par thighs that I trained them with 10 sets of squats and 10 sets of leg curls every day for an entire year. My thighs did improve on this

Squat.

Leg press.

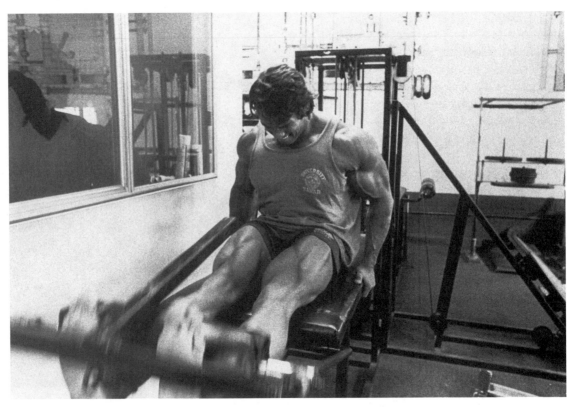

Leg extension.

arduous routine, but I finally discarded it because my legs were still lagging far behind the rest of my body.

Most of my training knowledge in the early days came from the muscle magazines. I devoured each magazine I could lay my hands on from cover to cover. One particular article that really helped me when I was in Munich described how to shock the muscles into new growth and prevent staleness with a routine of heavy weights and low reps alternated with higher reps and less poundage. I decided to apply this approach to my thigh training. During one week, I performed all of my thigh exercises for 6 to 8 reps with maximum poundages, and in the next week I did the same exercises for 15 to 20 repetitions. I made excellent progress on this system. The low reps gave me more power and mass, while the high reps built up my endurance so that I could do more reps with heavier weight. Not only did I acquire more shape and definition, but the higher reps helped improve my stamina so

much that I was soon blasting all of my sets with no more than 60 seconds' rest, regardless of how heavy the poundage.

The main ingredient of any thigh-building program is the squat. It's not the sissy squat, the hack squat, the half-squat, the bench squat, or the front squat. It's the full, parallel back squat that builds both the foundation and the complete development of the thighs. Other exercises help add shape and definition.

If you were to concentrate all of your effort on just heavy squats, you'd probably get results similar to mine. I actually worked up to where I could do reps with 700 pounds. My thighs were twice as massive, but they lacked shape and cuts. Through a system of trial and error, I finally found a great thigh program that gave me size, shape, and definition simultaneously. It works the thighs thoroughly from all angles to build the front, side, and back of the legs. It builds mass, power, contour, and deep cuts—the whole package.

MY FAVORITE THIGH EXERCISES

The following exercises are the ones I've found most valuable and productive for me. They enabled me to add more than 10 inches of quality muscle to my upper legs.

Heavy barbell squats

This is the best exercise for growth. Place the bar across your shoulders at the base of your neck and the trapezius. Keep your back straight at all times. I look at a spot directly ahead when squatting. This keeps my head up and my back straight. I wear a lifting belt to add lower-back support. I warm up with a light weight and do 20 reps. On my first set I don't quite lock out. This keeps continuous tension on my thighs and allows for a better warm-up. On the second set, I pile on some weight and do 10 reps. Then I add more weight and do 2 sets of 8 reps; I add weight and do 2 sets of 6 reps; and finally, I go for maximum poundage for 4 or 5 reps. I finish with a tapering-off set of 10 to 15 reps to fully flush the thighs with blood.

Front squat

This exercise adds mass and shape to the quadriceps just above the knee and accentuates the teardrop look of the vastus medialis. Place the bar high across the front of your shoulders with your elbows high at all times. Place your heels on a block to help maintain balance. Again, I warm up the area by doing a light set of 15 non-lock reps to start. This gets you into the proper groove and lessens the chance of injury. Keep your head up and your back straight throughout the exercise. I do 5 sets of 10 reps with as much weight as I can handle.

Leg curl

My front thighs now get rest while I bomb the back area, or hamstrings. I do this one on the leg curl machine. Your hips must remain flat at all times so that the hamstrings, not the

glutes, do all the work. For my first set, I do a 20-rep warm-up. Then I increase the weight and do 8 sets of 12 reps in a strict manner—no cheating.

Leg press

This exercise adds size to the outside portion of the thighs, or vastus lateralis. It seems to work better if I do leg curls first, because the quadriceps have had a rest and are now ready for a final assault. I warm up with a light set of 15 reps, and then I blast out 5 sets of 8 to 10 reps with 600 pounds. Every rep is done in strict form—I let my knees come all the way into my armpits, then press the legs out slowly and tense and flex my thighs at the top. I might add that this superb exercise also puts mass on the middle of the thighs.

These four exercises are the core of my thigh training. I have found it necessary to work my thighs extremely hard with lots of sets to get results. After the leg presses, I often go back and do 2 or 3 more sets of leg curls. When I'm finished, my thighs have been

Squat	5 × 12, 10, 8, 6, 5
Leg press	3 × 12
Leg curl	4 × 12

The following is another good program for intermediate bodybuilders.

Parallel bench squat	6 × 12
Leg extension	5 × 12
Leg curl	5 × 12

I used this program strictly to build mass, but I did more sets. I did 12 sets of squats and 10 sets of leg extensions and leg curls. This was a very tough but extremely effective regimen.

Here's another heavy thigh-bombing routine that proved to be very helpful in building size, shape, and cuts:

Squat	6 × 8
Leg press	4 × 10
Superset with	
Front squat	4 × 10
Leg extension	5 × 12
Leg curl	5 × 12

As you can plainly see, my thigh programs are all comprised of various combinations of the same productive exercises. There are a great many other thigh exercises, but in my opinion these are the cream of the crop.

worked from every angle to their absolute limit.

Another exercise that I've used for getting deep, razor-etched definition without losing any size is machine leg extensions. On each rep, I extend my lower legs until they are as high as possible, hold each rep at the top to tense the thighs for maximum contraction, and then slowly return to the starting position. When you do the last rep, your legs should be burning. I perform 12 reps on this exercise. I sometimes modify my usual thigh program by adding leg extensions to the routine in order to bring maximum shape and cuts to the quads during the last six to eight weeks before a contest.

My thigh program is only for the most advanced bodybuilders, so I would recommend a lot less work for those who have less experience. Here's a program that will add size and shape to less-advanced trainees' thighs:

TRAINING TIPS

- Work the legs on one day and the upper body on the next.
- Work the thighs first so that you can blast them with full intensity while your energy level is at its peak. Work your calves after your thighs.
- The first set of each exercise should serve as a warm-up to bring blood into the area and get you into the groove of the movement, so use a lighter weight and do more reps.
- I train my thighs three times a week. Some people find that twice a week is better for growth. Experiment and decide what works best for you.
- To improve the shape and definition of your thighs after you've attained sufficient size, always train them three times a week.

- Work out with a partner whenever possible. It gives you more incentive, relieves boredom, and makes you train harder because of the rivalry. It also helps ensure that you don't pause too long between sets and exercises.
- Don't rest too long between sets, or you lose the benefits of the flushing effect, which keeps the blood and nourishment in the area you're trying to make grow. I never rest longer than one minute on squats and leg presses. On other exercises, I rest for about 30 or 45 seconds.
- Always use good form and concentrate on the movement from beginning to end to force your thighs to work harder.
- I squat barefoot with my feet flat on the floor. I have good leverage and balance this way, and my thighs work harder when I'm not using a block under my heels. Try it without the block, but if you need greater stability, use it.
- Add weight to each exercise whenever possible. You must force your muscles to work against constantly increasing resistance.

Don't neglect your legs, or you may find, just as I did, that it can take years to get a perfect balance between your legs and your upper body. Start bombing your thighs the way they deserve, and don't give up until you reach your goal. I'm positive that you will be amazed, just as I was, at how much your thighs will improve when you start blasting them from all angles with a hard and heavy program.

Next, listen to a champion powerlifter, Judd Biasiotto, Ph.D., explain the biomechanics of the squat and how it can be used to develop ultimate leg power and mass.

THE ALMIGHTY SQUAT
Judd Biasiotto, Ph.D.

I want to talk to you about developing massive legs, legs that Tom Platz would envy. Well, maybe not Platz, but you'll be the envy of 99 percent of the rest of the world's lifters. Before

George Olesen.

we start, however, I want you to get up and drive over to your gym. Go ahead. Put the book down, go over there, and look around a little. Stay away from the mirrors; just check out the lifters and then come back to this article.

What did you see? Did you happen to see a number of lifters walking around wearing baggy pants? Did you also notice that just about every one of them has massive shoulders, chest, and arms, and a nice little tapered waist?

Let me tell you a little secret. The reason those guys wear baggies is that when they take them off, their legs look like a pair of pliers in shorts. In other words, they have the upper body of a Dorian Yates and the legs of a Schwarzenegger—Maria, not Arnold. This is a mistake of significant magnitude.

To begin with, your legs are the foundation for your entire body. Without a pair of powerful legs, you have nothing on which to build. It's like putting a huge house on a pair of sticks: it's just not going to work. Powerful legs will also help you generate greater force in just about every lift you perform, from the bench press to the military press. World bench press champion Ken Lain probably says it best: "Your legs are the most important part of lifting, because all of your power is generated from your legs. If you don't have strong legs, you're not going to be able to handle massive weight, and if you can't handle massive weight, you can't grow. If you look at all the great lifters, they all have big, powerful legs."

Need I also mention that legs that look as if they belong on a high chair just don't look good, not even in baggies? And let's be honest. With legs like that you're not going anywhere in powerlifting or bodybuilding. More important, you're not going to look good at the beach.

Massive, powerful legs are a must, and the best way to get them is to perform power squats. Believe me, with power squats you can convert Lilliputian legs into a great set of wheels. All you have to do is do them.

Now, before you run over to the gym and crawl under a squat bar, you'll need to know a little about the biomechanics of power squatting. In fact, here's a little tip: don't even consider starting your training until you have picture-perfect form. I've seen numerous lifters, including world-class athletes, who started training before they developed sound form. Inevitably, after two or three years they either got injured or they plateaued. You don't want that to happen to you. What's more, if you don't perfect top-notch form, you'll never come close to reaching your potential for lifting weight—and, to paraphrase Ken Lain, if you don't handle massive weight, you can't become massive.

So sit back and relax. There's nothing more conducive to learning than being in a comfortable environment, munching on a Power Bar. (I read that in *Ironman* once and adhere to it religiously.) Pay attention, though, as you'll be tested in the squat rack later.

From a biomechanical standpoint, the squat is the most difficult to master of the three powerlifts. *Biomechanics* refers to the exact method by which you perform the lift. This includes the way you position your body as well as the speed of the movement. Correct biomechanics in the squat will direct most of the stress of the lift toward the muscles instead of the joints and connective tissues. With proper biomechanics, not only do you use your body more efficiently, but you're less likely to sustain an injury.

Although squatting is a relatively simple skill, it requires you to focus on many more environmental cues than either the bench press or the deadlift. Of course, if you don't recognize the cues, your form deteriorates.

BAR PLACEMENT

With the weight still in the rack, you have four options. First, you can carry the bar high on your back. With the bar in that position, it's easier to keep your back upright when you squat. That affords you a number of advantages: it's safer, you'll break parallel more quickly, and it looks pretty. Of course, if you're not going to enter a powerlifting competition, breaking parallel is of no consequence. In fact, if you're not into powerlifting, it's probably smarter to stay a little above parallel to the ground. By breaking high, you take a lot of

George Olesen and Michelle Sorensen.

stress off your lower back, which is primarily used to get you out of the bottom of the lift when you break parallel. On the downside, by carrying the bar high, you raise your center of gravity, thereby making the lift a little harder.

Your second option is to carry the bar on your back at the legal limit, which is 13 centimeters (about 3½ inches) below the posterior deltoid. Again, if you're not a powerlifter, the legal limit is irrelevant. You don't want to carry the bar any lower, however. That could be hazardous to your back.

As you might expect, the advantages and disadvantages of placing the bar at this position are pretty much the opposite of carrying the bar high. The lower placement lowers your center of gravity, thereby increasing your mechanical efficiency and, consequently, making the lift much easier. The problem with a low bar placement is that it's hard to keep your back erect—and it doesn't look pretty. Fortunately, there are no points subtracted for ugliness, and with practice you can learn to keep your back fairly close to upright. I prefer

George Olesen and Michelle Sorensen.

this type of bar placement. For me, the key point is that it makes the lift easier. Remember, the more weight you handle, the more mass you build.

Your third option is to place the bar somewhere between the first and second options. Your fourth option is to leave the weight in the rack, go home, get a cold one, and do some channel-surfing. The advantage of this option is that it's a lot easier and safer, and it's a heck of a lot more fun. The disadvantage is that you can only watch.

PERFORMANCE: THE STANCE

If you choose any of the first three options, it's time to squat. After you unrack the weight, take one very short step backward. Ten inches is plenty of distance between you and the rack. There are a couple of excellent reasons for this. Not only do you not get any extra points for walking the weight all over the place, but you burn up a lot of energy doing it and scare the heck out of everyone in the gym—none of which is good.

When you're in a position to set up as described, you have a few more options to consider. First, you can squat with a wide foot spacing. For what it's worth, most world-class powerlifters use an extremely wide stance. By taking a wide stance and keeping your back in an upright position during your descent, you can break parallel much more quickly than if you use a narrow stance. Of course, by breaking parallel quickly, you shorten the distance that you must lift the weight and, consequently, do less mechanical work. Again, this is only an advantage if you're a powerlifter. The advantage for bodybuilders is that a wide stance involves more muscle groups, so you lift more weight—and build more mass.

The disadvantages of using a wide stance are few. It's been said that wide-stance squats broaden your hips. I'm not sure about that, and I could find no research to substantiate the theory. I will tell you this, though: be prepared for some serious soreness or pain in your hips when you start squatting with a wide stance. Also, from a strictly empirical

Smith machine squat.   Greg Kovacs.

standpoint, I believe that a wide stance can predispose you to more back injuries than a narrow stance does—but significantly fewer knee injuries.

If you have trouble with your back and you have superstrong quadriceps on the order of Fred Hatfield's, you might want to experiment with a narrow stance. For the life of me, however, I can't think of many other reasons that you should learn to do this. For every reason you give me in favor of squatting narrow, I can give you five for squatting wider. Still, there are lifters, like Hatfield, who have done quite well using a narrow stance—and who's going to argue with Hatfield? Maybe Mike Tyson or Hulk Hogan, but certainly not Judd Biasiotto.

If you're a bodybuilder, you probably squat narrow in order to stress your quads more. After all, you don't want to have mass without shape (powerlifters don't care about shape, just mass and power). For ultimate mass—and shape—I suggest that you power squat with a wide stance in the off-season and then shape up during competition time.

Of course, you can find yourself a foot spacing between the two extremes, or you can go home and watch TV. One thing you do need to be aware of concerning foot spacing is the very specific nature of strength. Even a slight deviation in your foot spacing can cause a significant change in muscle involvement and a decrease in strength. For that reason, once you decide to change the stance you use, make sure you use that same stance every time—especially if you're a powerlifter. Also, if

Jonathan Lawson.

you decide to change your stance and/or form, you can expect a decrease in strength at first due to the specificity factor. With training, your strength will come back and most likely improve, especially if the change was for the better.

THE ASCENT AND DESCENT

The descent is the easy part. In fact, I've never missed a descent. It's getting up that's the trick. As mentioned above, when descending with the weight, you want to try to keep your back in an upright position. It's important to keep your calves straight and your knees

directly over your feet. Try to keep the weight back over your heels, aligning your position so that your power is centered vertically. In addition, it's a good idea to point your toes slightly outward, which lets you lift the weight farther back over your heels. It also helps you to flare your knees outward at the bottom of the lift, which lets you break parallel more quickly and helps you lock in your hips.

One big no-no is to squat so rapidly that you bounce at the bottom. That could result in stretching or tearing ligaments in your knees. You should keep the weight under perfect control as you lower your body.

Now for the fun part, getting back up. As soon as you get to the bottom of your lift (note that you don't get points for going deeper than parallel), tilt your back slightly forward, thereby causing your hips to lead your ascent. As you drive the weight upward, gradually move your thighs inward and upward. This will help channel your power vertically. When you reach your sticking point, drive your shoulders backward and your hips inward until you're in an upright position.

Although you should avoid bouncing at the bottom, you must drive up quickly and powerfully while maintaining perfect form. This explosion upward ultimately stimulates the greatest number of motor units, which in turn produces greater muscle stimulation.

KEEP LEARNING

That's the power squat in a nutshell. Don't think for a second that you know everything there is to know about this movement. Keep searching for new and different ideas that will improve your performance—never stop learning. Learning is a lifelong journey; the more you learn, the more powerful you become. In bodybuilding, bigger has come to mean better, and there's no better way to become bigger than by using the ultimate powerlift—the squat. Powerlifters have known that for years.

DR. JUDD'S POWER SQUAT PROGRAM

In general, jump 5 pounds each week, stretch before each set, and rest approximately 5 minutes between sets.

Monday	
Power squat	
Warm-up	2–3×6–8
	$1 \times 5 \times 60\%$ of 1RM
	$1 \times 3 \times 70\%$ of 1RM
	$1 \times 3 \times 80\%$ of 1RM
	$1 \times 3 \times 90\%$ of 1RM
	$1 \times 3 \times 75\%$ of 1RM*
Leg press	3–$4 \times 8 \times$ maximum
Leg curl	$2 \times 8 \times$ maximum
Leg extension	$2 \times 8 \times$ maximum

Leg extension.   Mike Mentzer.

Hack squat.   Paul DeMayo.

Thursday
Power squat

Warm-up	2–3 × 6–8
	1 × 5 × 55% of 1RM
	1 × 3 × 65% of 1RM
	1 × 3 × 75% of 1RM
	1 × 3 × 85% of 1RM
	1 × 3 × 70% of 1RM*
Leg press	3–4 × 8 × 90% of 1RM
Leg curl	2 × 8 × 90% of 1RM
Leg extension	2 × 8 × 90% of 1RM

* Pause for 3 to 5 seconds after each rep.

This terrific article by Gene Mozée draws on his exhaustive knowledge of bodybuilding to tell you exactly how to build powerful legs.

BUILD SHAPE, SWEEP, AND SIZE INTO YOUR THIGHS Gene Mozée

There are few things more disappointing than to see a bodybuilder with real contest potential who has a terrific upper body and legs like a stork. Believe me, I've seen many. Some people are lucky enough to have thighs that respond rapidly—just about any exercise seems to make their thighs grow bigger and more impressive. Obviously, you wouldn't need to read this article if you were one such fortunate individual. Don't feel alone. Ninety-nine percent of your fellow bodybuilders—including yours truly—have to bust their buns to make any type of thigh improvement.

Usually, if the thighs respond slowly, most of us tend to concentrate more on the muscles that grow more quickly and are easier to work (chest, arms, back, and so on). Not to worry, because I discovered a training program that added 3 inches to my thighs in just six weeks; that is, quality muscle—shape, sweep, and size. I have seen dozens of guys at my gym use it with similar results. It will work for you.

Chris Duffy.

I didn't invent this sensational, result-producing thigh program; I learned it from the man who did. His name is Millard Williamson. He was just about unbeatable in Best Legs subdivision competition. His thighs were the epitome of the teardrop appearance; they were 25 inches when measured 3 inches above the kneecap!

Not even Tom Platz's amazing thighs could surpass Williamson's lower-thigh development—although Platz probably would have prevailed in a Best Legs event if the two had competed against each other, because his overall thigh mass, density, definition, and vascularity may have been the best in bodybuilding history. But as for shape, different strokes (and bone structures) for different folks. I prefer the teardrop look, just as Steve Reeves did. Besides, no matter what you do, how could you truly expect to build the equal of Platz's thighs? You can, however, make the best of what Mother Nature gave you structurally and try to attain your maximum potential. The routines in this article are designed to help you do just that.

Years ago there was a young guy named Don Rhondo who trained at Ernie Phillips's gym in San Francisco. Don would squat, squat, and squat with nothing to show for it. His thighs just refused to grow no matter how hard he trained. One day, Don had Millard Williamson design a program for him, and six months later he was winning Best Legs events in local competitions.

If you want to see dramatic improvement in your thighs, try one of Mel Williamson's programs. After 30 years in bodybuilding, I have never seen anything that works better or faster for the average bodybuilder. Here are the exercises Williamson favors:

NON-LOCK SQUAT

Mel said, "This is the most effective exercise I have ever used for building both mass and shape." It is performed in the same manner as the regular squat (heels elevated on a 2-inch board), except that you never fully lock out the thighs—you stop about 3 inches short of

Sissy squat.   B. J. Quinn.

straightening your legs. This technique keeps continuous tension on the quadriceps. With no hesitation in this top position (knees are slightly bent), do another full squat, continuing until you hit 12 reps; then lock out fully and tense the thighs as you take three or four deep breaths. After that, blast out another 8 reps for a total of 20 (12 plus 8). Your thighs will be screaming for mercy.

FRONT SQUAT

Front squats differ from regular squats in that the bar is held on the shoulders in front of the neck. Also, they attack the thighs from a different angle and, if done correctly (with the back always straight), there is no danger of injuring the lower back. Generally, only one

Aaron Baker.

deep breath between reps is recommended to prevent the thighs from getting too much rest. Five to 8 reps in strict form stimulates the best gains.

LEG CURL

Again, using only strict form, you'll get best results with 12 to 15 reps. Always keep your butt from arching up as you contract the leg biceps, otherwise you'll be working the glutes more than the hamstrings.

REGULAR HIGH-REPETITION SQUAT

This is probably the best all-purpose thigh exercise. It ranks second only to non-lock squats for building mass and shape. Using strict form, take only one deep breath between reps, and lock the knees at the top on every rep. Most trainees prefer 20 reps, but it's possible to do well with as few as 12 reps.

REGULAR LOW-REPETITION SQUAT

The only difference between these and high-rep squats is that you perform fewer reps and can use greater poundage. Also, you can allow a longer rest period between reps—take sev-

eral (three or four) deep breaths between reps. Any number of reps between 3 and 10 will be effective, depending on the individual.

Although there are well over 100 effective exercises for the thighs, these are the ones Williamson has found to work the best—not only for him, but for hundreds of bodybuilders and athletes he has helped train. Here are a few of his favorite routines:

ROUTINE 1

This routine will take you through 10 sets of low-repetition squats. Perform 10 reps on the first set. Then add 10 pounds to the bar and do 9 reps on the second set. For each succeeding set, increase the weight 10 pounds and do one less rep until finally, on the tenth set, you're using 90 pounds more weight than you began with for a single rep. To make the routine progressive, every week Williamson added 10 pounds to his starting poundage. This is Williamson's favorite program for building leg strength.

ROUTINE 2

Front squat	4 × 8
Non-lock squat	4 × 20

Williamson used this routine for several months, adding at least 5 pounds to each exercise every week. This is one of his favorite programs for building shapely mass.

ROUTINE 3

High-rep squat	4 × 12

Training tip: Use very heavy poundages. Williamson and his training partner at the time, Mr. Universe winner Jack Delinger, were using 405 pounds for 4 sets of 12 reps. They used this as a change-of-pace routine, adding 5 pounds a week to their training poundage. They also performed a light warm-up set of 15 to 20 reps in addition to the 4 heavy sets.

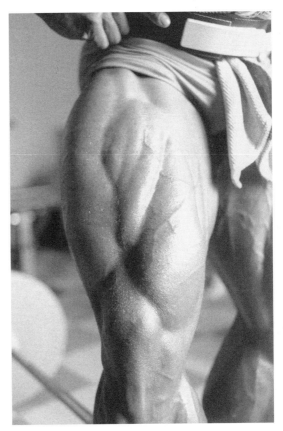

Aaron Baker.

ROUTINE 4

Low-rep squat	
Non-lock squat	5 × 8 × 20%–30%

Training tip: One light warm-up set precedes the 5 heavy sets. The one set of non-lock squats should be done as follows: Start the first workout on this routine with 1 set of 10 reps. Add 1 rep each workout until you reach 30 reps, then increase the weight, but now work up from 20 to 30 reps on this "pump set."

ROUTINE 5

Non-lock squat	10 × 20

Training tip: This routine is strictly for advanced bodybuilders. It is the most rugged and result-producing routine Williamson ever used. He said, "I can guarantee anyone willing to do this routine for six weeks will get amazing results." Start within your capacity and add 5 pounds each workout. You'll get fantastic improvement in development and endurance.

ROUTINE 6

Non-lock squat	5 × 20
Front squat	3 × 8
Leg curl	4 × 15

Training tip: I couldn't keep up with Williamson, but I gained 3 inches in six weeks, working up progressively to 5 sets of 20 reps with 225 in the non-lock squat. Very few people can handle 10 sets of this brutal exercise.

These are only a few of the many exercise routines that can be formulated from Williamson's five super thigh blasters. Here are a few major points to remember about these terrific routines:

• Be sure to perform all movements just as described. All squats must be full, with

Leg lunge.   Aaron Baker.

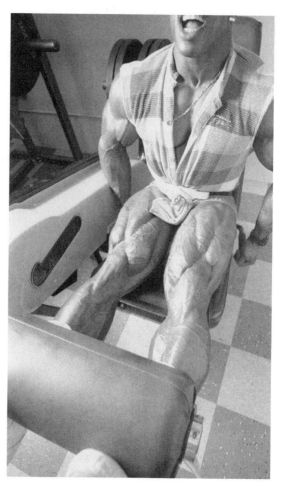

Leg extension.

no hesitation between reps on the non-lock squats except as described.

- Don't rest too long between sets—only as long as it takes to get the recommended reps for the following sets.
- Use intelligent planning on your progression of poundage increases; be realistic.
- Perform squatting movements with the heels on a 2-inch board.
- Williamson got best results when using any of the routines three times a week, but two times per week may be sufficient for most trainees.
- Use all the weight you can possibly handle in strict form.
- Don't do any running or outside athletic activities that work the legs (cycling, football, basketball, tennis, and so on) while on these routines.
- Get plenty of rest and sleep; you'll need it. And you must keep your nutrition program 100 percent, with no missed meals or junk foods.
- Maximum effort—no missed workouts or half-effort training sessions—produces maximum gains.

If you need to improve your thighs, give one of Mel Williamson's routines a try for six weeks. If you work, they'll work!

Finally, Ironman *editor Steve Holman gives us this "no-bull" approach to calf training. Follow his guide to lower-leg development—it can't miss.*

NO-BULL CALF TRAINING Steve Holman

Many bodybuilders make one heckuva big mistake when it comes to learning how to build calves: they look at the training of those with outstanding lower legs, like Chris

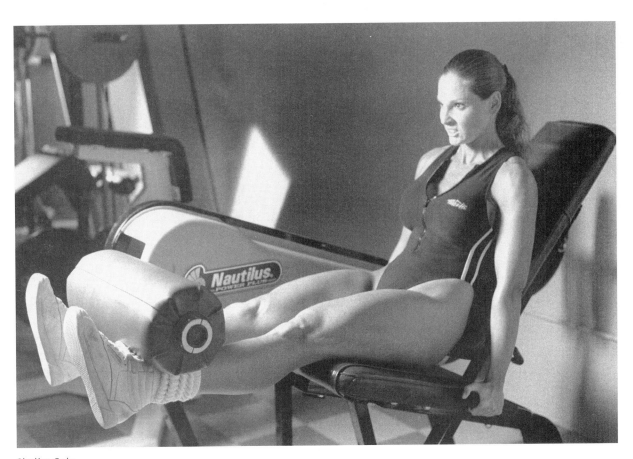

Shelby Cole.

Single leg standing calf raise.   Michael Ashley.

athletic activity. It's mostly in the genetics, and not all that much in the training.

The right strategy for learning about calf building is to look at the training of someone who has had to struggle to overcome a genetic weakness. In the case of calves, Robby Robinson is a prime example.

Robby's lower legs seemed to be cursed from the very beginning of his bodybuilding career. The "high-calf" look knocked him down in every contest he entered. But he didn't give up. Eventually he discovered an approach that blew his calves up to respectable proportions, which eventually helped him reach the winner's circle in bodybuilding.

TOES IN, TOES OUT

Robby's five-point plan to overcome his genetic disadvantage was simple:

1. Hit the calves from as many angles as possible.
2. Use a slightly higher rep range because of the calf muscles' density.
3. Feel each repetition through the entire range of motion.
4. Don't neglect the soleus muscles.
5. Avoid overtraining the calves at all costs.

Let's look at the first point. Robby's multi-angle approach simply consisted of doing some sets with toes in, some with toes out, and some with toes straight ahead. Why did this approach work? Primarily because of the calves' form and function. In other words, Robby hit his calves' primary positions of flexion, which caused some startling progress.

The calves have two positions of flexion: In the stretch position, your torso is bent at a 90-degree angle (as in donkey calf raises) and your heels are angled outward (toes in) at the bottom of a calf raise on a high calf block. In the flexed position, your torso and legs are on the same plane (as in standing calf raises) and your toes are pointing out and heels are angled inward, almost touching at the very top of a calf raise.

Dickerson, for instance, and figure his training is the reason for those fabulous inverted hearts perched so majestically below and behind his knees. But there's a problem with this rationale. Some men are simply gifted in the calf area—like Chris—and will have great lower legs from just walking around and other mild

So what Robby was doing, in effect, was correct; he was working the two positions of flexion by turning his feet on various sets so that all of the angles were covered. Although this "shotgun" approach works, there is a more efficient way to ensure full and complete development in your lower legs with fewer sets.

EFFICIENT CALF-BUILDING

If you analyze the positions of flexion, you'll notice that the calf (gastrocnemius) muscles require only two exercises—if they're done correctly—to cover all the angles: donkey calf raises and standing calf raises.

The way to do these two calf builders is with a slight twist of each foot throughout the range of motion. For example, during donkey calf raises, start each rep from the bottom, stretch position with the heels out, toes in with about 8 inches between the big toes. As you start to rise up, begin rotating the heels inward until you reach the top, flexed position. At this top point, your toes should be angled out, and the heels of your feet should almost be touching. Hold this position for a count of two, and reverse the procedure on the downward stroke of the rep. Use the same foot-rotation procedure on standing calf raises, and both of the gastrocnemius's positions of flexion will be worked completely with these two exercises.

One last point about these foot rotations: the amount of foot movement isn't that great, and it shouldn't cause your feet to slide off the block. You may need to adjust your feet slightly after every few reps, but nothing drastic.

Since we've refined Robby's multi-angle training approach to a slightly more efficient method, let's take a look at the other parts of his plan.

Seated calf raise.   Katsumi Ishimura.

HIGHER REPS

The calves are one of the densest muscle groups in the muscular system. In other words, there are more muscle fibers per square inch of calf muscle than other muscles. This is the reason it takes a few more reps to get that painful-but-oh-so-productive growth burn

Seated calf raise.   Terry Mitsos.

from a set of calf raises—there are simply more muscle fibers to move the load and then fatigue. For best results, all gastrocnemius exercises should have rep ranges between 12 and 25.

FEEL

As with any muscle group, you must get the mind in the muscle and avoid bouncing or throwing the weight. Rep speed is also important: three seconds up and three seconds down is just about right. This slightly exaggerated rep slowness is a must for complete calf development.

Another aspect that must be exaggerated is range of motion. Many trainees work only

through the midrange and then wonder why their calves don't respond. Ever seen the guy with the pipe cleaner lower legs pumping out his calf raises with a movement of about 3 inches per rep? Well, it doesn't matter how many sets of partial calf raises you do; your calves will never get that complete look until you work from complete stretch to complete contraction. Stretch down as far as you can on each rep, come up, and then get as high as you can at the top; then, for a count of two, try to get higher.

SOLEUS

The soleus is a broad, flat muscle situated right under the gastrocnemius that runs from knee to ankle. Developing this muscle not only gives the gastrocnemius a fuller appearance, but also makes the area between the gastrocnemius and the ankle meatier. Those trainees with high calves should never neglect soleus work. A developed soleus will give the illusion of a lower gastrocnemius and will slightly diffuse a glaring high-calf appearance.

The best exercise for soleus development is the seated calf raise. If you do these on a machine, be sure that your lower leg is at a 90-degree angle to your thigh—no more, no less. This is the optimum angle for soleus involvement. One other point concerning soleus development: this muscle isn't as dense as the gastrocnemius, so keep your reps in the 8-to-12 range on seated calf raises.

OVERTRAINING

Walking, climbing in and out of cars, and getting up out of chairs all have an effect on the calves. But unless you're a mail carrier or have some other leg-oriented job, the calves really don't receive much work from this low-intensity, low-duration daily activity. Nevertheless, the calves are still susceptible to the perils of overtraining, just like any other muscle group. That being the case, there is no reason to ever do more than 8 sets for the calves, soleus included, if you're working hard.

And never work your calves more than three days per week—two days per week is preferred.

CALF-BUILDING ROUTINES

For the rank beginner, a productive calf routine is a relatively simple proposition. Two sets of standing calf raises will get the job done, no foot rotation necessary. The feet should remain parallel throughout the range of movement.

Beginner routine a

Standing calf raise   2 × 12–25

Start with this routine if you have less than two months of training. After about two months of training, donkey calf raises should

be done in place of standing calf raises for 2 sets; once again, no foot rotation necessary. This will get your calves accustomed to the stretch this exercise places on your gastrocnemius muscles.

Beginner routine b

Donkey calf raise   2 × 12–25

This routine should be appropriate for those with two to six months of training. At the four-to-six-month interval, the beginner will be moving into the intermediate phase. This

Standing calf raise—start position.   Aaron Baker.

Donkey calf raise—start position.   Jean-Pierre Fux.

means it's time to combine the two movements like so:

Intermediate routine

Standing calf raise	2 × 12–25*
Donkey calf raise	2 × 12–25*

* Incorporate foot rotations on the first set only.

The intermediate routine is for those with six months to one year of training. After a solid year of training, you will be considered a late-intermediate bodybuilder. At this point, you can use a routine like this:

Late-intermediate/advanced routine

Standing calf raise	3 × 12–25*
Leg press calf raise	3 × 12–25*
Seated calf raise	2 × 12-25

* Foot rotations on all sets.

This routine works the calves from all angles and really gets the blood pumping. If you're doing each rep correctly, 8 total sets should be enough. In fact, after you use this routine for six weeks, you may want to cut back to 5 sets per calf workout for about a month. This will allow the calves to recuperate more fully and produce a new growth spurt when you go back to the slightly longer version with more foot-rotation sets.

Roger Stewart.

Here's a rundown on things to remember when using this late-intermediate routine:

1. Only on rare occasions should you do more than 8 total sets for calves, even when specializing.
2. Cut back on your total calf sets every six weeks to allow for recuperation.
3. Feel every rep with a three-second-up/three-second-down performance.
4. Hold each rep in the contracted position for two seconds while you attempt to get higher on your toes.
5. Use an exaggerated range of motion on every rep of every set.
6. Keep your knees locked on all gastrocnemius work.
7. For seated calf raises, make sure your knees are bent at 90-degree angles—no more, no less—for optimum soleus involvement. (No foot rotations on seated calf raises are necessary; you're working the soleus here, not the gastrocnemius.)
8. If you're an intermediate-to-advanced bodybuilder, do foot rotations on some or all of your gastrocnemius sets; rotate heels from down and out (stretch) to up and in (contraction).

EXERCISE EXPLANATIONS

Contracted position of flexion

Standing Calf Raise These are best performed on a machine, but can also be done on a calf block with a barbell on your traps while you're leaning with the top of your head against a wall (a towel is a good idea here). Keep the torso and legs on the same plane with the knees locked. Simply rise up and down with as full a range of motion as possible.

Hack Machine Calf Raise Some hack machines are set up with a calf block so that you can face the machine and do a version of standing calf raises. On these, remember to keep your torso against the pad and knees locked throughout every rep.

Toe press—start position. This is a good alternate stretch position calf exercise.

Toe press—finish position.

One-Legged Calf Raise Hold a dumbbell in your hand (the hand on the same side as your working calf) and position yourself on a calf block. Bend the non-working leg up behind you and begin doing calf raises in normal fashion. Foot rotations will be too difficult on these, so keep your foot pointing straight ahead.

Stretch position of flexion

Donkey Calf Raise Bend at the waist and rest your elbows on a waist-high bench or bar. Place your feet on a calf block and have someone about your same bodyweight sit up on your hips facing forward. Begin doing full-range calf raises with foot rotations or without, whichever your current program calls for. Keep your knees locked throughout the movement.

Leg Press Calf Raise Position yourself in the leg press and place your feet on the foot plate with your heels hanging off the bottom. Begin doing full-range calf raises with or without foot rotations, whichever your current program calls for. Once again, keep your knees locked for maximal gastrocnemius involvement. Also, your legs and torso should be at a right angle to each other for optimal calf stretch.

Soleus

Seated Calf Raise   Position yourself on the seated calf machine. Make sure your legs are bent at 90 degrees—no more, no less. Rise up and down on your toes in a controlled fashion, and really feel the soleus work.

Aaron Baker.

Chapter 9

TRAINING WITH A SYSTEM

You can't be involved with bodybuilding or strength training very long before being exposed to someone's "system." Generally speaking, a system consists of one or more training theories (often unproven) that are integrated into a method of training. By some definitions, there are probably hundreds of training systems that have been used over the years.

Debates will rage forever over which ones work best. But perhaps the most common benefit that trainees garner from trying different systems is to discover something that works well for them and, at the very least, to prevent staleness and boredom from always doing the same thing in the gym.

First, Steve Holman gives us a very thorough look at how to use supersets for supergrowth.

SUPERSETS FOR SUPERGROWTH
Steve Holman

Supersetting, or alternating two exercises for antagonistic muscle groups, was a popular mass-building method back in Arnold's illustrious heyday in the 1970s. The Oak was notorious for supersetting chest and back exercises, which would blow up his torso to immense proportions and have him strutting around the old Gold's Gym in Venice, California, like a peacock spreading its feathers. And with feathers like his, who could blame him? Most of the big men used this technique to get even bigger during this era—athletes like Ken Waller, Franco Columbo, and Mike Katz.

Bill Pearl was another bodybuilder who often used this method, especially in his arm training. In fact, he wrote an article for *Muscular Development* in which he proclaimed that supersetting biceps and triceps was one of his favorite methods for jarring his arms out of hibernation—and jar them it did. His arms reached a gigantic 20 inches, the sight of which caused more than one neophyte trainee to pursue bodybuilding with the obsession of a heroin junkie.

Arthur Jones, the creator of Nautilus machines, quantified the success that these and other bodybuilders were having with this technique in the November 1971 *Ironman* as follows:

Since working the triceps muscle also involves a far lighter form of work for the opposing muscle, the biceps, you can produce faster and better recovery by working your upper-arm muscles alternately—the slight amount of work provided for the biceps by working the triceps will cause the biceps to recover better than it would if it were rested entirely, and vice versa. Thus, by working the triceps heavily during the rest period between heavy sets for the biceps, you will perform better during your second set for your biceps than you would if you did nothing between the two sets for your biceps. Far better results are produced by working faster. Rest periods actually have an effect exactly opposite to that which might be expected in this case; instead of doing two sets for the biceps and then two sets for the triceps with rest periods between sets, do the sets alternately with no rest at all. Far better results will be produced in much less time.

Although Jones specifically targeted the biceps and triceps with his explanation, the question arose as to whether lifters might experience this training effect by working other opposing muscle groups in this superset manner. Arnold certainly found it to be just as result-producing for chest and back.

Ronnie Coleman.

So why aren't more of today's bodybuilders taking advantage of this tried-and-true technique? Good question. The answer lies in the way trends occur: in cycles. Although bodybuilders back in the early '70s found supersetting to be highly effective and efficient, as with any other technique in bodybuilding it had a few years of popularity and then became passé. Because variety is so important in the gym, even the most productive techniques lose their luster and get shoved back into the closet after a while. What goes around comes around, however, and every few years daring bodybuilders hungry for new gains venture into that dark closet and dust off an effective, old technique, causing a resurgence. Considering the impressive results that Arnold and the other aforementioned men achieved, perhaps you'll want to reach into the closet and start the superset ball rolling.

Using supersets is a much more realistic proposition for those bodybuilders who train in a home gym than for those who train in a commercial gym, because of the risk of inadvertent thievery. In a commercial gym, there's always the danger of someone taking off with your dumbbells or the barbell you've set aside for your second exercise, and this can blow the superset (not to mention your entire workout).

No matter where you employ this technique, however—at home or in a commercial gym—you must realize that it's difficult, especially when you superset two large muscle masses like chest and back or thighs and hamstrings. In this case, you may run out of aerobic steam during your second exercise and cheat that bodypart out of growth stimulation. If you find this to be the case, keep your reps low on both movements—around 6—so that you don't become so winded that you can't push your second muscle group to failure.

Here is a good routine that incorporates supersets and that will produce rapid results. It's a variation of the Efficiency-of-Effort workout from Ironman's *Home Gym Handbook*. Use this regimen on three nonconsecutive days per week—say, Monday, Wednesday, and Friday—or two nonconsecutive days if you're a hard gainer.

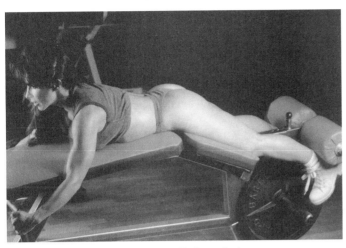

Leg curl—start position.   Tatiana Anderson.

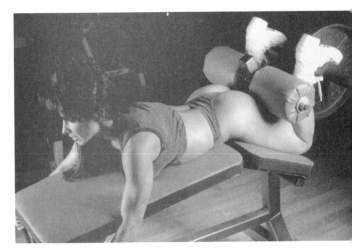

Leg curl—finish position.

Front thighs and hamstrings
Squat	1–2 × 6–8
Superset with	
Leg curl	1–2 × 6–8
Sissy squat	1–2 × 6–8
Superset with	
Stiff-legged deadlift	1–2 × 6–8

Chest and midback
Bench press	1–2 × 6–8
Superset with	
Bent-over row	1–2 × 6–8

Upper chest and lats
Incline press	1–2 × 6–8
Superset with	
Chin	1–2 × 6–8

Delts and midback
Dumbbell press	1–2 × 6–8
Superset with	
Behind-the-neck chin	1–2 × 6–8

Lateral delts and teres major
Lateral raise	1–2 × 6–8
Superset with	
Pullover	1–2 × 6–8

Triceps and biceps
Barbell curl	1–2 × 6–8
Superset with	
Lying triceps extension	1–2 × 6–8

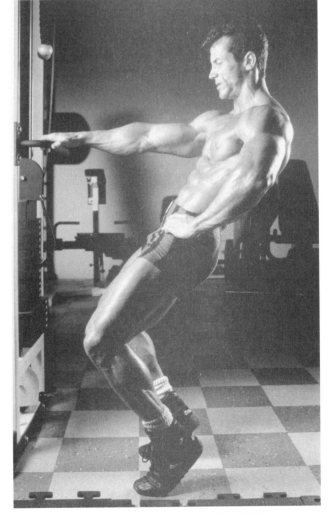

Sissy squat.   B. J. Quinn.

Abs and calves *

Crunch	1–2 × 20
Superset with	
Donkey calf raise	1–2 × 20

*Abdominals and calves aren't antagonistic muscle groups, but alternating them keeps you in the superset mode and saves time.

Keep in mind the following suggestions when you use this routine:

- Do a light warm-up set for each movement before beginning a superset.
- Do not rest between exercises in a superset. Go from the first exercise immediately to the second.
- Rest one to two minutes between supersets.
- Do 2 sets for the exercises that work your weakest areas, and only 1 set for other movements. (Of course, if you do 2 sets for the first exercise in a superset, you'll do 2 sets for the second movement as well, even if the second works one of your strong bodyparts.)
- Always keep your set total at around 20; supersetting is intense, so don't overdo it.
- Maintain strict form on all sets.
- Use this routine for a maximum of six weeks.

Another reason this workout is so effective is psychological—when you superset two antagonistic muscle groups, you get an enormous pump in two areas at the same time, and you therefore feel huge. Imagine your biceps and triceps simultaneously engorged to the bursting point, your arms looking more gigantic than ever before. Don't you think you'd feel invincible and get one heck of a mental boost? You'll probably end up doing the peacock strut around your home gym, but go ahead—Arnold would encourage it. In fact, because you're using one of his favorite techniques, he'd probably demand it.

Stiff-legged deadlift—start position.

Stiff-legged deadlift—finish position.

Bench press.   Ronnie Coleman.

Bent-over row.

Incline press—start position.   David Liberman.   Incline press—finish position.

Chin—start position.   Ronnie Coleman.   Chin—finish position.

Dumbbell press—start position.

Dumbbell press—finish position.

Lateral raise—start position.
Don Long.

Lateral raise—finish position.

Pullover—start position. Henrik Thamasian. Pullover—finish position.

Barbell curl—start position. Jonathan Lawson. Barbell curl—finish position.

Lying triceps extension—start position.

Lying triceps extension—finish position.

Crunch.

Decades ago, bodybuilders experimented with "isometrics," exercises without movement or weights, and experienced mixed results. Bodybuilding author John Little theorized that isometrics could be improved by holding real, known weights in a static position and then gradually increasing the load. He and I used this technique to develop Static Contraction Training.

STATIC CONTRACTION TRAINING

John Little

Arthur Stanley Eddington (1882–1944) was a brilliant British astronomer whose work was instrumental in proving, mathematically and experimentally, Einstein's theory of relativity. Eddington is also remembered for an analogy he used to explain a complex problem involv-

ing sensory perception and scientific inquiry. He compared a fishnet to the human senses and to the parameters of an experiment. If the net has holes of a certain size, he said, we can predict what size fish it will catch, but we cannot assume that the net will catch everything in the ocean. Hence, differently designed nets will catch different objects. Human senses have the same limitations. So do experiments.

We set up the Static Contraction Research Study (SCRS) to learn the following about static contraction training.

- Does it cause an increase in muscle mass?
- Does it cause a reduction in bodyfat?
- Does it cause an increase in muscle size?
- Does it cause an increase in both static and dynamic, or full-range, strength?

We refer to these as bottom-line benefits to bodybuilders in contrast to some of the parameters that are usually measured in the few strength studies that are done. These parameters include blood gases, blood chemistry, muscle-fiber activity and chemistry, electrical impulse variations, and other esoterica. Make no mistake, they are important scientific questions and useful measurements to know (all knowledge is beneficial), but in the final analysis they don't matter to bodybuilders.

The fact that lifting a 5-pound weight increases neuromuscular stimulation is interesting, but does it put more mass on you? Does it increase the size of your biceps? Does it increase your bench press? Ultimately, that's what bodybuilders want to know, so that's what we designed our fishnet to find.

We recruited test subjects directly from our Power Factor Publishing customer list, asking a small percentage of our best customers—that is, those who purchased multiple products over time and thus appeared to be serious bodybuilders—if they'd volunteer to participate in a research study involving 10 weeks of static contraction training. They would perform no other strength training during this time and would make no changes in their diet, supplementation (if any), or aerobic exercise schedules. People who took growth drugs of any kind were not permitted to participate.

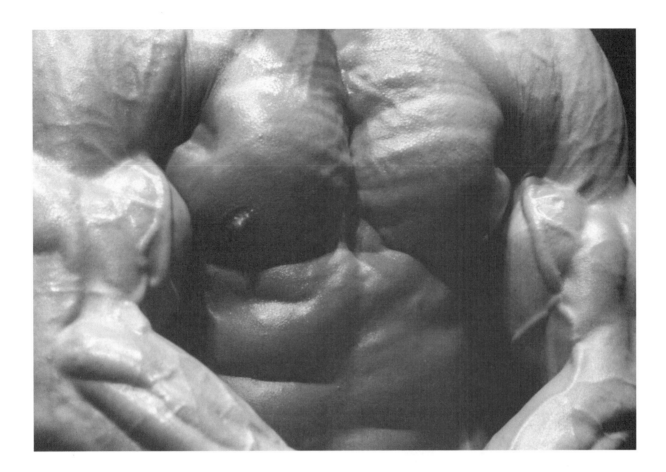

At the beginning of the study we recorded the following data for each subject: age; weight; bodyfat percentage; and chest, waist, shoulder, biceps, forearm, wrist, thigh, and calf measurements. In addition, we asked each subject to characterize his own muscular development on a scale of 1 to 10, with 1 representing "terrible muscular condition, very weak" and 10 representing "top of your genetic muscular limit, could not be stronger."

Next, we had the subjects take the following three measurements of strength for 17 specific exercises:

1. A conventional full-range 1-rep maximum
2. A conventional full-range 10-rep maximum
3. A static hold, in the strongest range, of the maximum weight possible for 15 seconds; that is, a weight sufficiently heavy that after 15 seconds the subject can no longer hold it and it begins to descend

Tatiana Anderson.

The exercises tested included the deadlift, weighted crunch, bench press, barbell shrug, lat pulldown, close-grip bench press, preacher curl, squat, leg press, calf raise, toe press, cable row, cable pushdown, standing barbell curl, leg extension, and leg curl. Because of equipment limitations, some subjects couldn't perform all of the exercises. In those cases, all the exercises they were able to measure were included in the before-and-after test comparisons.

After 10 weeks, the subjects took all of the mass, size, and strength measurements again.

The subjects were divided into groups that used three major protocols: one set, two sets, and three sets. Each set consisted of one static contraction repetition, which is very different from a conventional repetition, as there's no movement of the weight. In this study, a repetition consisted of holding the weight slightly out of the locked position—in the strongest range—for a period of 15 to 30 seconds.

There were also three training frequencies used: three times per week, two times per week, and a variable schedule that began as three times per week but decreased as the study progressed.

All subjects used programs that consisted of 10 compound exercises divided into two workouts of 5 exercises, each performed on alternate training days. Thus, it took two different workouts to exercise all major muscle groups.

Here's how they performed a static hold. Using the bench press as an example, they lifted the weight from a resting point at the top of their reach, lowered from the point of lockout to two or three inches below lockout—the strongest range—and held it there without any up or down motion.

The duration of the sets followed the principle of progressive resistance. The subjects selected a beginning weight that was sufficiently heavy that they could only hold it statically for 15 seconds. After 15 seconds, the weight would begin to descend—or ascend, in the case of a lat pulldown or similar pulling movement. At subsequent workouts, the subjects achieved progression of intensity by holding the weight for longer periods of time, such as 21 seconds, working up to 30 seconds.

Lee Apperson.

When they could hold a given weight for 30 seconds, they increased the weight, choosing a poundage that they could hold for only 15 seconds, and so on. For example, a subject who could hold 100 pounds statically for 15 seconds would, at his next workout, try to hold it a little longer. At the next workout, he'd use the same weight but try to hold it for a still longer time. As soon as he was up to 30 seconds with the 100-pound weight, he increased the weight to, say, 125 pounds so that he was again able to hold it statically for only 15 seconds.

Note that total workout time was extremely short. With one set per exercise, the five-exercise session took a total of 75 seconds to 2½ minutes. That's 2½ minutes for an entire workout! Of course, as a practical matter, additional time was spent setting up equipment and resting between sets. While this is an extremely brief duration of maximum muscular contraction, the intensity is, proportionately, enormously high. This kind of training must be experienced to be fully appreciated.

THE SUBJECTS

As mentioned before, we solicited volunteer subjects from our customer list, male bodybuilders who'd been training for up to two years with the Power Factor Training and/or Precision Training systems. That means they'd been training for a long time with ultra-high intensity and progressive maximal overloads and had already seen some very impressive gains. Most of them had been training for years and considered themselves to be near the upper limits of their potential. In general, it would be far more difficult for them to add new muscle to their bodies than it would for the average person. Furthermore, their average age was 38.4—about 20 years older than the test subjects in most training studies. We knew that if we could find a way to make these subjects put on new muscle, we'd have a system that would be of enormous value not only to the average person but to very experienced bodybuilders as well.

NO DOUBLE-BLIND PROTOCOL

The technique of conducting double-blind studies is very important and is widely used in experiments in which the subjects' (or the test giver's) attitude could influence the outcome. Double-blind techniques are used in drug testing and some psychological tests in which neither the test subjects nor the test giver knows which of the subjects are receiving the test drug.

This technique cannot be used in weight lifting, however, as there's no way to get subjects to lift weights without knowing that they're doing it. There's no way to put them in a situation in which they're unaware that they're trying to get stronger or that they're exerting themselves maximally. Our test subjects knew they were trying to get stronger.

NO CONTROL GROUP

Another technique often used in research studies is to have a control group. For example, one group of subjects, the control group, might make no change whatsoever in its diet while another, otherwise identical group of subjects, the test group, changes its protein

intake by 300 percent. At the end of the study, the two groups are compared for certain characteristics related to protein intake and observations are made.

For this study we decided against using a control group, for a very simple reason: What strength-training routine would they have used? Periodization? Heavy Duty? Positions of Flexion? Pre-exhaustion? Supersets? Bulgarian training? Russian bear training? Superslow? Power Factor Training? Sets of 100? Three sets of 12? Four sets of 8? Instead, we decided that the control group consisted of everyone else. For example, regardless of how you normally train, examine the results of the subjects who spent 10 weeks on the SCRS and compare those results to your own progress over the past 10 weeks. In the final analysis, that's all that matters to you anyway. The question is, Will static contraction work better than what you're doing now?

THE DATA

We deliberately recruited far more test subjects than we would have needed in order to have conclusive results. It's important to note that many academic, clinical studies involve as few as four or five subjects. We have complete and meaningful data from 12 subjects, representing a wide cross-section of ages and degrees of success on the SCRS.

Figure 9.1 is a summary of the results of those subjects after 10 weeks of training on the SCRS. In case the numbers don't jump off the page at you, let us state now that these findings are very significant. There were sub-

stantial increases in static strength; dynamic, full-range strength; lean mass; and muscle size. The fact is, 100 percent of the subjects got stronger.

The average static strength, measured on the 17 exercises, increased 51.3 percent, and, in what will come as a major surprise to virtually everyone, dynamic strength—over a conventional full range of motion—also increased.

ARISTOTLE MEETS GALILEO—AGAIN

As usual, having more facts means we now have fewer myths. Ever heard this one? When you exercise a muscle statically at only one point, you only get stronger at that limited range. Your static strength gains don't transfer to full-range strength gains.

In fact, that's not just a myth. It's the orthodox teaching encountered in every exercise physiology class. Ask anyone who has a degree in exercise physiology if static strength will transfer to dynamic strength, and he or she will tell you, "No way." But 100 percent of the subjects on this study had a positive, significant transference to full-range strength from the gains they made in static strength. The transference averaged 60 percent. That

	Strength (percent gained)				Frequency		Mass (pounds gained)			Size (inches gained)			
Subject	Average static	Average 1RM	Average 10RM	Transfer of static to full	Sets	Days off between	W/O per week	Lean	Fat	Age	Biceps	Chest	Shoulders	Waist
Joaquin M.	57.7	16.4	22.1	33.4	3	8.1	0.9	28.9	-18.4	20	0.38	0.75	1.50	0.00
Matt C.	55.9	26.0	47.7	66.0	2	3.1	2.3	21.1	2.9	31	1.00	1.50	0.75	0.00
Gary J.	54.1	34.8	40.6	69.6	2	4.2	1.7	12.7	-10.7	52	0.25	0.00	0.50	-1.00
Kimball M.	36.9	35.0	23.5	79.2	3	2.8	2.5	12.6	-9.6	44	1.00	3.75	0.25	1.25
Shane P.	58.6	25.7	25.9	44.1	3	3.0	2.4	7.8	-0.8	24	0.75	2.00	3.13	1.63
Reg P.	15.7	11.0	12.0	73.4	2	7.1	1.0	6.6	-8.6	50	0.25	0.25	0.50	-2.00
Dave T.	92.4	57.8	69.1	68.7	1	2.6	2.7	6.3	-1.3	44	1.75	3.00	4.00	-2.50
William L.	35.5	12.5	12.2	34.7	3	2.4	2.9	5.6	-9.6	29	0.31	0.63	1.13	-1.00
Michael A.	76.8	60.8	77.1	89.8	2	3.8	1.9	4.1	3.4	34	0.13	-0.50	0.00	0.50
Paul S.	44.2	19.4	19.1	43.5	1	3.7	1.9	2.3	-1.3	51	0.25	0.00	0.00	0.00
Bruce B.	28.1	19.6	20.4	71.1	2	2.3	3.0	1.9	-1.9	44	-0.19	1.50	1.25	-1.25
Tim P.	59.7	12.8	42.3	46.2	2	3.3	2.1	-1.5	-2.5	38	0.50	0.50	1.50	0.00
Averages	51.3	27.6	34.3	60.0	2.2	3.9	2.1	9.0	-4.9	38.4	0.5	1.1	1.2	-0.4

Static Contraction Research Study (SCRS) Data Summary (Ordered by Lean Mass Gains)

Figure 9.1.

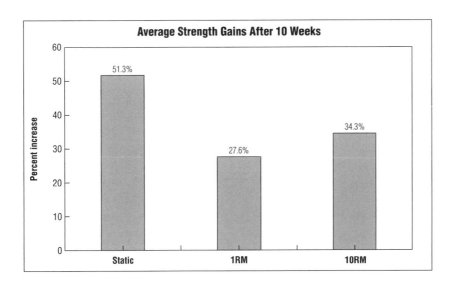

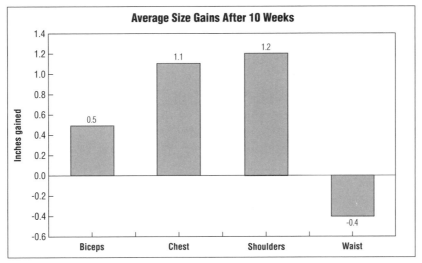

Most bodybuilders spend months in the gym working out and don't see improvement like this. Instead they overtrain week after week.

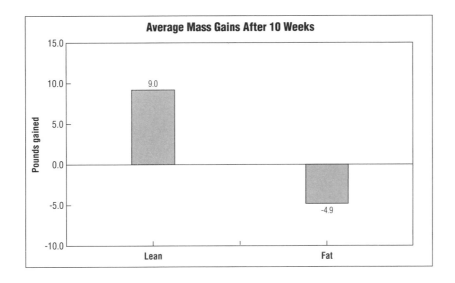

means a person who added 100 pounds to his static bench press would add, on average, 60 pounds to his full range 1- and 10-rep maxes.

This reminds us of Aristotle, who declared that heavier objects fall at a faster rate than lighter objects. That so-called law was taught for nearly 2,000 years. Finally, Galileo decided to test the law by rolling objects down incline planes. Sure enough, objects of all weights accelerated at the same rate. Think about that story when an incredulous fellow bodybuilder insists that training statically will not increase your full-range strength. More to the point, be like Galileo and test for yourself.

THE IMPORTANCE OF RANGE OF MOTION

Here's another bit of institutionalized mythology: you need a full range of motion in the muscle in order to stimulate growth. Guess what? The importance of range of motion falls somewhere between little and none. Every gain in mass, strength, and size achieved by everyone on the SCRS was acquired with no range of motion whatsoever. Look at Joaquin M., who gained 28.9 pounds of new muscle with zero range of motion. The fact is, you can make substantial gains with no movement (static contraction), some movement (partials, as proved by Power Factor trainees), and full movement (conventional training). Therefore, the range of motion has no significance.

MASS AND SIZE GAINS

The figures in the columns for mass and size speak for themselves. Take a look at them and ask yourself one question: when was the last time you had gains like that in 10 weeks of training? Note that only Tim P. had a decrease in muscle mass. We suspect that this was actually the fault of an inaccurate bodyfat measurement, as his strength was increased significantly and his biceps, chest, and shoulders all got bigger—virtually impossible to achieve during a decrease in lean muscle and fat. The likelihood is that Tim P. actually

gained muscle and lost even more fat, as his total weight was down by four pounds.

FREQUENCY OF TRAINING

Much was learned on the subject of training frequency. Figure 9.1 shows two columns under the heading "frequency." These measurements of "days off between workouts" and "workouts per week" are actually two ways of expressing the same thing.

Note that the subjects averaged just 2.1 workouts per week. At the beginning of the study, one group was required to train three days per week. Guess what happened to them? Approximately three weeks into the study, they began to report classic symptoms of overtraining. Some could not continue. Their training schedules had to be altered due to the increased demands put on their bodies by the increased loads they were lifting due to their increased strength. That proves it's useless to set fixed training schedules—for example, that you'll always train on Monday, Wednesday, and Friday. If you're getting stronger, you must work out less frequently. It's a biological law. Remember Sisco's maximum: Every day is kidney day. In other words, it doesn't make the slightest difference to your kidneys (or your liver, or your pancreas, or whatever) that yesterday was leg day and today is shoulder day. Growth is systemic, and so is recovery; and the stronger your muscles get, the longer it takes your supporting organs to clean up the waste by-products of your workout.

Also, if we compare the top six subjects with the bottom six subjects, as ranked by lean gains, we see further corroboration of this trend. The top six subjects worked out, on average, 1.8 times per week. The bottom six worked out 2.4 times per week—33 percent more frequently—but achieved poorer results.

CONCLUSIONS

The fact that this group of experienced bodybuilders, with an average age of 38.4, achieved such tremendous increases in mass, strength, and size in only 10 weeks of training is quite possibly without precedent in exercise physiology. That they achieved such results using zero range of motion is certainly unprecedented.

Moreover, they have unequivocally proved that, contrary to popular belief, static contraction strength training does make a very significant contribution to dynamic, full-range strength and that the range of motion has no role in the stimulation of new muscle growth, increased muscle size, or increased strength.

A quick glance at the average transference of 60 percent might cause you to ask, Why exercise statically if it only yields a 60 percent increase in dynamic transference? There are two answers to this. First, the 60 percent of transference yielded the average subject a 27.6 percent increase in his 1-rep max and a

Lee Apperson.

34.3 percent increase in his 10-rep max in 17 different types of lifts. So the question is, Has your conventional training given you the same or better increases in full-range strength over the past 10 weeks?

Second, look at the mass and size gains these subjects achieved. Bodybuilders who want more mass and size shouldn't care what technique they use to get it, even if it means standing on their heads and chanting. Remember, there's nothing sacrosanct about conventional training. If unconventional training gets you to your goals faster, do it. (*Static Contraction Training* is available from NTC/Contemporary Publishing Group, Inc.: ISBN 0-8092-2907-2.)

Henrik Thamasian.

Steve Holman is the developer of the successful Compound Aftershock system of training. In this article, he provides a complete program for arm training.

COMPOUND AFTERSHOCK
Steve Holman

Are you looking for a training routine that will inflate your arms to eye-popping proportions in record time—a program based on scientific principles and exercise analysis so it absolutely, positively can't fail? Then you've come to the right article. After only three workouts with the following Compound Aftershock routine, your arms will feel fuller than ever before, and with some diligent effort you'll eventually look as if you have 20-pound hams stuffed in your shirtsleeves—or perhaps 15-pounders, depending on your genetics.

How much discomfort must you endure for this transformation to occur? Well, the routines do require a high pain threshold, but the entire program takes less than 15 minutes.

We all need a little convincing before we start a new program, so here are the reasons this science-based arm program produces such spectacular results:

USES THE MOST EFFECTIVE EXERCISES

According to the book *Muscle Meets Magnet* by Per A. Tesch, Ph.D., which takes an MRI look at which parts of leg and arm muscles are hit hardest by certain exercises, the movements in the Compound Aftershock superset hit the target muscle structures completely, rather than focusing on certain heads.

Decline extension

This exercise puts maximum stress on the lateral, long, and medial heads of the triceps. You get total target-muscle stimulation with one efficient exercise. According to *Muscle Meets Magnet*, lying extensions on a flat bench, the most common version of this exercise, somewhat neglect the lateral and medial heads and

Close-grip barbell curl—start position.

Close-grip barbell curl—midpoint position.

Close-grip barbell curl—finish position.

focus on the long head. If you want to totally torch your triceps, do your extensions on a decline.

Overhead dumbbell extension

This exercise also puts maximum heat on all three triceps heads when you use two dumbbells. What's interesting is that the same movement done with a bar instead of dumbbells ignites only the lateral and medial heads, leaving the long head lagging behind. The reason the dumbbell version may be more effective is that your palms are facing each other. MRI analysis proves that varying your grip can have a substantial effect on target-muscle stimulation, as you'll see with the biceps exercises as well.

Close-grip barbell curl

This exercise puts a total hit on the medial and lateral heads of the biceps. The brachialis muscles even get complete stimulation. If you do the exercise with a wide grip, however, MRI analysis shows that the medial head, the one closest to your torso, takes the brunt of the stress and the lateral head and brachialis lag behind. Keep your grip close on curls, about 10 inches between your hands, and you'll get a more complete overall biceps hit.

Incline curl

Once again, you sledgehammer the medial and lateral biceps heads: the unusual stretch you get on this exercise may be the reason.

Incline curl—start position.   Mohamed Makkawy.   Incline curl—finish position.

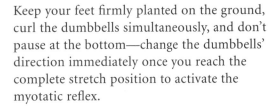

Keep your feet firmly planted on the ground, curl the dumbbells simultaneously, and don't pause at the bottom—change the dumbbells' direction immediately once you reach the complete stretch position to activate the myotatic reflex.

MAXES OUT FIBER RECRUITMENT

The myotatic reflex, or pre-stretch, helps max out fiber recruitment. This is especially true when you place the stretch exercise before a big midrange movement in a superset. For example, you can superset incline curls with close-grip barbell curls. Let's go through the entire Compound Aftershock biceps routine so you can see exactly how and why it's so effective:

- After a couple of warm-up sets, you train the mass of the muscle with a heavy set of close-grip curls to failure— muscle synergy from your front delts makes this heavy overload possible.

- After a brief rest, you move to the Aftershock superset. First, you use incline dumbbell curls to trigger the myotatic reflex for some extraordinary fiber recruitment—a call to arms for the reserve fibers. With a preponderance of fibers in a heightened state, you immediately follow up with a lighter set of close-grip curls—about 20 percent lighter than your first set—so that synergy once again forces maximum fiber recruitment.

- After a two-minute rest and some massaging of your incredibly pumped biceps, you finish them off with 1 or 2 sets of concentration curls, squeezing hard for a count at the top of each rep for a peak-contraction effect.

Your biceps can't help but grow after this on-target attack.

Triceps get the same treatment:

- Do one set of decline extensions—it's okay if your upper arms move so that

Shawn Ray.

you get some synergy from your lats and teres muscles. Just don't overdo it.

- Rest for a minute as you decrease the weight on the bar, then do 1 set of overhead dumbbell extensions supersetted with a second set of decline triceps extensions with the reduced poundage. Your triceps fibers will be screaming for mercy and pumped to the bursting point.

- Rest for about two minutes and notice how your triceps are so full, they feel as if they're a couple of inflated tire tubes hanging from your rear delts. Now finish them off with dumbbell kickbacks, making an effort to get your upper arms back past your torso on every rep as you contract your triceps hard. One set of this peak-contraction pain is all you have to endure—two if you're a real masochist.

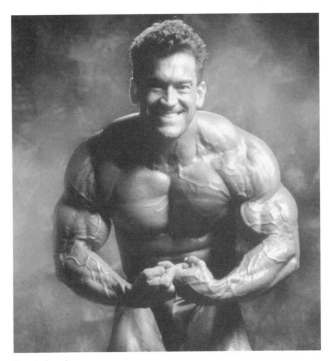

Lee Labrada.

BETTER PUMP AND BURN

New research suggests that supersetting helps lower the blood pH, which can force more growth hormone release. These findings may verify why bodybuilders have been instinctively chasing the pump for years—it may be a growth stimulus after all.

Roland Kickinger.

BRACHIALIS WORK FOR HIGHER PEAKS

The brachialis runs under the biceps, and when you develop this muscle, it can give your biceps more height, much like a developed soleus gives the lower legs more fullness. While close-grip barbell curls put a lot of stress on the brachialis, you may want to do a direct finishing set to give it that extra jolt. *Muscle Meets Magnet* says incline hammer curls, with your thumbs up and palms facing each other, provide a focused hit on the brachialis.

MORE RECOVERY FOR ACCELERATED GROWTH

You stimulate each target muscle to the maximum with only 4 or 5 sets, which means you have more recovery ability left for hypertrophy. Remember, the more sets you do, the more you deplete your system's ability to recover from intense exercise, so efficiency is key. Obviously, this is one heck of an efficient arm-building program, as you fatigue as many fibers as possible with as few sets as possible.

How should you use the Compound Aftershock arm routine for best results? An every-other-day split is the program that will help most intermediate bodybuilders make the best gains. Here's a sample:

Workout 1: Quads, hamstrings, calves, chest, and triceps
Workout 2: Back, delts, biceps, and abdominals

Always take a day of rest between workouts and you have a recovery-oriented split that will produce impressive size increases.

If you prefer full-body workouts, a different approach is necessary, as follows:

Monday	
Squat	2 × 8–10
Leg extension	1 × 8–10
Leg curl	2 × 8-10
Standing calf raise	2 × 12–20
Seated calf raise	2 × 12–20

Bench press	2 × 8–10
Pulldown	2 × 8–10
Bent-over row	2 × 8–10
Dumbbell upright row	2 × 8–10
Full-range crunch	2 × 8–10

Wednesday

Compound Aftershock arm routine—you may want to do two supersets instead of only one (or any arm-specialization program), since you have more time to recover.

Friday

Same as Monday

With this program you train arms only once a week, on Wednesday, with the full Compound Aftershock routine. Consequently, you may be able to get away with a few more sets, such as doing two supersets instead of one, but keep in mind that biceps and triceps get indirect stimulation on Monday and Friday from the pressing, rowing, and pulldown movements. This indirect work will pump blood into your arms for heightened recovery, but you want to make sure you don't overtrain. You'll see impressive results from this type of program in a matter of weeks, guaranteed.

If buggy-whip arms is the disease, Compound Aftershock is the cure. Give this routine a try and watch as your biceps and triceps swell to hamlike proportions in record time.

Vince Taylor.

Eric Sternlicht, Ph.D., gives us this examination of "negatives," or eccentric movements, a technique commonly used by bodybuilders trying to squeeze every last bit of growth stimulation from an exercise.

TRAINING WITH NEGATIVES
Eric Sternlicht, Ph.D.

Many of us regularly use negatives and forced reps in our training. Forced reps enable us to do a few more reps than we can handle on our own, while negatives let us use more weight during the lowering part of a movement than we can lift at the start—or so most bodybuilders believe. What does science say about the aforementioned intensity techniques? Are they really beneficial? And if so, how much weight should you use? How many forced reps should you perform?

While it's widely accepted in the athletic community that negatives and forced reps do work, the scientific community has only recently begun looking at training methods that focus on eccentric muscle contractions. The research appears promising, as it shows that optimal gains in muscle size and strength require eccentric, or negative, muscle contractions. Both the United States military and NASA are now funding further research involving eccentric exercise in an effort to develop more-effective training programs for the troops and astronauts. You'll benefit from all the research as well, as the knowledge gained will lead us to create more effective and time-efficient programs to meet your training goals. Rather than doing forced reps or negatives because you think they work or because they feel good, you'll actually have the answers to questions like How much? and How many?

As you probably know, every rep of every weight exercise includes two phases: the concentric (shortening) phase, in which you raise or push the weight, and an eccentric (lengthening) phase, in which you lower the weight or otherwise return it to its original position. Many people think their muscles contract only during the concentric (positive) movement, but the fact is, whenever you control the eccentric phase by slowing the weight's movement as it returns to the starting position, the muscle

continues to contract as it resists the force of gravity acting on the weight. In other words, eccentric contractions involve a lengthening of the muscle as it contracts to resist gravity or momentum. Anytime you get a spot, you're using some form of advanced eccentric training, even if you're not aware of it.

While a vast amount of research on muscle physiology and biomechanics exists, most of it involves concentric muscle contractions and traditional modes of resistance exercise. At present, there's a limited amount of research regarding eccentric muscle contractions, and only speculation as to the mechanics at work. Several recent studies report significantly greater improvements in muscle strength and size when programs focus on the negative phase of lifting movements as compared with more traditional training—exactly what many people had observed in the gym.

Negative dip—start position.   Bruce Patterson.

Negative dip—finish position.

Negative leg press—start position.   Aaron Baker.

Negative leg press—finish position.

Negative one-arm cable curl—start position.

Negative one-arm cable curl—finish position.

Tom Varga.

Despite those results, eccentric training has some limitations. The first is muscle soreness: both eccentric exercise and exercise the body isn't accustomed to can lead to delayed-onset muscle soreness, or DOMS. There are conflicting reports as to the effect of DOMS and/or prior muscle damage on subsequent muscle function, with some research showing no change and some showing a decrease in performance. In terms of rehabilitation, however, eccentric exercise appears to be beneficial for both injury prevention and rehabilitation.

Eccentric muscle contraction also makes unique metabolic demands on the body. In one study, the addition of negative loads following concentric muscle contractions increased metabolic costs by 14 percent. Another limitation is that you have to have a partner: Not many machines let you vary the resistance between concentric and eccentric phases of an exercise.

There are limits to how much weight a muscle can resist during any eccentric movement. Theoretical and applied research suggests that the optimal load is between 104 and 140 percent of the muscle's maximal isometric contractile force, or MICF. The neuromuscular systems interact to function optimally while protecting themselves from injury. In this case, the nervous system not only directs your muscles to contract and lift a weight, but it also receives feedback that limits the force of contraction to protect the tissue from excessive stress, damage, and injury.

Looking to rectify at least one of the limitations of eccentric exercise, Flex Equipment, Inc. commissioned Stuart Rugg, Ph.D., and me to perform a series of pilot studies to determine the optimal resistance for eccentric movements. Under the auspices of Simply Fit, Inc. and Occidental College, we designed studies involving traditional resistance-training equipment and electromyography (EMG). The EMG recordings allowed us to examine the degree of muscle activity during the entire range of motion.

Five subjects who had weight-lifting experience, including one professional bodybuilder, participated in the study. While the subjects performed numerous exercises, the results for the barbell curl are typical of our findings for the other machines and muscles tested.

Each subject performed multiple sets of barbell curls for four repetitions, each using four different workloads, with the concentric load remaining constant at 80 percent of the subject's 1-rep max. The eccentric load was increased in increments of 10 percent, producing negative workloads of 100, 110, 120, and 130 percent of the positive load. The subjects all took rest periods between sets to minimize fatigue.

With respect to muscle physiology and biomechanics, it's well documented that when the load is kept constant during an exercise, both the energy expenditure and mean EMG values decrease during the eccentric phase. In other words, when the weight remains constant during the entire movement, there's less muscle activity during the negative phase.

Our data confirm that—at least on the second set of barbell curls. However, on the third set, on which the eccentric load was increased by 20 percent, the muscle activity went back up. It wasn't just the elite bodybuilder either. For all five subjects, the mean eccentric EMG values started to maintain or increase when the negative workloads increased to 110 to 120 percent of the positive load. When the subjects used 130 percent on the eccentric load, though, the mean EMG values once again dropped below those for the corresponding concentric phase. That decline may be due to the fact that the subjects could no longer control the descent of the load; so it represents a decrease in recruitment of the target muscle.

Based on our preliminary data, we believe the eccentric load should not be more than 20 percent greater than the concentric load. Although the theoretical limit for eccentric overload has been reported at as high as 140 percent of a muscle's maximal isometric contractile force, our five subjects were incapable of controlling eccentric overloads of 130 percent. Using a negative load of no more than 120 percent MICF enables you to control the movement and limits your potential for muscle damage. Any more weight would make it difficult for you to perform multiple reps with proper form, would most likely produce a drop in muscle activation, and would increase the probability of your sustaining muscle, connective tissue, or joint damage during training.

Strictly speaking, the power rack probably doesn't constitute a training system; but it is so magnificently useful and productive in bodybuilding that it should be considered as essential as a barbell.

In this article, Bill Starr makes the case for power rack training.

POWER RACK TRAINING Bill Starr

For anyone who's honestly trying to get stronger, a power rack is an essential piece of equipment. I'm not just talking about advanced strength athletes, either, because

Ted Arcidi in the power rack.

the power rack is extremely useful for rank beginners as well. The beauty of the power rack is that it takes up so little space and is so versatile.

If you have an Olympic set and an adjustable bench, you can do a tremendous range of exercises inside and outside the rack—and the fact that it's compact makes it ideal for a home gym. You can, conceivably, work out in a 10-by-10-foot space. I know this is true, because I've trained in such confined areas. It's tight, but you can accomplish the same amount of work as you can in a commercial gym. All it takes is desire.

Whenever I see a television commercial about some new exercise gadget and hear the announcer going on and on about how little space it takes up, I have to laugh. I can do 10

times as many exercises in a power rack, and it's less intrusive than the machines.

Perhaps the most outstanding advantage of the power rack is the safety feature. This, again, makes it the ideal equipment for those who train alone. Racks come in many shapes and sizes. Some cost a small fortune, but you can find excellent racks for less than $300. For home use, or for use by only a small group of trainees, the rack doesn't have to be heavy-duty construction. Many racks use 4- to 5-inch metal, and that's sort of overkill. Even in my gym at Hopkins, we only have racks that are made of moderately heavy metal, and they've held up perfectly for nine years. The heavy-gauge metal is for show more than for function.

There are some important things to look for when you buy a rack. Is it tall enough to let you do some overhead work? Are the uprights set wide enough apart to let you do movements without being restricted, and are the holes set close enough to give you a wide variety of positions to choose from? The rack must have four pins, and I'll explain the reason for that later.

The feeling of security is probably the main reason that people like to work inside a rack. They know that if they get stuck, say, in a squat, they can simply sit down and place the bar back on the pins. That eliminates damage to the equipment, floor, and, even more important, themselves. The sense of security enables them to put a greater effort into the exercise, a factor that's doubly true for the bench press, which in my opinion is the riskiest exercise of all. You can always dump a squat. Sure, you may lose some skin, but people are rarely injured while dumping a squat. What's more, there's no risk in pulling movements, because you can just drop the bar.

The bench press, on the other hand, is a horse of a different color; if you miss a bench press while you're training alone, you're in deep doggy doo-doo. At best, you're going to get a lot of bruises. At worst, it could actually be tragic. With the pins properly situated inside a power rack, however, you can always squeeze out from under a missed attempt. And, as I mentioned before, knowing that you're safe lets you apply greater effort to the

Darin Lannaghan.

lift. I believe I have more guts than most people who train, but I have to admit that I'm reluctant to go for a max attempt or even that extra rep on my back-off set when I'm alone and don't have the benefit of a power rack.

One of the greatest uses of the power rack is for injury rehab. By setting the pins at specific positions, I can direct athletes to do many exercises that wouldn't be possible outside the rack. For instance, when athletes are recovering from any sort of shoulder injury, they usually cannot do full-range bench presses because the bar aggravates the injury when it's lowered past a certain point. By placing the pins just above the range that hurts, which is usually right above the chest, they can perform bench presses. That not only enables them to maintain some degree of shoulder girdle strength, but it helps the healing process because it flushes blood into the damaged area.

The same holds true for pulling and squatting movements. When athletes are com-

ing back from a knee injury, it's imperative that they don't go low in the squat right away. That doesn't mean they can't do squats at all. By setting the pins in the rack above the point where it hurts, they can do partial squats quite safely. This is a much sounder idea than doing partials outside the rack. For one thing, it's often difficult to tell how low you're going on each rep, and there's also the fear of going too low and reinjuring the knee.

Inside the rack, however, lifters are secure. They know exactly when they're going as low as they want to, and they also know that if they experience any discomfort, they can simply dump the bar.

It's extremely important to feel secure when you're rebuilding an injured area. Since you don't have to worry about aggravating the injury, you can apply your full attention to doing the exercise precisely. In some cases, I've even had athletes ride the bar up and down the railings of the rack so they don't have to concern themselves with balance. It's much like doing squats in a Smith machine, which is another point for the rack's versatility.

In that case, even though the athletes are unable to do full squats, they're still way ahead of people who don't do any form of squatting. The partials help strengthen their hips, backs, and quads, as well as flushing blood and healing nutrients into the injured area. What's

Ronnie Coleman.

more, doing something positive to rebuild the injured area puts athletes a step ahead mentally, for they have some degree of control.

Obviously, some muscle groups are neglected when athletes do partials, primarily the adductors and leg biceps. Knowing this, I have them do extra work for those groups in order to maintain some degree of proportionate strength. Stiff-legged deadlifts and good mornings hit the leg biceps nicely, and the adductor machine is the best weapon for strengthening those muscles. In the event that trainees cannot do either stiff-legged deadlifts or good mornings, I have them do lots of work on the leg curl machine.

People can also work around a back injury inside the rack, since it affords a variety of positions. Breaking the bar off the floor may be out of the question, but by setting the pins at a higher level, you can still get in plenty of back work.

Except for those gym mullets who believe racks were designed to hold the bar between sets of curls, most people only use a power rack for squatting. Nevertheless, you can perform a wide range of exercises in a rack. You can do all sorts of pulling and squatting exercises, and if you have an adjustable bench, you can do inclines and seated presses as well as regular flat-bench presses.

Some people prefer to work outside the power rack and use it much like a staircase squat rack, performing their benches, inclines, overhead presses, push presses, shrugs, stiff-legged deadlifts, and good mornings in that manner. Most racks also have a built-in chinning bar. Olympic-style lifters use racks to do heavy supporting exercises, drop snatches, and jerks.

While the power rack is extremely useful for anyone who trains alone, it's an absolute necessity for those who desire greater strength. The reason is that it allows motivated individuals to isolate and identify their weaker areas and bring them up to par—and sometimes way beyond par.

For example, a great many bench pressers have developed the habit of rebounding the bar off their chests. They don't pause with the bar on their chests at all, but kick-start it in

order to move heavier poundages. There are several good reasons not to do this, but I don't want to get off-track. My point is that rebounding the bar vaults it through the middle portion of the lift—that is, until the lifter attempts a max single. In that case, the bar sticks in the middle. The reason is simple, but often overlooked: the muscles that are responsible for driving the bar through the sticking point, in this case the middle range, have been neglected because of the rebounding, so they haven't been strengthened at the same rate as the others used in the lift.

The first step is to identify the weak area in any lift. Until they admit to it, they'll do nothing to correct it. I once trained with an exceptional bencher who couldn't move past 440. He had the problem just described, so I suggested he use the power rack to overcome his weak area, which was obviously the middle. When he was unable to budge 350 off the pins from the middle position, however, he was so embarrassed in front of his buddies

that he never did rack work again. And he never moved past 440.

You can improve a weak area in a variety of ways inside a rack. For the bench press, one method is to set the pins slightly below the weak area and press the bar to arm's length. For the first few weeks, you may do lots of reps just to increase the workload for that range. Then you start lowering the reps and moving the poundage up.

Another technique is to isolate the weak area by positioning two or more pins directly over the bar and start doing isotonic-isometric movements, which are the ultimate strength builders. That's the reason it's essential to have four pins for your rack. You'll eventually need them to do isotonics-isometrics.

The power rack became a part of strength training because of isotonics-isometrics. Doc Zeigler may not have had the very first power rack in the country, since a number of the old-time strongmen like Bob Peoples used some form of rack training, but Doc was the first to

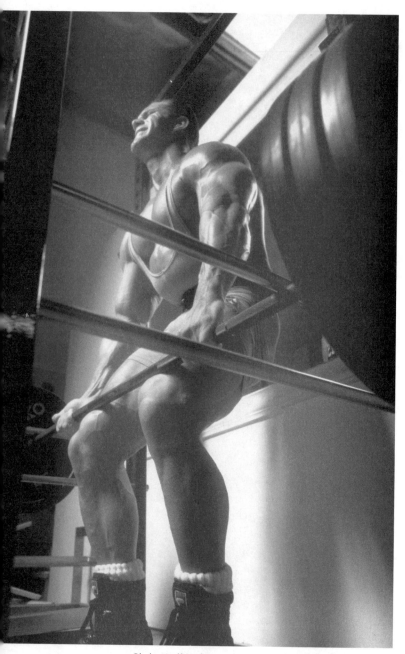

Chris Kadlecek.

marry a program with the rack. Bob Hoffman of York Barbell took all the credit for developing isometric training and all the money from the sales of the racks, but in truth the concepts all came from Doc Zeigler.

He proposed that if lifters could fully contract their muscles and corresponding attachments for a certain period of time, they'd get stronger. Of course, Doc understood that it's

impossible to contract any muscle 100 percent, for that only occurs in fight-or-flight situations. He meant that lifters should try to apply 100 percent effort. Doc's rule of thumb was 8 to 12 seconds, and it was pure isometrics, pushing or pulling against a stationary object.

It's been my observation that very few people can actually know if and when they're applying their full effort against a stationary object, so I suggest using a short isotonic movement prior to locking the bar against the pins for the isometric phase. You do that by moving the loaded barbell a short distance, only a few inches at most—and even less is desirable if the rack lets you set the pins closer. When there's weight on the bar, you know for sure if you're pushing or pulling hard enough, since the bar will either be touching the pins or it won't. There's no guessing.

The time factor is more important than the amount of weight you load on the bar. If you can hold easily for 12 seconds, you should add weight the next time you do the movement. If you can't hold for 8, you need to take some weight off the bar. Admittedly, I often have my athletes hold beyond a 12-count, but that's for my own amusement more than their development.

How many sets and reps? Three total sets at a given position are enough once you find out where your limits are. By that I mean the first few times you try doing this form of exercise, you really don't know how much weight you can handle. So it takes a bit of experimenting—which means the first few times you do isotonics-isometrics you may end up doing 5 or 6 sets. Eventually, however, 3 sets is plenty, for the 2 warm-up sets are only preparing you for 1 work set.

Always do at least 1 warm-up set using a full range of motion before going to the rack. That will ensure you're warmed up sufficiently, which is very important because you'll be going all-out on the isometric movement.

Keeping with the idea of improving the middle portion of your bench press, let's say you're currently benching 315. Do a set of 10 with 135 on the regular bench as a warm-up. Your first set in the rack will be with 185 for 3 reps. On the first two reps, touch the pins but don't hold there. On the third rep, hold the bar against the top pins for a short count of three. That helps you get the feel of what's to come. For your second set, use 225 and do the same drill, touching the top pins twice, then holding the third rep for a short count of three. The third set is the money set, and there's really no way to know how much weight you can handle until you try it.

Nevertheless, assuming that you're weak in the middle, use 255. It's better to use a bit less initially, for, again, the time is more important than the amount of weight on the bar. With 255 you once again touch the top pins twice, but on the third rep you lock it in and hold it for the minimum 8 and maximum 12 count. If you manage to barely hold it for 8, stay with that poundage the next time around. If you hold for 12, you can increase the weight next time.

One work set is enough. This is very concentrated work, and more is not better; it's detrimental. I've seen lifters add two or three more work sets, stating they didn't feel as if the one set did anything. That's a mistake. Zeigler preached that once you've fully contracted any set of muscles for the required length of time, that's all the strength you're going to develop that day.

How often should you do isotonics-isometrics? I believe once a week is enough for most people because the work is so demanding and requires recovery time. Typically, I put them in the program on Friday to allow two days' rest before the Monday session. I've also used this idea by having lifters do just one set after their regular routine for the exercise. I substitute it for the back-off set, for I don't advise doing both. So after completing a bench press routine, you can go inside the rack and do one work set at your weak position. The technique works with a squat or pulling routine as well.

You can also build strength in those hard-to-reach areas, like the deep bottom of a squat or the very top of a pull. Not everyone is interested in doing that, but you can work them inside the rack. Set the pins very low for the squat and high for the pulls. This is one of the very best ways to increase strength on the top of the pull, both for cleaning and snatching. When you do either of those dynamic exercises, the bar stays in the top position for only a very short time—not enough time to make them much stronger—but you can really lean into those groups with an isotonic-isometric movement. It's positively one of the best methods for increasing rear deltoid strength.

Another way you can use the rack to build strength by overloading is to remove the top pins and lift the bar from whatever position you choose to lock out. If you're especially weak in the middle, start from there. If you're weakest at the top, work that position. The lockout position on any lift is typically the strongest, and I use it to let lifters handle extremely heavy weights. That not only enhances structural strength, but it also does wonders for the mind. After 400-pound squatters lock out 800 or 900 pounds, which they can usually do the very first time, the next time they try 400-plus, it feels ridiculously light when they back out of the rack.

If you don't have a rack at your disposal, consider getting one. You can even build one if you're so inclined. During the 1960s, I built and worked out on quite a few homemade racks and got exactly the same results. It's a most versatile piece of equipment, and every gym should have one.

Arnold Schwarzenegger and Franco Columbo.

Chapter 10

TRAINING WITH THE CHAMPIONS

Ironman magazine has enabled its readers to work out with champions for over 60 years. In this chapter, you'll get the insight of pros who have gleaned years of experience through countless workouts and who pass that hard-won information on to you. Learn from these top athletes, and your growth will never get derailed.

First, let's look over the shoulder of Mike Mentzer as he trains Aaron Baker.

MIKE MENTZER TRAINS AARON BAKER T. C. Luoma

During the 1970s, millions of Americans sat down in front of television sets every week as a blind Chinese priest offered the following challenge to his disciple: "When you can snatch the pebble from my hand, it will be time for you to leave." If his disciple, or "Grasshopper," as the priest called him, could perform this feat, he would be ready to leave the monastery and live a spiritual life, which apparently involved kicking the butts of a lot of American Westerners.

Although he's hardly some blind priest in a bathrobe with white eyes like frozen mackerels, Mike Mentzer is a veritable holy man in bodybuilding. He, too, has his disciples, and WBF star Aaron Baker is the latest. Unlike Grasshopper, however, Aaron doesn't have to snatch a pebble from Mike's hand in order to leave the gym. Heck, if he works out hard enough, he can leave in about 45 minutes.

Baker is hardly a beginner, but after 17 years of working out, he'd reached a point where his training was becoming a little stagnant—he wasn't making the same gains as before, and he had actually lost mass. One evening, after his third workout of the day, Aaron was complaining to Mentzer and a friend that he was tired and had lost faith in his current training methods.

"I told Mike about the routine I was following, and without blinking an eye, he said I was overtraining," Aaron remembered. "Then my friend said, 'You should let Mike train you.' It was funny because I had never really thought about it. Here was this virtual gold

Mike Mentzer spots Aaron Baker on the incline press.

mine of information that I had never taken advantage of before. Even though I've been training a long time, I'm not closed-minded, and I hardly think that I know it all. So I was willing to put myself in Mike's hands."

This, to paraphrase Bogart, was the start of a beautiful friendship. What Aaron learned from Mike was to shorten his workouts by about 50 percent and increase the intensity by 100 percent. "The whole philosophy boils down to this one simple statement: You can train long, or you can train hard, but you can't do both successfully," Aaron explained.

What Mike has been preaching since the early '70s is to try to get away from the assumed necessity of always doing more and more sets. He believes that the bigger and stronger a person gets, the more likely it is for that person to overtrain. Not only does he believe that it's more important to shorten the duration of the workout, but he also feels that it's sometimes necessary to get more rest than what's traditionally dictated.

"When I first started training with Mike, we were working a three-days-on/one-day-off routine, but it was a joke because I'd come back after my day off and I'd still be beat up," Baker said. "Now I sometimes take two days off.

"You know, when you tell people that you're only doing a 45-minute workout, they tend to think that you're not working hard and don't deserve two days off, but I'm now doing more work than I used to. In fact, I will match the amount of work I do with anybody. I'll match intensity with anybody. No one can tell me I'm not busting my ass."

Aaron teased us so much about his new workout without telling us how it works, we were beginning to think he was in cahoots with those scientists who claimed they invented a way to produce cold fusion in a test tube but never proved it. He finally relented.

"It's gonna sound just as crazy as it did in the '70s when Mike first came out with this method," Baker explained. "More often than not, I'll only do two for a bodypart. Take chest, for example. Say we're doing incline-bench presses on the machine. With a very light weight, I'll do maybe 20 reps. Then Mike will increase the weight by about 50 percent, and after about a 10-second rest I'll do another maybe 15 to 20 reps. So in effect, I've done 2 back sets, which serves as a warm-up before I get to the meat sets.

"Okay, so I've done my second set, and then Mike really loads up the bar—maybe to about 435 pounds—and I have to do it after only 15 or 20 seconds of rest. I'll do as many

as I can, and I'll rack them up. But after 10 seconds, he'll make me do it again. He'll say, 'Okay, let's get it while it's still hot,' and I'll wanna shout obscenities at him.

"We'll continue that way, with Mike adjusting weights as necessary, and we'll employ any and all advanced techniques such as strip sets, negatives, or whatever it takes to make it more intense, and it'll go on for minutes. It's hard to tell exactly how long it takes, though, because I lose track of time, and I'm hanging off the end of the bench slobbering and moaning and making ugly faces. You can't be cool when you're in the middle of a set like this."

After Smith machine inclines, Mike sometimes has Aaron attack flat-bench dumbbell flyes, and they employ the same sort of gut-wrenching, exert-till-you-squirt, curl-till-you-hurl methods. "I'll do a couple of the same kind of hold-back sets that serve as warm-ups," Aaron continued, "and then I'll do a heavy set using maybe 105-pound dumbbells, and I'll do as many as I can. Then, after a very short rest—say, 10 seconds—I'll do some more. And then, using forced reps and drop sets, I'll continue doing flyes until I've exhausted the muscles."

Other times, they may superset the two movements; that is, after the first two warm-up sets on the incline bench, Aaron immediately does a set of flyes, rests 10 seconds, and then does another set with the big-boy dumbbells. After he goes to complete failure on those, they hustle back over to the incline, which in the meantime Mike has politely loaded up, and Aaron explodes out as many reps as he can. This back-and-forth method continues until Mike thinks Aaron is sufficiently blue in the face.

Aaron summarized the workout as follows: "We've taken what a regular lifter might spend 30 or 40 minutes doing and condensed it down to 10 or 15 minutes. By the time most people have done their fourth set, they're feeling pretty good—their muscles are gorged and they're warm—but imagine feeling that way after one set. Unbelievable!

"When I finish a set, I'm panting, I'm out of breath; and about halfway to the next machine, all of a sudden a sea of blood flows to the area I just worked. It's like, 'Everybody to the chest area,' and—wham!—saturation without warning!"

Aaron and Mike use this type of training on each bodypart. Imagine, however, how a leg workout of this nature would feel. Unfortunately for Baker, he doesn't have to imagine it. "There's snot coming out of my nose, 10 ugly faces crammed into one, and I'm on the floor hyperventilating. Sometimes I feel like I'm gonna pass out, and I haven't felt the luxury of being nauseated while training in a long time."

Although they usually do two movements for larger bodyparts, smaller bodyparts such as triceps or biceps may only get one set each. Shoulders, however, usually get a total of 3 sets: one exercise for each head of the deltoid. Since Aaron and Mike work two bodyparts per workout, an average training session takes about 45 minutes.

Mike Mentzer.

Aaron is quick to point out that contest training differs slightly from off-season training. "When I'm getting ready for a show, I will do quite a few more exercises—mostly isolation-type movements."

Despite the intensity of their workouts, Aaron insists that you have to keep increasing the intensity every time. "If you do what you did last week, it's old muscle doing it. But if you fight to go beyond what you did last week, whether it's a weight increase or a rep increase, it's gonna be new muscle doing that."

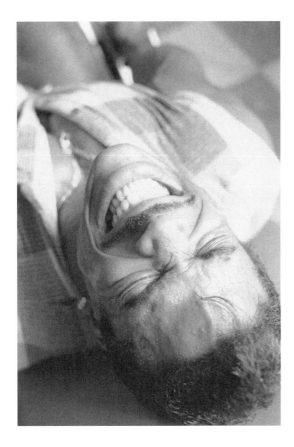

Aaron is obviously exuberant about his newfound training method, but it took a few weeks for his body to become conditioned to this type of training. "In the beginning, I didn't have the capacity to get that explosive in one set—I didn't have the muscle endurance. I had to learn to do it better," he said. "Within a month or so, my ability to jam on 1 set or 2 sets was much greater than it was in the beginning. I had to learn to go through the pain barrier."

Would Aaron recommend this type of training to everyone? "No, you have to be open-minded to it. Some people will just not accept that this could work. You know what I say to them? 'Fine, I'll see you in about 30 pounds.'"

I have a feeling I know what that blind Chinese priest would say to people who aren't open to Mentzer and Baker's training methods. He'd probably say, "Ah, yes, Grasshopper, your mind is like the gym in the silence of the night—it is closed, and all the lights are out."

AARON BAKER'S HIGH-INTENSITY BODY BLITZ

Day 1
Back

Close-grip pulldown	1 set
Seated cable row or	
Hammer machine row	1 set

Traps

Hammer machine shrug	1 set

Chest

Incline barbell press or	
Smith machine incline	1 set
Flat-bench dumbbell flye	1 set

Day 2
Shoulders
Behind-the-neck press or Nautilus press
Superset with
Nautilus lateral   2 sets
Rear delt flye
    (on the pec deck)   1 set

Biceps
Preacher curl or
    Nautilus machine curl   1 set

Triceps
Lat machine
    pushdown or dip on
    seated dip machine   2 sets

Day 3
Calves
Seated calf raise   1 set
Standing calf raise or
    leg press toe raise   1 set
Quads
Squat or leg press   1 set
Leg extension   1 set
Hamstrings
Leg curl   2 sets

Aaron cautioned that none of this routine is "carved in stone"; he often makes changes from workout to workout. Also note that to work his abs, or "biscuits," as he calls them, Aaron prefers doing weighted sit-ups. Although he uses the characteristic Mentzer intensity, every third or fourth day he may not restrict himself to only one set. It depends on what his instincts tell him.

Perhaps no one man in bodybuilding knew more about the sport than the late Vince Gironda. His friend, Gene Mozée, allows us this look inside the knowledgeable mind of the Iron Guru.

VINCE GIRONDA'S TRAINING SECRETS   Gene Mozée

When you talk to bodybuilding champions from the past—superstars like John Grimek, Steve Reeves, Clancy Ross, Bill Pearl, Larry Scott, Robby Robinson, and others too numerous to mention—they all agree that the science of bodybuilding has suffered in the current drug era. Today's bodybuilders have a real shortage of information on the best training techniques and nutrition procedures, and they make up for it by ingesting more steroids, growth hormone, and thyroid drugs than is safe or healthy.

Vince Gironda.

Only through progressive magazines like *Ironman* can today's bodybuilders learn the valuable exercise and nutrition secrets of the great and enduring muscle stars of the past who did it all with scientific training and proper nutrition—without chemicals. Vince Gironda is the most controversial and talked-about bodybuilding trainer in the history of physical culture. In his more than 50 years of practical experience as a competitor, instructor, and gym owner, he's earned the reputation of being an honest, outspoken original. When it comes to bodybuilding, Vince is a nonconformist. He accepts nothing at face value and is constantly striving to improve old concepts and experiment with new ones. Although he's remarkably creative in his thinking, he takes a very scientific approach to bodybuilding. He evaluates each exercise and training principle by the results it produces.

Here, in his own words, are these four pillars of wisdom.

USE POSITIVE VISUALIZATION

Champions obviously possess something that others don't. How often do we see somebody use the same routine—set for set, rep for rep—as the champions, but not get the same results? I've even observed champions training in a manner I don't agree with, but getting phenomenal results. What is it they possess? What do they do that's different?

In my opinion, the answer is that they use mental suggestion, or self-hypnosis. When I first observed this many years ago, it puzzled me. The bodybuilder in question was San Francisco's Walt Baptiste, a former gym owner and the publisher of the now-defunct Body Moderne. Baptiste promoted the early Mr. California physique contests, in which I placed second and third several times. He eventually opened a chain of yoga studios in the Bay Area.

I noticed that Walt would touch his abdominals backstage before going out to pose at physique contests. He seemed to be saying something to his abs as he stroked them, sending a message to them, because I could actually see them sharpen and grow more outlined than they normally were. I later discovered that Walt was actually sending mental images to his subconscious to produce this phenomenon.

I learned that you can actually produce the desired condition by picturing in your mind what you want to happen. Walt also breathed deeply and regularly in through his nose and out through pursed lips. As you may know, many bodybuilders use this type of breathing between sets. The idea is to form a clear image in your mind of the muscle or area of the body you wish to develop, and then hold that image throughout the next set.

The technique of mental suggestion is what all physical culture writers are trying to explain when they throw that nebulous term *concentration* at you. They seem to recognize that concentration is necessary, but they don't know how to trigger the mechanism that produces the phenomenon. The subconscious "believes" anything you perceive and stores it. It accepts what you think or say, if you accept it as the truth. So if you repeat the thought over and over until the subconscious accepts it as fact, it will produce the condition you picture in your mind.

I believe that the champions use this technique, whether or not they're aware of it. They're convinced of a successful outcome, and they get it. This awareness can be more important than any steroid drug, diet plan, supplement, or exercise routine.

FOLLOW MY WEIGHT-GAIN SUGGESTIONS

The great majority of people who have come to my gym over the years are those who need greater bodyweight. Our improved system of training has allowed us here at Vince's Gym to help them gain it. Everyone can build more

solid muscle tissue. Some people take longer, but in the final analysis the results do come. I repeat: everyone can gain.

While it's true that the exercise program is of primary importance, the following hints can help you gain many pounds of solid muscle:

- Drink water during your workout. Drink one pint after each muscle worked, but don't drink out of a fountain, because you swallow air.
- Eat three good, generous meals a day. Even more beneficial, if time permits, is six small meals per day. Include a lot of broiled meats, baked potatoes, stewed fruits, eggs, brown rice, thick soups, stews, nuts, and natural grains. Be sure also to include lots of green and yellow vegetables.
- Drink a pint of certified raw milk in addition to your regular meals at 10 A.M., 2 P.M., 4 P.M., and one hour before bedtime.
- Give your food a chance to digest thoroughly by lying or sitting with your feet propped up on a high footstool after each meal.
- If you take your lunch to work, be aware that the best sandwiches for gaining weight are made with 100-percent whole wheat, such as pumpernickel or rye breads. Ground beef patties, tuna with mayonnaise, turkey, meat loaf, avocado and bacon, peanut butter and bacon, and cream cheese all make excellent high-protein, high-calorie sandwiches.
- It's my observation that 90 percent of trainees who smoke can't gain weight. Consequently, I cannot guarantee that anyone who smokes is going to achieve substantial weight gain.
- Don't miss a workout unless you're ill or it's absolutely imperative. Remember, your whole bodybuilding program is based on regular habits.
- It's essential to get sufficient rest and sleep in order to fully recuperate from your workouts and for muscle growth to occur. I recommend eight to nine hours of sleep each night.

TAKE KELP TO INCREASE YOUR METABOLIC RATE NATURALLY

Bodybuilders have been stimulating their metabolism to help burn fat and increase definition for many years with drugs such as Thyroxin, Cytomel, and Synthroid with sometimes very unpleasant results. These drugs do the job that the thyroid gland should be doing—they replace the natural flow of organic thyroxine—and they're prescribed for patients whose thyroids don't function properly. They can't heal the gland; they can only boost its activity by supplementing its thyroxine output. The thyroid, then, totally shuts down production of thyroxine because it's being supplied by an artificial source. So what do you think happens when lifters stop using these thyroid drugs? Their metabolic rates drop below normal, and fat accumulates rapidly. Based on current data, I firmly believe that there's a decline in our output of thyroxine as we grow older, whether the gland is healthy or not. Therefore, it would appear that a thyroxine precursor—that is, an element that stimulates the production of thyroxine naturally—is highly desirable. Consequently, it's a good idea to add a thyroid-feeding supplement to your diet. Iodine is the only element that will properly nourish the thyroid, and sea kelp is the richest source of iodine.

Modern people live under stressful conditions and are subjected to a greater variety of stresses than were faced by early civilizations. There's an amazing amount of evidence that modern stress subtly causes the metabolism to shift into an unbalanced condition. The thyroid gland, whose primary function is to maintain a balanced metabolism, takes a beating under stress. The number of people on thyroid drugs staggers the imagination. (It's important to note that these dangerous thyroid drugs are usually prescribed only after tests show the thyroid gland is in marked decline, which is often too late.)

I believe the key to a healthy thyroid is supplementing the daily diet with kelp. Understand that I'm talking about iodine that's supplied in food, not synthetic iodine.

Due to its amoebic activity, ocean kelp absorbs all of the ocean's trace minerals and nutrients and locks them in. Tremendous amounts of iodine are stored in this treasure chest of nutrients.

Kelp contains more trace elements and iodine than any land vegetation. During erosion, many of these vital minerals disappear from the soil, leaving some 20 to 24. But there are 44 minerals and trace elements that are believed to be essential for human nutrition, and the ocean—and no other source—contains all 44. Incidentally, the most nutritious salt comes from the sea—it contains all of the essential mineral elements not found in foods that are grown in soil.

The trace minerals have proved highly effective in the treatment of arthritis; bursitis; strained ligaments, tendons, and cartilage; skin dryness and underelasticity; and hair loss. Many cases of infant arthritis have been halted by giving the babies purified seawater—1 to 2 ounces three to four times a day—with results occurring within three to six months.

How can you incorporate these vital elements into your diet—especially that all-important ingredient, iodine? The answer is kelp tablets, which are made from pure, cleaned ocean kelp and sea lettuce powders compressed at low temperatures to maintain all of the naturally occurring elements. The iodine content of kelp is higher than that of any other food.

I recommend that everyone jump on the kelp bandwagon—especially bodybuilders who want their thyroids to function optimally without drugs.

AVOID USELESS TRAINING PRINCIPLES

Once upon a time, some 50 years ago, there was a well-known training system called the "Course Number One." It described "peripheral flushing," which was a popular training method of that era. It was no good then, and it's no good now.

The peripheral flushing system consisted of doing an exercise for one bodypart, then another bodypart, and so on, and was touted as a training approach that would keep you from tiring too quickly. It was supposed to enable you to work for longer periods of time, getting in more sets and reps. Now, isn't that just great? Can you think of a better way to discourage beginning bodybuilders than by telling them that they may someday find themselves able to work out for eight hours a day? The fact is, most of the advanced trainees who come to my gym have planned routines that will definitely work their bodies too hard to make the kind of gains they're looking for. I've had people come to me who were actually doing 50 sets for a muscle—and they wondered why they were not making progress.

I've learned over the years to teach my pupils that there's a fine line between just enough and too much work. Twelve sets per muscle for the advanced bodybuilder is the theme I constantly hammer.

There are three very important elements that you should include in every bodybuilding routine if you want it to be effective: burns, supersets, and pain barrier. It's been my experience that if you want to bring up a hard-to-develop bodypart, 10 sets of 10 repetitions consistently works well. I've known champion bodybuilders who had a lagging bodypart and brought it up to par on this system.

Just ask Dominic Juliano—a physique star who always won the Best Back and Best Chest awards—how well it works. His arms never really responded satisfactorily until he used 10 sets of 10. That brought them into proportion with the rest of his sensational torso.

It's important to remember that you can't do 10 sets of 10 for *every* bodypart—just selected slow-gaining muscles. Unless you concentrate the work where you need it, you'll be doing exactly what the peripheral flushing system advocated—overworking. And speaking of peripheral flushing, isn't it funny how we're impressed by jargon that includes a little pseudoscientific terminology? It sounds so good, people are liable to keep on trying it even after they find out it doesn't work! Remember the "isometric contraction" fiasco of the early

1960s? Some equipment manufacturers sold thousands of "isometric power racks" to a gullible public before this worthless concept was proven false.

No system that advocates overwork is going to accomplish much. In fact, such approaches are the pitfall of most bodybuilders. Remember that fine line between overwork and enough work. One way to get enough work is by concentrating more, using better form, and taking shorter rests between sets. Champs like Arnold Schwarzenegger concentrated so deeply when they trained, they appeared to be in another world. Compare their results with those of men who used the peripheral flushing system—when a 16-inch arm was considered big!

Whenever the debate on "the greatest bodybuilder of all time" comes up, the name Bill Pearl is offered. Such debates can never be definitively settled, but there is much to support the claim that Pearl is the greatest. When Gene Mozée interviewed Pearl, he offered these training routines and tips on how to maximize results.

TRAINING WITH BILL PEARL
Gene Mozée

Bill Pearl stands as a colossus in the world of bodybuilding. From the time he won the Mr. America title in 1953 until he won the Pro Mr. Universe in 1971, he remained in near-peak condition. No other bodybuilder has come close to remaining at the top for that long. He went out a champion of champions, having beaten Sergio Oliva, Frank Zane, Dave Draper, Franco Columbo, Serge Nubret, and Reg Park. Perhaps even more astonishing, he weighed 40 pounds more at the Pro Universe than he had at the Mr. America—with more cuts. In 1971, he was the heaviest, at 242 pounds, and the oldest, at 41, man to ever win the NABBA (National Amateur Bodybuilders' Association) Mr. Universe.

Remember, this was before anabolic steroids ruled the competitive bodybuilding world. Bill was the first to sport more than 230 pounds of hard, muscular mass, and he did it without human growth hormone supplements or any of the other sophisticated drugs that are producing the mass monsters in vogue today. Not only that, but he was on a totally vegetarian diet.

Bill has trained thousands of people at his gyms over the years. He estimates that more than 90 percent of the training queries he has received have to do with building mass. The following is designed for the average bodybuilder who wants to get bigger and stronger as quickly as possible.

Muscle mass is generally associated with power. A big man is considered a strong man—if he has the right kind of weight. For some people, of course, mass is an asset regardless of shape—sumo wrestlers, football linemen, shot-putters. For bodybuilders, however, the object is to build muscle mass without fat.

The following workout routines are designed to increase muscle mass throughout your body and to lay the foundation for developing a complete physique, one without weak points.

Bill Pearl.

Program 1[1]

Dumbbell swing	1 × 10
Bent-knee leg raise	1 × 30
Good morning	1 × 10
Breathing squat[2]	2 × 15
Bent-arm lateral raise[2]	2 × 12
Calf raise	3 × 20
Shrug	2 × 8
Bench press	2 × 8
Row	2 × 8
Behind-the-neck press	2 × 8
Curl	2 × 8
Bent-legged deadlift	3 × 5

[1]Do this workout three times a week with a day of rest between workouts, and follow the program for six weeks.

[2]Alternate sets on the squats and laterals.

Program 2[1]

Dumbbell swing	1 × 10–15
Bent-knee sit-up	1 × 15–20
Dumbbell side bend	1 × 15–20
Alternate leg raise	1 × 10–30

Parallel squat	3–5 × 6–8
Bent-arm pullover	3–5 × 8–10
Calf raise	3 × 15–20
Upright row	2 × 8
Military press	2 × 5–6
One-arm row	3 × 8
Bent-legged deadlift	2 × 8
Incline dumbbell press	2 × 6–8
Bent-arm lateral raise	2 × 6–8
Dumbbell triceps extension	3 × 6–8
Standing dumbbell curl	3 × 6–8

[1]Follow this routine three days a week for six weeks.

Program 3[1]

Bent-knee sit-up	1 × 25
Bent-leg raise	2 × 25
Bench press	5 × 5
Behind-the-neck press	5 × 5
Pulldown to the front	5 × 5
Barbell row	3 × 6
Barbell curl	4 × 6
Barbell triceps extension	4 × 6
Bench squat	5 × 5

[1]Follow this routine three days a week for six weeks.

If you want to gain 25 or more pounds of muscle, start by doing program 1, regardless of how long you've been training. It may be a lot less than you've been doing, but it will give your body a chance to rebuild and prepare your ligaments and tendons for the stress that will be placed on them later. It's important to do these exercises in the exact order presented. You must get a full extension and contraction on every rep. Use lighter weights at first—about two-thirds of your maximum—so you can do the recommended number of reps.

Don't hurry through your sets. Rest for about three minutes between sets. This pace will let you use heavier weights as your stamina improves. Your recuperative power is the true measure of the pace you should maintain. Because of the long rest periods between sets, I suggest that you wear a sweatshirt to keep from cooling off too much.

Keep an accurate record of your training. Record your bodyweight and measurements before you begin this program, and remeasure every six weeks. If, after several weeks, you haven't gained weight, experiment with your calories. Don't expect a big increase in weight in the first week or two, because your system must adjust to the increased workload and expenditure of energy.

TRAINING HINTS

It's very important to breathe correctly when training for mass and power. Do not hold your breath during the hardest part of a lift. Remember to exhale.

Start with a light weight on each exercise, about two-thirds of your maximum. When you can easily do two more reps than the recommended number, add poundage. Keep trying to increase the weight on all exercises as long you can do them with correct form. Always do a full extension and contraction on each rep.

Program 3 focuses on heavy weights. Start with a warm-up set and then use poundages that force you to work very hard. You'll need more rest between sets, but three to five minutes should be adequate.

Sleep and relaxation are very important. While some people may need more sleep and some need less, plan to get at least eight hours of sound sleep. Going to bed at the same time every night helps the body to regulate itself and produce faster muscle growth.

A proper attitude plays a large role in building size and strength. Think positively about all of your daily activities, not just your gym work. A healthy, positive attitude will improve your body and make you a better person.

DIET

It's difficult to recommend a diet that works for everyone. People have differing tastes and finances, and the availability of foods varies from area to area and season to season. Some people are allergic to certain foods. You must choose the foods that work for you, but there are some general guidelines that apply to virtually everyone.

Eat a good breakfast. You'll give your body the fuel it needs to operate efficiently. Start the day with at least 50 grams of protein, plus some fats and carbohydrates.

Eat at regular times and intervals. If you find that three meals a day don't provide enough calories to add muscle size, eat smaller meals—one about every three hours. If you're very underweight, you can make outstanding gains by drinking a quart of milk during your workouts.

If your goal is rapid weight and muscle gain, you need 4,000 to 5,000 calories a day and 150 grams of protein. Try to get most of the protein from food rather than from supplements. A good protein drink or two is useful, but shouldn't replace your regular meals. You should also take vitamins B, C, and E with your meals.

The great English philosopher John Locke wrote, "We are born with faculties and powers capable of almost anything, such as at least would carry us further than can be easily imagined; but it is only the exercise of those powers which gives us ability and skill in anything, and leads us towards perfection." By using your faculties and powers, you can have a more massive and powerful physique. These basic programs provide a proven route to physical perfection.

Want to train alongside a current champion whose physique could make him the next Mr. Olympia? David Prokop was in the gym with Jean-Pierre Fux to learn exactly how he does it.

Jean-Pierre Fux.

IN THE GYM WITH JEAN-PIERRE FUX David Prokop

The man most likely to become bodybuilding's next superstar would seem to be Jean-Pierre Fux (pronounced *fooks*), a blue-eyed, soft-spoken former soccer player from Lucerne, Switzerland.

The 6′, 280-pounds-in-contest-shape 1994 World Amateur Bodybuilding champion made an impressive pro debut in 1996. He finished ninth at the Olympia, in 1997, and in 1998 the

29-year-old placed a respectable seventh, with many believing he should have been higher. As American pro bodybuilder Jeff Poulin has said of Jean-Pierre: "He's more massive than Dorian Yates, and he doesn't have a weak bodypart on his body."

Plus, Jean-Pierre is very serious and intelligent in his approach to training, and he's improving at a remarkable rate. The training

philosophy that has enabled him to achieve that level of development is summarized in these comments from interviews we conducted with him in the weeks before the Olympia, when he was training at Gold's Gym in Venice, California. Jean-Pierre, who, despite his first name, is actually of Swiss-German descent, speaks passable English, but his comments were translated from his native language by his training partner, Daniel Scherrer.

Although we use a lot of variety, the basic approach is to really work very intensely. Only with more and more intensity can you bring your body up from one level to the next. If you always do the same things, just longer, that doesn't give you more muscles. You have to overload the muscle more and more, and that you can do with short workouts, more intensity, not working more. You have to work harder, not longer.

I think the body falls asleep when it knows from one workout to the next what it has to do. For example, if Monday is your chest day, and you always go in and do 2 or 3 sets of bench presses to start, always with the same number of reps, the body gets used to it and your improvement stops.

In our approach, we may do a chest workout a certain way one week, but the next time we come in, we may change the exercises or the order of exercises, change the number of reps, change the angle, change the grip or the foot placement, so it's a whole new situation for the body. We try to surprise the body every time.

If you go to any gym—in Switzerland or here—you'll see people training. A year later, you'll see the same people training the same and looking the same, so nothing has happened. You need the type of approach we use to get better.

Right now, here in California, preparing for the Olympia, our training schedule is a little bit different than it is back home. Since we're in a precontest phase, we're training twice a day, but normally during the off-season we only do one workout per day. We're not doing more weight lifting right now; we just break it up because we do posing every day, which we don't do during the off-season, and we do more cardio work.

Normally, Monday is our leg day—we train quads and calves. Tuesday we train hamstrings, followed by chest and front delts. Wednesday is usually a rest day. Thursday we train back, traps, and rear delts. Friday is a rest day. Saturday we train calves again and arms. Sunday is another day off, so we take three days off. Our training is very intense—not many sets, but most of the time very heavy weight.

We train abdominals only during our contest preparation, not all year long. I think when you're training a lot of other muscles, you're working the abdominals indirectly. I trained my abdominals year-round early in my career, but I think now it's better if I just work them the last 10 to 12 weeks before a contest, using only my own bodyweight.

In the gym where we train at home, we don't have as great a variety of equipment. We don't have 20 different leg machines like they do here at Gold's. I think if we had this gym in Switzerland, my physique would be even better because there's more variety.

But I think there is also a danger here that you could get a little bit lazy just working on machines and forgetting about basic stuff with dumbbells and barbells. So in Switzerland, our training is mainly free weights.

The feeling is not the same when you're using machines. I don't know, maybe it's because more muscle is activated when you're using free weights, since you have to be stable and balance the weight as you're lifting it. I can't get the same feeling out of it if I'm using machines. Not that I'm against machines. There are some machines I like to use, but training has to be, at the least, a mixture of free weights and machines. And in our approach, the bigger part is free weights.

Whenever I come to California, the first week I get very excited about all the machines in the gym. I go from machine to machine. After a week of that, though, I'm back to my old exercises with dumbbells and barbells. I can't get the same out of a heavy set of squats in a machine as I can out of a heavy set of squats with a barbell.

We normally do between 4 and 12 reps when we're using heavy weights, and we may do between 15 and 25 if we're using lighter weights. If we do descending sets, it may be 18 to 20 reps—three times six as we decrease the weight. It can be only one rep if I'm doing deadlifts with a maximum weight, or I may do as many as 100 reps with a light weight to pre-exhaust a muscle before the heavy exercises.

I have a half-hour drive to the gym, so that's when I decide what I want to do. Sometimes I have an idea a few days before, but it's on the way to the gym that I decide what to do that day.

Most of the time, we train with very heavy weights. The most I've used on squats, for example, is 700 pounds for 7 reps. That's deep squats—rock bottom. We do donkey calf raises with 1,300 pounds or more. I've used about 750 pounds in the deadlift. I've done alternate dumbbell curls with 90 pounds, and

200 pounds in the triceps French press behind the head.

Even though I train heavy, I think the form always has to be correct. With the poundages I use, it would be easy to use a lot of body motion and slip into incorrect form, but I always use strict form. Heavy, but correct. That's the key.

We do forced reps but only one or two, maybe three, on the last set of an exercise. If you used a lot of forced reps, I think the body would get overloaded.

Usually for the bigger bodyparts, like legs or back, we'll do 6 to 7 total sets in a workout of 2 to 3 exercises. And for the smaller bodyparts, like arms, we'll do 3 to 4 total sets. Now, we're talking about work sets here; we're not counting warm-up sets. Our approach is quality, not quantity. But as I said, sometimes—just to pre-exhaust or to shock the muscle—we may do 50 to 100 reps with a light weight.

I think our training, which is very high-intensity, basically low sets and short work-outs, and a lot of variety, has a lot to do with the mass I've achieved. The genetics is also a part of it, because someone who is very skinny maybe cannot get so big. But I think our training approach is responsible for most of the mass.

You cannot go high-intensity all year around. You get too tired. So we go 12 weeks on a heavy cycle, using the approach I've described, and then we go on a lighter cycle, maybe three or four weeks, to recuperate. During this time, we do what we call a fitness workout, which is a whole-body routine done three times a week with more reps and lighter weights. We do one exercise per bodypart, and we don't go to our limit. After a few weeks of this, your body is hungry to get back to hard training, and we start in again with a heavy phase.

Ronnie Coleman.

Chapter 11

TRICKS AND SECRETS TO BOOST GROWTH

Here is where Ironman *magazine is worth its weight in muscle. When a bodybuilder spends decades in the gym performing thousands of workouts, he tends to learn tricks and secrets that improve his progress. Just as important, he learns what mistakes thwarted his progress. Taken together, these tips can save you years of unproductive workouts and virtually guarantee you success with every workout. Pay close attention to this chapter, and your progress will rocket ahead of those in the gym who are still using trial and error.*

SEVEN SECRETS THAT PACK ON POUNDS OF MUSCLE Ron J. Clark

Sorry, I lied. No real secrets here. The topic of how to increase size and strength has been beaten to death so severely that it takes an extreme approach to get your attention. Secrets are like quick fixes, and everybody wants a quick fix—even me.

Aside from anabolics, however, there really aren't any shortcuts to building size and strength. These qualities are best achieved through consistent application of the funda-

mental principles of training and diet. And you're in luck, because that's just what this article is about.

To begin with, there are no mysteries or secrets. The information I am about to reveal is not available at the great low price of only $29.95, as so many secret training and supplement programs are these days. Why not? Because everyone thinks that he or she already knows the basic facts of size and strength increase. Consequently, my manual wouldn't sell, and I wouldn't be able to make the payments on my new sports car. Don't be a schmuck and fall prey to these gimmicks. Read this article. At least it's free, and you'll probably learn something, too.

If you are confused about your approach to size and strength training, which most people are, keep this information close at hand. Anything or anybody that contradicts the principles outlined here is wrong and should be ignored—I don't care who it is who disagrees.

While this may seem pretty cocky, it's not, really. This information is based strictly on science and muscle physiology applied to resistance exercise.

USE THE RIGHT ROUTINE

Split the major muscle groups into three to four workouts, and train about five days per week. Since we are talking basics here, break up your major bodyparts any way you see fit. Do abs, calves, and forearms randomly, and try to split up the total mass of tissue equally among your workouts.

USE THE RIGHT EXERCISES—HEAVY, BASIC COMPOUND MOVEMENTS

Always select movements that allow you to stress the target muscle with as much resistance as possible in its strongest position of leverage. For example, if you're working chest, flat-bench presses with 250 pounds will be more effective for size and strength than

dumbbell flyes with 40 pounds. For triceps, between-bench dips with 200 pounds will be more effective than triceps pushdowns with 80 pounds.

Although kinesiology is an exact science, "gym jock kinesiologists" sometimes take it a bit too far. You typically hear comments like, "There's too much chest involvement in that triceps movement," or "There's too much shoulder involvement in that biceps exercise." If a target muscle group can move a greater amount of net weight with the less-than-maximum assistance of another muscle group, is there really that much harm done? That's what compound movements are all about, and they offer target muscle groups what is indisputably the greatest growth potential. Furthermore, it is physiologically impossible to isolate a muscle group, even if you want to—which you don't, because the closer you come to isolating a target muscle group, the less growth-stimulating resistance those target muscles can withstand prior to failing. With this in mind, you should avoid partial isolation

movements such as triceps kickbacks, concentration curls, cable crossovers, and flat-bench flyes while training for size and strength.

The notion that you can "shape" a muscle group through extreme variation in movements during a single workout is a crock, disproved by the scientific principles of innervation. A muscle group's shape is strictly genetic. The idea that you can stimulate further growth by selecting a variety of movements from workout to workout is also a crock, but this type of variation will at least alleviate boredom and call on fresh new nerve pathways, rejuvenating your workouts. If and when you do use variation in exercises, always alternate basic heavy and compound movements. Flat-bench presses, incline presses, deadlifts, barbell rows, T-bar rows, pulldowns, close-grip cable rows, barbell curls, between-bench dips, squats, leg presses, upright rows, military presses, and shrugs are key movements to include.

CHOOSE BODYPART SET TOTALS WISELY

When you are determining the number of sets for each muscle group, take into account the size of the group. The smaller the target muscle group, the fewer the number of sets you should perform; the larger the target muscle group, the greater the number of sets. Here are a few rough guidelines: biceps, 4 to 5 sets; triceps, 5 to 6 sets; shoulders, 6 to 8 sets; chest, 7 to 9 sets; back, 8 to 10 sets; thighs, 10 to 12 sets.

Intensity is the all-important factor. It is only by using maximum intensity that you can justify performing so few sets. Don't wimp out and cheat yourself. Also, short, intense training sessions provide "leftover" recovery energy that will start building tissue right after your workout. This is a must. Almost all of the resistance athletes I know drag themselves out of the gym after an overexhaustive workout thinking they are superheroes, but in reality they are cheating themselves out of better gains.

The bench press is a compound movement.   John Terilli.

Gay Francois.

Take adequate time to recover before returning to the gym.   Eddie Robinson.

USE THE CORRECT NUMBER OF REPS

Take every set except warm-ups to absolute, positive failure in strict form with continuous tension through both the negative and positive parts of the rep. Training heavy with low reps will ensure the earliest possible recruitment of the motor units that have the greatest potential for growth. Intensity is once again the most important factor. Without it, it doesn't matter how many reps you do or how much weight you use—you'll never get anywhere. Do 4 to 6 reps to failure, with the possible exception of going slightly lighter on extension movements to prevent injury. Also, avoid the pump like the plague.

If, after a long period of strict, productive, heavy training, you hit a plateau, try adding a set of 12 to 15 reps to absolute, positive failure. This will optimize the involvement of other motor units and, most importantly, other cellular components. Never replace intense, heavy, low-rep training with higher-rep sets, however; just add them to your routine.

We all have different proportions of motor units and cellular components. Some of us are at a genetic advantage because we have a greater proportion of the right types of these elements, so we respond to size and strength training more readily.

ALLOW FOR COMPLETE RECOVERY

You must rest between sets as long as it takes you to be able to get out the same number of reps in every set of every movement while training to absolute, positive failure at maximum intensity. Each rep you lose by training too fast cheats the target muscle out of growth stimulation. When in doubt, wait longer. It's also of paramount importance to extend the recovery period between workouts. For one thing, if your metabolic rate is fairly slow, then your recovery time will be equally slow and you will require extended recovery periods.

If some of these suggested set totals bother you, I should point out that one intense set taken to absolute failure is more valuable for generating size and strength than performing 10 less-than-intense sets taken to less-than-absolute failure.

Once again, the greater the intensity, the greater the stimulation or damage. And the greater the damage, the longer the healing process. For example, after subjecting your chest to incredible punishment, give it three to four days' rest—maybe more. You are always better off to undertrain slightly than to overtrain.

USE A SIZE-AND-STRENGTH DIET

Eat every three to four hours, and ingest a considerable amount of complete protein at each meal. Take in enough carbohydrates to fuel your energy needs and then some, but keep your fat intake to a minimum. The nutrient percentage in a weight-gain diet should be about 30 percent protein, 60 percent carbohydrate, and 10 percent fat. As for total calories, when in doubt, eat more. Use high-calorie protein and carb-load drinks as a source of additional calories. Instead of guessing or trying to calculate total calories, purchase skin-fold calipers to intermittently check your own bodyfat percentage. Maintain a fairly strict high-calorie intake; and if your diet is producing more fat weight than is desired, slowly reduce your fat and carbohydrate intakes; or better yet, increase your low-level activity expenditures. It is always better to increase activity than to decrease total calories.

TRAIN CAUTIOUSLY

Performing exclusively heavy training is not without risks. Such heavy training strengthens soft muscle tissue more than it strengthens hard tissue like tendons and ligaments. This results in an increased tension on the tendons of insertion, possibly leading to an acute tearing of the tendon from the bone. Strict concentration and continuous tension are your best weapons against serious injury. Also, from time to time you should consider performing a few high-rep sets to strengthen the hard tissue and improve fluid movement in and around the joints. This will assist in preventing injuries that are commonly associated with heavy training. Moreover, an injury is most likely to occur in the first repetition of a set rather than toward the end of a set because your rep speed slows as your muscles become fatigued, gradually reducing the intensity of the contractions.

That's it. Cut this out and use common sense in implementing these principles into your size-and-strength diet and training program.

Joe Spinello.

Before you let your newfound enthusiasm get the best of you, read what Eliot Jordan says on the subject of overtraining. Follow this excellent advice and you'll build up instead of burning out.

BUILD UP—DON'T BURN OUT
Eliot Jordan

Arthur Jones used to say that the major mistake most bodybuilders make is overtraining. Jones, the inventor of Nautilus exercise equipment, never developed a massive physique—but his bank account would have impressed even Arnold Schwarzenegger. Jones hypothesized through what he called "self-evident logic" that the human body has a finite recovery ability from exercise and that if a bodybuilder exceeds his or her recovery ability, muscle gains will screech to a halt.

Mike Mentzer later echoed Jones's theories about recovery ability. He also espoused Jones's recommended training methods, which consisted of high-intensity, short workouts. Mentzer appropriately called his system of training "Heavy Duty."

Dorian Yates feels that the reason why many bodybuilders fail to make regular gains is that they simply do too much. For example, Yates's chest routine consists of 6 heavy sets—and that's a total, not per exercise—whereas most bodybuilders do upward of 15 to 20 sets for chest as well as other bodyparts.

When you first begin training, just about anything you do will make you stronger. This is because initial gains result more from nervous system accommodation than actual muscular size increases. As your muscles do begin to show changes, however, it's a natural impulse to want to do more exercise. Unfortunately, more is not always better.

Beginners often lapse into overtraining because of what they read in the bodybuilding magazines. They read about a champion's workout and try to duplicate that same routine. Even if the listed routine is accurate, most top bodybuilders have been training for several years and thus have developed a tolerance for a large volume of training. A novice attempting to use a similar routine will only lose muscle, because his or her body isn't ready for that much training.

Does this mean that Jones, Mentzer, and Yates are right? Is intensity more effective than sheer volume for producing rapid muscular gains?

While it is vital to making gains at all levels of training, intensity is a relative commodity. When Mentzer and Yates train, they go to failure on every set. Many bodybuilders think they are training hard, but actually stop a set long before they reach a point of failure. These trainees will make only small gains, because one or two sets not worked to failure is just one or two plain sets. For many people, this isn't enough to produce size increases.

Then you have those who claim that you can't become overtrained no matter how much you work out. Some of them do, in fact, train with weights for several hours each day and seem to make gains. It could be that these people have developed a high tolerance for excessive exercise. More likely, however, they use substances such as anabolic steroids that artificially increase exercise tolerance and recovery—at least temporarily.

If you don't want to use steroids but you do want to avoid the effects of overtraining, you must consider stress and its effects on your system.

THE STRESS FACTOR

Former Mr. Universe Mike Mentzer liked to use the development of a skin callus as a metaphor for the effects of overtraining. He pointed out that if you rub a piece of your skin regularly with a certain firmness, a callus will form, but if you rub the area too much, the callus will disappear.

Exercise is a form of stress, albeit a potentially beneficial form. Without applied stress, such as training, the body has no reason to adapt. You have to push it to change. According to Dr. Hans Selye's general adaption syndrome, the body reacts to stress in three stages:

Alarm

This is where the body recognizes and begins to make changes to account for a stress factor.

Resistance

Here the body adapts to stress by making changes. For example, when you apply stress to a muscle through resistance exercise, the body adapts by increasing the size of the muscle to deal with increased weight loads.

Exhaustion

This occurs when the body is overwhelmed by stress and can't accommodate in time— roughly what occurs with chronic overtraining.

The trick, then, is to apply stress, or exercise, without overwhelming your body's recovery ability.

CAUSES OF OVERTRAINING

Knowing what causes overtraining allows you to recognize when you're falling prey to the syndrome. The following situations can lead to problems:

Frank Zane.

- **Sudden increase in the amount of training.** If you add too many sets or increase the frequency of your workouts too quickly, your body may fail to adapt in time. This leads to a catabolic, over-trained condition.
- **Not enough recovery.** Many competitive bodybuilders train twice a day, believing that this method maximizes limited energy stores. If you haven't recovered from the first workout, however, you can quickly slip into a chronic over-trained state.

- **Monotonous training routines.** This is a more subtle form of overtraining in which your nervous system adapts to training and fails to stimulate growth. Some bodybuilders make the opposite mistake of changing their exercises too often. By doing this, they fail to overload the muscle through the gradual weight progression that comes from adding poundage to the same exercises.

You don't need to change your exercises at every workout, but it's a good idea to vary the weights, repetitions, and sets that you use. This keeps you motivated, because no two workouts are exactly alike. You go by the way you feel that day. If you feel strong, train heavier. If you feel off, train lighter and use higher repetitions. This means you must heed your body's signals. Be honest about it; don't cheat yourself by being lazy.

Some signs of overtraining include a lack of motivation, anxiety, depression, fatigue, and the inability to concentrate. In other words, your get-up-and-go feels like it got up and went.

You may also notice a loss of muscle. What happens here is probably this: When you train intensely, you increase the blood testosterone levels. Since testosterone is an anabolic hormone, it promotes muscular growth. If you overdo the training, however, catabolic hormones such as cortisol, which breaks down muscle tissue, predominate over the testosterone. In addition, since the body secretes excessive cortisol under stress conditions, if you don't overtrain, the body compensates for the increased cortisol by increasing testosterone secretion.

Some researchers suggest that a short period of overtraining may even be beneficial for overcoming sticking points. They theorize that the body becomes more sensitive to testosterone after overtraining ends, and a rebound effect occurs. This translates into increased muscular growth. Many bodybuilders commonly observe increased growth after a short layoff from hard training. The rebound effect theory may explain this phenomenon.

Craig Licker.

Does this mean that you should purposely overtrain to foster muscle growth? The problem here is in gauging exactly how much overtraining is necessary to get out of a rut. A good method is to occasionally increase the volume of your training for a short time and then return to your usual number of sets, reps, and exercises. You must listen to your body, however. Too much of this may do more harm than good.

Not following a proper diet causes another type of overtraining. If you don't supply your body with the nutrients it needs, you won't recover properly between workouts. For example, consider what happens when you don't eat enough carbohydrates. Your body needs carbohydrates to synthesize muscle glycogen, the main source of energy for anaerobic weight training. Without glycogen, your body can't repair the microdamage that your muscles incur every time you train. Within a short time, you feel the effects of chronic unrepaired muscle damage. In short, you lose muscle.

Not getting enough protein can cause an overtrained condition, although this is admittedly rare among protein-conscious bodybuilders. About the only time you may slip into a negative nitrogen balance is when your caloric intake is too low or if you're not eating sufficient carbohydrates. Hard-training bodybuilders definitely need more protein, although exactly how much is still a matter of guesswork. Some experts suggest that 1.7 grams of protein per kilogram (2.2 pounds) of bodyweight should cover all needs.

HOW TO AVOID OVERTRAINING

The best way to avoid overtraining is to vary your workouts. Many experts suggest using a periodization program: this means dividing your training year into sections that emphasize different goals. For example, the first three months may be a conditioning period in which you lift lighter weights and do higher reps to prepare your body for the later, heavier training.

The next phase may be a moderately heavy period in which you use weights that allow for a repetition range of 8 to 12 and you gradually increase the poundages you lift. Next may be a power/size phase in which you train as heavy as possible using a rep range of 6 to 8. From there, you can slip into a precontest mode in which you again switch to moderately heavy weights while increasing aerobic exercise.

This type of training system is ideal for people who want to make maximum muscular gains without using drugs such as anabolic steroids. Periodization, which is also called *cycle training*, works because it allows you to train hard while promoting recovery. The inherent variety in the system also forestalls staleness because you continually change the focus of your training.

Many champion bodybuilders use a variation on the periodization concept by training heavy at the first workout, then lighter at the next workout for the same muscle. They use this technique mostly to prevent injuries that may occur through constant heavy lifting, especially before a contest.

Rome wasn't built in a day, and neither is your body. You must allow adequate rest time.

It's a bodybuilding truism that your body doesn't grow during training; it grows when you rest. This means not just resting between workouts, but also getting sufficient sleep at night.

You must also heed the signals your body sends. If you feel excessively sore or fatigued, it may be telling you that you overdid it and that you are not sufficiently recovered from the last workout. When that happens, take a day off and let your body recover. Eat plenty of complex carbohydrates, such as whole grains, pasta, and vegetables, to supply your body with the fuel it needs both to power hard workouts and to help you recover from them.

Since everyone responds differently to exercise, some people can make good gains on more exercise than others can handle. Only you can find the amount of exercise that will allow you to reach your bodybuilding goals. Forget how much training Lee Haney or Gary Strydom does. Instead, observe your own progress and make adjustments or cutbacks as needed to avoid slipping into overtraining.

In bodybuilding, avoiding the wrong things is just as important as doing the right things; one big mistake can short-circuit all progress. Jerry Brainum gives us book, chapter, and verse, on common mistakes to avoid.

COMMON BODYBUILDING MISTAKES TO AVOID Jerry Brainum

> It's not a fool who makes a mistake; it's a fool who makes a mistake twice.
> —Chinese proverb

Many bodybuilders make the same mistakes repeatedly. They aren't fools, as the proverb at the beginning of this article might suggest; they just don't know any better. You'd think that with all the available information on training in books, courses, videotapes, magazines, and from private trainers today, few people would err so often—but they do.

These errors stem from a common origin: ignorance. Often, it's a case of the blind lead-

ing the blind. Some people, for example, are trained by self-styled experts who call themselves personal trainers. I've seen dozens of people hire a personal trainer, train with him or her for two months, and then start their own personal training business. Such people are under the vastly mistaken impression that you can learn everything you need to know about exercise in two months.

Other sources of information are inaccurate. I once interviewed a top professional bodybuilder, who then was interviewed by two other writers within a two-day period. He told each of us a totally different version of how he trains. When questioned about this,

he replied, "Why should I tell my competitors what I'm really doing?" Most bodybuilders aren't reticent about revealing their true training/dieting methods, but some are as insecure as this fellow.

The problem is that many people believe the hogwash handed out in some magazine articles. The person who ends up in trouble is the hapless bodybuilder who tries to follow some of this poor advice.

Here, then, is a partial survey of common mistakes made by many bodybuilders. Since these mistakes often stem from false beliefs, I hope this article will serve to enlighten those lost in the mire of bodybuilding falsehoods.

GENERAL TRAINING ERRORS

Using too much weight

It's true that muscles grow in response to over-load; that is, to make a muscle larger, you must gradually increase resistance until a muscle adapts to the resistance through added size. Some bodybuilders take this truth too far, however. They sacrifice proper form for sheer weight. Very often, this removes stress from the targeted muscle and disperses it to assist-ing muscles, thus reducing the benefits.

In barbell curls, for example, some body-builders cheat by throwing the weight. This removes resistance from the targeted muscle (biceps) and deflects it to the lower back and shoulders. By lowering direct resistance to the biceps, you nullify the benefit of added weight and increase injury potential.

Overtraining

Contrary to what some people think, the human body has a finite ability to recover from intense training sessions. Some aspects of recovery, such as muscle glycogen repletion, can take 48 hours. If you train a muscle before its glycogen supply is replenished, you risk damage to the muscle and loss of muscle size. To paraphrase an old wine commercial, "Never train a muscle before its time."

What constitutes overtraining, however, varies with training experience. Arthur Jones, inventor of the Nautilus machines, was a bit dogmatic about what he called the "recovery factor." He claimed that no one needs to do more than 2 sets of any exercise. Later, his fol-lower, Mike Mentzer, a former Mr. Universe, echoed similar training ideas. The problem

Chronic overtraining leads to chronic fatigue.

Art Dilkes.

was that Jones and Mentzer were too narrow in their estimate of recovery ability. In essence, some people have better recovery ability than others.

There is a limit, though. The only way to find your personal tolerance is through experimentation. If you feel burned out and tired, you obviously are overtrained. By cutting back on your training, you'll experience a new surge of both gains and enthusiasm.

Following someone else's routine

No two people are exactly alike; therefore, no training program is ideal for everyone. You must make adjustments for your body. Back in the early '70s, I watched Arnold Schwarzenegger go through dozens of training partners. Arnold would train with anyone in those days, the only requirement being the other person use his routine. Arnold constantly improved, especially before a contest; but many of his training partners didn't fare as

Sandy Riddell.

Franco Santoriello.

well. Their mistake was in believing that training exactly like Arnold produces similar results. Such a system would work only if Arnold had an identical twin (sounds like a good movie idea!).

This doesn't mean that you should completely eschew training partners; it means that you must make adjustments necessary for your body and not blindly follow someone else's exact routine.

Midsection mistakes

Probably the most frequent training mistakes occur with abdominal training. Twenty years ago, bodybuilders did hundreds of reps of ab work in the belief that high reps burned fat. What they were burning was calories; they could have obtained better results from aerobics, since spot reducing proved to be a false idea. Today we know that the body burns fat systemically, not just in one specified area.

Surprisingly, many people still do abdominal work to "reduce the gut." Abdominal exercise does tone the waist area, but losing fat is largely a matter of combining fewer calories with aerobic exercise. Aerobic exercise is a superior fat burner because it uses large muscle groups (such as the legs) that burn larger amounts of calories. Because of the characteristic high oxygen intake associated with aerobics, this type of exercise is also the most direct fat burner.

While many abdominal exercises aren't harmful, some are ineffective. This relates to the function of the abdominals, which is to shorten the distance between the sternum and the pelvic bones. It's a limited range of motion. The clearest example of this is the crunch, or partial sit-up. If you go past the crunch, you are no longer training abs; you are training the deep hip flexor muscles.

Most abdominal exercises are actually hip flexor exercises. An example of this is knee raises, in which you hang from an overhead bar and bring your bent knees up toward your chest. The only way to involve the abs in this exercise is to curve your torso and bring your knees up to your face. The way most bodybuilders do this exercise does little or nothing to develop impressive abs.

Regular leg raises are also a hip flexor exercise, but have the added disadvantage of causing an inward curvature of the lower back (lordosis) that aggravates lower-back problems.

You may say at this point, "But why do I feel these exercises so strongly in my abdominals?" The answer is that the abdominals remain under tension when you're doing these exercises, but the muscle doesn't fully contract—so the exercise has little or no value. Imagine holding a barbell in a curling position but not moving the weight. You would definitely feel muscle tension, but would you get big biceps from such training?

Chest training mistakes

The common error here is doing too many bench presses and neglecting the upper-pectoral area. In most people, the lower pecs are easy to build, especially by doing lots of bench presses. But after doing only flat-bench work, you'll develop an imbalance between the upper and lower pecs, with a noticeable lack of muscle density in the upper area.

You can do bench presses, but make sure you include more upper-pec exercises, such as incline presses and incline flyes. Doing bench presses to the neck is also great for thickening a deficient upper chest.

Shoulder training

While various types of shoulder press exercises help to thicken the shoulders, they do little to improve the shape in this area. For this, you need to do side laterals and rear laterals. Many bodybuilders frequently neglect the rear deltoid, which results in a lopsided, unbalanced deltoid development that looks especially bad from side and back angles.

Usually, doing more than one pressing exercise during a shoulder routine is wasted effort. Top professional bodybuilder Vince Comerford succinctly points out why he does only one pressing exercise for shoulders: "Why travel down the same street twice." All pressing exercises concentrate mainly on the front deltoid, so why do two or three press exercises when they all work the same area?

Back mistakes

The problems here involve poor form and incomplete range of exercise motion. In bent-over rowing exercises, it's common to see excessive body motion, or throwing the weight. This places excessive strain on the lower back that often results in serious injury.

Another problem is not doing a full contraction. Many bodybuilders like to use a 150-pound dumbbell for one-arm rows and raise the weight about four inches. Then they wonder why they lack back development. Take a hint from Lee Haney, who uses only a 75-pound dumbbell in one-arm rows, yet has developed one of the most impressive backs in bodybuilding history. He goes all the way up.

Michael Francois.

Thigh training

When doing squats, some bodybuilders drop down too fast and bounce on their knees. This inevitably leads to damaged knees. Research shows that squats don't harm knee joints unless you use poor form. Do the exercise slow and controlled for best results.

If you do leg extensions, start the exercise with your knees in a 90-degree angle to your feet. Any more than this hyperextends the

knee joint, which lacks protection at this angle. Doing leg extensions in poor form is just as dangerous as doing squats in poor form.

Calf training

When doing standing calf raises, always keep your knee joint locked. Doing this exercise with bent knees shifts the focus from calves to the large, flat muscle lying beneath the calves (soleus). It's better to reserve the soleus work for exercises such as seated calf raises.

Arm training

The primary error with arm training is excessive cheating and failure to do a complete range of motion. Make sure you do full reps, and lower the weight all the way for full muscle development.

With triceps training, it's important to warm up the elbow joint with a few light, high-rep (15 repetitions or more) sets to prevent injuries.

This list is by no means exhaustive, but it does point out a few common errors that could slow down gains.

"Going to failure" is such blanket advice in bodybuilding that it is bound to be misunderstood and misapplied. In this article, I tried to shed some perspective on the value of "failure" as a means to ensure intensity and its misuse by those who believe it is the only element necessary for success.

IS FAILURE NECESSARY?
Peter Sisco

Over the past 20 years, a great deal has been written about going to failure on weightlifting exercises. In our Power Factor books and audiotapes, John Little and I advise trainees to work to failure to ensure growth stimulation. As with every other aspect of bodybuilding, however, the concept of failure is one that has fallen victim to misapplication, misunderstanding, and faulty logic. Used properly, failure can be a constructive tool;

Chris Duffy.

John Terilli.

however, there's no valid reason for the near-mythic importance it's given by some body-builders, who believe that they cannot make progress unless they train to failure. In fact, exercising to momentary muscular failure is not—and never has been—a requirement for stimulating muscle growth.

Failure refers to performing a set until you are unable to complete one more rep; in other words, despite all effort, you fail to complete the last rep. The fact is, outside of a gym there's virtually no human activity that involves going to failure.

For example, a person who makes his living by digging with a shovel would never dig until he could not lift one more shovelful of dirt, nor would he swing a pickax until he couldn't lift it one more time. Yet people who perform such manual labor can develop tremendous muscularity. Similarly, sprinters often develop formidable hamstring and quadriceps muscles compared to the nominal muscularity of distance runners. This occurs because sprinting requires a great amount of muscular work in a unit of time. But who sprints to failure?

Indeed, you might find weight lifters in your gym who have made great gains in size and strength without ever training to failure. Those people are able to stimulate new muscle growth, so how can anyone say that failure is an indispensable requirement for growth? All the evidence goes against that assertion.

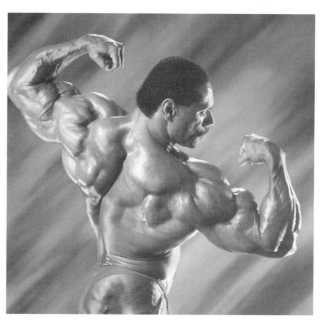

Mike Christian.

Michael Ashley.

Don Long.

The human body operates with very complex mechanisms that are always taking variables into account. In a normal day, your body adjusts to accept X amount of sunshine, Y amount of temperature variation, Z amount of humidity, and so on for hundreds of different environmental and biological factors. For every variable, the body makes calculations and adjustments in terms of blood viscosity, hormone levels, degree of skin tanning, and muscle growth. If, on average, you're exposed to the

same amount of sunlight every day of the year, your skin will darken to the point at which it has sufficient protection from that average level of sunlight—but no more. Similarly, if you lift weights on a regular basis using the same amount of intensity at every workout, your muscles will develop to a point at which they can comfortably handle that intensity without unduly depleting your body's resources.

In order to increase the thickness, or viscosity, of your blood, it's not necessary to subject your body to the absolute coldest temperature that it can stand before you lose consciousness. By the same token, if you want to increase the darkness of your tan, it isn't necessary to subject your skin to the most intense sunlight it can stand without blistering. Muscle-growth stimulation also operates on this principle. It's not necessary to operate a muscle to its absolute limit of failure in order to stimulate new growth.

You may have seen a new product on the market for sunbathers that uses a wristwatch-type device to monitor and measure the intensity of sunlight and compare that intensity to user-provided information like the color of your skin and the SPF of the sunscreen you're using. The device calculates the safe interval of sun intensity and sounds an alarm when you reach those limits. Bodybuilders would greatly benefit from the same type of device if it could be adapted to measure the intensity of muscular output.

Suppose at the end of the day the device indicated that your average muscular output was 100 pounds per minute. Let's call that your baseline muscular intensity. If every day for the next six months you engaged in an amount of muscular activity that caused the device to register an average of 100 pounds per minute, you wouldn't increase your muscle mass, because there would be no reason for your body to grow new muscle. Now, suppose that each day you engaged in an amount of muscular activity that caused the average intensity to rise by 5 percent; for example, 100, 105, 110, 116, 122, and so on. At the end of 30 days, if you could sustain such a steady increase in your average muscular intensity, your wrist monitor would indicate an average of 412 pounds per minute. In order to safely cope with 412 pounds per minute of muscular output, your body would have to make itself substantially more muscular than it has to be to cope with 100 pounds per minute.

Using the principles of Power Factor training, a method based on partials, if you were to construct a month's worth of bench press routines, you could begin by establishing baseline Power Factor and Power Index numbers, which represent a measurement of the

muscular intensity you're capable of generating in that exercise. You could then design a number of workouts for the next month that would always require you to use an intensity that was 5 percent higher than what you used at the last session.

That's all you'd need. You wouldn't have to go to failure. You wouldn't have to perform four different exercises in addition to the bench press, or periodize your workouts by including several workouts at 20 to 30 percent below your baseline intensity. You wouldn't have to stop all aerobic exercise for a month or train three days per week. You'd only have to increase the intensity of the bench press on a workout-to-workout basis.

SO WHAT GOOD IS GOING TO FAILURE?

While failure is a crude gauge, it can be an effective tool for finding your baseline intensity. For example, if you're performing 3 sets of 15 reps with 200 pounds and on your first set you do 15, on your second set you perform

Ron Coleman.

15, and on your third—to failure—you do 25 reps, you have a good indication that your first two sets were at submaximal intensity and that you should be using a heavier weight or more reps.

Furthermore, if you're seriously overtrained, you'll reach failure at a point lower than the progressive intensity you require in order to stimulate new muscle growth. For example, suppose you start with a baseline intensity of 100 pounds per minute, and a few sessions later your intensity is 160 pounds per minute on the same exercise. At that point you become overtrained, and the next time you're in the gym, you go to failure at 140 pounds per minute. There's no possible way that weight can stimulate new muscle growth, despite the fact that you went to failure. Why? Because going to failure is not a requirement for muscle-growth stimulation.

To exaggerate the point, consider what happens to your strength when you're recovering from a serious bout of flu. You can return to the gym and take every set to failure, but the intensity will be so low that it cannot stimulate new growth. That's the reason some people can train to failure on every exercise month after month and never show any sign of progress, even though they're convinced they're going all out and delivering 100 percent of momentary muscular effort. What matters is a tangible progression of overload intensity.

IS THE LAST REP THE MOST PRODUCTIVE?

Advocates of training to failure, particularly those who adhere to the Arthur Jones model of performing only one set, believe that the last rep is the most productive rep of the set. As the rationale goes, the first rep takes very little of your effort; then the second, third, and fourth take correspondingly more effort until you reach that last rep, which requires all the effort you can muster and still cannot be completed. Many people believe that this most difficult rep is the one that triggers muscle-growth stimulation. As we have already discussed, however, it's the progressive increase in intensity that trig-

gers muscle growth; and since you can accomplish that increase without ever going to failure, the last rep, which is described as being impossible to complete, can be entirely unnecessary.

For example, if you reach the required increase in intensity at the sixth rep of that set, then the sixth rep is the one that triggers growth, and anything beyond that is not even necessary. If you have a baseline intensity of 100 pounds per minute and you've set an intensity goal of 110 pounds per minute, then the moment you reach 110 pounds per minute of intensity, you can stop the exercise, even if you've completed only 5½ reps. The number of reps is irrelevant; failure is irrelevant. The only relevant factor is the amount of intensity generated.

In science, we measure the intensity of light not by squint factor or headache potential, but by lumens and candlepower. We measure the intensity of sound not by ear pain or gut vibration, but by decibels—precisely defined measurements that can be compared mathematically and then used to discover other properties.

How does the unscientific mind measure intensity? By feel, by burn, by pump, by soreness, by failure, by rep count—by intangibles that are not indispensable conditions of growth stimulation. How does a scientific mind measure intensity? With a mathematical system like the Power Factor and Power Index. Anyone who claims there is a science of bodybuilding but rejects a precisely defined objective measure of muscular intensity is either a poseur or a dogmatist—or perhaps both.

Specialization is a tried-and-true technique that has helped countless bodybuilders spur a lagging bodypart into growth. In this nearly exhaustive article by Steve Holman, he provides 50 different specialization routines from the biggest names in bodybuilding.

SPECIALIZE FOR MORE MUSCLE SIZE—50 SPECIALIZATION ROUTINES Steve Holman

You probably know this already, but bodybuilders can be a little insane . . . okay, a lot

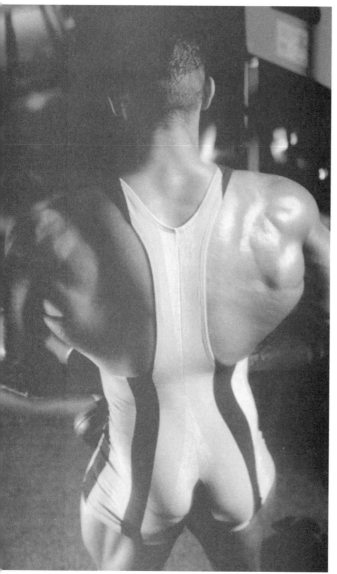

Ron Coleman.

ADDITION AND SUBTRACTION

When most bodybuilders think about specialization, they automatically think more sets. While more sets can be part of the answer, bodybuilders often forget to reduce sets for other bodyparts to keep the overall systemic stress about the same. That's especially important for drug-free trainees.

For example, if you're doing four bodyparts at a session for 6 sets each, you're doing 24 total work sets—and 24 sets at any one workout may already be pushing the limits of your recovery ability, placing you very close to the overtraining edge. Say one of those bodyparts is quads, and they just haven't been responding the way you want them to; so you add another exercise, like hack squats, for 3 work sets.

Now, 3 sets doesn't sound like a big deal. But if you were walking the overtraining tightrope to begin with, just 1 extra set has the recovery-draining power to knock you off-balance, sending your gains spiraling downward. A better strategy is to take a work set or two away from stronger bodyparts when you up your sets for your quads. That keeps your work set total the same, but allows you to do a few more sets for your lagging bodypart.

FEWER SETS, MORE EFFORT

Adding sets for a lagging bodypart is the easy part. It's subtracting sets from stronger bodyparts that's so difficult, because bodybuilders equate fewer sets with less stimulation. "Gee, I don't want my stronger bodyparts to start shrinking," you say. After all, the concept of workload has a lot of relevance. If you reduce sets for a bodypart and all other variables remain the same, it could atrophy. The solution is to up your effort a notch when you reduce the workload.

In other words, when you decrease the sets for a stronger bodypart or two in favor of a weak bodypart, slightly increase the stress level on the stronger bodyparts so they not only maintain their size, but keep growing as well.

insane. So insane, in fact, that they hear voices. We're not talking paranormal activity here, but rather paraplegic activity—comatose bodyparts suddenly coming to life for a few seconds just to taunt any thought of egomania into submission.

Try this test. Sneak a peek at your physique in the nearest mirror. If you hear a voice say something like, "Wow, you're starting to look like a badly drawn cartoon," it may be time to specialize—unless your friends see you talking to the mirror, in which case you may be heading for a padded room.

Say you want to reduce your volume on biceps work. If you've been doing 3 sets of barbell curls and three sets of incline curls, try switching to 1 set of barbell curls to failure with a few forced reps, followed by a superset of incline curls and barbell curls. That gives you half the volume—dropping from 6 sets to 3—but an intensity uptick with forced reps followed by a superset that counterbalances the set decrease. Now you can add 2 or 3 extra sets to your lagging bodypart on the same day without sacrifice—and your biceps may even grow faster with the shift to high-intensity, low-duration work.

Keep in mind that a little extra stress goes a long way. A study by Frank G. Shellock, Ph.D., verifies this. In the study, untrained subjects performed one set of positive-only curls with one arm and a set of negative-only curls (with the same weight) with the other arm until they reached positive failure. The results were quite interesting, if not startling. The positive-work-only biceps showed no damage, while the negative-work-only biceps showed damage that peaked five days after exercise. Also, while the subjects' soreness was completely gone by the ninth day, some didn't regain all their strength in the trained muscles for six weeks.

While the test subjects were untrained individuals, it nevertheless appears as if high-intensity weight training is much more severe than was previously believed, even for those who do it on a regular basis. Because of their extensive adaptation to exercise, bodybuilders who are used to heavy training won't experience the type of extreme damage exhibited in the study; however, the results do suggest that bodybuilders should take more time between workouts to completely recover and/or drastically reduce the number of sets when they use high-stress techniques, such as negatives and forced reps.

In other words, too many stress techniques, even with a volume reduction, can lead to overtraining rather quickly, so don't get carried away.

INTENSITY FOR IMMENSITY

If supersets, as well as other high-stress techniques, have the power to increase mass, then why not continue to use the same sets and intensity for your strong bodyparts and just attack the lagging one with more intensity? That's not a bad idea, but note the caveat at the end of the last section. Ramping up stress for a bodypart can lead to overtraining, just as too many sets can. The solution is more stress and fewer sets. That's right, keep everything the same for your stronger bodyparts, but do fewer sets for your weaker bodypart. Just show it no mercy by incorporating supersets, forced reps, and negatives—even more intensity than that in the biceps example discussed earlier.

In our hypothetical 24-set workout—6 sets for four target areas—you would reduce the sets for your lagging bodypart to 3 or 4 and put that bodypart through a living hell in those work sets. Go for the quick kill. Keep in mind that intensity and volume are inversely proportional. The more intensity you use, the fewer sets you should do. Once again, it's a balancing act.

The downside of this tactic is that if you work your lagging bodypart into the ground first, which is what you should do in most cases in order to prioritize, you'll be more drained than usual when you get to your other bodyparts. You may just go through the motions for your stronger bodyparts after your all-out attack on the lagging muscle group—and that could result in stagnation or, worse, atrophy. Wouldn't it be much more effective to train your lagging bodypart alone on its own special workout day? Now we're talking total focus.

Greg Kovacs.

THE SPECIALIZATION SPLIT

Okay, so you want the perfect program that will enable you to bring that lagging bodypart up to speed most efficiently. We've already discussed how increasing sets, using stress techniques, and balancing workload can help in a standard routine if you use them correctly. Now let's talk nonstandard routines—the perfect split for your level of bodybuilding experience, with one day a week set aside for specialization.

Early intermediate specialization

If you have around six months of hard training under your belt, you've probably been doing primarily compound movements and using about 2 to 3 sets per bodypart. If that sounds like you, you probably shouldn't consider specializing until you have more training experience. Sometimes, however, lagging bodyparts are so severe that you have to do something early on in your training career, or your symmetry will get way out of whack.

If you feel strongly about your need to specialize, you'll want to follow something similar to the Early Intermediate Specialization Routine that accompanies this article (page 293). With that routine, you do a full-body schedule on Monday and Friday, with your specialization workout on Wednesday. Try hitting two lagging muscle groups on Wednesday with about 7 sets each. Also, when Friday rolls around, skip the direct work for the bodyparts you trashed on Wednesday. That will provide more recovery time until you do direct work again on Monday.

Early advanced specialization

If you're more advanced, with, say, a year to 18 months of hard-training experience, you need a few more sets—4 to 6—for each muscle group. You're no doubt using a split routine already, dividing the body over two days, which is a good strategy; however, you need to somehow squeeze in a specialization day. The solution is to split your routine on Monday and Tuesday, use Thursday as your specialization day, and then do a full-body routine on Friday. As with the early intermediate specialization, you should not include direct work for the bodyparts you annihilated on Thursday in your Friday session. See Early Advanced Specialization Routine (page 293) for the complete program.

Advanced specialization

Once you've been training hard and consistently for one and a half to two years, training most bodyparts once a week is sufficient for maximum growth—if you train intensely with various stress techniques such as forced reps every so often and/or you use enough sets to require seven days of recuperation. With this routine, you split the body over three days, as follows:

> Monday: Chest, delts, and triceps
> Tuesday: Quads, hamstrings, calves, and abdominals
> Wednesday: Back, biceps, and forearms
> Thursday: Rest
> Friday: Specialization

You rest on Thursday and then come back to the gym on Friday for specialization. Note that you may have to shuffle the Monday, Tuesday, and Wednesday workouts to allow for sufficient recovery before or after your specialization day, depending on the lagging bodypart. For example, if you're specializing on back, switch the Tuesday (legs and abs) and Wednesday (back, biceps, and forearms) workouts. That will give your back an extra day to recover before your specialization routine on Friday.

As for the back end of the workout week, if you specialize on chest on Friday, you want to switch the Monday (chest, delts, and triceps) and Tuesday (legs and abs) sessions to give your chest an extra recovery day after the specialization routine. That may be a bit confusing, but once you analyze the Advanced Specialization Routine that accompanies this article (page 294), you should understand the shifting concept a little better.

Specialization is the best way to get your physique in line aesthetically, and there are more than 50 bodypart attacks that you can plug into the core routine that fits your experience level. No excuses. No bodybuilder in his or her right mind (Are we ever in our right minds?) wants to look like a bad caricature, with pipe-cleaner arms dangling from cannonball delts. If you follow the appropriate strategy, don't overtrain, and give your lagging parts total focus, you'll look at your physique with more satisfaction than ever before, and maybe one day you'll mistake your reflection for Flex Wheeler. Just don't start talking to him, or somebody may call the guys in the white coats.

EARLY INTERMEDIATE SPECIALIZATION ROUTINE[1]

Monday

Squat[2]	2 × 8–10
Leg extension	1 × 6–8
Leg curl[2]	2 × 6–8
Standing calf raise[2]	2 × 12–20
Bench press[2]	2 × 8–10
Incline press	1 × 8–10
Pulldown[2]	1 × 8–10
Undergrip pulldown	2 × 8–10
Cable row[2]	1 × 8–10
Dumbbell upright row[2]	2 × 8–10
Lying extension	1 × 8–10
Barbell curl	1 × 8–10
Full-range crunch	2 × 8–10

Wednesday

Specialize on one or two bodyparts and do ab work—but that's all. Simply plug in one of the Specialization routines (pages 293–294), but in most cases do fewer sets. Early intermediates should never do more than about seven sets per bodypart, even during a specialization phase.

Friday

Repeat Monday's routine, but delete the direct work for the bodyparts you trained on Wednesday. For example, if you hit arms on Wednesday, eliminate the barbell curls and lying extensions on Friday.

[1]For those with at least six months of training.

[2]Do one or two warm-up sets with 50 to 70 percent of your work-set weight prior to your work sets.

EARLY ADVANCED SPECIALIZATION ROUTINE[1]

Monday[2]

Squat[3]	2 × 8–10
Sissy squat	1 × 8–10
Leg extension	2 × 8–10
Stiff-legged deadlift[3]	2 × 8–10
Leg curl[3]	2 × 6–8

Leg press calf raise[3]	2 × 12–20
Standing calf raise	2 × 12–20
Seated calf raise	2 × 12–20
Incline knee-up	1 × 8–10
Ab Bench crunch pull	2 × 8–10

Tuesday[2]

Bench press[3]	2 × 8–10
Cable flye	2 × 8–10
Incline press	2 × 8–10
Pulldown[3]	2 × 8–10
Dumbbell pullover[3]	1 × 8–10
Undergrip pulldown	2 × 8–10
Cable row[3]	2 × 8–10
Dumbbell shrug	2 × 8–10
Dumbbell press[3]	1 × 8–10
Incline one-arm lateral	1 × 8–10
Lateral raise	2 × 8–10
Lying extension	2 × 8–10
Barbell curl	2 × 8–10

Thursday

Specialize on one or two bodyparts—but that's all. Simply plug in one of the Specialization routines (pages 293–294), but in most cases do fewer sets. Early advanced trainees should never do more than 10 sets per bodypart, even during a specialization phase.

Friday[4]

Squat[3]	2 × 8–10
Leg extension	1 × 6–8
Leg curl[3]	2 × 6–8
Standing calf raise[3]	2 × 12–20
Bench press[3]	2 × 8–10
Incline press	1 × 8–10
Pulldown[3]	1 × 8–10
Undergrip pulldown	2 × 8–10
Cable row[3]	2 × 8–10
Dumbbell press[3]	2 × 8–10
Lateral raise	1 × 8–10
Lying extension	1 × 8–10
Barbell curl	1 × 8–10
Ab Bench crunch pull	1 × 8–10

[1]For those with at least one year of training.

[2]You may want to switch the Monday and Tuesday workouts, depending on your specialization bodyparts. For example, if you're specializing on chest on Thursday, switch the Monday and Tuesday workouts; this will give

your chest an extra day to recover before your specialization routine on Thursday.

[3]Do one or two warm-up sets with 50 to 70 percent of your work-set weight prior to your work sets.

[4]Remember to delete the direct work for the bodyparts you trained on Thursday.

Steve Cuevas.

ADVANCED SPECIALIZATION ROUTINE[1]

Monday[2]

Bench press[3]	2–3 × 8–10
Dumbbell flye	1 × 8–10
Cable crossover	2 × 8–10
Incline press[3]	2 × 8–10
Incline cable flye	2 × 8–10
Dumbbell press[3]	2 × 8–10
Incline one-arm lateral	1 × 8–10
Lateral raise	2 × 8–10
Lying extension[3]	2 × 8–10
Overhead extension	2 × 8–10
Kickback	2 × 8–10

Tuesday[2]

Squat[3]	3 × 8–10
Sissy squat	1 × 8–10
Leg extension	2 × 8–10
Stiff-legged deadlift[3]	2 × 8–10
Leg curl[3]	2 × 6–8
Leg press calf raise[3]	2 × 12–20
Standing calf raise	2 × 12–20
Seated calf raise	2 × 12–20
Incline knee-up	2 × 8–10
Ab Bench crunch pull	2 × 8–10

Wednesday[2]

Pulldown[3]	2–3 × 8–10
Dumbbell pullover[3]	2 × 8–10
Undergrip pulldown	2 × 8–10
Cable row	2 × 8–10
Bent-over bent-arm lateral	2 × 8–10
Dumbbell shrug	2 × 8–10
Barbell curl[3]	2 × 8–10
Incline curl	2 × 8–10
Concentration curl	2 × 8–10
Reverse curl	1 × 8–10
Wrist curl	1 × 8–10

Friday

Specialize on one or two bodyparts—but that's all. Simply plug in one of the Specialization routines (pages 293–294). In most cases, you should be able to handle the routine as listed; however, try not to do more than 24 sets at this workout—that's 24 total sets, not per bodypart.

[1]For those with at least one and a half years of training.

[2]You may want to switch these workouts around, depending on your specialization bodyparts. For example, if you're specializing on back on Friday, switch the Tuesday and Wednesday workouts; this will give your back an extra day to recover before your specialization routine on Friday. You must also be aware of the back end of this routine. For example, if you specialize on chest on Friday, you want to switch the Monday and Tuesday workouts to give your chest an extra recovery day after the specialization routine.

[3]Do one or two warm-up sets with 50 to 70 percent of your work-set weight prior to your work sets.

SPECIALIZE-FOR-SIZE: RULES TO GROW BY

1. All workouts should include fewer than 30 total work sets, be it a specialization workout or a full-body session.
2. Don't get carried away on your specialization day. Early intermediates should do 7 sets per bodypart, early advanced trainees should do 10 sets per bodypart, and advanced bodybuilders can do 10 to 20 sets per bodypart. Advanced trainees should keep in mind, however, that if they do 20 sets per bodypart, they should do only one bodypart at that workout, not two, or the set total for that day will be too high (see item 1 above). They should also keep in mind that 20 sets is a hell of a lot of work, and the target muscle may not be fully recovered by the next workout, which can hamper gains. If you choose Arnold's 32-set chest workout (page 299), for instance, you may want to reduce the number of sets for each exercise so your total is less than 20.
3. Specialize on a bodypart or bodyparts for four to six weeks, then specialize on two other bodyparts or go back to a standard routine in which all bodyparts are trained equally.
4. Use stress techniques such as forced reps, negatives, and static contraction periodically if you're in the early advanced or advanced categories. Early intermediates should steer clear of

stress techniques, other than adding weight to the bar.

BACK WORKOUTS

Dorian Yates
Machine pullover[1]	3 × 7–10
Undergrip pulldown[1]	2 × 7–10
Bent-over barbell row[1]	2 × 7–10
One-arm machine row	1 × 7–10
Rear delt machine	1 × 7–10
Bent-over lateral	1 × 7–10
Hyperextension	1 × 7–10
Deadlift[1]	2 × 6–8

[1]Pyramid weight on each set; the last set is all-out to failure, often with forced and/or partial reps.

Steve Reeves[1]
Behind-the-neck pulldown	3 × 8–12
Cable row	3 × 8–12
One-arm dumbbell row	3 × 8–12

[1]From *Building the Classic Physique the Natural Way* by Steve Reeves.

Mike Mentzer (Traps)
Superset
Shrug	2 × 6–9
Upright row	2 × 6–9

Michael Francois
Overhand-grip deadlift (warm-up)	3 × 5 singles to max
One-arm dumbbell rows	3 × 8–10
Leaning T-bar machine row	3–4 × 8–12

Tom Platz
T-bar row or front lat pulldown	30 × 6–100[1]
Seated cable row	4–8 × 15–30

[1]That's not a misprint. He performs the exercise for a solid hour.

Shawn Ray
Chin	4 × 12
Seated cable row	4 × 8–10
Bent-over row	4 × 8–10
T-bar row	4 × 8–10
Deadlift	4 × 8–10

Dorian Yates.

Hypercontraction X-Rep[1]
Lats

Pullover[2]	2 × 8–10
Pulldown[3]	3 × 8–10
Undergrip pulldown[4]	1 × 1

Midback

Close-grip cable row[2]	2 × 8–10
Behind-the-neck pulldown[3]	3 × 8–10
Bent-over bent-arm lateral[4]	1 × 1
Upper traps	
Forward-lean	
dumbbell shrug	2 × 8–10

[1]From the book *Underground Mass-Boosting Methods.*

[2]Do two warm-up sets with 50 percent of your work-set weight prior to the work sets. Remember that the work sets should be medium intensity—don't go to failure. Focus on perfect form with a quick twitch at the bottom stretch position.

[3]Do one warm-up set with 50 percent of your work-set weight prior to your heavy sets.

[4]Use a poundage that allows you to hold the weight in the contracted position for 15 seconds. Once you reach contraction overload and can no longer hold the weight, slowly lower through the negative range of motion for six seconds. Try to increase your contraction time at each workout until you reach 25 seconds, at which point you should increase your resistance by 10 to 20 percent at your next workout.

Aaron Baker

Undergrip close-grip	
pulldown	3 × 10
Seated pulley row	2 × 15, 10
Behind-the-neck pulldown	3 × 10
Deadlift	2 × 6–12

BICEPS WORKOUTS

Arnold Schwarzenegger

Barbell curl	4 × 10
Incline dumbbell curl	4 × 10
Concentration curl	4 × 10

Craig Titus

Barbell curl[1]	4 × 9–12
Cable preacher curl[1]	4 × 9–12
Standing cable curl[1]	4 × 9–12
Concentration curl	3 × 12–15

[1]Pyramid weight and drop reps by one on each successive set.

Larry Scott
Superset

Dumbbell preacher curl	6 × 6

Larry Scott.

Barbell preacher curl	6×6
Barbell reverse curl	4×8

Hypercontraction Training[1]

Incline curl[2]	4×8–10
Barbell curl[3]	2–3×6–9
Concentration curl[3]	2–3×8–10

[1]From the video *Hypercontraction Training*.

[2]Add weight on each successive set; all sets are low- to medium-intensity.

[3]Take all sets to positive failure.

Paul Jean-Guillaume

Wide-grip preacher curl	4×8–12
Close-grip EZ-curl bar preacher curl	4×8–12
Alternate dumbbell curl	6×8–12
Standing barbell curl	4×8–12
Lying cable curl (to forehead)	4×8–12

Arnold Schwarzenegger.

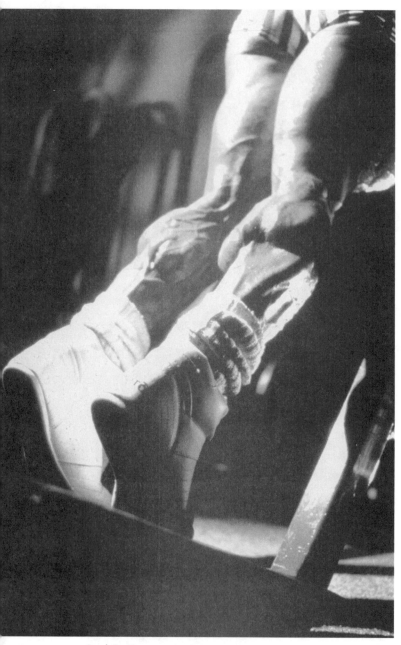

Paul DeMayo.

CALF WORKOUTS

Cory Everson

Donkey calf raise	4 × 15–25
Standing calf raise	4 × 15–25
Seated calf raise	4 × 15

Jodi Friedman-List

Seated calf raise	4 × 12–20
Standing calf raise	4 × 12–20

Paul DeMayo

Standing calf raise	3 × failure
Seated calf raise	3 × failure
Leg press calf raise	3 × failure

Arnold Schwarzenegger

Standing calf raise	10 × 10
Seated calf raise	8 × 15
One-leg calf raise	6 × 12

Positions of Flexion[1]

Toes-pointed leg curl	2 × 8–10
Donkey calf raise	2 × 12–20
Standing calf raise	2–3 × 12–20
Seated calf raise	2–3 × 12–20

[1]From *Critical Mass.*

CHEST WORKOUTS

Bertil Fox

Barbell bench press	5 × 4–8
Dumbbell bench press	5 × 6–8
Barbell incline press	5 × 6–8
Superset	
Dip	5 × 8–10
Flye	5 × 5–8

Mike O'Hearn

Bench press	8 × 5
Incline press	4 × 12
Incline flye	4 × 12
Cable crossover	4 × 12

Target Overload POF[1] **(Positions of Flexion)**

Lower chest	
Bench press	3 × 8–10
Flat-bench flye	2 × 8–10
Pec deck flye	2 × 8–10
Upper chest	
Incline press	3 × 8–10
Incline flye	2 × 8–10
Low-cable crossover	2 × 8–10

[1]From *Critical Mass.*

Chris Faildo

Dumbbell bench press	4 × 8–12
Incline flye	4 × 8–12
Cable crossover	4 × 8–12
Dip	4 × 8–12

Chris Faildo.

Arnold Schwarzenegger.

Arnold Schwarzenegger

Bench press	5 × 8–10
Flat-bench flye	5 × 8
Machine incline press	6 × 8–10
Parallel-bar dip	
(bodyweight)	5 × max
Cable crossover	6 × 12
Dumbbell pullover	5 × 10

DELTOID WORKOUTS

Pre-Ex Positions of Flexion[1]
Superset

Lateral raise	2 × 6–9
Behind-the-neck press	2 × 6–9
Incline one-arm lateral	2 × 8–12

[1]From *Critical Mass*.

Skip La Cour

Barbell press[1]	3 × 4–6
Dumbbell press	2 × 4–6
Lateral raise	3 × 4–6
Bent-over lateral	2 × 4–6

[1]Prior to his work sets, Skip does 2 to 3 light warm-up sets.

Michael Ashley

Lateral raise[1]	5 × 10–12
Bent-over lateral raise	4 × 10–12
Seated dumbbell press[1]	5 × 10–12
Shrug	4 × 10–12

[1]Add weight on each successive set.

Don Long.

Melissa Coates.

Steve Reeves[1]

Upright row	3 × 8–12
Behind-the-neck press	3 × 8–12
Bent-over lateral	3 × 8–12

[1]From *Building the Classic Physique the Natural Way.*

Don Long

Front press	4 × 16, 12, 10, 8
Behind-the-neck press	4 × 16, 12, 10, 8
Lateral raise	4 × 16, 12, 10, 8
Cable lateral raise	4 × 16, 12, 10, 8
Bent-over dumbbell lateral	4 × 16, 12, 10, 8

Melissa Coates

Lateral raise	4 × 12–15
Upright row	4 × 8–12
Bent-over lateral	4 × 12–15
Dumbbell press[1]	4 × 8–10

[1]Optional.

FOREARM WORKOUTS

Larry Scott

Wrist curl	4 × 8
Reverse curl	4 × 8

Positions of Flexion[1]
Flexors

Incline wrist curl	1–2 × 8–12
Decline wrist curl	1–2 × 8–12

Extensors

Hammer curl	1–2 × 8–12
Incline reverse wrist curl	1–2 × 8–12
Decline reverse wrist curl	1 × 8–12

[1]From *Critical Mass.*

Note: Static-contraction squeezes with a Super Gripper can help finish off your forearms with a severe fiber burn. Try them at the end of either of these routines.

Larry Scott.

Karl List

Seated leg curl	3 × 15
Lying leg curl	3 × 15
Stiff-legged deadlift	3 × 15

Paul DeMayo

Lying leg curl	4 × 10–12
Standing leg curl	3 × 10–12
Stiff-legged deadlift	3 × 10

Karl List.

HAMSTRING WORKOUTS

High-Intensity Pre-Exhaust[1]
Superset

Leg curl	2–3 × 6–9
Stiff-legged deadlift	2–3 × 6–9

[1]From *Mass-Training Tactics*.

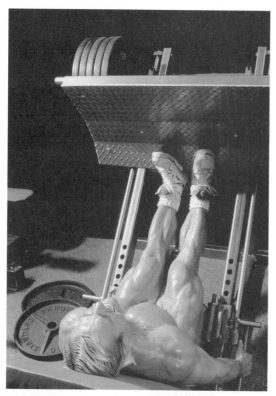

Tom Platz.

QUADRICEPS WORKOUTS

Compound Aftershock[1]

Squat	1–2 × 8–10

Superset[2]

Sissy squat	1–2 × 5–7
Leg press	1–2 × 5–7
Leg extension	1–2 × 8–10

[1]From *Compound Aftershock.*

[2]Research indicates that the muscle burn from supersetting can increase growth hormone release.

Tom Platz

Flat-footed	
Olympic-style squats[1]	6 × 15, 10, 10, 6, 5, 1

[1]Pyramid the weight.

Note: Platz did leg extensions, leg curls, and hack squats on his other leg day, 5 × 8–12 on each.

Cory Everson.

Cory Everson

Squat	8 × 10–20
Hack squat	4 × 10–15
45-degree leg press	6 × 10–15
Leg extension	6 × 10–15
Lunge	4 × 12–15

Note: Set totals include warm-ups; pyramid weight on most exercises.

Jeff Poulin

Smith machine lunge	4 × 10–15
Leg press	4 × 10–20
Hack squat	4 × 10–20
Leg extension	4 × 25–50

Paul DeMayo

Squat	4 × 10–12
Hack squat	3 × 10–12
Leg extension	3 × failure

Dave Palumbo

Leg extension	2 × 10–15
Squat	3 × 6–12
Hack squat	2 × 8–12

TRICEPS WORKOUTS

Shawn Ray

Lying extension	4 × 8–12
Close-grip pushdown	4 × 8–12
Dumbbell kickback	4 × 8–12

Dave Palumbo.

Mike Mentzer.

Mia Finnegan.

Mike Mentzer
Superset[1]

Triceps pushdown	2 × 6–9
Dip	2 × 6–9

[1]Take each set to total failure with forced reps and sometimes negatives after the forced reps.

Hypercontraction Training[1]

Overhead extension[2]	4 × 8–10
Lying extension[3]	2–3 × 6–9
One-arm pushdown[3]	2–3 × 8–10

[1]From the video *Hypercontraction Training*.

[2]Add weight each set; all sets low to medium intensity.

[3]All sets to positive failure.

Aaron Baker

Lying EZ-curl bar extension	4 × 8–10
Pushdown	4 × 10
Seated machine dip	3 × 10
Dumbbell kickback	3 × 10

Lee Labrada

Pushdown	3 × 10–15
Lying extension	3 × 10
EZ-curl bar overhead extension or close-grip bench press	3 × 10

Sue Price

Rope pushdown	2 × 9–10
Bench dip	3 × 12
Lying dumbbell extension	4 × 10–12

ABDOMINALS WORKOUTS

Mia Finnegan

Incline leg raise	4 × max
Incline reverse sit-up	4 × max
Incline double crunch	4 × max
Hanging leg raise	4 × max

Cory Everson
Giant set

Pulldown crunch	3–4 × 25–40
Decline sit-up	3–4 × 100
Leg raise off bench	3–4 × 10–40
45-degree twist	3–4 × 50–100
Crunch	3–4 × 40–80

Granite Abs Routine 2

Synergy and hip-curl function

Incline knee-up 2×8–10

Pre-stretch and torso-curl function

Ab Bench crunch pull 2–3×8–10

Paul Jean-Guillaume

Leg lift 4×20

Cable crunch 3×20

Crunch 200 reps

Twist with bar 200 reps

Chapter 12

TRAINING FOR MASS

Mass—it's what every bodybuilder covets. In smaller or larger quantity, it's what everybody who picks up a weight is looking to obtain. Fortunately, the folks at Ironman *know plenty about exactly how to get mass and get it as fast as possible.*

Gene Mozée has advice from three champions who each gained 50 pounds of muscle. After their insights, Gene offers more of his own formidable knowledge on the subject in this article.

GAIN 50 POUNDS OF MUSCLE: ARNOLD SCHWARZENEGGER, BILL PEARL, AND LARRY SCOTT REVEAL THEIR TECHNIQUES FOR MAXIMUM MASS Gene Mozée

Gaining muscular weight and size is by far the most important goal of almost every bodybuilder. Approximately 99 percent of all bodybuilders start out underweight.

To increase muscle size, you must gain weight—solid, muscular weight—and to gain weight, you must exercise the muscles progressively by constantly imposing greater demands

on them. The muscles will respond when they're pushed and properly nourished. More muscle mass is nature's way of accepting these demands.

If your goal is to gain muscular weight in the major muscle groups, the following workouts from three bodybuilding legends will help you reach your goal of new size and strength.

ADVICE FROM ARNOLD

I would like to clear up any confusion you may have about anabolic steroids. Every serious bodybuilder should know the truth about steroids. It is my opinion that you can gain all the weight you want without them. Steroids are a very radical departure from physical culture. Far too much emphasis is placed on their value in the quest for an improved physique. Personally, I think the usefulness of steroids is overrated and, needless to say, overdone. Superstars of the past such as Reg Park, John Grimek, Steve Reeves, Clancy Ross, Jack

Delinger, and Bill Pearl reached the ultimate in massive muscularity without them. So can you, with proper training and diet.

Some advanced bodybuilders can train three hours a day and show amazing gains, while others cannot make any kind of improvement if they train much more than one hour or so. When I was trying to get more massive in my early years of training, I followed a routine I called the Golden Six. I made tremendous gains on this program, and so did hundreds of others who trained at my

gym in Munich, Germany. All agreed that this simple system of training produced excellent gains in muscle size and bodyweight. Here are the Golden Six:

1. **Barbell squat.** This exercise not only develops the thighs, but it strengthens the heart and lungs and improves the general circulation. Use a weight that will permit you to perform 4 sets of 10 reps. Always lower yourself until your upper thighs are parallel to the floor, and keep your back flat. To ensure better balance and to put more stress on your quadriceps, place a 1-inch board under your heels with your feet about 15 to 18 inches apart. Inhale deeply as

you squat down, and exhale as you
come up. Do 10 reps, rest two minutes,
and repeat.

2. **Barbell bench press.** This is my favorite
upper-body exercise, and almost every
training program that I've used includes
it. Take a fairly wide grip, with your
hands about 32 inches apart. Inhale as
you lower the bar to your nipples, and
exhale as you push the weight back to
arm's length. Don't bounce the weight
off your chest. Perform 3 sets of 10
reps. Pause about two minutes between
sets.

3. **Chin or lat machine pulldown.** If you
have limited training experience,
you may find chins difficult at first.
If you have a lat machine, you can perform pulldowns until you've developed
sufficient strength to do chins. Use a
wide grip on the chins, and try to bring
your chin over the bar. Do as many reps
as you can for 3 sets.

4. **Behind-the-neck press.** This exercise
reigns supreme for widening and thickening the shoulders. I prefer to do it
seated. Use a wide grip, with your
thumbs about 6 inches wider than your
delts on each side. From this position,
push the bar upward to arm's length
while exhaling. Lower the weight slowly
while inhaling, and don't pause at the
bottom. Repeat for 10 reps. Do 4 sets
with about two minutes of rest between
sets.

5. **Barbell curl.** This is the great mass
builder for the biceps. The triceps have
already been thoroughly exercised during the bench press and the behind-the-
neck press. Use a shoulder-width grip
and a weight you can curl without any
body movement. Exhale as you curl the
weight up until the biceps are fully
flexed. Don't let your elbows move away
from the sides of your body. Inhale as
you lower the bar in a slow, controlled

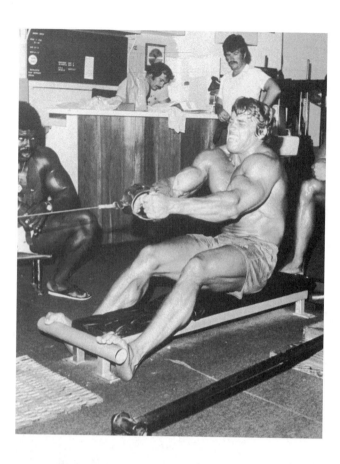

manner back to your thighs. Make sure you straighten your arms completely before doing the next rep. Do 3 sets of 10 reps, and rest about 90 seconds between sets.

6. **Bent-knee sit-ups.** It's only sensible to keep your midsection firm and toned when gaining muscular weight. Sit-ups help improve digestion and elimination as well. I prefer to do this exercise with my hands behind my head, but if you are just starting out, you may find it more beneficial and easier if you hold your arms straight out in front and touch your toes. The knees are kept in a bent position throughout the exercise. This helps focus the stress more on the abdominals, not the hip flexors or the lower back. Don't pause between reps, but continue for 20 or as many reps as you can do without stopping. Exhale as you sit up; inhale as you lower your torso. Do 3 or 4 sets, resting one minute between sets.

I feel sure that if you use these basic exercises for a minimum of three months without missing any workouts, doing them three times a week on alternate days, you can gain many pounds of new, impressive muscle size. Paul Grant, former Mr. World, used almost this exact same program and gained 65 pounds of muscle in less than a year. All he did was increase the sets on the first five exercises to 4 after three months, and after six months he went to 6 sets. Always strive to continually add more weight to each exercise when you can do 2 or 3 more reps over the recommended amount.

Larry Scott.

LARRY SCOTT'S MASS-BUILDING TECHNIQUES

Gaining muscular weight is a problem faced by nearly everyone at one time or another during his or her bodybuilding career. I was no exception, weighing in at only 120 pounds as a beginner. The first few years of my training were primarily devoted to gaining additional muscular weight and size. Through scientific training and proper nutrition, I reached a bodyweight of 215 pounds, a total gain of 95 pounds of muscle.

When it comes to gaining weight, the real secret is diet. Only by supplying your body with the proper nutritional elements that it requires will you be able to build maximum size and strength. It is my opinion that 75 percent of the battle to build a championship physique is proper nutrition. Exercise and proper rest and sleep are also of major importance, but diet builds muscle tissue when the exercise stimulates the body to grow.

One of the best mass-training routines that I used was to select one exercise for each major muscle group and do 6 sets of 8 reps on each. The following workout is intended for the intermediate bodybuilder who wants to pack on a lot more bodyweight and muscle mass:

Bench press to the neck	6 × 6–8
Barbell squat	6 × 8
Machine calf raise	6 × 15–20

Behind-the-neck press	6 × 6–8
Front pulldown	6 × 8–10
Lying barbell	
triceps extension	6 × 8
Preacher bench curl	6 × 8
Bent-knee leg raise	1 × 100–150

This is a rugged routine. You might wish to begin with just 3 sets of each exercise and add an additional set every 30 days until you work up to 6. Do this program three days a week.

Think big, and train with all the enthusiasm you're capable of. You can go as far as you want when it comes to getting more massive if you train intelligently, eat properly, and get enough growth-inducing sleep and rest.

BILL PEARL'S ADVANCED MASS TRAINING

A lot of time has passed since I first began training seriously. At first, I employed a basic all-around training program for conditioning. Then I began to work on my weak spots, which at the time included just about everything. I weighed about 165 pounds at 5'11". I wasn't skinny; I just had an average athletic build. When I competed and won the Mr. Universe, however, I weighed 241 pounds in my final competition.

My plan when gaining muscular weight was to eat five meals a day so that the digestive system was not overtaxed. Often when a person

is using all-out effort to gain bodyweight, the average individual eats to the point of force-feeding and in doing so stretches the stomach. When you eat smaller meals more often, not only is the food more easily digested and utilized to build muscle and produce energy, it also helps keep the waistline under control. Generally speaking, when trying to reach a maximum bodyweight, I consume mostly fresh vegetables, fruits, baked potatoes, cheese, meat, and fish (at least I did before converting to a vegetarian diet in later years). All foods are either baked or broiled for easier digestion.

Here is the mass program that helped me win Mr. Universe. I trained down to 190 and then slowly massed up to 241 pounds.

Monday-Wednesday-Friday

Incline flye	5 × 6
Bent-arm flat-bench flye	5 × 6
Decline flye	5 × 6
Behind-the-neck press	5 × 6
Military barbell press	5 × 6
Dumbbell lateral raise	5 × 8
Lying triceps extension	5 × 6
Lying dumbbell triceps extension	5 × 8
Triceps pushdown	5 × 8
Barbell curl	5 × 6
Incline dumbbell curl	5 × 6
Concentration curl	5 × 6
Sit-up	100–200
Alternate leg raise	100–200
Dumbbell side bend	50

Tuesday-Thursday-Saturday

Sit-up	100–200
Alternate leg raise	100–200
Dumbbell side bend	50
Wide-grip chin	5 × 10
Close-grip chin	5 × 10
Shrug	5 × 10
Stiff-legged deadlift	5 × 8
Partner-assisted neck work	
Wrist curl	5 × 20
Reverse curl	5 × 20
Squat	5 × 8
Hack squat	5 × 10
Leg curl	5 × 12
Standing calf raise	6 × 10
Donkey calf raise	6 × 10

Bill Pearl.

There you have it—advice and routines from three legends of bodybuilding. They each gained more than 50 pounds of muscle, and you can too. If you put in plenty of effort on a mass-building routine, along with lots of good food and enough rest, you'll pack on loads of new size and strength.

Now expert Gene Mozée shows how working heavy is the indispensable condition for putting on significant amounts of muscle.

POWER-MASS TRAINING: WORK HEAVY AND GET HUGE Gene Mozée

Why can't you build impressive muscle mass and density? Is something stopping you from getting huge? Maybe you need a dose of power-mass training!

When I first began training many years ago, my goal was to get bigger so that I could play football and, of course, have a better physique. I gained 30 pounds in the first six months, and the additional muscle size and strength greatly enhanced my athletic ability. I became stuck, however, at 158 pounds and just couldn't gain another ounce, no matter how

hard I worked out or how many calories I consumed. I bounced around from gym to gym and tried every workout program used by bodybuilding champs like Clancy Ross, Jack Delinger, and Reg Park. I was so confused that I was just about ready to throw in the towel and hang it up.

Fortunately, I met John Farbotnik at Muscle Beach in Santa Monica, California, and he invited me to his gym in Glendale. Farbotnik, who had won both the Mr. America and Mr. Universe titles in 1950, took my measurements and evaluated my physique and training program. He explained to me that I was overtraining and overeating.

"To build greater muscle size and bodyweight, it takes proper activity, proper nutrition, and sufficient rest and sleep; to develop

Terry Mitsos.

greater muscle mass, you need to use progressively heavier poundages and build greater power.

"Light warm-up exercises will never build the muscle size you want," Farbotnik continued. "Light dumbbell movements like concentration curls, which are necessary for shaping and peaking the biceps, are fine, but who needs them to work on 15-inch arms? Hack squats are great for shaping the thighs, but if you want real muscle mass, you need heavy squats. You must handle consistently heavier weights in combination with eating a more scientific weight-gaining diet to reach your goals."

I soon found out that John knew his stuff. I joined his gym and gained 30 pounds in three months. My bench press went from 275 to 360. My arms went from 15½ inches to 18 inches, and my chest increased from 45 inches to 48 inches. At the same time, I found out that a substantial increase in body power produced a simultaneous increase in muscle mass.

BOMB THE DEEP-LYING FIBERS

The most effective way to produce greater muscle mass is to blast those deep-lying muscle fibers with heavy poundages. These submerged muscle fibers are rarely activated if you don't use heavy weights. A basic, scientific law, the all-or-none principle, operates in relation to muscle use—that is, an individual muscle fiber either reacts with all of its contractile power or it doesn't react at all. There is no in-between, no compromise.

Your muscles are very economical, operating with as few fibers as they can. Light weights activate only a few muscle fibers, while heavy poundages stimulate the maximum number possible. As a muscle gets progressively stronger and larger, you must continually add more poundage to stimulate the maximum number of fibers. You have to constantly challenge your muscles to work harder and harder if you want to build dense, quality mass.

Unless you are a student of anatomy, you may be wondering what these deep-lying mus-

Jason Arntz.

cle fibers are. They are the auxiliary muscle fibers that attach to a major muscle group such as the biceps, pectorals, triceps, deltoids, or quadriceps and often surround its base. When they are bombarded with heavy power exercises, they thicken and increase in size, thus giving the muscle greater strength, more stamina, larger girth, improved shape, and increased fullness.

Generally speaking, performing an exercise with a moderate weight will produce only limited improvement. It will help shape and enlarge a particular muscle, but unless the deep-lying fibers of that muscle are aroused, it will never reach maximum development. Therefore, to activate those fibers and force your muscles to grow larger, you must blast them with the heaviest weapons in your arsenal—heavy power-mass exercises.

OVERALL GROWTH

When you attack the major muscle groups (chest, legs, back, and shoulders) with heavy power-mass exercises, all the other related muscle groups—primary, secondary, and tertiary—are stimulated into new growth. For example, when you do heavy bench presses in power-mass style, your deltoids, triceps, and even upper back receive extra benefits that make them larger and stronger and capable of handling heavier poundages on specific deltoid and arm exercises. This increased power is one of the keys to building the muscle mass and density you seek.

POWER-MASS TRAINING PROGRAM

The following program was used by Marvin Eder, possibly the strongest bodybuilder who ever hoisted a barbell. In the '50s, Eder, along with George Eifferman, had the most massive pecs west of the Pecos. Eder was so strong that he bench pressed 510 pounds and did standing presses with 365. He weighed 198, had 19-inch arms, and could do 5 sets of 10 reps with the 120-pound dumbbells in the seated press. He also did 12 one-arm chins with his right hand and 11 with his left.

Eder told me that his secret to building record-breaking power and incredible muscularity was power-mass training. The following exercise routine is the one he used, and it is the one he recommended to me. It not only helped me gain many pounds of muscle, but it pushed my bench press and overhead pressing strength to new heights.

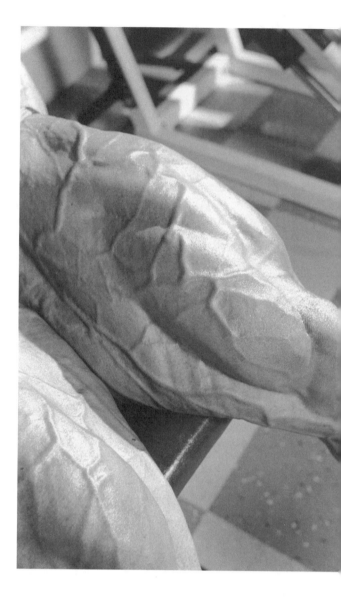

1. **Squat.** Keep the feet fairly close together. Elevate your heels on a 1½- to 2-inch board. Squat to slightly below parallel to the floor, keeping your knees pointed forward. Inhale on the way down, and exhale when you come up.
2. **Bench press.** Use a medium-wide grip, with your hands about 26 to 32 inches apart. Lower the bar slowly to the highest point on your chest while inhaling, and immediately ram it back to the top as you exhale.
3. **Heavy bent-over barbell row.** Use the same hand spacing as for the bench press. Bend forward with your back parallel to the floor and pull the bar up until it touches your upper abdomen just below the top of the rib cage. Lower the bar slowly close to your body, but don't let it touch the floor. Inhale on the way up, and exhale on the way down.
4. **Standing barbell press.** Use a slightly wider-than-shoulder-width grip. Take

Dave Palumbo.

Art Dilkes.

the barbell off a squat rack rather than cleaning it, and preserve all of your energy for pressing. Wear a lifting belt to support your lower back. Exhale as you press the weight upward; inhale as you lower it. Do the reps rapidly without pausing at the top or bottom.

5. **Lat machine pulldown.** Using a fairly wide grip with your hands 6 to 8 inches wider than shoulder width, pull the bar down to just below your collarbones until it touches your upper chest. Inhale during this pulling movement. Exhale as you slowly let the lats stretch as much as possible while returning the bar to the starting position. (You may substitute chins for this movement.)

6. **Heavy dumbbell curl.** Do this exercise while seated on a sturdy bench. Use a slight cheating motion as you inhale, curling the dumbbells upward until they touch your delts. Exhale as you

lower them all the way until your arms are straight.

7. **Cool-down.** 100 leg raises.

TRAINING TIPS

- Train three times a week on alternate days.
- Perform each exercise for 3 sets of 8 reps to start.
- After two weeks, increase to 4 sets of 6 reps.
- After 30 days, increase to 5 sets of 6 reps on each exercise.
- On the third month, increase to 6 sets of 6 reps.

Craig Licker.

- Relax and rest between each set and exercise until you have recuperated enough to go on. (This should be about two minutes.)
- Schedule your workout so that you will have enough time to go through it completely without rushing.
- Don't add any other exercises.
- Don't engage in any strenuous sports or recreational activities while on this program. Save your energy for your workouts.

- Do one light warm-up set of 10 to 12 reps with a light weight—about 50 percent of your heaviest poundage—for each exercise. Then work up to as much weight as you can handle without straining.
- Follow the exercises in the order given.
- Stay with this program for at least three months without missing any workouts.
- Remember, to get maximum results you need maximum effort. Increase the weight when you can do more reps than what is listed.

POWER-MASS NUTRITION

Get on a five-to-six-meal-per-day diet, eating a protein-rich meal or snack every three hours or so. Consume at least 1 gram of protein for every pound of bodyweight, plus an additional 10 percent for maximum growth. If you weigh 160, you need 160 grams of protein, plus an additional 20 to 25 grams (180 to 185 grams total). Eggs, milk, meat, fish, and poultry are the best sources of first-class muscle-building protein. To develop mass and make continuous weight gains, you need about 30 calories per pound of bodyweight every day, so stick to that if you want to gain 20 to 30 pounds of muscle in the next three months.

REST AND SLEEP

Eight to nine hours of sound, restful sleep *every* night is recommended. Also, never run when you can walk; never walk when you can stand still; never stand when you can sit; never sit when you can lie down; and when you do lie down, try to drift into a pleasant, growth-promoting sleep. Heavy power-mass training demands that you conserve energy outside of the gym whenever possible.

If you have been training regularly for at least six months and have gotten stale or reached a lack-of-progress plateau, try this power-mass training program to jolt your muscles into new growth. It has been used

Lee Labrada.

Leg extension. Dave Palumbo.

successfully by hundreds of bodybuilders and athletes. See what it can do for you.

Steve Holman shows you how to tweak common exercises so they deliver maximum gains.

TEN DYNAMITE MASS BOOSTERS
Steve Holman

Some exercises pack mass on just about anyone. Take the squat, for example. You have to be pretty handicapped in the leverage department to squat for any length of time without gaining some appreciable muscle. It trains your entire body, not just your legs, to grow bigger and stronger. The same goes for the deadlift.

Other exercises, however, take some tweaking if you're going to get the most stimulation from them—triceps pushdowns, for instance. Some bodybuilders can slam out set after set with a straight bar and not feel a damn thing happening. When they switch from a straight bar to a rope, including a twist of the wrist at the bottom of each rep, it's like

somebody stuck white-hot horseshoes under the skin on top of their triceps.

How do you know if an exercise is a waste of your time? The answer is pump and sensation. If you get a pump in the target bodypart and you have the sensation that the muscle is going to explode after a few sets, the exercise is stimulating growth. On the other hand, if you have a hard time determining which bodypart you're training with an exercise, it's time to either look for a new movement or try a variation.

One little technique tweak can make an exercise 20 times more effective. Here are 10 basic movements that you can turn into mega-mass boosters with simple variations or substitutions. If you decide to try them, make sure your partner is standing by with a fire extinguisher to douse the incredible burn.

LEG EXTENSION

Finishing off the quads with leg extensions is a common practice, and for good reason—you get resistance in the contracted position, which makes the muscle fibers almost burst through the skin. Most bodybuilders know that to get the most out of leg extensions, they should flex their quads hard at the top for a count. If you want an even better contraction—and to make those quad fibers really scream—try to raise your thighs off the seat during that part of the rep. You probably won't succeed, but that's not the point. It's the attempt that makes the difference. One or two sets of leg extensions in this style, and you may need a walker to get to your next exercise.

BENT-OVER ROW

Many bodybuilders turn bent-over barbell rows into a completely new exercise: the half-assed deadlift thrust clean. They bring their upper body to an almost upright position as they heave the bar into their waist—or, worse, their upper thighs. That doesn't work the back—at least not the midback, which is the primary target. If you really want to attack your midback, grab a pair of dumbbells and lean forward, resting your chest on an incline bench or other support. Now do strict rows, squeezing your scapulae together at the top of each rep. Be sure to keep your arms angled away from your torso so you don't hit too much lat. This exercise will thicken your back and etch in detail you didn't think you could ever achieve there.

CROSSOVER

When you do standing cable crossovers, you have a cable handle in each hand, and the

Bent-over row.   Berry DeMey.

Crossover.   Dave Palumbo.

cables are attached to heavy weight stacks that pull your arms up. It's almost impossible to keep your torso still when you pull the handles down in front of your waist. That's the problem with cable crossovers: you get a whole lot of swaying going on, which tends to bring the front delts into play, and that minimizes chest involvement. Try dragging a flat or decline bench over to the crossover apparatus and attaching the handles to the low hooks. Now recline on the bench with a handle in each hand and, with a slight bend in each arm, pull until your hands touch above your sternum at the lower end of your rib cage. That will give you much better pec isolation because your torso can't move. Remember to keep your chest high and squeeze those pecs hard on every rep. And don't let the weight stacks drop. Perform the reps slowly, and try to keep tension on your pecs throughout the range of motion.

BARBELL SHRUG

Ask a bodybuilder what the problem is with barbell shrugs, and the answer will be, "The damn bar drags against my thighs." That's only part of the problem, however. When you use a bar, your hands can't move freely, which limits your range of motion and your muscle gains. A better way to zap your traps is to shrug with dumbbells and shoot for an enhanced range of motion. Start with a forward lean and the dumbbells touching in front of your thighs, with your shoulders down and stretching your traps. As you shrug, allow the dumbbells to move out to your sides. When your traps are fully contracted, the dumbbells will be at the sides of your thighs, parallel to each other. This gives you more scapulae rotation and thus more trap stimulation.

Barbell shrug.

STANDING CALF RAISE

One of the big reasons bodybuilders have trouble building calves is they don't pay attention to the negative (eccentric) phase of each rep. Because of the skill you develop in walking and running, your calves are very efficient when it comes to performing work. That means you have to force them to do something they're not accustomed to—like controlled negatives. On each rep of your standing calf raises, keep your knees locked, drive up into the contracted position, then count to three as you lower the weight. Do this on every rep.

Standing calf raise.   Jodi Friedman-List.

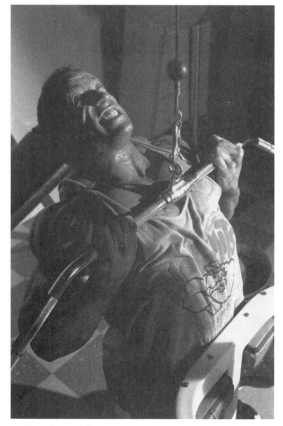

Undergrip pulldown.   Dave Palumbo.

the book *Muscle Meets Magnet*, a magnetic-resonance imaging (MRI) look at how exercises affect leg and arm muscles, the one-leg calf raise hits more of the overall calf than the two-leg variety.

UNDERGRIP PULLDOWN

Most bodybuilders keep their bodies perpendicular to the floor when they do undergrip pulldowns. That style, however, tends to put too much stress on the biceps at the expense of lat contraction. To remedy this, you can either try to lean back so your torso is close to a 45-degree angle to the floor when you pull the bar to your chest, or you can try rope pulls. Hook a double-rope attachment to a low pulley, grab the rope with both hands, bend over until your torso is about 45 degrees to the floor, and pull the rope to your waist. Be sure to keep your arms close to your sides and

Yes, you'll probably have to decrease your poundage somewhat, but your calf growth won't suffer in the least; it will kick into high gear. Speaking of suffering, be prepared for some ungodly soreness for the next few days after you perform these sets with negative emphasis. You may want to try them one leg at a time for even better results. According to

squeeze the heck out of your lats at the top. Go for a scapular squeeze and try to keep your torso as still as possible.

CONCENTRATION CURL

Concentration curls are a great biceps movement; you can really focus on the peak contraction. Even so, you can get a better contraction with another exercise. First, you must realize that the contracted position for the biceps occurs when your upper arm is next to your head and your forearm is pointing downward, flexing your biceps. When you're in this position, you look like you're doing a one-arm triceps extension, except your palm is down, twisting outward. You can see how the concentration curl doesn't quite get you there. A better exercise is the double-biceps curl performed in the cable crossover apparatus. If you do these on your knees, you'll get even closer to the biceps' fully contracted position because you'll be pulling from more of an overhead position. This is one of the best exercises for finishing off your biceps training.

Concentration curl.

CRUNCH

If you read *Ironman* on a regular basis, you know that the crunch is a good exercise for contracting the rectus abdominis, the rippled muscle on the front of your abdomen; but for best results you should begin the exercise with your lower back arched. This pre-stretches the rectus abdominis and also brings into play the surrounding ab muscles like the obliques and the transverse abdominis. The total impact of full-range exercise on abdominal development is tremendous, and the Ab Bench is the best way to get pre-stretch and total contraction for that chiseled-granite look from sternum to pelvis. Arch your back, don't pause, then pull forward to a full contraction. You'll work your rectus abdominis from top to bottom and through a full range of motion, which means faster gains than you could achieve with inefficient half-range on-the-floor crunches. If your gym doesn't have an Ab Bench, you can

Crunch.   B. J. Quinn.

always use a high pulley and a preacher bench to simulate the full-range movement, but be sure not to overstretch. The Ab Bench prevents overstretch and spine compression, but with a cable setup it's entirely possible to injure yourself if you're not careful. Remember, the key is the pre-stretch with an arched back, which standard crunches lack.

STANDING LATERAL RAISE

Almost everyone who does lateral raises does them incorrectly. A strong statement? You bet, but it's the absolute truth. Here's how the faulty form goes: Stand, keep your arms bent, and heave the dumbbells up, with your torso taking on a pronounced backward lean as the dumbbells reach the muscles' contracted position. This is a great delt exercise—front delt, that is. To hit your lateral (side) heads, you must lean forward and keep your delts rolled forward as well. This activates the important lateral head that's so necessary if you want to

build that wide-as-a-barge look. Most bodybuilders have trouble sticking with this form, however. For that reason, the best way to target your lateral heads for some radical new stimulation is to perform the movement while sitting backward on a high-incline bench. Try holding the dumbbells at the top for a count for even better hypertrophy. If you can't stand reducing your poundage for this stricter version, do 2 sets of your regular "front-delt" laterals to satisfy your ego and end with 1 set of these strict side-head burners.

LUNGE

To perform standard lunges, you step forward with a weight across your shoulders, plant your foot, and bend your knee. Then you push off, step back, and step forward with your other leg. This can be somewhat dangerous if you lose your balance or you land too hard. A better way to lunge is to step back with the non-working leg instead of forward with the

Standing lateral raise.

working leg. This allows you to focus on each slow negative as you lower into a lunge, and turns the exercise into more of a one-leg squat than a knee-torquing balancing act. Plus, if you have a Smith machine, you can perform the exercise even more safely.

Do you consider yourself a hard gainer, someone who has to fight hard for every scrap of muscle? Well, Steve Holman has a comprehensive solution in this article. Follow these guidelines for exercise and nutrition, and your body will be transformed—hard gainer or not. This is the very program that Steve used to go from hard gainer to an easy gainer.

HARD-GAINER SOLUTION TO AMAZING MASS GAINS
Steve Holman

Your metabolism races faster than a revving Testarosa, your wrists and ankles have the diameters of twigs from an undernourished sapling, and your muscle growth is about as fast as a snail on Quaaludes. In bodybuilding, you're known as a hard gainer, but a better description would be genetically cursed. You believe you have about as much chance of hitting poses in front of a cheering crowd as Howard Stern has of becoming president of the Daughters of the American Revolution—even if he does look mighty fetching in a skirt and panty hose. It's impossible for you to attain a competition-worthy physique, right? Not so fast, there, fellow hard gainer.

Allow me to revert to first person for a few paragraphs and regale you with my own story. It's important for you to know that I'm not some genetic Dorian Yates–type superfreak telling hard gainers how to train. That would be like Troy Aikman trying to teach a guy with no arms how to throw a football 50 yards.

I'm far from gifted in the muscle-building department. Talk about genetically cursed! My father weighed all of 115 pounds—no doubt after a big meal—when he married my mother, who weighed a whopping 95, fully clothed and holding a large purse. It was a union of two string-bean physiques: Barney

Lunge.   Craig Titus.

Fife meets Olive Oyl. At 16, I was the spitting image of my rail of a father in his teenage years (okay, so I had him by about 5 pounds; I weighed in at just under 120).

When you're that skinny in high school, you do one of three things: You turn into an introvert and get beaten up a lot, join the chess club and get beaten up a lot, or lift weights so the thought of beating you up crosses fewer people's minds.

Of course, I was still damn skinny all through high school, even with my intense weight-training sessions. I was 5'10", and my bodyweight hovered around 160 during my senior year. I'm sure many readers can

Mike O'Hearn.

identify with that plight, but even at 160 I had enough visible muscle on my frame to ward off the majority of beatings. If bullies see a hint of sinew, they tend to look elsewhere for a victim.

Nevertheless, I was the living embodiment of Jolly Roger, the skull-and-crossbones figure on pirate flags, when I entered college, which may account for my voracious thirst for body-building knowledge. I knew it held the key to overcoming my physical inadequacies—if only I could determine the perfect training routine that would pack mass on my bamboo-shoot body.

At the University of Texas at Austin, I hit the books hard, doing most of my research papers on muscle growth and the best way to trigger it. I combed the science libraries for hypertrophy-related studies and abstracts; and, lo and behold, I actually uncovered a number of things that made efficient muscle building much easier, especially for hard gainers.

For example, I learned that the myotatic reflex occurs when a muscle is stretched and then forced to contract soon thereafter. The stretch puts the target muscle in an emergency-response mode, which can cause an inordinate number of muscle fibers to fire. In other words, you get more growth stimulation from each rep when the myotatic reflex is engaged. If you use it right, this technique can cause you to leapfrog genetic growth limitations by tricking the nervous system into believing it must grow in order to prevent severe trauma, as in muscle tears.

I took this knowledge into the gym and made some of the best gains of my life. My bodyweight eventually shot over the 200-pound mark, and I entered and won my very first bodybuilding contest. People were even accusing me of being an easy gainer.

This metabolic shift out of the genetic trash bin didn't just magically happen, how-ever. It took a lot of experimentation. While it's true that, once I identified and began using a stretch-position movement for each bodypart, my gains increased significantly, I also had to go back to my research and hone the other factors that contribute to muscle growth.

TRIGGERING HYPERTROPHY

According to Michael Wolf, Ph.D., the following changes are associated with increases in
muscle size and strength:

1. The actin and myosin protein filaments
   increase in size.
2. The number of myofibrils increases.
3. The number of blood capillaries within
   the fiber may increase.
4. The amount of connective tissue within
   the muscle may increase.
5. The number of muscle fibers may
   increase.

If you train in the 7-to-12-rep range with
heavy weights often enough, you stress the
type-II, or fast-twitch, muscle fibers, which
will positively affect the actin and myosin
filaments and increase the number of
myofibrils (1 and 2 in the list). Most bodybuilders know this is the appropriate mass-
building rep range and use it at every workout,
so there's no real insight for the hard gainer
there. However, item 3—increasing the number of blood capillaries—holds some real
muscle-building possibilities.

Forcing blood into the muscle and induc-
ing a pump causes new capillaries to form in
the target muscle, which increases the muscle's
size. How much bigger does the muscle get?
It's hard to say, because the percentage of
increase may depend on genetics. Ah, but isn't
this article about breaking through those barriers? Absolutely. So here are a couple of
things that facilitate the pump and force more
capillarization, no matter what your genetics.

Jonathan Lawson.

Carbohydrates

While dietary carbs are getting a bad rap these
days because of their association with insulin
and fat deposition, you, as a hard gainer,
shouldn't worry about that. Your blast-furnace
metabolism won't allow for much fat storage,
and any excess glycogen you can infuse into the
muscles will help you attain a skin-stretching
pump in the shortest time possible. Remember,
with your limited recovery ability, you can't
waste time and energy doing endless sets to

get a pump that increases the number of
capillaries. You have to blow up the muscle in
a few sets and then get out of the gym so you
can grow.

Try to eat some carbohydrates at every
meal, which means six times a day, along with
your feedings of 30 to 40 grams of protein.
Don't be afraid of taking in some fat at a few
of your meals, either. New research says that
fat can help bolster testosterone production,
which in turn can help you build muscle.

"Research shows that this type of training not only increases GH levels, but it also increases GH receptors located on the trained muscles." This is truly exciting research. Go for the burn, and you'll definitely pack on mass faster.

CONNECTIVE TISSUE AND FIBER SPLITTING

What about items 4 and 5 in our list (page 327)? How do you increase the amount of connective tissue and/or perhaps increase the number of muscle fibers?

Connective-tissue generation has to do with using heavy weights, so relying on the big compound movements like squats, deadlifts, and rows is key. Most hard gainers know that those exercises are best for mass stimulation, so they use them as the core of their workouts. In addition, stretch-position movements, such as sissy squats for quads and stiff-legged deadlifts for hamstrings, help increase connective tissue because they elongate the target muscle, creating more stress at the origin and insertion points.

As for increasing the number of muscle fibers, or *hyperplasia*, this is still a controversial topic. Some researchers believe it to be fantasy. Nevertheless, one animal study showed that muscle-fiber hyperplasia does occur as a result of—get ready—"stretch overload" (Antonio, J., and Gonyea, W. J. 1993. Skeletal muscle fiber hyperplasia. *Medicine and Science in Sports and Exercise.* 25:1333–45). The possibility of even small increases in the number of fast-twitch fibers is reason enough to use stretch-position movements. Another reason is fascial stretching.

Stretch-position movements stretch the fascia, or the membrane that encases the muscle fibers. A looser encasement can mean there's more freedom for a muscle to grow because there's less fiber constriction. A good example of this constriction/slow-growth connection is the former Chinese tradition of binding girls' feet. Because tiny feet were considered attractive in the Chinese culture, wealthy families had their daughters' feet

Supersets

Combining two exercises for the same muscle will do tremendous things for growth. Not only will it help you achieve a mind-blowing pump fast, spurring capillary generation, but new research suggests that it can also lower the pH of the blood and stimulate growth hormone (GH) release. As European researcher Michael Gündill wrote in "The Science of Supersetting," in the August 1997 *Ironman*,

tightly bound for years at a time so that growth would be stunted—and it worked, although it was extremely painful. Fascia can act in the same constricting manner and restrict a muscle's growth, according to a number of trainers and researchers, one of whom is John Parrillo.

Parrillo suggests performing separate fascial-stretching sessions to facilitate faster muscle growth, but when you incorporate stretch-position movements into your routine, you don't need special sessions. The stretch position movements do a good job of elongating the target muscles to the maximum and thus produce a fairly severe fascial stretch with each rep. To enhance the effect, you can hold the stretch position of your last rep on these exercises for 5 to 10 seconds, but don't do this on every rep or you diffuse the myotatic reflex.

UNLEASH NEW SIZE

One of the catch-22s of hard-gainer training is that to build a muscle to extraordinary levels, you must train it from a number of angles; but when you do that, you can overstress your recovery ability and overtrain, which slows or halts growth. The bottom line is, if you want tremendous muscle growth in every bodypart, you have to figure out a way to use multi-angular training without overtraining. Of course, many experts will tell you that all you need is one exercise per bodypart to get maximum development, but don't be fooled. It's just not that simple. If you follow that logic, you'll be using the hard-gainer excuse for the rest of your days. The reality is that only certain fibers, those that have the best leverage during a particular exercise, will grow as a result of your doing that exercise, so you have to make sure the fibers contract in a variety of positions if you want to maximize the number of fibers that get total growth stimulation.

Here's a quote from Jaci VanHeest, renowned exercise physiologist at the United States Olympic Training Center in Colorado Springs, Colorado, that will help you under-

stand the need for more than one exercise per bodypart:

Muscles contract when tiny levers on myosin, a muscle protein, fit into grooves on actin, another protein, and push it forward exactly like a ratchet wrench. But myosin can latch onto actin in any of several positions, not all of them ideal. Only when the myosin heads are in the right register can the muscle have the optimal tension. But optimizing every actin–myosin pairing is less an achievable goal than a Platonic ideal.

Essentially, that means almost every exercise optimizes a different configuration of actin–myosin pairings. While there's some overlap, you have to exercise a muscle in a number of positions to optimize as many of the actin–myosin pairings as possible.

After reading this quote, you may think that you, the hard gainer with limited recovery ability, are doomed. You can't possibly train every muscle from a variety of angles without smashing headfirst into the overtraining wall. Ah, but what if you used different exercises at different workouts to cover all the angles—say, in two workouts—rather than trying to do all angles at one session? You would leap over your so-called genetic barriers and grow beyond your wildest imagination.

THE ULTIMATE HARD-GAINER ROUTINE

To construct the Ultimate Hard-Gainer Routine, we must first identify what *multi-angular training* means. Each muscle essentially has three positions, or angles, you should strive to train in order to optimize as many actin–myosin pairings as possible: midrange, stretch, and contracted. Many of you will recognize this as Positions of Flexion (POF). For those of you unfamiliar with POF, here's a quick example using triceps.

- You train the midrange position with close-grip bench presses or lying extensions.
- You train the stretch position with overhead extensions—upper arms next to your head.
- You train the contracted position with kickbacks—upper arms behind the torso for a maximum contraction.

Note that you train three different points along the arc of flexion—from the overhead position to the hands-over-the-chest position to the behind-the-torso position.

This arc isn't as simple to define for some bodyparts, such as quads, but you can still put

B. J. Quinn.

every exercise into one of those categories. Squats, leg presses, and hack squats are midrange movements because they do not completely stretch or fully contract the quads and they use synergy from other muscles to help the quads perform work; a sissy squat is a stretch-position movement for quads because the torso and thighs are on the same plane, and when the hamstrings and calves meet, the quads are completely stretched; and leg extensions are the contracted-position movement because the torso and thighs are at almost 90 degrees to each other and there is resistance in the contracted, or knees-locked, position.

On this mass-boosting program, you do the midrange and contracted exercises on Monday and superset the stretch and midrange movements on Friday for an awesome pump and fiber hypercontraction. On Wednesday, you train arms, calves, and abs, hitting all three positions for most of these bodyparts.

Give the Ultimate Hard-Gainer Routine a fair trial, make adjustments where necessary, and you may be surprised at just how much easier it is to put on muscle. In fact, after you add slabs of new muscle to every bodypart, you may even be accused of being an easy gainer—by the other four finalists standing on stage with you waiting for the winner's name to be called.

1. Each workout takes about one hour—with fewer than 20 work sets—which is perfect for the hard gainer's limited recovery ability. You can keep your intensity high without burning out.

2. There's a day of rest between workouts, and then two days' rest at the end of the cycle, which facilitates systemic recovery.

3. The big compound movements are at the core of each workout—the first exercise for each bodypart on Monday and Wednesday and the second exercise in the supersets on Friday. They train the mass of the target muscle and also help develop tendon and ligament size and strength.

4. The use of supersets and drop sets helps develop more capillaries in the target muscle and also can increase growth hormone release. Plus, by using stretch-position movements as the first exercise in a superset, you kick the muscles into hypercontraction, which activates extreme fiber recruitment during the second exercise in the superset.

5. The use of stretch-position movements on Wednesday and Friday helps stretch the fascia to allow for more muscle growth, develops tendon and ligament size and strength, and produces more fiber recruitment through neurological stimulation and by placing the muscle in an emergency-response mode. Stretch overload may also cause hyperplasia, or fiber splitting, which can increase the growth potential of a muscle.

6. The rep ranges listed are ideal for activating type-II muscle fibers, which

Steve Cuevas.

are the fibers with the most growth potential.

7. By training each muscle from three distinct angles, or positions—midrange, stretch, and contracted—you optimize as many actin–myosin pairings as possible and therefore stimulate complete development in every target muscle.

8. Arms get only one direct hit a week, which prevents overtraining them. Remember, you get indirect arm work from all the pressing, rowing, and pulling at your other two workouts.

Monday
Quads and hamstrings

Squat or leg press*	2 × 7–10
Leg extension	1 × 7–10

Hamstring

Leg curl*	2 × 7–10

Chest

Bench press*	2 × 7–10
Crossover	1 × 7–10

Delts

Dumbbell press*	2 × 7–10
Lateral raise	1 × 7–10

Lats

Front pulldown*	2 × 7–10
Stiff-arm pulldown	1 × 7–10

Midback

Behind-the-neck pulldown*	2 × 7–10
Forward-lean shrug	1 × 7–10

Wednesday
Triceps

Lying extension*	2 × 7–10

Superset

Overhead extension	2 × 5–8
Kickback	2 × 5–8

Biceps

Barbell curl*	2 × 7–10

Superset

Incline curl	2 × 5–8
Spider curl	2 × 5–8

Calves

Superset

Donkey calf raise or leg press calf raise*	2 × 10–15
Standing calf raise	2 × 10–15
Seated calf raise	2 × 12–20

Abdominals

Incline knee-up	2 × 7–10
Full-range crunch or Ab Bench crunch pull	2 × 7–10

*Do one or two light warm-up sets with 50 to 70 percent of your work-set weight prior to your work sets.

Friday
Quad superset

Sissy squat	2 × 5–8
Squat or leg press	2 × 5–8

Hamstrings drop set*

Stiff-legged deadlift	2 × 5–8

Chest superset

Flat-bench flye	2 × 5–8
Bench press	2 × 5–8

Delt superset

One-arm incline lateral	2 × 5–8
One-arm dumbbell press	2 × 5–8

Lat superset

Dumbbell pullover	2 × 5–8
Front pulldown	2 × 5–8

Midback drop set*

Forward-lean shrug	2 × 5–8

* To perform a drop set, do one set to failure, then quickly reduce the weight and perform another set to failure.

Note: Do one light warm-up set of each exercise before doing your superset. Also, stop your stretch-exercise work set a few reps short of failure, but push the second exercise till you can't get another rep in perfect form.

Using stretch-position movements has a number of hypertrophic benefits, including the following:

- Loosens fascial constriction to facilitate more fiber growth
- Develops tendon and ligament size and strength
- Increases neuromuscular efficiency for better fiber recruitment
- May stimulate hyperplasia, or fiber splitting (this is still debatable from a scientific standpoint)

Here's a list of the best stretch-position exercises for each bodypart:

- Quads: sissy squat
- Hamstrings: stiff-legged deadlift
- Calves: donkey calf raise or leg press calf raise
- Chest: flye
- Delts: one-arm incline lateral
- Lats: pullover
- Midback: close-grip cable row
- Biceps: incline curl
- Triceps: overhead extension
- Abdominals: full-range crunch

Incorporating these exercises into your routine—using correct form—at least once a week can significantly increase muscle growth.

POINTS TO REMEMBER

Allow your system to recover

Power Factor Training author Pete Sisco has been saying for years that "every workout is a kidney workout," and Mike Mentzer has said practically the same thing. The statement refers to the fact that your whole body must recover from a workout, not just the muscle group you trained. In other words, it makes no difference to your nervous system that yesterday was leg day and today is back day. That's the first thing people need to understand when they begin training or when they're not making gains. Overtraining is the number-one culprit. If you're not making progress, make sure you're not working out more than three days a week—Monday, Wednesday, and Friday, for example. Also, you don't have to train your whole body on each day. Split it up, but don't train two days in a row.

Use the best exercises

There are good exercises, and then there are the best exercises. You should always pick the best exercises over the good ones. For example,

Mike O'Hearn.

pulldowns are good for lat width, but wide-grip pullups are best. The bottom line is neuromuscular adaptation, or NMA.

Muscles ultimately grow from stimulation to the nervous system—or perhaps don't grow because of too much stimulation (remember item 1 from our list [page 327]). The more neural activation you get from an exercise, the better the results. Generally, the harder the

exercise, the more neuromuscular activation. That's why free weights are better than machines, and compound free-weight movements are better than isolation exercises with free weights.

The best exercises are ones in which your body moves through space—squats, dips, chins, and deadlifts. Harder usually means best.

Change routines often

Your body is amazingly adaptive. The more advanced you are, the better your body is at adapting to workouts. Once your body adapts to the routine you're doing, growth stops cold in its tracks.

Great bodybuilders have an innate ability to determine when they need to change things. Arnold Schwarzenegger was a master at this. He changed his routine almost every time he went to the gym—and his muscle growth was almost continuous.

How often should you change your routine, and what type of changes should you make? After three to four weeks of the same training regimen, your body has adapted and you're ready for change.

The reason your body adapts to your workouts is due to your nervous system, which learns to do an exercise more efficiently at each workout. Let's say you attempt a new chest workout this week. During the first week, since the stimulus is new, you might recruit 75 to 80 percent of your pec muscle fibers. At the next workout you recruit fewer, and by about the fourth week you may only be recruiting 40 to 50 percent of your pec muscle fibers. Now it's time for a new stimulus.

Research suggests that your body adapts to your choice of exercises the slowest. In other words, changing exercises is not as good as changing the manner in which you perform your workout.

For maximum results, try a new workout style every three to four weeks. For example, do high-intensity, short-duration Heavy Duty workouts for four weeks, then switch to 10 sets of 10, then move to a Positions of Flexion program, and so on.

René Endara.

Pick your protein and eat regularly

You can choose the best exercises, train correctly, and get enough rest between workouts, but if you don't consume sufficient calories and protein, then it's all for nothing.

The most important aspect of nutritional muscle building is consuming enough calories to facilitate the growth of muscle. Many bodybuilders fail to gain because they don't eat enough. Studies have shown that when people overeat, they not only gain fat, they gain muscle as well. It's a big myth—albeit a widely accepted one—that when you eat too much, you only store excess calories as fat. You also gain a lot of muscle, so if you're a hard gainer, you need to eat the world.

Next to not eating enough, it's inadequate protein intake that prevents people from gaining muscle. Be sure to consume at least 1 gram of protein per pound of bodyweight, and 1½ to 2 grams is probably better.

Eat-to-grow rule number one for the hard gainer is to feed yourself at least 20 grams of protein every three hours. Rule number two is to add some carbohydrates to your protein feeding—throw a banana in the blender with your protein powder, or eat some raisins.

Everyone knows that protein builds muscle tissue, but why eat carbs? Carbohydrates fill your muscles with glycogen so they'll pump to the maximum at every workout, and that facilitates capillary generation. Carbs also stimulate insulin, one of the most powerful anabolic hormones the body produces, which may be the very reason teenagers crave junk food—so they kick insulin production into overdrive and grow. That's only the beginning, however. A high-carbohydrate diet has also been shown to suppress cortisol. This is a stress hormone that can cause your body to eat its own muscle tissue. It's an emergency reaction from your body, the so-called fight-or-flight mechanism.

For example, let's say you're living a few million years B.C. and you're in your cave, eating barbecued mammoth. A 500-pound sabertooth happens to catch a whiff of your meal and enters your cave for a bite. Of course,

you've just polished off the last mouthful, and all that's left for him to fill his stomach is you. Once you realize this, your adrenaline level skyrockets, giving you the ability to jump about 20 feet over the sabertooth, fly out the door of your cave and then run like hell—right past a gazelle sprinting at full speed. This episode causes your body to pump immense amounts of cortisol into your bloodstream, which helps your system break down tissue, including loads of muscle, for immediate energy. As a bodybuilder today you want to minimize cortisol surges so that you avoid the catabolism they can cause. You say you don't confront sabertooths too often? Well, it's not just life-and-death situations that stimulate cortisol production, especially in high-strung hard gainers. Any stress can cause it, from high-intensity workouts to not eating to relationship problems to deadlines at work to final exams.

Hard gainers are especially susceptible to cortisol surges, so in addition to a high-carb diet, a phosphatidylserine (PS) supplement may help facilitate the muscle-building process. Ps was shown in two Italian studies to suppress cortisol by up to 33 percent—which can create a muscle-building bonanza for ectomorphs. Champion Nutrition makes a PS supplement called Cortistat, and Muscle-Linc has its best-selling Cort-Bloc. Either of these is a great addition to the high-carb, medium-protein, medium-fat hard-gainer diet that follows.

Other supplements worth a try include a whey protein powder, to make those three-hour feedings more convenient, and creatine monohydrate. Creatine affects the anaerobic energy mechanisms in the muscle, which means it can help you train harder. It also helps increase muscle volume, possibly through water retention in the muscle cells. Reports of 10-pound muscle gains after just a few weeks of creatine supplementation are not uncommon—especially in athletes who don't eat a lot of red meat, a high-creatine food. There are a number of good powdered creatine products out there, including Twinlab's Creatine Fuel and EAS's Phosphagen HP.

Steve Cuevas.

Hard gainers should also take a good multivitamin and mineral supplement as well as the antioxidants—vitamins C (500 milligrams) and E (500 international units) and beta-carotene (20,000 international units). These compounds will help the body optimize its recovery ability and prime the system for spectacular hypertrophy.

Here's a good eating schedule, adapted from the 10-Week Size Surge Diet, that gives you about 3,000 calories, with 25 percent protein, 25 percent fat, and 50 percent carbs, along with a basic supplement program.

Meal 1
Milk (2%), 8 oz
Oatmeal, 8 oz
Eggwhites, 2 (stirred into oatmeal)
Dates, ¼ cup (about 5 whole dates)
Supplements: vitamin and mineral tablet

Meal 2
Whey protein powder in milk with
* banana*

Meal 3
Roasted chicken, 6 oz
Lima beans, 6 oz
Rice, 1 cup
Sherbet, 3 scoops

Meal 4
Cottage cheese, 6 oz
Pears (canned in own juice), 4 halves

Meal 5
Peanut butter and jelly sandwich on
* whole-wheat bread*
Milk (2%), 8 oz

Meal 6 (right after training)
Whey protein powder in milk with
* banana*
Supplements: creatine, PS (cortisol
* blocker)*

Meal 7
Tuna sandwich on whole-wheat bread
* (tuna packed in water)*
Apple
Peanuts (handful)

Before bed
Supplements: PS (cortisol blocker),
* antioxidants*
(C, E, and beta-carotene), amino acid
* capsules*

If all of that information from Steve Holman was not enough to convince you that there are answers to even the most challenging hard-gainer mass problems, look at his article on "Size Made Simple." These proven techniques are taken from some of the greatest names in the sport.

SIZE MADE SIMPLE   Steve Holman
Exercise programs come and go, and some even stay around for a while. Every now and then, an old lifting technique is revived because some researcher declares it's the ultimate way to put on muscle size; for example, partial reps. An old system may also get new life because a certain bodybuilding star uses it. That was the case when Dorian Yates revived

Mike Mentzer's Heavy Duty training. Five years ago, no one trained that heavy. Things changed overnight when Dorian started talking about his training.

There's a training system that hardly anyone uses today that's due for a revival—the one-exercise-per-muscle-group technique. There are no champs touting its effectiveness in magazine articles. No one uses it in this modern age of multiple exercises. Even so, it's not likely you'll ever find a better way to train for size.

There are several benefits to using the one-exercise-per-muscle-group technique, not the least of which is that it works well with a number of different bodybuilding programs. Probably the best feature is that you don't lose your pump. You know how that goes: you're training really hard on an exercise and getting an excellent pump when you decide to move on to another exercise; the next thing you

know, the pump is gone and your workout goes downhill from there. Have you ever thought about just sticking with that exercise for 6, 8, or maybe 10 to 15 sets?

This training style is also excellent when the only thing you want is sheer muscle mass. There have been several champs who used it almost exclusively, and their progress was remarkable. The most prominent example is Sergio Oliva. The three-time Mr. Olympia's favorite way to train chest and back was to alternate sets, performing one for his chest and one for his back. The trick was that he stayed with only one exercise for each muscle group, primarily bench presses and chins.

Oliva would pyramid his weight on the two exercises. On bench presses, for example, he'd start off with a light weight and work up to a heavy triple, double, or single on about his tenth set. From that point on, he'd reverse-pyramid, dropping weight and adding reps.

Now, Sergio was no slouch in the genetics department. He'd probably have grown muscle no matter what routine he performed. He did, however, prefer this style above all others.

Reg Park is another legend of bodybuilding who liked to train this way. He believed it to be the ultimate for building mass. He'd pick one exercise for whatever bodypart he was working and just hammer at it, using 6 to 10

reps until that bodypart was engorged with a monstrous pump.

Tom Platz is also a proponent of one-exercise-per-bodypart training. He often performs up to 30 sets per exercise. On back, for example, he usually does T-bar rows for a full hour using sets of 6 to 100 reps. The key to his success with this technique is that he allows at least seven days of rest before he blitzes the same bodypart again.

The point of these examples is that the one-exercise-per-bodypart routines are some of the most effective you'll ever find for working any of your muscle groups.

THE PYRAMID/REVERSE-PYRAMID SYSTEM

This is the technique that Sergio Oliva used. When it comes to adding bulk and power, I don't believe it can be beat. You can either work one muscle group until you complete all the sets or alternate antagonistic muscle groups the way Sergio did, using what Platz calls jump sets. Either variation is great. Following is a sample routine for the bench press in which you work straight through before going on to the next bodypart. Note that the weights listed are only hypothetical, to give you an idea of the jumps.

Set 1:	135×12
Set 2:	185×10
Set 3:	205×8
Set 4:	225×6
Set 5:	245×4
Set 6:	265×2
Set 7:	275×1
Set 8:	225×6
Set 9:	205×8–10
Set 10:	185×8–10
Set 11:	135×12–15
Set 12:	135×12–15

If you feel that you grow better with fewer sets, then you don't need to perform so many. Just make sure you're warmed up well before you jump to an extremely heavy set. Also, don't try a heavy single or double every time you lift. You'll only burn yourself out. It's best to hold a little back most of the time. That keeps you from overtraining and also keeps you hungry for the iron at every workout.

Another variable that makes this particular routine effective is that you perform a wide range of reps, which ensures that you hit every muscle fiber. Every once in a while you might try some really high reps on your final 2 to 4 sets. I'm talking the 20-to-50 range. That type of training helps build your blood vessels, capillaries, and neuromuscular pathways, which are needed for a huge pump.

René Endara.

DROP SETS

You've no doubt heard of drop sets. They're also called strip sets, down-the-racks (when used with dumbbells), and descending sets.

Most of the time when people incorporate drop sets, they tend to let their reps drop with each drop in weight. The most effective way to perform these, however, is to maintain your reps or increase them as you decrease the weight. Popular IFBB (International Federation of Bodybuilders) pro Eddie Robinson trains that way almost exclusively. He claims it's the best method he knows for adding mass. Eddie picks one exercise and performs it for only 4 drop sets. Most of the time he finishes each bodypart in about eight minutes.

If you think you can handle that, try Eddie's system. Pick a single exercise and do 3 or 4 heavy sets that drop from heavy to moderate to light, and see how tough you really are.

BURNOUTS

Perform one exercise for an all-out war with no mercy: that's the philosophy behind burnouts. Paul DeMayo regularly shocks his muscles with this single-exercise technique, and it's hell—so consider yourself warned.

The best way to do burnouts is with a training partner. If you haven't got one, you'll need one. Pick one exercise and challenge each other with what DeMayo calls *burndowns*. Take turns going back and forth until you can get only 1 or 2 reps. The trick is to keep the action moving. Your partner starts his or her set as soon as you finish yours, and vice versa.

If you decide to do this with either squats or—God forbid—deadlifts, be sure you have what Platz calls a "breathing bench" nearby. That's a bench for you to lie on between sets, gasping for breath.

TEN SETS OF TEN

This is probably the most common one-exercise-per-bodypart routine, and for good reason: it works. Vince Gironda has touted this training technique for years because, he says, it's probably the single best way to train, and it's really helpful in bring up a lagging bodypart.

When using the 10-sets-of-10 approach on any bodypart, don't start out with your heaviest poundage for 10 reps. Pick a weight that you can probably handle for a few more reps. The trick here is to hold your rest between sets to less than a minute, preferably 30 seconds. You're guaranteed a monstrous pump from this workout.

AND IF ALL OF THIS HASN'T CONVINCED YOU . . .

Here's a little information about one-exercise-per-muscle-group training you may not have known: the great Arnold Schwarzenegger, when he wanted to blast a particular muscle group into oblivion, would perform this kind of workout. Once a week he and a training partner would drive into the country with some weights, limiting the workout to one exercise. As he described it in *Education of a Bodybuilder*:

> I remember for the first day we carried 250 pounds into the forest and did squats for three hours straight. I began by doing 20 repetitions with 250 pounds, then my partner did whatever he could. Then it was my turn again. We ended up doing something like 55 sets of squats. The last hour was endless. Our thighs pumped up like balloons. That first day we gave our thigh muscles such a shock that we couldn't walk right for a week, and each of us put something like an eighth or a quarter of an inch on our thighs.

Now, Arnold took this to a maniac level. He and his partner always brought girls with them, and after they finished their shock training, they'd guzzle wine and beer, have a barbecue, and get drunk. As Arnold put it, "We carried on like the old-time weightlifters—sometimes it became pure insanity."

But it worked.

ONE EXERCISE PER BODYPART

If you're looking for a routine that will pack on some serious mass, this one-exercise-per-bodypart routine will pack it on and pack it on fast—if you're consistent with it for the next two to three months. Are you ready? Here it is:

Monday and Thursday

Squat	5 × 10, 8, 6, 5, 4*
Leg curl	5 × 8–12
Standing calf raise	5 × 12–20
Seated calf raise	5 × 12–20
Full-range cable crunch or Ab Bench crunch pull	5 × 8–12

Tuesday and Friday

Bench press	5 × 10, 8, 6, 5, 4*
Incline bench press	3 × 8–12
Undergrip pulldown	5 × 10, 8, 6, 5, 4*
Bent-over row or cable row	5 × 10, 8, 6, 5, 4*
Dumbbell upright row or dumbbell press	5 × 10, 8, 6, 5, 4*
Barbell curl	3 × 8–12
Lying triceps extension	3 × 8–12

*Your first 10-rep set should be light enough to count as a warm-up, then pile on the next poundage and go for broke on the 4 sets, adding weight after each set.

Ted Arcidi.

Chapter 13

TRAINING FOR POWER

An athlete who wants to develop awesome power has no choice but the iron: lifting heavy weights is the only thing that triggers the physiological response necessary to develop impressive muscular power. This chapter will show you the techniques, exact routines, and mental attitudes of powerlifters like world-record holder Ted Arcidi, Judd Biasiotto, Bill Pearl, and Don Ross.

TED ARCIDI'S BENCH PRESS SECRETS Ted Arcidi

If you've ever had the opportunity to see world-class powerlifting champions in action, you probably noticed that they don't just walk up to the bench, collapse on it, grab the bar, and attempt to press out a world record. In fact, it's a precise technique emphasis—coupled with considerable drilling on the mechanics of the bench press—that has enabled me to set the standard for twenty-first-century championship bench pressing.

I'm going to walk you briefly through my preparations prior to benching, say, 635 pounds for a triple and 650 pounds for a nice double. My lifting apparel includes a pair of sweatpants, a warm-up jacket, a lifting belt, and tennis shoes—but no bench shirt. I never wear a bench shirt during my workouts, for I believe it would weaken the integrity of my tendons and ligaments. Usually, I have a couple of training partners load up the bar for me—although I always make a point to check that the correct poundage is on the bar and that the spin-lock collars are tightened down. Sometimes, before an attempt I go over to the bench and get into position under the bar without actually unracking it, just to get the mind-set going.

In my workout attempts, I'm generally after pure power rather than Herculean muscle size, so I take a rest that's not going to give me a pump. My body usually needs at least 5 minutes to recover after most sets, and a minimum of 10 minutes (sometimes) between maximum lifts like 650 and beyond. If a powerlifter is looking for maximum muscle size along with some really big numbers in the big three, then I suggest taking 4 to 10 minutes' rest between sets of those lifts and 7 minutes' rest between sets on the assistance work.

Ted Arcidi.

I use the rest to focus on the next set, for I know that even a momentary lapse in concentration can throw off my technique emphasis just enough to make me lose a rep or two for a few extra bench press pounds. Just before I begin a set, I chalk the bench surface, pull up the sleeves of my warm-up jacket, and put on some full-length wrist wraps for support and to reduce wrist pain. Then I cinch my lifting belt tight, and I'm ready to go.

The gym buzzes with the electricity of encouragement as I approach the bench. I turn so my backside faces the foot of the bench. While I'm still standing, I take in a healthy gulp of air. Then I sit on the foot of the bench and place my feet 3 to 4 inches away from the base, with my toes pointed outward about 45 degrees. I make sure that the soles and heels of my shoes remain in contact with the lifting platform at all times. Usually at meets or exhibitions, such as the one I put on at the Mr. Olympia, I wear a pair of power shoes, which

provide good traction. At workouts, though, I usually wear a pair of high-cut suede sneakers.

I crack an ammonia capsule and inhale its contents to clear my head. A microsecond later, I lie back on the bench. I position my head so that my eyes are about an inch past the racked barbell, and my shoulders are 4 to 6 inches from the upright support rack. At this point my head, shoulders, upper back, lower back, and buttocks are in direct contact with the bench. I don't go for the big arch that most of the top powerlifters do, for I simply can't arch due to the extreme thickness in my back. I can only speculate how much more weight I could bench with a nice 8-inch arch than I'm doing with the flat-back style.

The next thing is hand placement. I take a conventional thumbs-under-the-bar grip, which is just narrower than the allowable 32 inches between the forefingers. As a matter of fact, during world-record attempts I move my hands an inch closer than what I do for regular workouts in order to use my powerful triceps and deltoid muscles to their maximum. To get a better idea of what I'm talking about here, I suggest you check out the cover photo of the November 1990 issue of *Powerlifting USA*.

I squeeze the bar as tightly as I can, and this in turn tightens my wrists, elbows, and shoulders. The action makes the whole bench press movement more fluid.

I'm now ready for a smooth liftoff. At the count of three, my spotter helps me lift the barbell out of the upright support racks—but not more than 3 inches or too far out in front of me. I might mention that my spotter does the liftoff from the center of the bar with an over-and-under grip.

After the bar is unracked and I'm supporting it under my own power, I take half a breath and begin lowering the bar to my chest. This action usually takes anywhere from one and a half to two seconds. There are times, though, when I do it a bit quicker, in one to one and a quarter seconds.

I like to let the bar touch my chest about one-half inch below the nipples. If I position the bar any higher than that, it affects the power groove by constricting my delts and puts major stress on my rotator cuffs, which are almost turned up at an angle rather than flat. When the rotator cuffs are flat, the stress is more evenly distributed, and there's less chance for injury.

I don't believe in tucking my arms into my sides when the bar touches my chest; in fact, I flare them out to about 45 to 50 degrees perpendicular to my body. That's the most natural movement for me.

I think of my chest as a minefield and my big, thick lats as the elastic cocking of a gun.

Using primarily those two muscle groups, I blast training poundages and world-record attempts off my chest. Most of the top world-champion powerlifters I know press the barbell off their chest in an arc toward the uprights, but not me. I've overdeveloped my deltoids and triceps just so I can power press the weight up vertically. I finish each and every rep without employing any performance tricks, and my spotter helps me re-rack the weight.

I hope my technique helps you blast your training poundages, too.

Ted Arcidi.

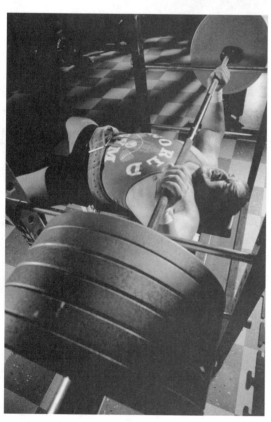

The late Don Ross, Pro Mr. America, was a hardcore bodybuilder if ever there was one. His "Secrets of Super Strength" are garnered from many years as a powerlifter and bodybuilding author.

SECRETS OF SUPER STRENGTH: UNLOCK YOUR BODY'S AWESOME POWER POTENTIAL Don Ross

A muscular physique indicates power. It's no wonder that average people stop bodybuilders to ask how much they lift. This question is often annoying to bodybuilders, whose routines produce primarily visual rather than functional results.

There are many different approaches to increasing muscle size. Although an increase in muscle size indicates increased strength, each of the approaches results in different types of strength. I've written a lot about sustained strength from heavy, nonstop descending-set and superset training. Endurance strength from high-rep training, on the other hand, allows you to do more with lighter poundages. When most people think of strength, they envision explosive strength—those huge bench presses, powerful squats, and overhead presses.

This is why people want to see you arm-wrestle the local tough guy at parties. If you can tear a telephone book or bend a spike at a get-together, they'll be more satisfied than if you just flexed your biceps. People want to see strength performances. Seeing is believing.

Practically speaking, that extra strength can bring about victory in athletics. It can save the day in an emergency situation where strength is needed at once to move a heavy object. Strength makes emergency tasks possible. All through life you will run into situations where you'll be glad you took the time to train for power.

The early bodybuilding champions all trained for strength, and the strongman bodybuilders remain legends—from Eugene Sandow, John Grimek, Marvin Eder, Reg Park, Chuck Sipes, and Franco Columbo. Those of you who do well in physique shows but don't approach world records in your poundages can improve your strength considerably if you incorporate the following secrets of super strength into your training.

In most cases, you should do your strength training during the off-season. Contest training requires full concentration on visuals. After the show and a short layoff to recuperate from the mental and physical stress is the best time to begin your power training. These workouts should be short and basic with days in between for recuperation and growth. Shorter workouts with fewer exercises and sets allow you much more energy for power. At first, while your mind is conditioned to those longer bodybuilding workouts, they'll seem too brief; but if you stay with the program, you'll experience that excess energy in the form of rapidly increasing strength.

THE POWER BODYBUILDING PROGRAM

The exercises may look simple—they're mostly basic movements—but any accomplished power bodybuilder will tell you that it's not so much the exercises you choose as it is the effort and form you use. We use these particular movements because they work muscle areas in groups rather than isolating specific aspects as in bodybuilding or specialized athletic training.

Begin each exercise with a light warm-up set. Do deep, slow movements to stretch ligaments and tendons while "waking up" the muscle fibers. Do 20 easy reps.

Next, do your heavy sets. Explode on the initial (positive) movement, and use slow, controlled return movements. Have a reliable spotter standing by to give you just enough assistance to complete the prescribed reps.

Day 1: Chest and Triceps Power
Bench press. Medium-wide grip to the mid-chest, elbows out. $2 \times 6, 2 \times 4,$ $2 \times 2, 2 \times 1$

Incline press. Use a barbell and set the bench to 35 degrees. $2 \times 5, 2 \times 3$

Don Ross.

Dip. Add weight, lean forward, and keep your elbows out.   4 × 4–5

Lying triceps press. Lie on a bench with a barbell overhead. Bring the bar to your forehead while bending the elbows and keeping them pointed up. Don't move your upper arms. Push back up, flexing your triceps.   6 × 5–6

Day 2: Shoulders and Pulling Strength
Military press. Take a bar off the squat rack onto your front delts. Hold it at your chest with a medium grip, and, without bending back, push the bar overhead.   2 × 6, 2 × 4

High pull. High pulls are similar to upright rows, but with a medium grip. Start with the weight at your thighs. Pull the bar up to your chin using your legs and body momentum. Use your shoulders and traps to control the return movement.   3 × 6, 5, 4

Shrug. Do shrugs with a barbell (and wrist straps if necessary). Bring your shoulders as high as possible. Hold, then lower slowly.   3 × 8

Bent-over row. Take a medium grip on a barbell. Keep your body parallel to the floor. Pull the bar to your body. Hold and lower slowly. Don't use body momentum: it's hard on your lower back.   2 × 6, 2 × 4

Power chin. Use a weight on a weight belt (and straps, if necessary). Stand on a crate or other support as you take a wide grip on the bar. Boost yourself up off the crate. Touch your chin to the bar, then lower yourself slowly. Do the second set with a medium grip and the third with a close grip. Do 6 reps per set. Finish with a nonweighted set of medium-grip chins for as many as possible.

Power curl. After a set of strict curls for 10 reps, take a heavy barbell. Rock forward, then swing the weight to your chest, using momentum and keeping your back slightly bent. Lower the bar very slowly, then immediately begin another rep. $2 \times 6, 2 \times 4$

Day 3: Off

Day 4: Leg Power
Warm up.
Do stretches and no-weight squats.

Half-squat. Inhale deeply as you squat down halfway. Exhale on the way up. You may need a board under your heels if you can't keep your heels down. You might want to use a power rack or Smith machine for safety. $2 \times 8, 2 \times 4, 2 \times 2$

Day 5: Off

Now let's review the strength techniques you should incorporate during the first five days:

- First, you use lower reps and ascending-set progression. This allows good warm-ups as a prelude to all-out effort.
- Take longer rests between sets—around three minutes, or enough to completely regain your energy for the next set.

- Use a reliable assistant and go beyond your natural strength capabilities with one or two forced reps at the end of your final sets.
- Use slow negative movements (you should always use these, but they're especially important now, as they provide extra work for the muscles and prevent bouncing or momentum reps).
- On Day 2, use the cheating principle on three exercises: high pulls, power curls, and power chins. You employ body momentum movements for these exercises in order to overload the muscles and tendons, which causes physical strength increases and helps you overcome psychological barriers when handling heavy poundages. It is most important to use slow negative movements during a cheat exercise; this focuses on the negative part and also prevents injury on what is an otherwise dangerous practice.
- On leg day, use partial movements, breaking the squat into two exercises. This way you don't limit yourself to

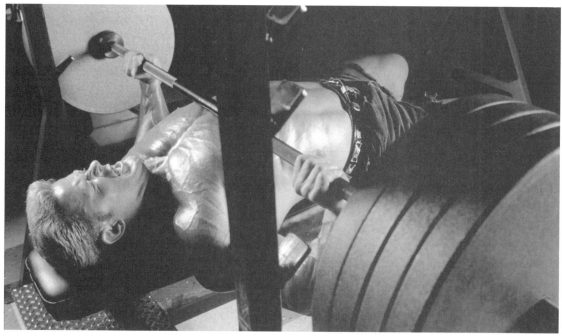

Art Dilkes.

the weight that you can do during the difficult part (low squat) of the movement.

On Day 6, you apply little-used techniques guaranteed to break all physical and psychological strength barriers!

Day 6: Supports and Lockouts

These methods were taught to me by Chuck Sipes back in the late '60s. Chuck was Mr. Universe and a runner-up in the Mr. Olympia. At a solid, ripped bodyweight of just under 220 pounds at 5′9″, Sipes bench pressed 570 pounds in strict form! When I added these techniques to my routine, my strength increased 15 percent in just a few weeks.

Bench press support. Begin with 20 percent more than your maximum bench press. Lie directly under the racks. Have two spotters help you lift the weight. Support it at arm's length for 10 to 20 seconds or until the weight forces itself down to the racks. Do 3 sets, trying for 20 seconds. Now remove 20 percent of the weight and resume the same position. This time, do a set of 6 to 10 lockouts, pushing the weight from the rack to arm's length. Do 1 set of lockouts.

Squat support and lockout. Perform this exercise as you did the bench press supports. Keep your legs locked for 3 sets of up to 20 seconds. Conclude by reducing the weight 20 percent and doing a set of lockouts.

Overhead press lockout. Set the bar on a rack so it is level with the top of your head. Stand beneath the bar and take a medium press grip. Push the weight overhead, straightening your arms. Use a poundage that enables you to do 6 reps. Do 3 sets.

Deadlift. Keep your back straight and knees bent. Use an alternate grip on the bar. Take two or three deep breaths between reps. Do 3 sets of 4 reps. This is a full-movement exercise.

Day 7: Off

SECRETS OF CONTINUOUS STRENGTH GAINS

Having been around both lifters and bodybuilders, I have observed that power bodybuilders succumb to injury more frequently than lifters do. The reason is that many of these athletes try to apply bodybuilding philosophy to power training. They always go for more, always go to failure.

Experienced lifters, on the other hand, back-cycle frequently in poundages. Back-cycling amounts to taking one step backward and two steps forward. The results are continuous gains without those setbacks due to torn and pulled muscles, ligaments, and tendons.

Let's take the bench press as an example. You work up to sets of doubles with 300 pounds. On the next chest workout, increase all your poundages by 5 pounds so you end up with 305 for doubles. Increase again by 5 pounds on your third workout, finishing with 310. For your fourth workout, go back down 5 pounds so you finish with 305.

Ted Arcidi, the first man to bench press more than 700 pounds, uses another method. On the first workout, he goes all out for maximum efforts. The second time he trains those bodyparts, he uses the same exercises for the same number of reps but lifts 40 to 50 percent less weight! The object is to work the neural pathways so as not to lose strength while allowing the microtraumas (slight, undetectable injuries that always occur during all-out efforts) to heal and the muscles to fully recover. In applying Arcidi's technique to this routine, you alternate heavy weeks with maintenance weeks.

Stay with this program for six to eight weeks. Your raw power will increase amazingly. When you return to your bodybuilding routine, you'll have even more muscle mass to work with. Once your stamina is restored, those poundages will seem easy.

Paul DeMayo.

Franco Santoriello.

Finally, in our quest for power, Judd Biasiotto, Ph.D., gives us his examination of what goes into a "big bench."

BIG BENCH Judd Biasiotto, Ph.D.

If you took a survey of American lifters, I'm sure you'd find that the bench press is by far the most popular lift. Actually, you'd probably find that it's the most popular lift in the world. Everyone benches, even the Russians, and just about everyone loves to do it—except for me, that is. For the longest time, I hated the bench press with a passion. Just the thought of it would turn my stomach. Of course, I had a few good reasons for the way I felt. First, but certainly not foremost, was the fact that I never had what you'd call an awesome bench press. It's true that I once out-benched Pee-Wee Herman, but not by much. Generally, I used my bench press as a rest period between my squat and my deadlift.

Another thing that bothered me about the bench press was that everyone and his brother consider it the ultimate criterion for strength. No matter where you are, if people find out that you're a weight lifter, the first thing they ask you is, "How much do you bench?" If you don't come up with some great big numbers, they look at you as if you're someone who trains at Spa Lady. It's absurd—especially when you consider that the bench press is the least important of the three powerlifts because you lift significantly less weight on it. You can be blown away in the bench by 50 pounds—whereas in the squat and deadlift you can be blown away by 250 pounds. Obviously, if you're a powerlifter, you'd be better off with a good squat and deadlift than a good bench. On the other hand, if you're a bodybuilder, it doesn't matter if you can bench press your own bodyweight, as long as you look as if you can bench press an apartment complex.

In the past, when I'd try to explain that to powerlifters or bodybuilders, they'd look at me as if I were intellectually constipated. In short, it seemed that everyone wanted a big bench, whether it was important or not. The thing that grated on me the most, though, was that a lot of guys were cheating on the lift. In fact, in my opinion, there was more cheating going on involving the bench press than you'll find being discussed in most divorce courts.

So what changed my mind about the bench press? It's simple. I learned how to cheat. That's right, I learned how to cheat, and my bench jumped from 285 pounds to 320 at a bodyweight of 132 in less than four months—without my using a bench press shirt. What's even more amazing is that I honestly don't believe my strength increased during that time. In other words, by learning to cheat—which in this case means correcting my form—I increased my bench by approximately 35 pounds without significantly enhancing my strength.

I'm sure you'd like to know how to cheat the way I do, right? The major secret is in the arch. According to powerlifting rules, you're allowed to arch your back as much as possible during the bench press as long as your shoulders and buttocks remain in contact with the bench—so it's not really cheating. The idea is to roll your shoulders under and then inch your buttocks in the direction of your shoulders as much as possible. In other words, you want to position your body so it looks like an inverted U. By arching your back that way, you can significantly increase the height of your chest above the bench; and the higher you can elevate your chest relative to your arm length, the less mechanical work you have to do to perform the lift. Arching also helps you increase the horizontal distance that the bar travels in the lift.

I've taken a good five inches off my bench press stroke by arching. Obviously, that makes the lift a lot easier because I'm not moving the weight as far. Another technique is to learn to drive with your legs. That's right, you can use your legs to do exactly what most great benchers have done: taken a chest exercise and made it a near total-body exercise. By supporting the weight with your shoulders and legs and by just grazing the bench with your buttocks—thus, staying within the rules—you can generate momentum from your legs to your upper body. According to Dr. Thomas McLaughlin, a biomechanics expert who's done an extensive analysis of the bench press,

David Liberman.

the preferred leg position is with your legs parallel to the bench. As he said, "When the legs are positioned at this angle, the momentum generated by the legs can be channeled horizontally through the body much better than if the legs are out at an angle to the bench."

Also, according to McLaughlin, "The effect of the momentum—especially in the more dramatic cases when bridging/arching is used to help this even more—is to move the bar toward the shoulders. In fact, the result of this momentum transfer is to cause the bar path to be transferred horizontally toward the head and for the bar to move at lower angles toward the head. These changes in bar path caused by the momentum transfer in bridging/arching are exactly what constitutes superior technique in bench pressing. This is the main reason that bridging helps bench pressing—by focusing a better bar path."

There's only one little problem with arching like that to enhance your bench press—it's dangerous. You significantly increase your potential for injury to the lower back due to extensive lower-back hyperextension. In addition, any transfer of momentum from the legs to the upper body will result in more lumbar hyperextension, so there's an even greater potential for injury. Obviously, lower-back flexibility is not only necessary if you're going to perform a bench press with an extreme arch, but it's also necessary to help protect

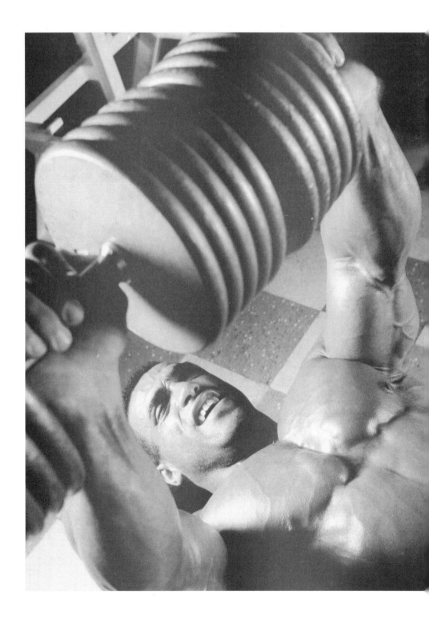

Joe Spinello.

against injury. Still, even with superior flexibility, there's a chance for injury. You should consider this point before deciding to use the bridging technique.

There are a few other considerations I'd like to discuss. The first consideration is your grip. Generally speaking, most top bench pressers use a wide grip, and there's some scientific evidence indicating that a wide-grip bench is potentially better than a narrow-grip bench. While there must be more research before we can draw a definite conclusion about bench press grips, I believe I can present a good argument for the wide grip from a strictly empirical standpoint.

First of all, in terms of mechanics, the wider your grip, the shorter the distance the bar has to travel. I've seen some guys, like Lamar Grant, cut out a good foot of their bench press by using these techniques. Think about that for a second. How much could you bench if you shortened the distance the bar travels by a foot? I guarantee it would be a dramatic improvement. Another plus for using

a wide grip is muscle involvement. As you're probably aware, a wide-grip bench involves the pectoralis major more and the triceps less. With a close grip, the reverse is true. Since the largest muscle mass used in the bench press is the pec major, it seems logical that you'd want to involve that muscle more. The closer your grip, the more the triceps are brought into play. Then, as you move your hands outward, the more the combination of triceps, deltoids, and pecs takes over.

Obviously, the more muscles you bring into play, the greater your strength potential. Plus, your potential for strength is much greater in the pectoralis major than the triceps because of the pec major's much larger muscle

mass. While I won't deny that there are some top bench pressers who use narrow grips, they're few and far between. Not only that, but I honestly believe that even those lifters would improve their benches if they moved their grips out.

The next consideration is the bar's ascent and descent. There are two very important points. The first is that we're all anatomically different. Consequently, each and every one of us has to develop his or her own groove. Not everyone's bench is going to look exactly the same. There are, however, some general rules to follow when developing your groove.

The second point is that strength is very specific. Even a slight deviation in your groove

can cause a significant change in muscle involvement and a decrease in strength. I've experienced that phenomenon on numerous occasions. I'd attempt a weight in competition and miss it badly. Even so, I'd add more weight to the bar for my next attempt and smoke it. Of course, the difference between the two lifts was that on the first one I missed my groove, and on the other I nailed it. It all boils down to the fact that you need to develop your groove, and then make a conscious effort to follow it on each lift you attempt—even on your warm-up lifts.

As for the descent, there are only two things to remember. First, let the bar descend straight down to the highest point on your chest, and try to stay as tight as possible. Be careful not to let the bar free-fall from the straight-arm position to your chest. There's considerable research indicating that it takes more strength to stop the bar and reverse inertia when you let the weight free-fall than when you let it descend at a controlled rate. Of

course, it's also dangerous to free-fall the weight.

The second point about the descent concerns your elbows. They should be tucked near your sides during the descent. Whatever you do, don't let them flare outward, because you'll decrease your mechanical efficiency for driving the weight off your chest and through your sticking point. On the ascent, according to McLaughlin, "Lifters should develop a horizontal bar path that's as close to the shoulders as feasible. The displacement of the bar path toward the shoulders reduces the torque that the lifter is required to generate at the shoulders. The initial movement of the bar from the chest should therefore include a substantial horizontal component toward the head and shoulders and should gradually continue along this path until completion of the lift." In gym terms, that means that when you push the bar off your chest, you should gradually drive it back over your eyes until you reach a straight-arm, or lockout, position.

Chapter 14

MENTAL ASPECTS OF TRAINING

Any experienced bodybuilder will tell you that the mental aspect of training is just as important as the physical. Without the will to perform hard workouts, or to even go back to the gym, all other knowledge is moot.

Still, bodybuilding is a grueling, demanding sport, and a tough mind is indispensable if you are going to achieve your goals. Indeed, tough-mindedness should be one of your goals.

Randall Strossen, Ph.D., explains where you should lay blame as a first step in developing the right attitude toward your training.

BLAME Randall Strossen, Ph.D.

What makes one person succeed, no matter what? Why do some people fold in the face of the slightest opposition? Why do some people make excuses for everything that goes wrong, while others simply go about trying to make things right? What can you do to develop the ability to forge forward through any obstacles that appear in your path?

More times than I can remember, I've watched a world-class lifter, back to the wall, pull off a lift that nobody would have believed possible. Maybe the lifter missed his first two attempts and, down to his last shot at staying in the contest, he makes the lift. I've even seen people in this situation ask for an increase and then make a good lift. We're talking big-time contests here: world championships, the Olympics, and the like. These people know how to dig deep, how to not only keep going in the face of adversity but also go a little harder when things get tough. Consider, for example, Olympic gold medalist in weight lifting Naim Suleymanoglu, who was doing snatches in the training hall at the Atlanta Olympics, and before too long had the bar loaded to more than the world record. He missed it. He tried it again and missed it again. He took it a third time and missed it yet again. He took it an unbelievable fourth time and made the weight. A few days later, in one of the highlights of the 1996 Olympics, Naim went lift-for-lift with arch-rival Valerios Leonidas, held him off, and won a historic third gold medal.

Or there was the time in China when a guy named Marin Shikov, at the end of his

Tina Jo Bagne.

B. J. Quinn.

second tough workout that day of heavy snatches and clean and jerks, worked up to a heavy single in the squat. The single was so heavy that he missed it, and, since he wasn't surrounded by an army of spotters or the security of a power rack, he dumped the bar on the lifting platform. Obviously, when you've gone through a tough leg and back workout and miss a limit squat, you call it a day. But nobody told Marin this. He stripped the bar down, power cleaned it, put it back on the racks, reloaded it, and tried the squat again. And, just as in his first attempt, when he couldn't stand up with the weight, he dumped it. Surely anyone with any sense would know that it was time to call it a day, but once again Marin must have been clueless—because he stripped the bar down yet again, power cleaned it, put it in the racks, reloaded it and, voilà, ground out a very tough, successful lift.

You might not know Naim Suleymanoglu or Marin Shikov from Salvatore Ferragamo, or care a hoot about picking up an Olympic gold medal in weight lifting. But if you're serious about making progress in your training and in your life as a whole, developing a bit of their drive can open the door to a lot of really good things. Let's take a look at one aspect of how the way you think and act controls your ability to generate outstanding results.

Once upon a time, if you tripped and fell while walking down a sidewalk, you would quickly get up, brush yourself off, and hope that you were spared the embarrassment of anybody's noticing what had happened. Now, when the same thing happens, a lot of people look around for somebody to sue, someone to blame for their accident. They might try to claim that the sidewalk was poorly maintained, with anthills sprouting up here and there; or that there should have been signs warning pedestrians that walking is a potentially hazardous activity; or that, perhaps, the sidewalk contractor was insufficiently schooled in the chemistry of sidewalk composition and the physics of sidewalk design. We've come so far in our attempts to avoid personal responsibility that even if a dead-drunk driver goes several times the speed limit and has an accident that kills everyone in his car who wasn't wearing a seat belt, there's a massive movement to blame the whole thing on a bunch of guys waving cameras in the distance. Examples in bodybuilding and lifting are no less ludicrous and, more important, no less likely to obscure the path to progress.

For instance, it's amazing how many people blame others for misleading them about everything from training routines to diet. With straight faces they describe in exquisite detail how they were led astray, often for years at a crack, before they saw the light. Or they excuse their lack of progress by noting that they have this or that genetic deficiency that keeps them from becoming world champions—ignoring the fact that five years into training, they're still squatting with no more than a couple of plates. And let's not forget the drug line, either—that everyone who outperforms them is on some drug, even though they themselves have not made one iota of progress in the past year and their own accomplishments would have been insignificant decades before anabolic steroids were ever invented. Excuses like these shift responsibility to external sources, psychologists explain. Let's see how this works, putting the whole thing in the context of helping your lifting move forward.

When we look to external sources for explanations of our failures, it bolsters our self-esteem. This, of course, is a good thing a lot of the time, but it can also lead to some

very unproductive behavior. Consider, for example, the lifter who has made virtually no gains since starting to train. If the lifter lays the whole affair at the feet of an unproductive routine he was duped into following, he feels good about himself: after all, he was the innocent victim who was defrauded by a villain. Consider the challenge to his self-esteem if he says, instead: "Maybe I didn't do such a good job evaluating the training program in the first place," and "Maybe I didn't really train as hard as I should have or could have." This second approach, which gives what psychologists call an *internal focus* to your failures, is a little rough on your self-esteem, but it also carries a tremendous advantage: it provides

Shelby Cole.

the opportunity to do better in the future by taking direct responsibility for your progress. I know a general contractor who has little sympathy for anyone who is swindled on a building project: "It's their fault for not checking references before they started the project." It's a tough one to swallow if you prefer to play the victim's role, but it's hard to fault the logic of his stance: take some responsibility for how things turn out.

The same thing applies in the world of weights. What sort of idiot follows lame advice for week after week, month after month, year after year, and then tries to pin the blame on

Michael Francois.

anyone but himself? When you've been squatting with the same weight for so long that the plates are practically rusted in place on your bar, how can you blame anyone but yourself for your lack of gains? If you've missed more workouts than you can count in the last year, do you really have to look outside yourself for the causes of your failure?

Foster the belief that your future, for better or worse, lies largely within your control, and cultivate a belief that your ability to mold your destiny comes from your control of what you do right here and now. And remember that sometimes when things go wrong, if you take the blame, it will only help you gain.

Next, Randall Strossen, gives up perhaps the ultimate bodybuilding "secret."

GRINDERS Randall Strossen, Ph.D.

The iron game has a dirty little secret—it's the real key to most people's progress. It alone will transform a bag of bones or a tub of lard into something approaching an authentic husky. The secret isn't anything illegal, and it isn't linked in some obvious way to your DNA patterns. For all its wondrous benefits, there's no place you can buy more of it. It is, however, equally available to all, and it's just as useful whether you're a lifter or a bodybuilder. In fact, it transfers extremely well to all parts of your life. If you could put it in a bottle, you might think of it as something that enhances good fortune, because the results that follow are nearly always positive and often so stunning that you would think the stuff should be banned.

We call the secret *grinders*.

To back up a little, it's no secret that the movements that produce the most dramatic gains are the time-honored basic lifts. They're done with free weights, the poundages are substantial, and they're the type of exercises on which making your eyeballs pop out leads to another rep or two or ten. And that's the essence—you grind out more than you comfortably can; you stretch beyond what's easy; you stick doggedly with it way beyond what

most people would consider reasonable. Grinders call for having a quit switch that's set somewhere around the red line.

Grinders aren't flashy, they're never fashionable, and most people avoid them like the plague. Sure, they work like nothing else on earth, but at a price: you pay for grinders in the currency of hard work. If you want to succeed, you might as well learn about grinders as soon as possible, so you can reap the benefits.

Consider the average person who lifts weights. For starters, he or she probably chooses a gym for all the wrong reasons. Maybe the aerobics class looks good, or all the machines are strictly the latest generation; maybe the color scheme makes it easier to coordinate his or her training clothes. Once in the gym, the person picks a training routine that represents the course of least resistance: lots of machine work; most movements done sitting down; training frequency and intensity reduced; multijoint, basic movements avoided. That's not a good attitude for grinders.

Grinders tend to fit in places that lean toward the primitive. It might be that primitive surroundings inspire brutal efforts, but, at the least, your focus is locked on the rep you're struggling to complete, not the color or condition of the vinyl. One of the most famous lifting gyms in the United States had holes in the floor and a locker room that was so disgusting, the municipal health department told the owner to redo the whole thing or be shut down. The lifters barely noticed the surroundings, and nothing they saw deterred them from training there. Down the street was a slick gym with a nice this and an even nicer that; the lifters there were strictly local and regional level. The lifters from the first gym frequented the Olympics and the World Championships.

One of the best setups I've ever seen for grinders was in China. World-record holders, world champions, and Olympic champions were more common there than 300-pound bench pressers in any chain gym. How could athletes of that caliber be expected to produce their world-class results in anything less than a world-class environment, right? Consider the

James Demelo.

facts: For starters, the squat racks were the old-fashioned design that looks something like a pair of barstools. Many were made from wood, none adjustable, and all the wrong height for almost everyone. Short lifters had to pile up plates on the platform, under the bar, so they could reach it. Tall lifters had to stack plates on top of the rack and then balance the barbell on the stack to raise the bar enough to get under it. Some put plates under the legs of the racks to prop up the whole affair. Things

were shaky at best, and more than once the bar fell off the racks or lifters nearly ate it going up and down from their improvised step under the bar. Even though the local lifters kept the lifting area neat and tidy, more than once a rat greeted me in the bathroom—not exactly an advertiser's dream. Nonetheless, there was nary a whimper from the lifters.

It's tempting to write that despite all those suboptimal conditions, 700-pound high bar, rock-bottom squats with no belt, no wraps, no spotters were ordinary fare. In truth, because the lifters were unfazed by their surroundings, grinding through their training regardless of what went on around them, they produced elite performances. That gym witnessed some of the hardest training on the face of the earth, and the next year many of those lifters were competing in the Atlanta Olympics.

A grinder is any set that has at least one rep you could easily have failed to make, and a world-class grinder consistently gets rep after rep, lift after lift, workout after workout—each step marked by reps that surely might never have been born. Grinders might take the form of a world champion missing a huge weight a few times before making it, or a beginner gritting his teeth to make his full set of squats with 200 pounds.

Some movements are better suited to grinders than others. For example, quick lifts, such as snatches or power cleans, are executed with great speed, so you can't really grind through a dubious rep, although you might have to grind through a series of misses before finally hitting a successful snatch with a heavy weight. Isolation movements and just about anything on a machine can be attacked in grinder fashion, and the results will be good— although the leg extension machine is not well suited to grinders because of possible knee injury. Best of all, however, is grinding through the big free-weight movements. None rivals the cornerstone of them all: the squat. In fact, the squat is so well suited to grinders that in classic 20-rep squat programs, the tough guys end up grinding out 20 reps with their usual 10-rep weights—and as anyone who's been lifting weights for a while can tell you, the results of such programs are mind-boggling.

Skip La Cour

Some people fail on grinders because they try to go too fast, too soon, meaning they try to attack a weight that's too big for them. Because you have to be able to lift the weight in order to grind out reps, it's important to start with something within your ability. Always remember that when it comes to grinding, it's the size of the effort, not the size of the weight, that's important. If you do them properly, grinders will reveal their magical properties. Little grinders today lead to big grinders tomorrow, and that's the path to progress.

Bill Starr has been studying for years what makes the greatest bodybuilders successful. One of the mental attitudes he has discovered is to want to make workouts.

HARDER, NOT EASIER Bill Starr

At some point in your strength program, you have to become more aggressive and lean on the top-end numbers. If you continue to train with comfortable poundages for too long, you'll get lazy and your progress will come to a halt. The body seeks equilibrium, complacency. In fact, it would prefer to stay out of the gym altogether. Given a choice, it would much rather lie on a couch and have cold liquids and foods stuffed into it than sweat and strain in a hot gym.

To add to the problem of inherent indolence is the fact that there is, sadly, a trend in training philosophies that actually promotes making things easier. For example, some recommend using machines rather than free weights, since machines put less stress on the body. Other trendy but easier techniques include abbreviated workouts, split routines that barely raise a sweat, doing partial squats instead of full squats, and putting absolutely nothing heavy on the bar. How about performing seated presses over standing ones or clean and presses? Are the latter movements better? No, but they're easier. The same goes for using Smith machines instead of free weights, or hang cleans instead of full cleans. When I ask people why they do hang cleans instead of the full-range movement, they usually reply that it's safer. Horse fritters. People do hang cleans because they're easier to do— and also easier to teach—than full cleans.

I have a beef with today's mania for the trap bar. Proponents say it makes the movements easier than when they use an Olympic bar. That's its main selling point—but to me it's not a plus, but a negative. Anytime you make a lift easier to perform, other than when you're perfecting your technique on it, you're going to get less out of it. Many, many sets of huge, powerful traps were built before this device came along. What's more, I can still make any trainee's traps so sore that he can't sit down without pain, and all I need is an Olympic bar and lots of weight.

Another pet peeve of mine is the various apparatuses that are manufactured solely to ease workout pain. My favorite is the plastic cushion for the shoulders so the bar won't hurt your back when you squat. Another one is gloves. Since when are calluses a major problem—unless you happen to be a surgeon? Wraps and other supportive equipment are in this category too—anything to keep you from feeling any hurtful sensations while training.

Nevertheless, my biggest gripe is the all-you insanity that permeates the training halls of this country today. Whenever I hear the cry, "All you!," I can be 100 percent certain most of the lift is being done by the spotter, not the lifter. I believe I know how this nonsense made its way into strength training. It's supposed to be a form of forced reps. Now, forced reps do have a place in strength training, but only for advanced lifters, in which case you must do

Lee Labrada.

them with heavy weights and use two spotters, who must time their movements precisely.

That's not what's going on, however. What they're doing with the all-you goofiness is not really forced reps at all but rather trainees being assisted through the most difficult part of the lift. I compare it to helping runners go the final few yards in a race by carrying them across the finish line. After all, they were very tired. Perhaps even more ludicrous than the practice of making the lift easier for their partners is the interaction between lifters and spotters following an all-you attempt. The lifter will turn and ask, "How much weight did you take off the bar?" The invariable answer is, "Only about a pound," with the added note, "I barely touched it." Why not a gram?

Am I the only person who thinks this practice is totally stupid and counterproductive? To add to the absurdity, people who have been all-youed always count the assisted reps, having been convinced by their partners that they could have done them even if the partners hadn't touched the bar.

I finally came to the conclusion that the logic behind the all-you practice is, You scratch my back and I'll scratch yours. In other words, if I help you through the most difficult portion of a lift, then I can count on you to help me. While it's nice to have a reliable spotter in case you do fail, he or she isn't helping you get stronger by nudging the bar through the sticking point. In fact, he's hurting your progress. How am I going to learn to grind through that tough part of the lift if someone always helps me? It's called the sticking point for a good reason: it's the weakest part of the lift. Instead of helping me lift the bar, better to push down on it—which is what I generally do when I spot people who are accustomed to being all-youed. Of course, they only ask me to spot them one time, and that's fine with me.

All-youing is most common on the bench press and incline, but it also occurs during curling, overhead pressing, and squats. The behind-the-lifter, hands-under-the-armpits form of spotting for squats also drives me up a wall. I see people do that sort of thing even if the lifter is inside a power rack or in a staircase rack.

Johnny Moya.

Don't get me wrong. I understand the importance of spotting, especially for lifts such as the bench press and incline, where the bar is over your face. But I believe having a spotter hug you and help you through the difficult part of the squat limits your progress. If I have people squatting inside a power rack or staircase rack, where they're protected, I discourage them from using any spotters. A great many of my athletes prefer to squat without spotters. If they miss, they're covered, and they believe it forces them to put out more when they know they're not going to be helped.

The only time I ever use the behind-the-lifter spot is when there's no one else in the gym and no power or staircase rack. I've also noticed that people who use that type of spot never go very low. It's a good thing—if they did get stuck in the deep position, they'd be out of luck, for one person can't do much to save them. They'd have to dump the bar. So either squat inside a rack, or use two spotters. You can have someone hug you later.

Weight training isn't a team sport, and those who try to make it one only limit themselves. In the final analysis, you are alone with the bar. The only gains you make come from your efforts, not from those you train with. I believe that many people employ the all-you assistance on almost every single exercise so they'll never fail. In reality, they don't succeed, since the spotter does most of the work. In their minds, at least, they don't miss.

I encourage pushing to failure. I believe in the concept of getting your misses up. How else can you really know exactly what your limits are on any lift? Failing is part of the overall process. Lifting without failing is like skating without falling. There's nothing wrong with failing. In fact, it's necessary. In most cases, the failure serves to motivate you. You become irritated at missing a certain poundage, and work harder and harder so you won't miss it again. When my athletes miss a max attempt, they dwell on it for weeks until I let them take a crack at it again. In the mean-

Craig Licker gets focused.

time, they're strengthening the weak area that revealed itself with the failure. Seldom do they ever miss the second time around, and in the process they move to a higher strength level. It also builds a more aggressive attitude, which I want to promote in my athletes.

Fear of failure is also one of the reasons that so many programs don't include singles. Some experts suggest that singles are risky, but I don't find that to be the case if lifters have been taught proper form. Certainly, the Olympic lifts are riskier than any weight-training exercise, and Olympic lifters thrive on singles. Instead of singles, coaches encourage high reps. They use them to test the relative strength of their athletes as well. That practice actually came out of professional football and has filtered down to colleges and high school.

Milos Sarcev.

Take a given weight and do as many reps as possible. Proponents of high-rep testing say it's safer than trying a max single, but I find that the exact opposite is true. Typically, the lift of choice is the bench press. Once lifters tire, they revert to sloppy form in order to run the reps higher. They rebound the bar off their chest, bridge, and/or twist—anything to gain one more rep. That's much more stressful to the shoulder girdle than trying a max single.

Another common practice that protects lifters from facing the horrors of failure is the conversion chart, which enables them to convert reps done on a certain lift to a max single. I've always hated that idea, for everyone who has ever lifted anything heavy understands there's a world of difference between being able to handle 300 for 10 reps and 400 for one. It's a world of difference physically and, more important, mentally. It takes a certain amount of courage to deal with 400, and it fosters weakness to convert a light poundage to a heavy one.

When I first arrived at Johns Hopkins, the football coach, who left soon afterward, showed me the results of his off-season strength program from the year before. I was impressed because there were a half-dozen players squatting more than 500. My job was going to be easier than I expected, I thought. When I did get the football team in the weight room, however, I discovered that only one player could even manage 315, and he wasn't going low enough. Then I found out the former coach had used a conversion chart. Why? It's easier, for one thing. But the primary reason that so many use it, I believe, is that it boosts the numbers, even if they are artificial. High school coaches promote the conversion method so they can elevate the status of their players to the collegiate recruiters. It makes the coach look good to have 20 athletes benching more than 300 and squatting more than 400, even if they never handled that much weight, not even in their dreams.

Singles should be a part of every strength athlete's program. When I suggest that idea to older people or to people who are not trying to gain strength for a sport, they often come back with, "But I don't care how much I can single. I don't plan on entering a weight-lifting meet. I only want to improve my strength in order to look and feel better."

I fully understand, for I'm in the same boat. But if you're serious about getting stronger, for whatever reason, then you need to include singles in your routine. You may not want to do them often, but the singles will help you break through the numbers barrier, and numbers are what strength training is all about.

If, for example, the most you ever handle on the bench press is 275 for 5 and you decide to try 290 or 300, the odds are you'll fail. The reason for that is partly psychological, but there's also a physiological aspect. Lifting a maximum single opens up totally new synapses in the nervous system and forces the tendons and ligaments to work harder. The

René Endara.

A training partner who gives encouragement can boost workout intensity enormously. Henrik Thamasian and Shelby Cole.

the case for a max single. The line has to be very precise. Miss the groove even slightly, and you'll miss the lift.

By the same token, max singles help you locate your weak point. With a lighter poundage used for any number of reps, you can slide through your weak point—but not with a max single. Quite a few of my athletes power their squats out of a deep bottom position. So powerful are their starts that they seldom have to worry about grinding through the middle range. Their hips and glutes elevate the bar so forcefully that they only have to be concerned with the start and finish—that is, until the bar is loaded to a new max and the weakness shows itself. That's a good thing, however, because they can isolate that weak area inside the power rack and make it stronger. If they never attempted a max single, they might never discover the weakness.

Singles influence the numbers barrier in another way, also. Some numbers, such as 300 and 400, are formidable. Many shy away from singles because they are fearful of dealing with big numbers. If you include singles in your routine on a regular basis, though, you can slip right up to and over those numbers. Move your max to 285, then go back and work that lift until you can do the same 285 for 3 reps. Then single out again. This time you manage 295. Do the same thing again—work, work, work, and get a triple with 295. The next time you go for a max, you'll vault right over the 300 barrier.

Whenever I bring up the subject of singles, I'm invariably asked, "But are they safe?" Yes, if you satisfy two conditions. You have to learn good form on the lift and establish a solid foundation. Those conditions apply to any lower reps, even triples. Nothing is really more important to people interested in gaining strength than perfecting technique on all the exercises. And I mean all of them, even small-muscle movements like pullovers and dips. If you've been working out consistently for six weeks or more, your base will be sound enough for you to do some singles.

Singles serve the strength athlete in much the same manner as sprints serve the runner.

true sources of strength are the tendons and ligaments, so you must stress them positively in order to make them stronger.

Another advantage of doing singles every so often is that they help hone technique. Doing tens and even fives or triples allows a certain margin of error in form, but that's not

They trigger different responses in the body and help make it stronger. You may only want to single once a month, and that's fine. Many people like to spend adequate time firming up their base and increasing the workload on a lift before trying to max out for a personal record. That's a good idea. Singles are fun, since they allow you to set personal records, so people will quite often do them too frequently. Every four weeks is enough to get the desired effect.

Besides adding singles to your program, continue to incorporate newer, more demanding exercises as well. Once you've mastered the power clean, try doing full cleans. Do cleans and presses instead of seated presses or presses from the rack. Try front squats. They're tough, but they work the legs and hips quite differently from the way back squats work it. Keep challenging your body, and it will grow stronger. Baby it and you'll forever remain a mullet.

B. J. Quinn.

Chapter 15

NATURAL BODYBUILDING

Fortunately, one of the strongest current trends in bodybuilding is toward natural (read: drug-free) development. This can, and will, be a large enough subject for an entire volume in this book series.

This chapter, however, will give you a good look at the amazing results that can be achieved without the aid of dangerous, life-shortening drugs.

First, author Dave Tuttle shows how you can naturally control your bodyweight.

GET A LEAN, MEAN PHYSIQUE NATURALLY Dave Tuttle

The control of bodyweight, especially bodyfat, is highly prized in most sports. There is nothing to be gained and much to be lost from having excessive amounts of fat on your body. Even athletes who must have high bodyweights to compete, such as football linemen and heavyweight wrestlers, need to be concerned with their bodyfat levels.

Bodyfat slows down the athlete by increasing the amount of nonproductive weight he or she must carry during the performance of a sports movement. In bodybuilding it also hides muscularity, placing the athlete at great competitive disadvantage. The way to achieve a low level of bodyfat for a competition with the smallest possible loss in lean muscle tissue is to maintain a diet program that is reasonably controlled all year.

You have no doubt seen bodybuilders who gain large amounts of weight in the off-season only to go on crash diets and lose most of it for a show. It was once felt that this bulk/cut system permitted greater amounts of muscle growth compared to a relatively strict year-round diet program. Bodybuilders who took steroids were notorious for bulking and cutting. In the off-season they would fill up on everything that passed in front of their faces, figuring that this way they were assuring themselves of the greatest possible benefit from the drugs they were taking. Of course, when they dieted for a competition, they would then take even more drugs to maintain as much muscle as possible while they drastically reduced their food intake to make up for the excess of their previous overeating.

As it turns out, this bulk/cut system is not the best muscle-building program even for an athlete on drugs. It is definitely not recommended for the natural athlete.

The best way to achieve your sport goals is to keep to a diet that provides you with the nutrients you need—but only in the amounts that you need them—throughout the entire year. Excess consumption of calories in the off-season is not only pointless, but actually counterproductive.

Studies have shown that weight-loss programs always result in a loss of some muscle tissue along with the fat, especially when exercise is not included as part of the diet program. As a result, anytime that you try to drop

B. J. Quinn.

those pounds or kilograms for a competition, you will inevitably lose muscle. The best way to minimize this loss in muscle weight and muscle mass is to never gain excess fat in the first place. And the way to do that, of course, is by controlling your food consumption so you never take in more calories than your body needs.

There is no question that this requires discipline. Nobody said athletic excellence would be easy. Yet by following a few simple rules, you should be able to achieve your dietary objectives without a great deal of hassle.

Here are some guidelines for controlling your bodyweight:

COUNT CALORIES ALL YEAR

This may sound like a radical concept, but it really isn't once you think about it. It makes a lot of sense theoretically, and since it only takes a few minutes a day to do the arithmetic, why not give it a try?

Counting calories is the most effective system for controlling your bodyweight. Counting your calories in the off-season ensures that you make the greatest gains toward your sport goals without pointless fat buildup. Counting them during the competition season guarantees steady and accurate progress toward the fat-reduction goals you have set without a needless loss in lean muscle. When you think about it, that's a small investment to make to ensure that you get all you possibly can from your hardcore training.

Jennifer Goodwin.

TREAT YOURSELF TO A SPLURGE A DAY

Counting calories does not mean you have to lead a life of puritanical virtue, eating food that only a rabbit could love. While you should always watch your fat, salt, and sugar intake, you can still have a splurge a day without "breaking the rules" and getting overwhelming feelings of guilt. Everyone has his or her own idea of a splurge, and these ideas can

vary over time. The important thing to remember is that a splurge per day is fine as long as you limit the quantity of food involved.

If you go out with friends and they order pizza, it's okay to have a slice or two (unless your contest is just around the corner, of course!). Just count the calories in what you eat and add it to your total for the day. If the pizza pushes you over the top of your calorie

Danny Hester and Tina Jo Bagne.

INCLUDE AEROBIC TRAINING

Always include aerobic exercise in your program to control bodyweight. Studies have shown that when bodybuilders combined dieting with aerobic exercise, they lost less muscle tissue than when they tried to lose all of their weight through dieting alone. Therefore, you should always include aerobic exercise in your diet program. For weight-reduction purposes, you need only 30 to 45 minutes of aerobic activity per day to get results. The increased energy expenditure required by this activity, combined with a modest calorie reduction of 10 percent, trims off excess bodyfat while keeping your muscles full and ready for action.

Since aerobic training enhances your cardiovascular fitness and helps raise your basal metabolic rate, it is also a good idea to incorporate some aerobic training into your year-round program. This may run counter to what you have heard in the gym, but it has been shown in scientific studies that a moderate amount of aerobics (one to one and a half hours per week) has no negative effect on your strength or muscle development. Greater amounts of aerobics can negatively influence strength, however, so keep track of the quantity of aerobics you do.

ALTERNATE HIGH-CALORIE AND LOW-CALORIE DAYS

When trying to lose fat, alternate periods of high-calorie days and low-calorie days so that your metabolism does not slow down. The body is an incredible machine. When faced with a situation that it interprets as famine, it conserves needed energy by lowering the basal metabolic rate and increasing the efficiency at which food is utilized by the body. It also tries to hold on to the fat stores, sensing that they may be needed in the future for critical energy reserves if the famine continues. These safeguards have no doubt gotten us to where we are today instead of at some dead end on the tree of evolution, yet they can play havoc with the diet plans of bodybuilders if they are

count for that day, take the excess calories off tomorrow's total. Better yet, if you know you are going out for pizza later, save some room in your calorie count for the splurge. Chances are that you will find a modest splurge to be well within your diet parameters for the day. Let reason be your guide. It will make your diet a lot more interesting and will ensure that you stick to it over the long term.

not recognized and worked into the diet program.

Earlier it was noted that the most effective diet program includes a modest (10 percent) reduction in calories tied to an increase in aerobic activity. Yet in order to ensure that the body does not interpret this calorie reduction as the start of a famine condition, it is necessary to "fool" your body by alternating periods of high- and low-calorie days in your diet. That way it is hard for the body to decide what is going on and the metabolic rate will decline at a slower rate.

For example, if you are currently eating 3,000 calories per day, you would begin your fat-reducing diet by setting your average daily calorie level at 2,700. Instead of eating 2,700 calories every day, however, you would alternate two-day periods of 2,900 and 2,500 calories (200 calories above and below your weekly average). For instance, you might eat 2,900 calories on Monday and Tuesday, 2,500 on Wednesday and Thursday, and so on. This gives your body something close to the calorie level it was used to half the time, and should put a brake on the slowing down of your metabolism. The higher your metabolic rate, of course, the more fat you will burn at a given caloric intake, so make it a point to include this daily roller coaster in your diet. It really can make a difference.

The guidelines indicated here are geared toward the average athlete and will produce very good results for that person. Still, everyone is different. If you lose more than two pounds of bodyweight per week, you are dieting too severely.

INCREASE CALORIC INTAKE, REDUCE AEROBICS, OR BOTH

On the other hand, if your metabolism is on the slow side, you may find that you need a somewhat greater caloric reduction to reach your final weight goal. Take your time, though, and don't rush it. Stay with the guidelines noted previously until they no longer produce additional results. If you lose two pounds the first week, you may very well lose an addi-

Shelby Cole.

tional two pounds the second week with the exact same calorie count.

As in many things, patience is a virtue in dieting. Don't expect results overnight, because if you try to get them that quickly you

Jonathan Lawson.

will knock your metabolism out of kilter and wind up retaining fat. Look at bodyweight control as a long-term venture. Most people who lose weight rapidly put it back on just as swiftly, and often they have proportionally more fat and less muscle fiber than they had to begin with. Slow and steady wins the race. Let that principle be your guide, and you will never again have a problem with controlling your bodyweight.

Let's take a look at Steve Holman's case history of a bodybuilder who had fantastic success using all-natural methods to go from . . .

CHUNK TO HUNK   Steve Holman

Why do guys do it? What's the motivation? Why do they put themselves through the agony of liftng heavier and heavier weights day in and day out, year in and year out? Painful, burning reps. Buckets of salty sweat. For what? Sex appeal, plain and simple. Twenty-four-year-old drug-free bodybuilder Jonathan Lawson has no qualms about telling it like it is, insight he got directly from the mouths of babes:

"I had a lot of female friends in high school," said the Southern California bodybuilder. "As I started hanging out with them more and more, they began confiding in me, and I found out something many guys don't know: women talk about guys' physical attributes just like guys talk about girls' bodies. Women may act like they don't notice, but believe me, they do."

Once this juicy tidbit came to his attention, Lawson decided that maybe it was time for him to go from dud to stud, from chunk to hunk, from cream puff to big and buff, from—well, you get the picture. He wasn't playing any high school sports, so he joined a gym and began weight training with the hope of looking like Arnold—in a matter of months, of course.

While his workouts weren't all that consistent—when you have a lot of good-looking female friends who like to talk and cry on your shoulder, workouts can easily fall by the wayside—he did manage to add about 10 pounds of muscle, taking his skinny 150-pound body to a slightly less skinny 160-pound package. Unfortunately, that was far from his dream physique. Arnold he wasn't.

After Lawson graduated from high school, he decided to dedicate himself to solid workouts and follow the bodybuilding champs' advice he read in the magazines. "I figured if I wanted to be big, I should look to the guys who are the biggest," he explained.

He started training like a man possessed, six to seven days per week, up to 20 sets per bodypart, and his physique was transformed—

but not in a good way. He did put on a pound or two of muscle in the beginning, but soon his gains sputtered from overtraining, he began eating everything in sight, and he got the dunlop syndrome—that's where your belly "done lopped" over your belt. While his insight into women's admiration of the male form conjured the notion of James Bond, his bodybuilding knowledge was more along the lines of Jethro Bodine from the *Beverly Hillbillies.*

"I was naive, to say the least. I didn't realize the incredible impact anabolic steroids have on building muscle—and that all the pros are on them," he recalled. "The training routines I followed were geared to work for bodybuilders on drugs, not natural bodybuilders like me. I overstressed my system and overate to compensate."

Once he was up to speed on this little fact, Jonathan adjusted his training, backed off on his calorie intake, and actually progressed enough to enter a couple of contests. He never seemed to be big enough or cut enough to do very well, and after a few shows he thought that maybe this bodybuilding thing wasn't for him—that, or perhaps he should try it with drugs.

Anabolic steroids were fairly easy to get around his gym, and guys were coming up to him all the time offering him a trial run with Mexican Dianabol or Anavar. Ah, the fringe benefits of living in Southern California. It was tempting, but Lawson wasn't going to revert to the naïveté of Jethro again. Instead, he decided to research the topic thoroughly before taking the plunge. Now in college, he did one of his first research papers on anabolic steroids, and what he found changed his outlook completely.

"The negative health consequences that can occur are endless," he said, "and taking drugs just wasn't worth the risk. Plus, because it's illegal, I knew guilt would eat me alive. I would feel as if I were cheating somehow."

So his dreams of building a great physique and winning a bodybuilding competition went up in a puff of smoke—or into the glute of some less-cautious bodybuilder via a syringe. Or so he thought.

With disappointment looming but his integrity intact, Jonathan let his training slack off. At age 21, with his bodyweight leveled off at a marshmallowy 190 pounds at 5′11″, he began to refocus his priorities.

As chance would have it, he got a job in the product division of *Ironman* magazine around the time the 10-Week Size Surge program was being developed—at the end of 1994. At that point, Lawson was still training, but he had no direction. He didn't exactly look like a serious bodybuilder—more like a serious channel surfer. The Size Surge program made sense, and it motivated him to make a two-and-a-half-month commitment to double-check his potential. Was he really not cut out for bodybuilding? Ten weeks would tell the tale.

And how telling it was.

"To say I was shocked by the results I got from the 10-Week Size Surge program is putting it mildly. My muscle size took a radical leap: I added almost 20 pounds without an increase in bodyfat, according to caliper testing. My bodypart measurements and strength increases amazed me: arms, up 1¼ inches; thighs, up 1½ inches; waist, down 1 inch; bench, up from 200 × 10 to 290 × 6; squat, up from 205 × 8 to 335 × 7. And I did this with no steroids. Size Surge not only changed my physique, it changed my entire outlook on bodybuilding. I saw that I wasn't the hard gainer I thought I was."

After his successful Size Surge experience, which is chronicled in the book *20 Pounds of Muscle in 10 Weeks*, Jonathan shifted into a version of the Fat to Muscle program, added

some cuts to his new mass, and took home a couple of second-place trophies at drug-free contests—but first place continued to elude him. Bodybuilding is a continuous learning experience, and after tweaking his routine and diet to determine what works best for him, this past year he took first in his class, as well as the Overall, at the Southern California *Ironman* Naturally Novice and was in the best shape of his life.

Considering he was working full time as a customer service rep and going to night school for most of the year, Jonathan's victory was quite a remarkable accomplishment. What did he do differently? How did he make such dramatic progress from '96 to '97 and win his first Overall trophy? Here are a few things he learned that helped him get bigger and better, his seven natural laws, if you will:

1. **Maintain hard condition all year.** Lawson never lost sight of his abs, keeping his bodyweight at around 200 pounds for most of the year. Losing fat is a difficult process, because you can lose muscle as well.
2. **Don't overtrain in the off-season.** Since his time was so limited, his off-season training was three days per week, working each bodypart only once every seven days.
3. **Don't overtrain during the precontest phase.** At 10 weeks away from the '97 *Ironman* Naturally, Jonathan's school semester ended and he ramped up his training, but not as much as he had in '96. In '96 he split his bodyparts over three days with no days off—yes, he trained seven days straight for about 15 weeks; for the '97 show he split his bodyparts over four workouts and took Sundays off, and this precontest phase lasted only 10 weeks.
4. **Use supersets.** He incorporated Compound and Isolation Aftershock supersets, which improved his muscle size and vascularity immensely.
5. **Don't overdo aerobics.** In '96 he was running and walking the treadmill almost every day—and sometimes twice

a day. In '97 he walked the treadmill three to four times per week, relying more on small calorie cuts to get ripped. Reducing his aerobics decreased his cortisol surges, which resulted in much less catabolism than in '96. His bodyweight actually dropped way down to a depleted 175 in '96, with a lack of

separation and hardness; a year later he competed at somewhere between 180 and 190 pounds, ripped, with cross striations in his quads and triceps. He is looking to step on stage at close to 200 in solid condition in another two years—without chemical assistance, of course. Although he wants to get bigger, his primary concern is to maintain his proportions and symmetry and keep his Bob Paris–like lines.

6. **Use quality supplements.** Jonathan experimented with some new compounds, including So Cal's Turbo Blast 600 liquid creatine and Andro-50 (androstenedione) and Muscle-Linc's Cort-Bloc (phosphatidylserine, or PS). They produced more and better creatine absorption, higher testosterone levels, and less cortisol, respectively, which meant more overall muscle mass.

7. **Try not to be too obsessive about the contest.** In '96, Jonathan was so totally focused that he burned out. In '97, he took the show less seriously and saw it as an opportunity to have fun and even let his diet slide a little every so often—but not too often.

All of this culminated in his victory and an *Ironman* cover, much to his delight—and relief.

"Being on the cover of *Ironman* is a dream come true and has inspired me to take my bodybuilding to the limit of my drug-free potential," he said, his voice rising with anticipation. "My growing collection of runner-up trophies was beginning to make me wonder if I had what it takes. It just goes to show you that persistence in bodybuilding, along with an open mind and learning what works for you, can pay off big."

And speaking of payoffs, how have the women responded to his new larger, more-ripped physique? At the intermission after his contest win, Lawson was answering questions. A good-looking woman made her way up to him and asked if she could give his beautiful body a hug. She proceeded to put her arms around him, testing his hardness by grabbing handfuls of his glute muscle for a good minute and a half. (I know this happened; I was there, staring with disbelief.) Why do guys work so damn hard in the gym? I think it's obvious.

Day 1
Quads

Leg press	3 × 8–10*
Aftershock superset	
Sissy squat	1 × 6–10
Leg extension	1 × 6–8
Hack squat	2 × 6–10
Calves	
Leg press calf raise	2 × 10–20*
Aftershock superset	
Donkey calf raise	2 × 10–12
Standing calf raise	2 × 10–12
Standing calf raise	1–2 × 30–40
Seated calf raise	2 × 10–12
Abs	
Aftershock superset	
Ab Bench crunch pull	2 × 8–10
Incline knee-up	2 × 8–10
Day 2	
Chest	
Bench press	3 × 8–10*
Aftershock superset	
Dumbbell flye	1 × 6–8
Decline cable flye	1 × 6–8

Cable flye	2 × 8–10
Incline press	2 × 8–10
Incline cable flye	2 × 8–10
Lats	
Front pulldown	2 × 8–10*
Aftershock superset	
Dumbbell pullover	1 × 6–8
Undergrip row	1 × 6–8
Aftershock superset	
Pullover machine	1 × 6–8
Undergrip row	1 × 6–8
Midback	
Behind-the-neck pulldown	2 × 8–10*
Supported T-bar row	2 × 8–10
Shrug	2 × 8–10
Rear delts/Midback	
Bent-over lateral	2 × 8–10

Day 3

Hamstrings/Lower back	
Stiff-legged deadlift	2 × 8–10*
Leg curl	3 × 6–8*
Low-back machine	1 × 8–10*
Calves (light)	
Donkey calf raise (light)	2 × 20*
One-leg calf raise	1 × 12–15
Standing calf raise (light)	2 × 20–40
Abs	
Ab Bench crunch pull	1 × 8–10
Incline knee-up	2 × 8–10
Machine crunch	2 × 8–10
Neck	
Manual resistance at four positions[1]	1 × 10–15

[1]Press head against hands in left, right, forward, and back directions.

Day 4

Delts	
Smith machine press	2 × 8–10*
Forward-lean lateral	1-2 × 8–10
Aftershock superset	
One-arm incline lateral	2 × 6–9
One-arm lateral	2 × 6–9
Nautilus lateral machine	1 × 8–10
Triceps	
Decline dumbbell extension	2 × 8–10*
Aftershock superset	
Overhead extension	1 × 6–9

Close-grip pushdown	1 × 6–9
Aftershock superset	
Overhead extension	1 × 6–9
Kickback	1 × 6–9
Bench dip	1 × 8–12
Biceps	
Barbell curl	2 × 8–10*
Aftershock superset	
Incline curl	1 × 6–9
Close-grip curl	1 × 6–9
Aftershock superset	
Incline curl	1 × 6–9
Preacher curl	1 × 6–9
Spider curl (on vertical side of preacher bench)	1 × 8–10
Forearms	
Superset	
Reverse wrist curl	1 × 8–12
Wrist curl	1 × 8–12
Superset	
Reverse curl	1 × 8–12
Behind-the-back wrist curl	1 × 8–12

*Do one or two warm-up sets with 50 to 70 percent of your work-set weight prior to your work sets.

TRAINING TIPS

Lawson keeps Positions of Flexion and its midrange-stretch-contracted concept at the core of his routine because he believes "training each bodypart through its full range is important for the most complete development possible." He does, however, have some other important realizations concerning faster development in each bodypart, discoveries he's made "with the help of Steve Holman, a true innovator in bodybuilding training. I call him the Granite Guru." (Thanks, Jonathan. Let's hope that nickname doesn't stick.) Here are a few tips from his experience at the *Ironman* Training and Research Center that you may want to consider:

Quads

"I've squatted most of my training career, but after my second-place finish in 1996 I participated in the Hypercontraction-Training experiment and got very strong very fast. After I had been stuck at 405 for 5 reps in the squat for six months, Hypercontraction took me up to 500 pounds—for the first time in my life—in about six weeks, and I did that 500 for 6 reps! Because of this fast strength gain, I began feeling as if my spine was being compressed every leg day with so much weight on my back, so I decided to lay off squats for a while. Leg presses have given me some new development without back problems. As a change, I plan to start using Safety Squat Bar squats soon to replace leg presses."

Calves

"I believe in heavy weights for calves in order to build the fast-twitch fibers. But I think you also have to push lots of blood through your lower legs with high reps. To accomplish these two goals, I use fairly heavy weight for a few sets of one exercise, then move to supersets. After that, I finish off my calves with one or two sets in the 30- to 40-rep range. This high-rep attack creates a totally new kind of pain, but I've seen some spectacular growth in my lower legs, an area that I consider one of my weaker points."

Chest

"Standing cable crossovers used to be one of my favorite pec exercises, but after trying cable flyes on a flat bench, I don't think I'll ever go back to the standing version. You get absolutely no body movement when you're on a bench, so cheating is minimal. It's all pec, and you can squeeze harder to etch in deep striations without the front delts doing too much of the work."

Tatiana Anderson.

Henrik Thamasian.

Lats

"It's very important to get the upper-arms-into-the-torso contracted position, either with a pullover machine—at the bottom of each rep—or undergrip rows—at the top of each rep. So many bodybuilders neglect this position, relying instead on pulldowns or chins, on which it's almost impossible to hit the contracted position. If you want some new development in your lats, try one of those exercises and squeeze your lats hard."

Midback

"I try to think detail and concentrate on bringing my scapulae together on all of my midback exercises. Doing rows on a Nebula T-bar machine with my body supported so that my torso doesn't move has made a big difference. I also think doing bent-over laterals has added to my back detail."

Hamstrings

"Doing hamstrings first [Day 3 workout] has given me new development, as has doing stiff-legged deadlifts as the first exercise. Getting an initial stretch before doing any other exercise is the Hypercontraction principle, and it works. The backs of my legs had lots of new knots and vascularity due to this. I also like to do my final set of leg curls with a light weight and include Double-Impact reps (one-and-a-quarters) to make sure the muscle is completely spent."

Delts

"I have narrow clavicles but strong front delts, so building wide shoulders has been a challenge. I'm still working on it, but a few things have helped my side delts pop a little more. I do my laterals on a forward lean—I sit facing the pad on the Ab Bench. Also, supersetting a stretch-position movement, one-arm incline laterals, with a contracted-position movement, standing one-arm laterals, has created some new fullness." (Note: This is an example of an Isolation-Aftershock superset.)

Triceps

"Heavy lying triceps extensions have been the key to bigger triceps for me, but not the standard version. I use a fairly steep decline, which, from what I've read and from what I can feel, hits all three triceps heads. The supersets have also helped me develop a lot of vas-

cularity and detail that I never had before. I could finally see the insertion of the lateral head come to a point near my elbow, with cross striations running down the length of it."

Biceps

"The Aftershock supersets that follow heavy barbell curls really blow up both heads of my biceps. I finish the muscle with spider curls, which are preacher curls done on the vertical side of the bench. These allow me to squeeze in the contracted position for a final set. Spiders also seem to hit my brachialis muscles, which added height to my peak."

Abs

"I've used the Ab Bench for years now, and it's a great piece of equipment that works your abs from full stretch to complete contraction. The crunch pulls combined with incline knee-ups is all you need for a detailed midsection. For my second set of Ab Bench crunch pulls, I sometimes did a twisting version to bring in more oblique and intercostal detail."

One last thought: "For those bodybuilders who are looking to pack on a lot of mass, I highly recommend the 10-Week Size Surge program. It changed my whole outlook on bodybuilding. Adding almost 20 pounds of extra muscle tends to do that. Bodybuilders who believe they're hard gainers should try this program before they label themselves genetic underachievers."

Steve Cuevas.

Lonnie Teper has no shortage of case histories of bodybuilders who have made fantastic strides using all-natural methods. Here's one more success story that you can learn a lot from.

GOOD WILL PUMPING   Lonnie Teper

As a 15-year-old on his Temple City, California, Babe Ruth baseball team, Steve Cuevas was so puny he could have passed for the bat boy—or, perhaps, the bat. At 5'10" and 126 pounds, Cuevas might have replaced Kevin Costner as the title characters in *Tin Cup* and *The Postman*.

I mean, this cat was to skinny what Notorious B.I.G. was to obese. He was so slight, in fact, that when the catcher took the last spot on the end of the bench, he didn't even realize he'd knocked little Stevie into the dirt with a slight bump on the rump.

Being tossed to the ground with the greatest of ease wasn't the final straw, however. It was watching, day in and day out, assistant coach Shannon Kirkpatrick drive to practice in his handsome sports car with a lovely lass by his side. Kirkpatrick, a 6′2″, 225-pound former all-American football player at Steve's alma mater, Temple City High School, was often seen wearing a pair of tight shorts that showed off his physique, and Cuevas was so inspired he began pumping iron at home and at the high school weight room. He also started following the famous see-food diet—on which he ate everything he saw.

"I was so obsessed with getting bigger and more muscular that I really didn't know what I was doing for the first year and a half or so," said Cuevas, who now sports a solid 220 pounds on his 5′11″ frame, which he cuts back to 195 for contests. "I really overtrained. The first year I think I worked chest 364 out of 365 days. I worked out every single day, much of the time training twice a day. I wasn't exposed to a lot of the bodybuilding magazines back then, and when I did read something like *Muscle & Fitness*, they had all these routines the pros did. Basically, I was pretty much spinning my wheels."

When Cuevas graduated from high school, he was still tipping the scales at a paltry 157 pounds. By that time, though, he'd begun to read the magazines, and he'd learned that the first thing he needed to do was to put the barbells down, not lift them. He'd had enough of being a dumbbell when it came to proper workouts.

"I took three months off, which was really hard to do," Cuevas said. "Boy, just thinking about taking a few days off was frightening. But I knew I had to do something drastic. So when I graduated [in 1984], I took the entire summer off."

Upon his return to the gym, Cuevas was not only aided by a better knowledge of body-

building, but he was also fortunate enough to have several big-name stars training at his first gym, Astro's, in San Gabriel. Among them were Rory Leidelmeyer, Jon Aranita, Lonnie "Hams" Teper, Dennis Everly, Issac Curtis, and Derrick Cook. From the early to mid-1980s, Astro's was the Mecca of bodybuilding in Southern California's San Gabriel Valley.

Combining his newfound wisdom with his real life and aided by best buddy and training partner Bob Crowder, Cuevas slowly began to pack on the muscle he longed for. "By that point I was already a big fan of Arnold Schwarzenegger and Robby Robinson, so working out along with some of the more recognizable names in bodybuilding added to my ambition to achieve my ultimate physique."

A lifetime drug-free lifter, Cuevas already weighed 200 pounds—at 20 years old—before

he was even aware that anabolic steroids existed. "I never had a big desire to get really huge," he recalled. "My main goal was to achieve the most symmetrical, aesthetic physique I could, and steroids weren't the answer to getting that look. I had gone from 125 pounds to 200, and, even though I realized it would take extreme dedication, I was fully confident I could pack on another 20 pounds or so without ever touching a drug.

"However, perhaps even more important to me was the moral factor involved," he noted. His family—in addition to his parents, John and Terry, Cuevas has an older brother, Jeff, and two younger sisters, Gina and Marilyn—is very important to him. "Not only would it greatly disappoint my family and close friends if I took steroids, but the person I would let down the most would be myself. I have nothing against other people taking anabolics if that's their choice, but it's just not me."

Along with his size and physique, Cuevas's strength improved annually, leading to lifts of

500 for 8 reps in the squat, 550 for 8 in the deadlift, and 365 for 6 in the bench. At a top weight of 227, Steve has amassed 27½-inch thighs and 19-inch arms.

At World Gym, Pasadena, where he works as a personal trainer and hones his bod—he also works out and trains clients at Gold's Gym, Hollywood—he picked up the moniker "Hispanic Hercules" when a sleek, albeit small and smooth, reporter from this magazine was stunned by his physique. I mean, there was hair, muscles, and veins flowing all over the place, with thighs and hamstrings that reminded me of the world-class thoroughbred John Henry.

Although he's been noted for great muscu-lature since the late 1980s, Cuevas didn't put on posing trunks until 1994, when he entered the ABCC Natural Nationals. The contest was held in Victorville, California, which happens to be the current hometown of Cuevas's parents.

Ron Harris, *Ironman* columnist and asso-ciate producer for the American Sports

Network (which showcases bodybuilding and fitness on ESPN and ESPN2), persuaded the reserved 27-year-old Cuevas to enter the show. "I really never had an interest in competing," Cuevas said, "but after talking with Ron, I decided to experience the competition side of the sport."

Wise choice. At a weight of 184, Cuevas muscled his way to both the Tall and the Overall crowns. How good was his condition? According to a contest report that appeared in *Natural Bodybuilding,* Cuevas was "so cut he was almost bleeding." His parents, however, decided to pass on watching their son hit his poses live, choosing instead to watch the Junior Welterweight championship on TV, in which Julio Cesar Chavez's boxing opponent, Meldrick Taylor, got more cut than Cuevas while losing his battle for the title.

I was the next person to jump on Cuevas's back about competition, urging the muscle-bound lad of Mexican, Indian, and English ancestry to enter our Southern California *Ironman* Naturally Championships in 1995. I assured him of victory; he placed a disappointing fourth in the Light Heavyweight class, which saw Harris finish second and Karl List take first (as well as the Overall).

The only person more crushed than Cuevas was me, since my crystal ball looked clouded. What the heck happened?

"I made a mistake with my dieting," he said. "About a week before the contest I weighed 195 and felt I was in my best condition ever. I was really happy with my preparation at that point. But I panicked and overdieted, and by the time I hit the stage, I had dropped more than 10 pounds. Even though I was hard, I was way too flat."

Let's move forward two years. After more haranguing from yours truly (Cuevas set an NPC record by backing out of 17 contests in the next 23 months), he finally agreed to give the IM Naturally another shot.

This time his mistake wasn't coming in too flat, it was showing up too fat. "I was taking in too much sodium and didn't listen when my nutritionist at the gym told me I should incorporate some cardiovascular work

into my training," Cuevas said. "In the past I didn't need to do that to look sharp, but with the muscle I had gained in two years, cardio work would have made a big difference."

After finishing fifth in the '97 show, Cuevas dropped three to four pounds of water en route to taking the Tall Class two weeks later at Denny Kakos's ABA (American Bodybuilding Association) Natural World Championships, which were held a few blocks from World Gym. In that one, Steve held his own against the supershredded B. J. Quinn, winner of the Middleweight class at the IM Naturally and the Overall champ at the NWC (Natural World Championship).

These days, Cuevas, who has to slim down during certain periods of the year to accom-

modate his modeling and acting ambitions, spends more time in the aerobics room than Marvelous Mary Wong, a fitness fanatic who holds the gym's treadmill record of six hours in one day.

"I hope to get more into acting in the near future," said Cuevas. "I had a part last summer playing a hunk named Christian in the PBS television series *A Question of Citizenship*, where I weighed 220, but in a couple of recent Vallejo weight belt commercials I got down to 195 for a more athletic look."

As far as training goes, Cuevas has some standard advice for the natural athlete. "First of all, never set limits on what you believe can be achieved naturally," he said. "To set realistic goals, though, you must be willing to be very patient, as it takes a lot longer to build mature muscle naturally.

"I normally train with a three-on/one-off, two-on/one-off regimen in the off-season, and I use a three-day bodypart split. On Day 1 I work chest, shoulders, triceps, calves, and abs. On Day 2 I hit quads, hamstrings, and lower back. For Day 3 I do back, traps, biceps, abs, and calves. Currently I'm doing cardio on a daily basis, but that depends on what I have going on careerwise. I know it sounds like I'm hitting way too many bodyparts per day, but because I limit my sets, I never spend more than one hour with the weights. I do 8 to 10 sets for large muscle groups and 6 to 8 for smaller bodyparts.

"I lift moderate weight, with fairly high reps, and I don't rest much between sets. About every three weeks or so I'll go heavier and cut the reps back to 6 to 8.

"I eat six to seven meals per day, with a ratio of about 50 percent protein, 35 percent carbs, and 15 percent fat. For contest training the ratio stays the same, but I drop my calories a bit and add cardio. I also add a few sets for most of my bodyparts."

As if he weren't busy enough with his Sculpted and Fit Physiques personal training business and budding acting and modeling career, Cuevas still finds time to serve as head coach of the Alhambra Dolphins Youth Swim Team, a group of competitive athletes who range in age from 6 to 17.

"I swam for the Rosemead club swim team when I was a youth," he said, "and I continued to compete at the high school level. An opportunity came up six years ago to be a head coach; I started at the YMCA in Alhambra and got the Dolphin job three years ago. I took the position because I like working with kids, athletics, and building a team spirit that leads to camaraderie and values."

If the youngsters can build those components as successfully as Cuevas has built his body, they'll all end up in the winner's circle—in and out of a pool.

If you've ever even considered taking steroids or other "bodybuilding drugs," listen to the story of Ron Coleman.

RON COLEMAN: WORLD-CLASS MASS THE NATURAL WAY

Lonnie Teper

Considering the success 31-year-old Ron Coleman has achieved, it's hard to imagine him as a high school sophomore being laughed out of the weight room when he couldn't bench press 85 pounds on the Universal machine.

"It's true," Coleman said with a laugh. "I was on the wrestling team, and we went into the weight room to lift. I was about 5′8″ and 130 pounds, and was the weakest guy in the room. I was embarrassed, so weightlifting replaced wrestling as my number-one obsession."

Coleman eventually conquered the bench press, lifting 300 by the time he was 19, and ventured his first trip to the posing dais one year later at 190 pounds, winning the Overall crown in the '84 AAU (Amateur Athletic Union).

Two years and four pounds of muscle later, Coleman took it all at the '86 AAU Mr. Pennsylvania. He was still natural at that point, but the continued pressure of people around him in the gym changed that.

"You know, in bodybuilding you reach a point where everybody's telling you, 'If you want to go any farther, you've gotta use steroids,'" Coleman said. "I got married right after the Pennsylvania win, and we [Coleman and wife Beth] moved to Plymouth Meeting [just outside Philadelphia].

"I had met a gentleman at the Pennsylvania show who told me he'd get me a good job in transportation if I moved into his area, which was Philadelphia," continued the father of two. "I had no idea what that might entail— I figured probably a cabdriver—and after two or three months he finally got me a job in transportation, all right. I was a janitor, transporting furniture around at a computer company.

"People had been telling me about drugs since my first win," Ron related. "Everybody was hitting on me to 'work with them.' You know, trainers who could supply the stuff.

"One gentleman—I won't mention his name, of course—hooked me up with a doctor. I didn't want to do it, but I finally found something, sport-wise, that I was good at; I

went into a good number of competitions prior to that and did well.

"Nineteen eighty-six was kind of hard. I don't want to put blame on anybody. I decided to do it. The reason I finally did steroids was, the coach I was working with and [who I] really believed in told me I had to do it to be successful, period. So I decided to give it a try. I took steroids from the latter part of '86 through the middle of '88."

With added size and confidence, Coleman jumped into the '87 NPC (National Physique Committee) Nationals, which were held in Atlantic City, joining 41 other Light Heavyweights in pursuit of 22-year-old wunderkind and eventual Overall champ Shawn Ray.

"Now, guess who I had to pose after?" Coleman said, laughing. "Shawn Ray!" It didn't hurt him, however, as Ronnie placed eighth in what may have been the greatest Light

Ron Coleman trains heavy—naturally.

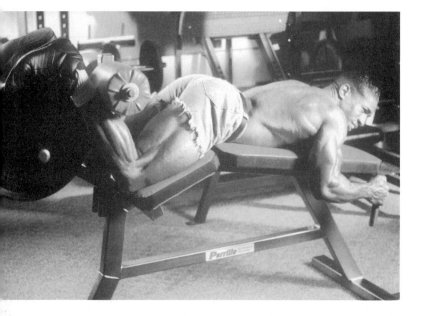

Ron Coleman.

Heavyweight division of all time. Brush off the cobwebs and check out the placings:

1. Ray
2. Daryl Stafford
3. J. J. Marsh
4. Vince Taylor

Have we heard much from those dudes since?

Despite the outstanding finish, Coleman was having problems with the pharmaceuticals, both emotionally and physically.

"Prior to the '87 Nationals I had won Jim Rockell's New York Gold's Classic as a Heavyweight," he recalled. "Ever since I started taking steroids, I had problems with water retention. I was told to go in as a Light Heavy at the '88 U.S.A. contest, but I couldn't get my weight down, entered as a Heavyweight, and didn't make the top 15.

"I had already been off drugs for a couple of months prior to the USA—I always got off that long before a show—but at this point I decided that was it for me with steroids. I never did 'em that much to begin with; if someone told me to take 'em 12 weeks, I'd do 6. I'd take half dosages of what I was being told to take.

"[The drugs] really depressed me. After doing so well at the '87 Nationals, I said I was going to do what I had to do to keep improving, staying on longer, whatever," Ron continued. "But I couldn't. I got so depressed—I had never felt this way before in my life. It wasn't worth it anymore. I was losing my family—my wife . . . we had one child at the time.

"But I wanted to do the Nationals that year, going back to doing things the way I did prior to taking steroids. I walked into Atlanta with my Burger King bag weighing 217 pounds" and placed twelfth in a Heavyweight class won by Johnny Ray Kinsey.

"It's funny because I still got so much attention from the media, it was amazing," he said. "So many of the photographers kept asking me why I didn't come in better shape, [saying] that I had such good lines, that I could have done this or done that. I was in shape at the USA, and nobody wanted to look at me."

Coleman retired from competition and left his so-called transportation job to sell cars and train people. He heard about a job running a gym in Easton, Pennsylvania, the hometown of former Heavyweight boxing champ Larry Holmes and a place that's situated midway between Philly and Scranton, and the Coleman family returned home.

Ron stayed in Easton for a couple of years, and he was eventually talked into getting back on the posing platform. In 1991, at his normal contest weight of 195, he took third at a show in Niagara Falls.

Angry about his placing, Coleman entered the East Coast Championships and moved up a notch. He also met a gal by the name of Denise Richardson, who looked at Coleman's aesthetic bod from the audience and decided they'd make a wonderful combo for Mixed Pairs.

"I was going to retire after the East Coast show, but since I had never tried couples before, I decided to give it a go," Ron said. They took second at the '91 Junior Nationals and third at the Nationals, in Pittsburgh, that same year.

Richardson not only talked Coleman into pursuing Mixed Pairs competition, but she also influenced him to try the Nationals again—with his main focus on landing a spot on the World Amateur team.

Although he placed only fifteenth, Ron did earn a position on the "clean team" that headed for Poland in '91, the show at which the other Ron Coleman earned his pro card. It was the slow-but-sure start of something big. Coleman took third in '92 in Graz, Austria, and second in Korea in '93, the year in which he also placed a lifetime-best sixth at the Nationals; and last year, in China, he was the only American to bring home a pro card from the Worlds.

Shortly after that victory, Ron and Beth opened up their own supplement and equipment store, International Body Gear, in a mall in Scranton, eventually setting up shop in the gym where Coleman trains, Northeast Fitness.

"The main difference is training and diet," he said when asked about his ever-improving physique. "I needed more thickness overall, and over time I learned how to properly train my body. I trained with more intensity, which

is something I lacked in the past. I used to be in the gym for about two and a half hours, with no aerobics, and now I go in the gym for an hour and a half, including aerobics.

"I used to do a three on/one off, two on/one off. I wasn't doing any more sets than I'm doing now. I would just rest longer. I used to lift, not train. I thought I had to do

500 pounds on the bench to get bigger, and that's just not true . . . I was worried more about how much I could lift than the results it would provide.

"I began changing my training little by little. Because they were a weak spot, I started training my calves differently. I gave myself less rest between sets, 10 to 15 seconds at the most and, after [I'd been] doing that for a couple of months, guys in the gym would say to me, 'Ron, your calves are growing.'" Coleman didn't need a degree in physics to figure that he should apply the same principles to his whole body—and it worked.

"My change of training is a little more complex than just decreasing rest periods between sets, but, for the most part, that's what I've done," he said. "I don't want people to think I'm not lifting any weight. I'm still going heavy for 8 to 15 reps, but with minimal rest. Sometimes my workouts are less than 30 minutes."

As for his diet, "I've become a huge believer in supplements," Ron explained. "They really do work. They work for me. I never used to believe in them. Guys used to say steroids work but supplements don't, so why waste your time and money?

"I would eat a lot of food and end up with added bodyfat, so now I supplement so much more, so heavy. I take a lot of Next Nutrition's whey protein powder, I use Met-Rx two to three times a day and also a lot of Twinlab products."

In the off-season, Coleman takes in 3,600 to 4,000 calories daily; for contest prep he drops it to no less than 3,000.

This is a man who, like Mike Ashley and Paul Jean-Guillaume, has proven you can be a champion without drugs. Any advice to the up-and-comers, Ronnie?

"You can be successful, but you have to train intensely and seek help from some of the top people in the field," Coleman emphasized. "The magazines today are great; they're filled with so much knowledge. Of course, you can't follow every bit of it, but I think you need to try different things and see if they work for you. If it doesn't work after a

couple of months, you move on and try something else.

"I give seminars all the time, telling people the evils of drug use," he continued. "It's hard—don't get me wrong. Most people laughed at me when I told them I wanted to be a pro bodybuilder even after I stopped taking drugs. I let kids know they have to knuckle

down in the gym and get smarter about the right way to train, learn more about the right supplements.

"For me, necessary supplementation includes good protein [not loaded with fat], creatine, chromium, carnitine, and, most important, a good multivitamin/multimineral twice a day."

Now that he's reached the pro ranks as a natural bodybuilder, what does he plan to do next?

"The thing I feel in my heart is that the sport has to change," Ron said. "I feel I can help it change. I plan to go outside the bodybuilding arena to do this. I have a lot of seminars and guest posings lined up, and I will be there to assure the natural bodybuilders they can do it. I did it naturally, and I'm sure I'm no freak of nature.

"As far as competition," he said, "I think I can hold my own against any drug-free bodybuilder in the world. Actually, I think I can hold my own against almost any bodybuilder in the world, period.

"I'll just keep doing what I'm doing," he said. "One thing that I found is God, and with God in my life I don't need drugs. I asked Him after the '91 Universe, if I'm meant to win this, please show me the way."

Hey, guy, I guess he was listening. Let's hope folks will listen to you the same way.

RON COLEMAN'S WORLD-CLASS-MASS TRAINING

Perform all sets to failure, using 8 to 15 reps per set and taking 15- to-30-second rest periods, unless otherwise noted.

Monday
Hamstrings
Lying leg curl	4 × 8–15
Standing leg curl	3 × 8–15
Stiff-legged deadlift	3 × 8–15

Adductors
Adductor machine	3–4 × 8–15

Abductors
Abductor machine	3–4 × 8–15

Tuesday
Take 30 seconds' rest between sets
Chest
Incline dumbbell press	4 × 8–15
Decline barbell press	3 × 8–15
Hammer machine press	3 × 8–15
Cable crossover	3 × 8–15

Triceps

Pushdown	3 × 8–15
Close-grip bench press	3 × 8–15

Wednesday
Back

Reverse-grip bent-over row	4 × 8–15
One-arm dumbbell row	3 × 8–15
Cable row	2 × 8–15
Wide-grip pullup to the front	3 × 8–15
Behind-the-neck pulldown	3 × 8–15

Biceps

Machine curl	3 × 8–15
Straight-bar curl	3 × 8–15

Thursday

Take 5 to 10 seconds' rest between sets

Traps

Dumbbell shrug	3 × 8–15
Barbell shrug	3 × 8–15
Neck machine	3 × 8–15

Calves

One-leg calf raise with bodyweight	3 × max
Seated calf raise	3 × 8–15

Abs

Machine crunch	3 × 8–15
Crunch on floor	3–4 × 8–15

Friday
Quads

Leg extension	4–5 × 8–15
Hack squat	3 × 8–15
One-leg leg press	3 × 8–15

Saturday
Delts

Lateral raise	4 × 8–15
Wide-grip upright row	3 × 8–15
Dumbbell press	3 × 8–15
Bent-over dumbbell lateral	4 × 8–15
Wide-grip machine row*	3 × 8–15

*For rear delts and lower traps.

Chapter 16

BODYBUILDING NUTRITION

This is another chapter that can, and will, be the topic of an entire book in this series. Rather than dive into the ocean of nutritional supplements and esoteric physiological arguments, this chapter gives you basic, sound advice on elements of nutrition such as protein, carbohydrates, fasting, and vegetarian applications to bodybuilding.

First we'll look at an excellent method of getting ripped and cut, and otherwise reducing bodyfat. Author Barbara Rosen looks at bodybuilders who fast.

FASTING Barbara Rosen

"Fasting? I've never fasted a day in my life," said Clarence Bass, bodybuilder columnist and Past-40 USA champ. "When you fast, you lose a good bit of muscle, and I don't think it comes back. Why would you want to spend weeks building bulging muscles only to throw all that hard work down the drain?"

Bass feels the way almost all bodybuilders do, but when you talk to lifters who fast, they tell the opposite story.

Take Susan Brickwood, for example. "I wanted to lose some fat, so my trainer recommended I fast on vegetable juice," she said. After eight days on juice, the 5′6″ lawyer was a scrawny 113 pounds. "But I started eating and working out again, and in two weeks my muscles came back even more cut than before."

Damon Welch, her trainer, agrees, "I wasn't surprised, because the same thing happens to me when I fast," he said. "It's like you're tempering the steel." Welch also noticed that Brickwood was more of a dynamo after her fast. "She just zipped through her workout—and she was lifting almost two-thirds more weight than she'd lifted before."

Bodybuilder Andreas Cahling has been doing fasts for about 15 years. He, too, agrees with Brickwood: "Your muscles come back more cut.

"Let's say you go on juices for a week. You may lose even seven or eight pounds, but you'll probably gain them all back the next week. And you don't have to work out any longer or harder to catch up."

Alan Goldhamer, D.C., of Penngrove, California, has put thousands of patients on therapeutic fasts, including several competitive bodybuilders. "When you don't eat," he stated, "your body has to get its fuel some other way. So it starts eating up some of those big muscles you've worked hard to build. But you don't lose any muscle cells. [That means] when you start working out and eating again, you pump those muscles right up." His bodybuilding patients tell him that they have to work to get back to where they were before, but the benefits of fasting are well worth it.

THE BENEFITS OF FASTING

What are the benefits? You can reduce your downtime in the gym. Meghan O'Leary, a competitive bodybuilder and personal trainer, said, "I've been doing fasts for four years. The biggest benefit I get is that it keeps me out of the sickbed and in the gym." O'Leary said that if she got a cold or flu, it would pull her off her strict training schedule. "Fasting cleans me out and keeps me from building up so many toxins."

"When you fast, your body doesn't have to eliminate your breakfast, lunch, and dinner, so it can concentrate on cleaning out the toxins you've accumulated over the years," agreed Goldhamer.

"For example, research shows that when you fast, your body seems to clean out tumors and abnormal growths before anything else. Other studies in Japan show that while people fasted, their bodies got rid of toxic chemicals."

Brickwood claims that fasting healed her of allergies, hypoglycemia, and chronic fatigue syndrome. "I was allergic to about 100 things—from cats to perfumes to tomatoes. My glands would swell up." After she had fasted, someone walked in reeking of perfume, and Brickwood didn't even react. "And I haven't since," she said.

She'd tried "everything in the world" to get rid of the hypoglycemia and chronic fatigue syndrome—acupuncture, herbs, vitamins, chiropractic. "It all helped a little bit,"

she said, "but the fasting put me right over the top."

It would take you a while to find an American doctor who recommends fasting. In Germany, however, for medical doctors in hundreds of clinics it is the number-one healing method. In both Germany and Sweden, patients are routinely put on fasts to cure them of just about every disease.

And you can concentrate better. Said Brickwood, "You're supposed to concentrate 100 percent when you're moving weights, but I used to think about my latest bankruptcy client instead. So my form got a little sloppy, and that's when I could have injured myself." After a one-week fast, Brickwood noticed that "I wasn't as stressed out, and I could focus more clearly in the gym." O'Leary, too, said she fasts to keep herself clearheaded "so I don't injure myself in the gym."

Fasting also helps you conserve energy. According to Cahling, "I feel younger after a fast. My workouts are easier."

Brickwood concurred: "Fasting gave me the stamina to do those extra three or four reps I needed to pack the muscle." And many people report they get a natural high when they fast.

HOW TO FAST

To fast safely, it's best to follow a few simple rules. According to Anthony Willimitis, M.D., family physician in Bonita Springs, Florida, it's okay for most people to fast, but don't do it in the following situations:

- If you have gallstones or a history of gallbladder trouble.
- If you have a serious, acute infection.
- If you have had a blood clot or heart attack within the past six months.
- If you are an advanced diabetic who depends on insulin.
- If you are a pregnant or lactating woman.

"Actually, this list could go on and on, but the general rule is if you're not healthy, consult a doctor before you fast," Willimitis said. He also advised that you consult a doctor if you've

ever taken anabolic steroids or if you're on water pills.

When should you fast? Andreas Cahling fasts in the off-season: "At least three months before or after a contest, when the schedule is less intense." Cahling says no to fasting before a contest, however. "A lot of bodybuilders look flat and small on stage," he commented.

Added Willimitis, "If you fast right before a contest, your heart might not have enough fat. Then you might not be able to do all that muscle flexing to win."

How do you start a fast? You don't want to shock your digestive system; so if you're fasting for three days or longer, take a few meals to slow down.

Goldhamer said that if you want to stay as massive as possible during a fast, drink juices—don't fast on water alone. "Your body will get glucose from the juices; then it won't have to eat up as much muscle. Besides, a water fast detoxifies your body so rapidly that you shouldn't do it without medical supervision."

It's best to drink freshly made juice, but it's "better to dilute your fruit juices half-and-half with water," Willimitis advises. "If you take too much concentrated fruit juice, your blood sugar could drop." He also tells bodybuilders not to drink coffee or black tea during a fast.

As far as activity goes, Goldhamer recommends that bodybuilders do only "minimal toning" while they fast. "You'll lose more muscle that way, but if you rest, your body has a better chance to cleanse and heal itself. And you'll easily get the muscle back later."

"Gradually reduce your workouts as the fast progresses," Cahling recommended. "If you push yourself too much, you might get dizzy." Some people do all their normal activities during a fast; others, like Cahling, prefer to limit themselves to reading, watching TV, and going for walks.

As toxins pass out of your body, you might feel weak, nauseated, tired, spacey, feverish, irritable, or achy. You could have other symptoms, such as insomnia, constipation, or cramps. "I drink some undiluted juice, and my energy goes right back up," Cahling said. "If that didn't work, I'd end the fast."

Dr. Paavo Airola, a nutritionist, advises in his book on fasting to take enemas so toxins won't get stuck in your colon and reabsorbed into your body. Cahling, O'Leary, and Brickwood take water enemas. Goldhamer said, however, "I rarely recommend enemas. They make you feel better, but they'll slow down the healing and irritate the bowels. If you feel weak or nauseated, drink more juice instead."

Also, keep in mind that if you end your fast too abruptly, you can get cramps, diarrhea, or even a serious illness. Bernard Jensen, a chiropractor-nutritionist, wrote, "A San Francisco newspaper allegedly reported a man who fasted about 15 days . . . was found dead a couple of hours after eating an extremely heavy meal of meat, potatoes, spaghetti, and pie." The newspaper said the man had starved, but Jensen knew that the man had died from breaking his fast too abruptly.

ONE LAST "BUT"

"But I'm afraid I'll deplete myself of too many nutrients if I fast," said Bill Pearl, four-time Mr. Universe, who used to fast one day a week.

"Not to worry," reassured Goldhamer. "After a fast, you assimilate nutrients even more easily. That will more than make up for what you've lost."

If you want to get leaner, healthier, stronger, and burlier, you might want to "juice up." But Goldhamer and Cahling both admit that "fasting is not a quick fix. The really important thing is to have a healthy diet and lifestyle all year long.

"After all," they said, "what good will it do to clean yourself out if you're just going to put the garbage in all over again?"

Three-Day Fast
Day before: Raw fruits and raw vegetables only
Three days: Fresh, diluted fruit, carrot, and beet juices
Day after: Raw fruits and raw vegetables only

Ten-Day Fast
Third day before: Fruits and vegetables, 2 1-cup servings brown rice, 2 baked potatoes
Second day before: Fruits and vegetables, ½ baked potato, ½ cup cooked brown rice
Day before: Raw fruits and raw vegetables only
Ten days: Fresh, diluted fruit, carrot, and beet juices and other fresh vegetable juices
Day after: Raw fruits and raw vegetables only

Second day after: Fruits and vegetables, ½ baked potato, ½ cup cooked brown rice

Third day after: Fruits and vegetables, 2 1-cup servings brown rice, 2 baked potatoes

If Barbara's fasting article was inspirational to you, wait until you learn what she has to say about vegetarian bodybuilding.

VEGETARIAN BODYBUILDING
Barbara Rosen

You turn on the television set, and there's your hero. Burly and muscle-packed, this 6′3″ hunk has just knocked down, with his bare hands, three no-goods at the local bar. Let's suppose this big guy could then pop his head out of your TV screen and demand, "I'm hungry! What's for dinner?" You offer him anything he'd like, but what do you envision your hero asking for? A peanut butter sandwich? A broccoli-and-tofu stroganoff? Not likely. Your idol calls out, "Give me a T-bone steak, bloody rare. If you don't have that, some nice, greasy fried chicken will do."

This macho guy wants red, bloody meat—not beans and rice. For the past few decades in America, eating flesh foods has been a symbol of masculinity and brute strength. The TV producers who portray your hero in this light won't tell you the rest of the story, however. They won't tell you that this meat-loving man has a 50/50 chance of dying from heart disease due to cholesterol and fats clogging his arteries, and that he is almost four times as likely to get prostate cancer as a man who eats a vegetable diet; nor will they tell you that with every piece of chicken or steak your hero eats, he's becoming a more likely candidate for one of America's biggest killers—colon cancer.

Why don't the image makers present the other side of the story? One reason is that the meat industry sponsors a lot of the programs, and producers are reluctant to bite the hand that feeds them.

Champion bodybuilder Andreas Cahling has seen through the fallacy that meat is necessary for strong muscles. "Meat is big business," he stated. "Commercial interests are perpetuating the myth that we need to eat meat. And many politicians feel they have to say yes to the meat industry's platform if they want to be reelected." Cahling carries the title of Mr. Pro International 1980, won fourth place in the Pro Gold's Classic 1990, and has published three books on bodybuilding. He knows it's a misconception that bodybuilders need animal flesh, since he hasn't eaten red meat, poultry, or seafood since 1978. And that hasn't kept him from winning two competitions. In fact, Cahling, who offers dietary consultations to bodybuilders, said he feels and looks better since he stopped eating meat.

Professional bodybuilder Bill Pearl, author of *Getting Stronger: Weight Training for Men and Women*, hasn't eaten flesh foods for more than 20 years. In an article in *Vegetarian Times*, he reported experiences similar to Cahling's: "With each succeeding year on the [non-meat] diet I've felt better. I'm healthier. I can train with more energy," Pearl wrote. He also said he no longer suffers from painful elbow and knee joints and that the high blood pressure, cholesterol, and uric acid levels that plagued him during his meat-eating days are gone.

But wait just a minute there. How are these two hunks making muscles if they're not eating flesh foods? With all those tough workouts, surely they need even more protein than the average Joe. "That's been the prevailing myth for decades," according to Michael Klaper, M.D., a physician with postgraduate training in surgery, anesthesiology, internal medicine, and obstetrics. "The meat industry pressured Washington to establish meat as one of the 'four basic food groups.' As one of the biggest distributors of educational literature to schools, this industry keeps this myth alive in our hearts from the time we're in first grade."

Klaper has been putting patients on nutritional programs for 10 years, and during the past two years he has lectured internationally on the benefits of a non-meat diet. "The human body has absolutely no nutritional requirement for animal flesh," he stated. "Just like the muscular elephant, we can synthesize all the protein we need from plant sources. The human body functions superbly without animal flesh, and I've repeatedly seen athletes perform quite well on a vegetarian diet." As to the question of whether bodybuilders need extra protein, Klaper pointed to two research studies showing that there is no muscle breakdown during a bodybuilder's workout. "If you're not breaking down muscle, you don't need extra protein to build up new muscle," he explained. Bodybuilders need about 5 grams more protein per day than the man on the street, and you can get that from a slice of whole-grain bread."

According to both Cahling and Klaper, meat is not only unnecessary, but it is also a stumbling block for bodybuilders. "Many bodybuilders have already dropped red meat from their workout regimen or cut down on it significantly," Cahling stated. "But I wish they'd realize that chicken is also hurting them. Chicken is still too protein-concentrated and causes fat and water retention that drain bodybuilders of their energy, keeping them from becoming as muscular as they could be."

Klaper asserted that when people eat chicken, fish, or red meat, saturated fats ooze out into their blood and tend to accumulate more easily in their bodies than do the poly- and monosaturated oils in legumes, nuts, and grains. That is why people who eat substantial amounts of animal flesh tend to have a harder time losing weight. "Many medical studies show that pure vegetarians are substantially leaner," he said. As bodybuilders accumulate fat under the skin, their muscle lines begin to get blurred under the fat, and any muscle definition that exists is lost.

Basically, people who fill up on animal protein and fat often don't have room for adequate carbohydrates in their diet. Klaper said that our bodies need lots of carbohydrates in order to make glycogen, or muscle fuel. "It is the muscles all pumped up with glycogen that makes them look so round and full," he explained. Cahling said that when bodybuilders use up their stores of glycogen, their muscles deflate like balloons.

Finally, eating meat saps a bodybuilder's energy. Klaper has seen evidence that eating meat increases body stress: the white blood cell count goes up, and body temperature rises. "The body puts a lot of energy into digesting this food, resulting in less available energy for muscular work," he said. "That's why a lot of people get sleepy after eating a heavy meat meal." Also, a person who doesn't eat flesh foods has fewer toxins to get rid of. Perhaps that is why research has shown that vegetarians recover more quickly after workouts. Numerous studies have also documented that vegetarians have more athletic endurance and strength than meat eaters.

Cahling said that while many of his fellow bodybuilders agree that a vegetarian diet is healthier, they are reluctant to give up stuffed salmon filets and fried chicken. It's boring, they say, to eat beans and rice at breakfast, lunch, and dinner.

Well, they ought to come over and get a taste of what Meghan O'Leary, Cahling's vegetarian fiancée, cooks at their home. "You can have some fabulously tasty vegetarian food," Cahling said. "And if you're hooked on the taste of meat and have a hard time giving it up, you can go to your local health food store and get soybean burgers, soy dogs, tofu, 'bacon,' and wheat gluten 'spare ribs.'"

Do Cahling's clients ever complain that they feel weaker after they stop eating meat? "Only rarely, and if it happens, they've usually been eating too few calories and/or training too frequently." To increase bulk, he recommends high-calorie foods like figs, avocados, and almond butter. Cahling's favorite foods include pasta dishes and brown rice, and for extra calories he eats bread and oatmeal. Every day he eats a salad, health cereal with soy milk, tofu, and fruit.

Klaper recommends that bodybuilders eat between 50 to 100 grams of protein a day, depending on their size and weight. "Accent the higher-protein foods like lentils, chickpeas, and nuts. A slice of whole-grain bread with almond or cashew butter, a few times a day, will easily give you that protein and caloric load you are seeking from meats."

Meghan O'Leary would probably agree that her vegetarian husband-to-be doesn't need an ounce of hamburger in him to make him more macho. She was so attracted to him that after they'd had only a few conversations, she decided she'd pick him up. Now, for a woman to pick up a man may not be so unusual these days, but Meghan is not your ordinary woman. She literally picked the 215-pound Cahling off the ground and held him horizontally. "Since I stopped eating red meat, chicken, and fish, I've still been able to lift Andreas over my head and even hold him on my shoulders," she declared. "It hasn't lessened my strength one iota to be on a vegetarian diet."

Wondering about protein? Here are the answers you need, along with some terrific recipes.

PROTEIN Dave Tuttle

You probably already know that it takes healthy eating and increased protein intake to build muscle. The trick is to translate that knowledge into meals.

In an effort to get plenty of protein, you may be taking in too much saturated fat, too little fiber, too much sodium, or perhaps too little of the essential vitamins, minerals, and phytochemicals (nutrients that stimulate the immune system). This can easily happen if you get carried away with protein powders, carbo drinks, pills, and food bars. The meal and snack suggestions that follow take all of this into account so you don't have to spend hours trying to figure it out.

Studies indicate that bodybuilders need anywhere from 1.3 to 3 grams of protein per kilogram of bodyweight, compared to .8 grams for the normal, nonbodybuilding man. If we settle on an average of 2, a 70-kilogram (154-pound) bodybuilder would require 140 grams of protein a day. To convert your weight to kilograms, simply divide it by 2.2. Here are a few examples:

- A 180-pound bodybuilder needs 164 grams of protein.
  ($180 \div 2.2 = 81.8 \times 2 = 163.6$, or 164)
- A 200-pound bodybuilder needs 180 grams of protein.
  ($200 \div 2.2 = 90.9 \times 2 = 181.8$, or 182)
- A 220-pound bodybuilder needs 200 grams of protein.
  ($220 \div 2.2 = 100 \times 2 = 200$)
- And a 250-pound bodybuilder needs 228 grams of protein.
  ($250 \div 2.2 = 114 \times 2 = 228$)

Once you determine your daily protein needs, you can take the hassle out of meal planning by using the meal and snack selections in this article. Whatever combination you choose will be low in fat, sodium, and sugar and high in protein, vitamins, minerals, fiber, and phytochemicals.

All the breakfasts contain approximately 30 grams of protein, the lunches and dinners

contain approximately 40 grams, and the snacks have approximately 30 grams. You can vary the number of snacks from one to three, as needed, to reach your protein requirement, eating them in midmorning, afternoon, and/or evening. Use the protein drink for all your snacks if you like, or you can have a variety from the suggestions.

Three meals and three snacks provide 200 grams of protein per day, which should meet the requirements of the majority of bodybuilders. If you are part of the small percentage who do need additional protein, you can work in another snack or add an extra ounce to each meal.

Those who are preparing for a contest, when the goal is to be as defined as possible, will have to modify the approach. Continue to eat lean protein foods while reducing the starches accordingly.

Don't let a busy schedule keep you from getting the kind of nutrition that will help you reach your bodybuilding goals. Use the winning combinations presented here and watch your progress soar.

BREAKFASTS

1. Egg or eggwhite omelette
   1–4 slices 100 percent whole-wheat toast

Nonfat margarine and/or small serving
sugar-free jelly
Beverage (coffee, decaf, tea)

Omelette
3 eggs or eggwhites
1 ounce nonfat cheese
Diced tomatoes and onions

2. Breakfast sandwich
Fresh strawberries
Beverage

Sandwich
1 whole-grain English muffin, sliced in
half
1 egg, over hard
2 ounces 98 percent fat-free ham

3. Instant power breakfast
1 cup Egg Beaters*
1 cup fruit sorbet
½ cup nonfat milk

Mix all ingredients in a blender.
*Do not use raw eggs!

4. Breakfast burritos
Sliced fresh papaya
Beverage

Burritos
2 12-inch whole-wheat tortillas
½ cup nonfat refried beans, heated
2 eggs or eggwhites
1 ounce 98 percent fat-free ham,
chopped
1 ounce nonfat cheese
Diced tomatoes

Spread half the beans on each tortilla.
Scramble the eggs with the rest of the
ingredients. Add half to each tortilla and
roll up.

5. Double serving of oatmeal topped with:
• 2 tablespoons raisins
• ¼ cup dry-roasted peanuts
• Sugar substitute or small amount brown
sugar (optional)
2–4 slices 100 percent whole-wheat toast

Nonfat margarine or small amount sugar-
free jelly
2 ounces Canadian bacon or 98 percent
fat-free ham, cooked in nonstick spray
1 peach
1 cup nonfat or 1 percent milk

6. 2 nonfat waffles* topped with:
• 1 cup nonfat cottage cheese
• Sliced peaches or strawberries
Beverage

*Commercial brand or make your own, omitting all
or most of the oil or shortening.

LUNCHES

1. Pita sandwich
Apple
Beverage

Sandwich
1–2 whole pitas, sliced in half
4 ounces chopped chicken
2 ounces fat-free cheese
Sliced tomatoes
Lettuce
Sprouts
Avocado
Nonfat or light mayonnaise (optional)

2. 1½ cups nonfat cottage cheese
Topped with 1–2 cups sliced fresh fruit
1 tablespoon raisins
1 tablespoon unsalted, dry-roasted peanuts
1 tablespoon unsalted sunflower seeds
8–12 low-salt whole-wheat crackers
Beverage

3. Submarine sandwich
Pear
8–12 low-salt whole-wheat
crackers (optional)

Sandwich
1–2 French rolls
1 ounce turkey pastrami
2 ounces turkey ham
1 ounce turkey bologna
1 ounce fat-free Swiss cheese

1 ounce fat-free cheddar cheese
Fat-free Italian dressing

4. Chef salad
8–12 low-salt whole-wheat crackers
Nectarine
Beverage

   Salad
   Lettuce
   Tomatoes
   Shredded carrots
   Sliced cucumber
   Other raw vegetables, as desired
   2 tablespoons raisins
   1 tablespoon unsalted sunflower seeds
   ¼ cup kidney or garbanzo beans
   2 ounces nonfat cheddar cheese, sliced
   2 ounces 98 percent fat-free ham, sliced
   2 ounces sliced turkey
   Nonfat dressing, any variety*

   *If you're concerned about sodium, use vinegar or lemon juice.

5. Cheeseburger
Raw vegetable salad
Nonfat dressing, any variety
1 slice watermelon
Beverage

   Cheeseburger
   4 ounces 7 percent fat or leaner
      ground round
   2 ounces nonfat sharp cheddar cheese
   1 whole-wheat hamburger bun

6. Tuna salad sandwich
1 cup nonfat yogurt, plain or flavored
Green salad
Nonfat dressing, any variety
Grapes
Beverage

   Sandwich
   3½-ounce can water-packed tuna
   2 hard-boiled eggs or eggwhites, mashed
   Nonfat mayonnaise

DINNERS

1. 6 ounces baked halibut
1–2 cups cooked brown rice
1 cup cooked carrots
Green salad
Nonfat dressing, any variety
1 slice oatmeal bread
Nonfat or extra-light margarine
1 slice fresh honeydew
Beverage

2. 6 ounces lean steak (filet, sirloin, round, or
      flank steak)
1 baked potato with nonfat sour cream
      and/or margarine
1 cup cooked broccoli
Carrot-raisin salad with nonfat or light
      mayonnaise
1–2 whole-wheat dinner rolls
Nonfat or extra-light margarine
1 slice watermelon
Beverage

3. Stir-fry shrimp
Lettuce and tomato salad
Nonfat dressing, any variety
1–2 slices whole-wheat bread
Nonfat or extra-light margarine
Pear
Beverage

   Stir-Fry Shrimp
   6 ounces shrimp
   Nonstick spray
   2 cups cooked brown rice
   1 cup mixed vegetables (broccoli,
      cauliflower, and carrots)
   Light soy sauce (optional)

   Spray a frying pan with the nonstick spray. Add the rice and vegetables, and sauté over medium heat until the vegetables are almost done. Add the shrimp and sauté another 5 to 10 minutes. Season with soy sauce.

4. Chicken with rice
1 cup cooked cut green beans

Green salad
Nonfat dressing, any variety
Nectarine
Beverage

Chicken
1 small can concentrated apple juice
2 chicken breasts, bone in
2 cups cooked rice

Pour the apple juice into a casserole dish; do not add water. Add the chicken, and make sure the pieces are covered in the juice. Bake covered at 375 degrees Fahrenheit for one hour. While the chicken is baking, cook the rice according to the instructions on the package. Serve the rice with the chicken, pouring the sauce over both.

5. Fajitas
   Green salad
   Nonfat dressing, any variety
   Mango slices
   Beverage

   ### Fajitas
   7 ounces flank steak, cut into strips
   Nonstick spray
   Sliced onions
   Sliced bell peppers
   Sliced tomatoes
   2 12-inch whole-wheat tortillas

   Spray a frying pan with the nonstick spray and sauté the meat and vegetables. Season to taste. Add half to each tortilla and roll up.

6. Quick spaghetti
   1 cup cooked Italian green beans
   Green salad
   Nonfat Italian dressing
   2 slices French bread
   Nonfat or extra-light margarine
   Fresh fruit salad
   Beverage

   ### Spaghetti
   2 cups cooked whole-wheat pasta

6 ounces 7 percent fat or leaner
  ground beef
Nonstick spray
1 jar lowfat pasta sauce

Spray a frying pan with nonstick spray and sauté the ground beef, breaking it up with a spatula as it cooks. Add the sauce and simmer. Cook the pasta. Top cooked pasta with the sauce.

SNACKS

1. Protein drink
   1 ounce protein powder*
   8 ounces nonfat milk**
   Mix all ingredients in a blender.

   *Whey protein seems to be the most popular form at present.

   **If you can't tolerate milk, use lactose-free milk, light soy milk, or a milk substitute such as Vitamite.

2. 1 cup nonfat cottage cheese topped with chopped fresh fruit
   Hard-cooked eggs or eggwhites
   6 ounces water-packed tuna

Finally, Dave Tuttle uncovers a lot of misleading information on the subject of sugar.

SUGAR Dave Tuttle
There's a lot of misinformation going around about sugar. Some bodybuilders claim that sugar (by which they usually mean sucrose) is plain old carbohydrate, just like a potato. Other musclemen avoid sugar like the plague, only to eat honey or molasses instead.

MOST PEOPLE EAT WAY TOO MUCH

It's been estimated that 25 percent of the calories consumed in the United States is actually sucrose. The average American now eats more

than 120 pounds of sugar each year! Studies have shown that large amounts of sucrose in the diet can produce obesity, which can lead to diabetes and an increased probability of glucose intolerance. The consumption of large amounts of empty calories in sucrose makes it easier to put on weight because sucrose-rich foods are long on calories and short on volume. That means you have to eat more calories to fill your stomach. Relying on those empty calories can result in nutritional deficiencies, even when you're eating a lot of calories. There's even been research that links high sucrose intake to increased cholesterol and blood triglyceride (fat) levels, as well as heart disease and, of course, tooth decay. So excess sucrose consumption is definitely not a good thing.

At the same time, the end product of all the carbohydrates we eat, including the sugars, is blood glucose. The polysaccharides require more processing than the disaccharides or monosaccharides in the digestive tract to break down their complex molecules into glucose, but the final result is always the same. There's no reason to get paranoid about consuming modest amounts of sugar. The main reasons you should eat lower-glycemic-index

foods are their greater nutritional values and the reduced impact they have on insulin production.

Here's another factor to consider: what most people think of as "sweets" are actually concoctions with lots of fat in them as well as sugar. Chocolate cake, for example, has plenty of fat in it, along with piles of sugar. That fat content makes a major contribution to the calorie count and can contribute to coronary problems. In fact, the fat is as bad for you as the sugar is. People need to look at the total composition of the foods they eat, especially the desserts. There are frozen desserts in the supermarkets now that use artificial sweeteners but have lots of fat in them. What sense does that make, unless you're a diabetic? Likewise, most of the fat-free baked goods on the market are chock-full of simple sugars. You may save a few calories, but your insulin levels will go on a real roller-coaster ride nonetheless. You're better off eating a piece of fruit.

THE DIFFERENT TYPES OF SIMPLE SUGARS

Some natural athletes feel that certain types of simple sugars are better for you than others. To some extent, that's true. Fructose has a much lower glycemic-index rating than sucrose, so it has less impact on insulin levels. It's also sweeter than sucrose, so you can get an equivalent amount of sweetness for fewer calories. Those are the reasons health-food stores frequently substitute fructose for sucrose. It is wrong, however, to think of fructose as a sugar substitute. It's sugar: better than sucrose, perhaps, but still sugar.

As for all the other forms of sugar, there really is no difference among them. Molasses is a by-product of sugarcane refining. It doesn't look like table sugar, but that's basically what it is. Brown sugar and turbinado sugar are sucrose with a bit of molasses thrown in, while powdered sugar is finely ground table sugar. Even maple sugar is predominantly sucrose. Only honey is somewhat different, since it is a combination of fructose, glucose, and water.

Keep well-hydrated during workouts.   B. J. Quinn.

Still, there's no scientific evidence that the body assimilates honey any differently than sucrose. If you like its taste, then have some, but don't think it's any better for you. In fact, studies show it can rot your teeth more quickly than sucrose. The choice depends on your personal taste.

TIPS FOR EATING SUGAR

Don't eat simple sugars before your workout. Sometimes, natural bodybuilders think that eating sugary snacks will provide a quick energy boost and increase their energy level throughout the workout. While foods that are predominantly sucrose are assimilated quickly, they also stimulate the release of insulin to counteract the rapid rise in blood sugar levels. So much insulin is released, in fact, that the level of blood sugar ends up being too low, requiring the release of glucagon to raise the level back to where it should be. During this period of overreaction, your energy level will be lower than normal, not greater. Your pre-workout meal should consist of a fructose-based product or, better yet, complex carbohydrates. That will provide a much better source of prolonged energy.

Eat mostly complex carbohydrates. As a general rule, complex carbohydrates have lower values on the glycemic index than the simple sugars. Complex carbs also have a lot more nutritional value than the calories found in sugary products. Spreading your carbohydrate consumption, including sugars, throughout the day will also help to maintain a relatively constant blood glucose level. That's yet another reason to eat five or six small meals per day instead of the traditional three. Of course, everyone craves sweets once in a while. There's nothing wrong with giving in to those cravings, as long as it doesn't happen too frequently. Just try to make such splurges the exception and not the rule. You'll have a healthier body, and your dietary discipline will produce a lot more natural muscle mass. What more incentive could you want?

Eddie Robinson.

Chapter 17

BODYBUILDING INJURIES

All the knowledge and all the iron will in the world will be of no use to a bodybuilder who has such a severe injury that he or she cannot train. If you learn to exercise properly and avoid injuries in the first place, you will reach your goals much faster.

This chapter gives you solid advice on how to stay in the gym and out of the doctor's office.

Richard A. Winett, Ph.D., has some terrific advice on how to prevent injuries.

PREVENTING INJURIES Richard A. Winett, Ph.D.

I am not a superstitious person; however, I knew there must be a danger in putting in print, as I did in an earlier column, that I was "injury-free" after 33 years of training. (Well, I did say no chronic injuries.) Such pronouncements, in an eerie way, set the scene for an injury. So in making that statement, I became an injury waiting to happen.

A few days after I finished the piece, I suffered a severe strain in my right hip area from squatting. A millisecond before the injury, I knew it was going to happen, but it was too late. And not surprisingly, after so many years of training myself to push through workouts, I made a bad situation worse by doing a few more reps to complete the set.

Fortunately, with age there does come a little wisdom. In my younger days, I would have finished the workout regardless of the injury. This time, I only did movements that would not further hurt my hip. That bit of gained wisdom probably prevented a major injury from occurring.

I was also determined that this time around I would learn something from the injury instead of just jumping back into training. Moreover, as I started to think somewhat more positively, I realized that my own experiences could help *Ironman* readers. While there have been a number of excellent articles in this magazine, particularly in the sports-medicine department, on injury prevention and treatment from a biomechanical perspective, less has been said about the behavioral perspective.

PSYCHOLOGICAL REACTIONS TO INJURY

For most athletes, an injury precipitates a crisis that can impair their ability to train or compete for a considerable period of time: They lose confidence in their training approach and their ability to profit from training. In my own case, the injury also led to depression, which I attribute partly to my reduced activity level, partly to the fact that my schedule of goals became derailed, and partly to loss of confidence.

The temptation is to escape the crisis by jumping right back into training and somehow "training around the injury." That's what I have always done, and it's worked out reasonably well in the past; I seem to have inherited a wondrous recovery ability and have always come back very quickly.

So we get past the crisis, but something is missing. We learn nothing from the injury. Specifically, we fail to find out the following crucial information: What conditions led to the injury? Were there enough warning signs—could we have foreseen and avoided the injury? What can we do to prevent injuries in the future?

LEARN FROM INJURY

As I've suggested, we can learn a great deal from these experiences if we pull ourselves out of a funk, avoid jumping back into training, and instead do some reflection and analysis. As we get older, there are also the haunting thoughts that it may now take a long time to recover or that a greater and more serious injury to the same area could end our productive training days altogether. If we start with the supposition that most injuries are not accidents, then we are in the position to analyze predispositions, warning signs, and preventive steps. Let's take my own injury. These were the warning signs:

1. The injury occurred in an area where I had been having some soreness from walking and from some aerobic exercises. The stress of training just found a weak, slightly injured spot that I had ignored.
2. I had changed my squat so that I could go deeper. In a prior workout, I noted that this position placed new stresses on my hips, but I ignored the feedback.
3. Furthermore, I ignored what I had noted in my training diary: that in order to get in my early-morning workouts, I had been going too quickly through my warm-ups and that I was letting my concentration drift to the day's activities that lay ahead.
4. I also noted in my training diary that going deeper for squats had not remedied my more basic problem of leaning too far forward, my original reason for trying that technique. I know that it's better to remain straighter than to worry about depth, but I ignored that insight.
5. In my warm-up squat sets for that day, I felt that something wasn't quite right. I never stopped, however. I ignored the feedback and plowed ahead.

These points support my major supposition: the vast majority of injuries are not accidents. Any one of those five pieces of information should have led to a change in training, not to mention my avoiding the injury, if I had not ignored the feedback.

TAKE POSITIVE PREVENTIVE STEPS

My forced, though brief, layoff and the pain and immobility that came along with the injury brought me face-to-face with those haunting thoughts I mentioned. More positively, however, the experience helped clarify my feelings about how very important training is to me and how it is something I want to continue doing for many years. More positive thinking, along with my analysis of the conditions that led to the injury, brought me to the following decisions:

1. I will always remain upright when I do squats. If that means using less weight in regular squats or focusing on safety bar squats, that's far better than constantly using heavy weights and asking for another injury.

2. I must pay as much attention to minor injuries and my overall recovery as I do to my training regimen itself.

3. Training is only productive when concentration is highly focused. I have to minimize all distractions—specifically, I need to sort out the day's activities before I train, not while I'm working out.

4. While in the past I have emphasized just warming up a specific area, I now try for a more complete warm-up. It prepares the body for better workouts and decreases the likelihood of injury. I have added a few minutes of easy riding on the Airdyne as a prelude to a regular, more specific warm-up.

5. I will not attempt any leg or lower-back exercises until all the pain is gone and my full range of motion has returned—an approach that as a young man I would have considered procrastination.

6. I also decided to experiment with using more moderate weights and focusing on specific muscle contractions—a process that as a power-oriented youth I would have considered heresy.

By definition, we "ageless athletes" are training for the long haul. While we delight in the day-to-day satisfaction of the process of training and the pursuit of short-term goals, our ultimate objective involves health and fitness through our lifetime. Prudence in preventing injury is one of the keys to long-term productive and enjoyable training.

Gene Mozée provides a dozen tips for avoiding injury that are worth their weight in gold. Follow these simple precautions, and your growth will never be interrupted by long layoffs due to injury.

SIMPLE PRECAUTIONS FOR SAFER WORKOUTS Gene Mozée

The worst thing that can happen to an athlete in any sport is a serious injury. When home run slugger Kirk Gibson of the Los Angeles Dodgers got hurt, the team almost lost the World Series. When Magic Johnson got injured, the L.A. Lakers lost four straight to the Detroit Pistons and failed to defend their NBA championship. When Joe Montana injured his back, the San Francisco 49ers were in deep trouble.

Bodybuilding, as an individual rather than a team sport, presents a different but equally critical set of circumstances if a competitor gets injured. Arnold once severely injured his knee when a posing platform collapsed while he was in a kneeling pose. He underwent months of rehabilitative therapy and was fortunate to come back and win the Mr. Olympia that year. Franco Columbo seriously injured his knee doing a stunt for some TV show. He was carrying a refrigerator on his back when the near–career-ending accident occurred. Ken Waller severely injured his elbow and never competed again.

Weight lifters and powerlifters are extremely susceptible to serious, sometimes permanent injuries caused by the enormous poundages they handle. Former world weight-lifting champions Paul Anderson and Dave Shepherd have had hip replacement operations. Dr. Eldon Beyerle, a former weight-lifting star, once told me that I was the only former powerlifting champ he had X-rayed who didn't suffer from disk degeneration of the spinal vertebra.

Lifting weights can be hazardous to your health if you're not careful. A case in point is the tragedy of Steve Massios, a former bodybuilder and weight-lifting star of the 1950s. Steve cleaned 375 pounds on an exercise (not Olympic) bar on the deck of a ship, lost his balance, and fell backward. The bar crushed his chest. It was reported that he died of a strep throat infection. Not true. He died because he did a foolish stunt without proper warm-up on the rolling deck of an anchored battleship.

Once, during a powerlifting meet in San Diego, I saw Wallen Piper attempt a record squat without a sufficient warm-up. You could hear his femur (thighbone) snap like a dry twig from the back of the room.

My personal horror story took place when I tore my left pectoral muscle while bench pressing 455 pounds. I had been doing nothing but power lockouts for the previous 30 days, and decided to go for a personal record without doing any bench presses. I made the lift, but the injury was so severe that I couldn't bench press for the next six months. If it wasn't for a brilliant doctor named Ken Sommer—a sports injury specialist—I would never have competed again. He saved me from an operation, and I completely recovered and later set two world bench press records.

Kenneth Sommer is a doctor of chiropractic medicine who also has degrees in orthopedics and nutrition. Located in Glendale, California, Sommer has treated numerous world-record holders such as Pat Casey (639-pound bench press) and Russ Hodge (former world-record holder, decathlon). Incidentally, Hodge could bench press 485, squat 680, run the 100-yard dash in 9.3, and throw the shot put over 60 feet.

According to Sommer, the three most important things in preventing an injury are:

1. Proper warm-up
2. Proper training techniques
3. Proper nutrition

I consider him to be one of the foremost injury specialists for lifters and bodybuilders in the world. He won the World Heavyweight Weightlifting Championship in the Masters division at the age of 53. Here, in his own words, are 12 tips to help prevent and overcome injuries that Sommer recommends to his clients.

WARM UP PROPERLY

Too much preliminary warming up will fatigue muscle fibers, making it impossible to get maximum effort with maximum poundages. Too little warm-up won't prepare

you for heavy work, however, and the result could be strain or injury. The first set of any exercise should always be relatively light. Pat Casey would warm up with 135 pounds for 20 reps on the bench press and work up to over 500 for reps using 50-pound increases on each succeeding set.

DRESS PROPERLY WHEN TRAINING

You have to keep the muscles and joints warm, especially on cold winter days. A pair of trunks and T-shirt are okay if you live in a warm climate or if it's summer. One of my former patients, Joe Baratta (winner of more than 20 physique titles) tore his pectoral while doing an iron cross in a cold gym. He had won the competition earlier that evening, but he came back later to give an exhibition at trophy time. It was cold, he didn't warm up enough, and his gymnastic uniform certainly didn't keep his muscles and tendons at an ideal temperature for his activities. Joe tore the pec so badly that it required surgery. It took him a year, starting with 2-pound dumbbells, to work his way back up to a 300-pound bench press.

AVOID SILLY STUNTS

One former Mr. America, who shall remain nameless, was showing off in front of a couple of ladies and the male members of his club. He tried to curl an Olympic barbell weighing 135 with his right hand. *Rip* went the biceps tendons as they tore loose from the insertion near the elbow. Corrective surgery was his reward.

FATIGUE CAN CAUSE INJURY

Excessive fatigue combined with repeated heavy effort that involves major muscle groups can result in injury. My colleague, Dr. Sam Homola, reported an incident where a famous strongman ruptured one of his biceps by lifting one end of a car several times for photographers right after completing a heavy arm workout. Ordinarily, this feat was well within his capacity, but his already fatigued biceps couldn't handle the tremendous load placed on them by the rest of his powerful development.

USE PROPER TRAINING TECHNIQUES

Many injuries occur when doing cheating exercises in which body movements are usually exaggerated. Never jerk relaxed muscles

into action. It is beneficial in some instances to bend your body in order to enlist the aid of other muscles while curling—but usually only on the last few reps. The muscles should be contracted smoothly against a steady resistance throughout a full range of movement. Also, letting a weight drop back freely to the starting point is a common cause of injury. Don't let momentum relax the tension on the working muscle area. I saw one fellow rupture a biceps while curling with a fairly light bar. He was warming up for heavier curls, but

Keep your back straight during bent-over movements.   Justin Brooks.

instead of curling with a smooth, even motion, he was swinging the bar up with body motion and then allowing it to drop back under its own weight. The momentum generated by the pull of gravity placed an abrupt jerk on his muscles, tendons, and joints at the end of the movement. Result: use of the arm was seriously impaired and required surgery.

Craig Licker.

DON'T USE EXCESSIVELY HEAVY POUNDAGES

Never let your ego exceed your talent. Everyone knows at least one diehard who uses such heavy weights that he can't even do a single rep in good form. There was one guy who trained at our gym whom we called "Mad Dog Mason." He used so much weight in his bent-over rowing motions that he had to jerk the weight from the floor and then drop his body down to touch his chest to the bar as the weight crashed back to the floor. One day, a heavily loaded bar smashed his left thigh and ruptured the big rectus femoris. His entire thigh turned black and blue, and it was several months before he could return to regular training. Trying to impress your gym buddies or spectators with incredibly heavy training poundages makes about as much sense as trying to impress your pals in a drag race down Sunset Boulevard. The results are often tragic and sometimes fatal.

EXAMINE YOUR EXERCISE EQUIPMENT

In top-quality modern gyms like Gold's and World, you probably won't have to worry about faulty equipment breaking down and exposing you to a possible injury. But in heavy-duty workout gyms, I've seen it happen. I saw one guy doing lat pulldowns with 200 pounds when the frayed cable snapped, knocking him unconscious and leaving a considerable lump on the top of his head. On another occasion, a 75-pound dumbbell fell apart when the end bolt came off one end, and the unlucky exerciser was rewarded with a broken big toe. One of the most dangerous gym accidents I ever saw was when I spotted a friend 350 pounds in the bench press. As he took the bar off the rack, he failed to notice that it was bent. He was using a thumbless grip, and the bar rolled right out of his hands as he started to lower it. The force of 350 pounds landing on his chest stunned him, and I grabbed the bar as it started to roll toward his throat. To this day, he claims I saved his life.

USE COMMON SENSE

Be careful. There is hardly any exercise you can do that won't result in an injury if you use too much weight in bouncing movements that utilize momentum. If you bounce your bench presses off your chest with too much weight and too much momentum, you might crack a rib. This is very painful, and it's the type of injury that might never heal. If you bounce off your heels doing heavy squats, you might damage your lower back or knees.

TRAIN WITH A PARTNER

If you handle heavy poundages as Franco Columbo, Bertil Fox, Kal Szkalak, and all 500-pound bench pressers do, you need spotters or a safety rack when training. Arnold never squatted alone. Who wants to get stuck on the last rep with 400 to 500 on your shoulders and no way to get up? If you push to the max on the bench press, sooner or later you won't be able to complete that final rep. Your training partner(s) can help you complete the rep. More important, you won't have to worry about a heavy barbell crushing your chest.

BREAK IN A NEW PROGRAM CAREFULLY

Whenever you try a new exercise, don't go for a maximum weight on the movement the first few workouts. There are complex neuromuscular factors involved in using certain muscles in specific ways efficiently. If an exercise is done regularly, you develop certain motor skills that allow you to give it maximum effort with minimum risk of injury. Too much weight in an exercise you are not accustomed to can lead to an injury. Even a change of grip can upset your control of an exercise. Going

from a close grip to a very wide grip on the bench press can injure the pecs or delts. Shoulder and elbow injuries heal slowly, so start easy and gradually increase the poundages on exercises that put stress on those joints. I once had a delt injury that took two years to completely heal.

DON'T RUSH A COMEBACK

One of the biggest mistakes I see is lifters and bodybuilders who try to get back in shape too fast after a layoff. Push yourself too hard too fast, and you will be a prime candidate for an injury. I've seen it happen time after time. Years ago, there was a Pro Mr. America named Floyd Page. He was a regional director for one of the big health club chains. Floyd decided he was going to get back in shape as fast as possible. He started training two to three hours, six days a week while working at his high-stress job. He also enjoyed the nightlife. Unfortunately, he had a heart attack and never saw his 44th birthday.

SLEEP, REST, AND PROPER NUTRITION ARE ESSENTIAL

You can't fool Mother Nature. If you don't get sufficient sleep and rest, you won't recuperate as quickly or as fully as you should. This increases the injury risk factor. Proper nutrition gives your body the materials it requires for tissue repair, muscle growth, and energy requirements. I recommend a minimum of 2,000 to 3,000 milligrams of vitamin C and 400 to 600 IU of vitamin E each day to help prevent tissue injuries. In the event of an injury, you can increase those amounts greatly to help speed the healing process.

An injury of any type can put you months behind in your training. It can result in a loss of some of the gains you've already made. But as they say, an ounce of prevention is worth a pound of cure, so be careful out there.

Getting into the mind of the athlete, Joseph M. Horrigan, D.C., president of the Soft Tissue Center in L.A., a rehabilitation clinic, looks at the psychology of an injury.

THE PSYCHOLOGY OF AN INJURY

Joseph M. Horrigan, D.C.

Injuries are the plague of all athletes, and that includes all weight-training athletes—from recreational trainees to bodybuilders, power-lifters, and Olympic weight lifters. They can range from minor nuisances to devastating, career-ending muscle tears or ruptures.

A severe injury generally requires a pro-longed and specific period of planned rehabili-tation, during which time the recuperative ability of the injured area is taxed, and what was once easy to perform seems completely out of reach. This taxes the athlete's patience and creates a variety of psychological responses. Some of these are expected and normal and will resolve in a healthy manner. Others, unfortunately, are inappropriate and should be of concern to the injured trainee's physician, family, and friends.

Physical rehabilitation requires a variety of therapy methods to address the specific diag-nosis and all the relevant factors, including the skills and demands of the patient's particular sport. The goal in sports medicine is to return an injured athlete to competition as soon as it is safely possible, which is not as simple as it sounds. The athlete must be as active as possi-ble while still being clinically safe. Too much too soon or too little too late will set him or her back in recovery.

Every health care provider has to deal with the frustration and despair of the injured trainee. I asked sports psychologist Michael Brannon, Psy. D., to help explain this complex subject. Brannon was a powerlifter for 15 years, an amateur wrestler for 12 years, and a professional wrestler for 10 years.

"There are common patterns of reactions to injuries," Brannon began. "Athletes react to losing their sport as if they were reacting to death and dying. It is not quite that extreme, but it is analogous. There are stages of denial, anger, bargaining, depression, and acceptance.

The emotional intensity of the reaction to the injury is proportional to the self-identity with sports. If they identify strongly with the sport, the reaction is usually severe.

"The loss is the biggest factor if the athlete is not able to train. The support group of friends and training partners provides a posi-tive reinforcement. The injured bodybuilder who is unable to train does not receive rein-forcement of the pump, growth, or training pain. The bodybuilder has a great deal of control and independence in his or her life. The control is demonstrated in the diet, train-ing, and sleep, [and it] is a powerful factor. Once the severe injury occurs, the physician or physical therapist is telling the bodybuilder what to do."

At the Soft Tissue Center, we see trainees who have what appear to be normal reactions, and others who seem very hard to reach. Those who are hard to reach and behave inap-propriately seem to have a slower recovery.

As Brannon explained, "The healthy reac-tion is usually a lack of compliance due to the denial stage. 'No pain, no gain' and 'It will go away' are the prevailing attitudes in the early stage of denial. Acknowledgment of the injury means time off from training. This is difficult because the bodybuilder's self-esteem is wrapped around the perception of body size. This is known as an *athletic body image disor-der* comparable to anorexia nervosa. The mir-ror is distorted in the mind. This creates real problems. One week off equates [in the mind of the injured bodybuilder] to seeing drastic changes in the mirror.

"A big factor in the psychological response to an injury is the athlete's health prior to the injury," Brannon added. "The age of the patient is a key factor. The same injury may be seen as severe in a young athlete, but in an athlete who is older it may be definitely career-ending. There may simply be different responses to the same injury in similar patients. One athlete may perceive the injury as career-ending, while another may perceive it as a normal course in [his or her] career."

The question is, then, What is a normal reaction versus an abnormal reaction? "There may be behavioral, emotional, or cognitive [thinking] reactions," Brannon said. "Normal reaction to an abnormal situation, of a behavioral type, may include isolation, increase of bad habits [like the use of drugs and alcohol], forgetfulness, argumentative tendencies, and a loss of interest in other areas of life. The normal emotional reaction will lead to moodiness, distractibility, guilt—'Should I have warmed up?' or 'Why did I do that exercise?'—depression, anger, nightmares, and sleep disturbance. The cognitive normal reaction is the negative mind-set—'I'll never be the same again,' 'Why me?,' 'Is the pain ever going to stop?' and 'I'll never be where I was.'"

Health care providers in sports medicine deal with these patient emotions on a regular basis. Their symptoms are still considered to be normal reactions to an abnormal situation. The abnormal reactions are another story.

"The abnormal reaction to an abnormal situation will demonstrate exaggerated and severe moodiness, fistfights, life being perceived as worthless, lack of socialization, continual angry outbursts with family and friends, and the exhibition of psychological signs of no adjustment to the injury," Brannon said. "No progress is fast enough for this person. Isolation may dominate. Alcohol usually becomes a bigger part of the picture. Other signs include hyperactivity, progressive loss of sexual activity, lack of compliance with the rehab schedule, and even behavior that is counterproductive to rehab. The patient may change to another doctor for 'the right answer.' There is a cognitive breakdown."

As there is rarely one simple answer with such patients, other issues must be examined. For example, if patients don't recover, they may use the injury to escape doing things that they don't want to do. The injury may even be used as a weapon against a spouse or family members. Both adults and children can get caught up in this; some are aware of what they're doing, while for others it is subconscious behavior.

I must emphasize at this point that these symptoms are not for the pop psychologist or person who studied Psychology 101 in college

to attempt to deal with. This is a clinical problem, and it must be handled by a clinical professional—either a psychologist, a psychiatrist, or a marriage and family counselor.

There is another issue that we touched on previously—exercise addiction. Brannon described this behavior as a negative reinforcement model; that is, the behavior—in this case the exercise—is increased to avoid something that is perceived as negative. The exercise

Fast movements invite injuries.

Keep the weight under your full control at all times.

controls the person; the person does not control the exercise.

"These people tend to be more restless, anxious, and depressed," he continued. "The exercise removes some negative aspects of the condition. The [person feels] euphoric [during the exercise], and after it the person feels drained and more relaxed, and the metabolism and the psychological arousal state decrease. They will experience withdrawal symptoms if they are not able to work out. The moodiness and nervousness increase, and they 'can't live without it.' This is dangerous when they are injured. There is no motive for health, well-being, or appearance. The factors outside of exercise must be addressed. This group has the lowest compliance of all. If you have a patient who is running with stress fractures, you must question if this is exercise addiction."

If you've been around the gym long enough, you've probably heard every type of rationalization in these situations. I have heard from injured patients that so-and-so said that

you must "work through the pain," "no pain, no gain," and other such trivial trash. Some trainees are not capable of distinguishing between what we call normal muscle burn and abnormal joint and tendon pain, and there are a variety of overuse symptoms that they also fail to recognize.

"Unfortunately, many champions display mild exercise addiction," Brannon said. "They may also be unhealthy both physically and psychologically. They must retire sometime. If they have not balanced their lives, their lives may become closed books upon retirement."

I suspect that none of you wants your training efforts to end in such a tragic situation. Very few trainees ever compete in anything, and of those who do, few are of state or national caliber. Only a handful are elite world-class athletes, and of that handful there is usually only one champion per year in any sport. It is unrealistic for the majority of us to copy the workout schedules of professional athletes. It's not the workout that makes an athlete an elite champion; that person had the necessary qualities, and he or she trained hard as well. Training in itself does not produce the prerequisite characteristics.

Please don't misunderstand these last comments. Weight training is a tremendous form of exercise. Olympic weight lifting, powerlifting, and bodybuilding are great sports as well. But remember that less than 1/100 of 1 percent of weight trainees compete.

Don't arrange your life around an unrealistic schedule. Structure intelligently planned workouts and, most of all, enjoy them and the rewards they bring. If you find yourself becoming obsessive about your training, step back and ask yourself why you're doing it in the first place and whether you're taking the appropriate steps to fulfill your goals. Do you have goals? Are you treating recreational training as if it were an Olympic regimen? Are your job and family suffering because of your workouts? Maybe you should ask the people around you how they feel about your attitude toward your workouts. As with anything else, your training may require a little juggling of time to fit it in, but it should not control your life.

Exercise addiction is a major issue in sports medicine. If your attitude toward your training has remained healthy, then you'll continue to derive the benefits of a terrific form of exercise. If you've lost your way and this type of destructive behavior is controlling your life, please seek professional help. If you have friends or family members who fall into this category, approach the situation with tact and concern. You may need the assistance of your family doctor, minister, school counselor, or a respected family member. Even so, the most important factor is that people who need such help must decide for themselves that they want it.

In this article, Joseph M. Horrigan, D.C., shows us the specifics of a common injury.

BACK TRAINING AND SHOULDER PAIN Joseph M. Horrigan, D.C.

It is well known that pressing movements cause injuries to the shoulder, particularly the rotator cuff. When this happens, you may feel pain in the back of the shoulder area (the rear delt) or in the front of the shoulder. Pressing movements don't have a monopoly on such injuries, however. Pulling movements can cause injuries just as easily, but these usually go unnoticed or, at least, unreported for reasons I'll outline here.

Once trainees develop shoulder pain, they start dropping exercise from their routines. Chest movements such as the bench and incline presses and shoulder movements like the behind-the-neck and military presses are usually the first to go. At this point, flyes, the pec dec, and various dumbbell laterals become the basis for the chest and shoulder workouts.

The same kind of changes take place in back routines. The mainstays of heavy back training fall by the wayside, and the trainees' workouts usually consist solely of pulldowns and dumbbell rows, especially if they have already switched to a lighter training regimen due to shoulder pain. The pain from the back movements often goes unnoticed, however, because the acute pain from the pressing movements seems to hurt more and because the bench press and related movements are generally more popular than back training.

It's not the *choice* of back exercises, but how you perform them that causes injuries to the rotator cuff. This is a group of four small muscles that originate on the scapula (shoulder blade) and insert into the humerus (upper arm bone) at the top. They are stabilizing muscles— the rotator cuff's function is to keep the head of the humerus stable in the shoulder joint. If you don't have this stability, it doesn't matter how strong your prime movers (pecs, delts, lats, and so on) are; you won't be able to lift.

Improper performance of heavy back movements can significantly contribute to, if not cause, a rotator cuff strain. To explain how this happens, I must first redefine an adage of bodybuilding that as it stands is partially true and partially a gym myth: a full range of motion is the correct way to train as long as you don't compromise the joint to do it.

The seated cable row is a perfect example. This is a good exercise for building strength and developing your back, particularly your lats and spinal erectors. When you perform it, it is fine to lean forward to obtain a greater range of motion and "stretch"; however, once you let your body lean forward and your elbows are completely straight, do not relax and let your entire arm and shoulder stretch forward to gain that "extra stretch." Simply stated, that extra inch is all it takes for injury.

That's all there is to it—that extra one inch. When your body is forward and your elbows straight, you have already achieved a full range of motion. To go for that extra stretch, you will relax your shoulders and let your arms stretch forward, and in doing so you will let your shoulders roll forward with them. This shifts the majority of the weight you are pulling onto the rotator cuff, which is not built to take it. The weight acts as a traction, or pulling, force that strains the small stabilizing muscles of your rotator cuff.

If you find that you are unable to perform seated cable rows because of shoulder pain, and that pain arises every time you add them to your routine, try the following: attempt to perform the seated cable row without leaning forward. Simply let the elbow and shoulder achieve a normal range of motion while rowing. Now, add the component of leaning forward and back while blending in the row with it. Do not attempt any further stretch.

If you traumatize your rotator cuff each time you attempt the cable row—by overstretching the movement—you won't be able to perform the exercise. And if you keep trying to see if the shoulder feels better after a layoff and you perform the cable row improperly again, the pain will still be there.

What happens to your muscle is a common pattern in such chronic, workout-related injuries. The overstretch and strain of the rotator cuff cause an inflammation; the body responds by forming fibrous adhesions (scar tissue) in the muscle, between the muscle groups, and between the muscle groups and the surrounding connective tissue. The adhesions restrict the normal, healthy lengthening and shortening ability of the muscle, which leads to loss of range of motion, pain, decreased stability in the joint, and decreased

sports performance (biomechanical function). As a result you are predisposed to reinjure your cuff.

When you have the same problem occurring with pullups and pulldowns, the injuries and subsequent trauma multiply. In performing these movements, try for a full range of motion, but do not relax and subject your arm and shoulder to the traction force that the weight is applying.

If your pecs have undergone adaptive shortening and/or have become fibrotic from repeated injury, the initial overhead stretch from the pulldown bar may even feel good. Stretching further, especially when you get it by relaxing and letting your shoulder blades rotate upward, is harmful to your shoulders and to your training.

Another exercise that belongs in this category is the shrug. Performing shrugs places a constant traction force on your shoulders. If you were to relax on a heavy movement like the shrug, an injury would follow immediately. Here's an example that involves two Mr. Olympia contenders:

One day at Gold's Gym in Venice Mike Christian and Gary Strydom found themselves at the power rack at the same time for their heavy shrugs. The bar was loaded to 525 pounds. Mike had matched Gary in the number of reps for that set, and due to their competitive relationship, Mike wanted to do the infamous "one more rep." In readying himself to do it, he took several deep breaths and relaxed his shoulders for a fraction of an instant in order to call on enough strength to get that last rep.

Pain shot through Mike's shoulder. He put the bar down and went straight to the gym telephone to call us at the Soft Tissue Center.

"I don't know what happened," he said over the phone. "I was just doing shrugs and bam!—a shoulder injury." Even a multiple-professional-contest winner like Mike wasn't able to see the performance error.

There is no such thing as ". . . just doing shrugs" or rows or pulldowns. How you perform the movement is vital. You can include it in your routine; just don't sacrifice the joint.

And that doesn't mean the more linear or the more 90-degree angles that are involved the better.

If you take an objective, honest view of your training, you may see some of the common training flaws that I have addressed in this column over the past nine months. If one or two exercises for each of the major upper-body muscle groups—chest, back, shoulders—is causing you shoulder pain, you might get the idea that you can't train like the others in the gym or like you "used to train." From there it's an easy step to the conclusion that maybe you "aren't really cut out for training." That doesn't have to be so.

If "everything hurts," then what you need is to completely reevaluate your training technique and choice of exercises so that you don't have to give up training. It's better to eliminate a few gym myths and exercises than to give up all of the wonderful benefits of weight training.

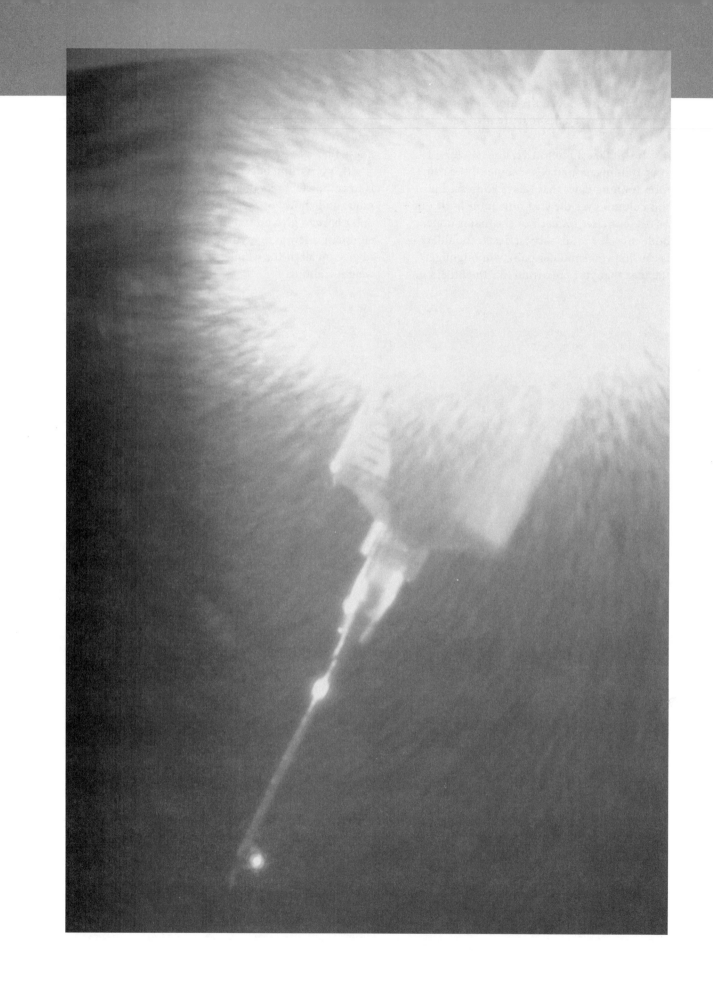

Chapter 18

DRUGS IN BODYBUILDING

Frankly, I could have chosen many articles for this chapter. I could have shown you studies of the effects of steroids, testosterone, and many other drugs bodybuilders use. We could have talked about the extreme danger of diuretics or of insulin shock.

But when it's all said and done, there is probably no better article ever printed on this subject than this candid interview with a top bodybuilder who is on the drug treadmill. Any reader who can't see the tragedy in having a magnificent physical specimen go from having his every waking hour consumed with the thought of crafting physical perfection to being lowered to the status of a drug-addicted lab rat scurrying around with an obsession for finding more illegal drugs, is beyond all reach of reason.

Please read this chapter carefully.

STOP THE INSANITY!
An IFBB (International Federation of Bodybuilding) Mr. Olympia Contender Reveals the Horrors of Doing What It Takes to Compete at the Top Anonymous

Warning: This is an extremely controversial interview. To be honest, we almost decided not to print it; however, because *Ironman* has always been an open forum, going to great lengths to tell the whole truth, we felt it was our responsibility to the sport and to you, the reader, to allow this athlete to speak his mind.

It took a lot of courage for this man to stand up and tell it like it is, and we are keeping him anonymous to protect his status as a professional bodybuilder. We're inserting [blanks] in place of names to help protect his identity—no process of elimination to narrow down the field—and also in place of drug names, so drug-using bodybuilders don't get any inadvertent "help" with their drug programs.

Keep in mind that we paid this man nothing, because we feel money can only corrupt the information. When people are paid a high sum, they feel as if they have to give the interviewer his or her money's worth, and that can result in exaggeration.

As you read this, remember that this athlete came to us because, like us, he loves bodybuilding and wants to see it prosper, not die a painful, drug-induced death.

Fasten your seat belts. This dose of reality is going to open your eyes like nothing ever printed in this or any other bodybuilding magazine.

IM: You want to get some things off your chest. You have the bodybuilding world's ear. What is it you want to talk about?

BB: Well, you know, most of the things nobody wants to talk about. I want to let everybody know how it really is.

IM: How it is with the drugs?

BB: Damn right!

IM: You're having to take too many, correct?

BB: Way too many, man.

IM: What kind of drug bill are we talking about?

BB: Well, growth hormone alone costs you $30,000 a year.

IM: Good Lord!

BB: And steroids, that's not a really big problem. I use a lot, but you can get them cheap. Mostly you gotta pay people to tell you how to use the growth hormone.

IM: And just the thought of putting all that in your body all at one time—that's gotta take its toll on you mentally too.

BB: Well, I don't mind a little bit, because I do like big arms, big back, big chest and legs and everything. But when it comes to the point where I'm as big as I want to get—

IM: They tell you that you have to get bigger, right?

BB: Yeah, I don't have a choice. I'm gonna be bigger. Next year you're going to see me 24 pounds heavier.

You know, it's the whole mind-set that you gotta get bigger and sacrifice your shape. I may not like the way my back looks. I mean, I've got improvements to make, obviously. But

those things come with time. Maturing into a physique is nice, but they want a monster.

IM: Do you think it can ever stop? I mean, if people keep getting bigger, what's going to happen to the sport?

BB: Well, the sport is already—

IM: Out of control?

BB: Yeah. It's an underground sport. It's [a cult that] likes to see the freaky mass monsters . . .

They really don't care. They just say, Whatever it takes to do that, that's what we want to see. But I think a lot of people want to see something that's somewhat attainable.

IM: Do you think the size of the competitors has caused the people to be a little blasé about it all? Like: Well, they're just going to have to do what it takes. We don't care; if they die, they die. We want to see 'em bigger, and we want to see 'em better.

BB: That's right. They want us to do it, and the judges want to see something bigger. In order for us to make a living and live our dreams, we gotta do whatever it takes, you know? You got guys like [blank, a bodybuilding columnist for another magazine] saying, "Well, nobody's making you." I guess nobody is, but a lot of us [have] this dream of being the best of the built.

IM: Absolutely. And it's a performance thing too. It's gratifying to be on stage. What do you think is a solution here? Do you think there is one at this point?

BB: Well, it's hard to say. Once you've seen extreme physique development, how are you going to train the eye of the audience to accept something less? You can practically see [some of these guys'] lungs when they do rear lat spreads. You just gotta accept something less.

By the way, before I go on, let me tell you right now, there's a lot of things in your hands.

IM: I understand. Your identity is completely confidential, I promise you that. We'll just say you're a top pro. That's all.

BB: Right. Okay. Ask anything.

IM: Do you think part of the solution is for the judges to start rewarding a more aesthetic physique?

BB: That would be the only way the sport would go into a positive direction. Like Bob Paris.

IM: Right, if Bob Paris came back. I think the problem is you have to have an eye for that type of physique, and the general public and most bodybuilding fans don't have it, so they look at size as the top criterion for victory.

BB: I think there's a certain presence, an aura to a really complete physique like Lee Labrada's, rather than someone who's just grotesque.

IM: Getting back to the whole drug thing, do you have to stay on the drugs year-round?

BB: Yes. I haven't gone off at all for years.

IM: You have to inject, what, three to four times a week?

BB: Every day.

IM: Every day you have to inject something into your body?

BB: Yeah. Every day. Let me go over my stack.

[He rattles off a list of injectibles and orals that's so long, my jaw hits the desk.]

IM: This is just off-season?

BB: Yeah. And of course I like to use [blank] that blocks estrogen and also increases testosterone levels. Also [blank] four times a day in the off-season to allow me to eat more calories. I also take half a tablet of [blank], which works better synergistically with growth hormone. Six weeks or so out I start taking some [blank] to stop some of the gyno. I did have to have it removed a few years back, but it kind of flares up now and then.

And I use [blank] to take some of the water out. And [every so often] I switch from the heavy androgens to the lighter anabolics, like [blank and blank], 300 milligrams every other day. Let's see, [blank], 200 milligrams a day. That helps you harden up your physique,

increase your vascularity. I take some [blank], which helps me harden, and I keep my insulin the same and my growth hormone the same.

IM: Whew! Quite a laundry list!

BB: Well, you know there's also many other things, like [blank], which keeps my gonadal system up and [blank] to boost my testosterone to make sure I don't atrophy down there. Also, anti-estrogens and other compound factors to combat the many side effects that I get.

IM: Have you ever noticed any serious health problems that you think are related to this?

BB: I piss a lot of blood come contest time.

IM: But in the off-season you feel pretty decent, even though you're taking all that stuff?

BB: Well, recently I started getting blood tests every two months.

IM: How about cholesterol count, blood pressure, and so forth? All that's pretty normal?

BB: No, everything is high. My blood pressure gets really high, and that must be watched, especially when I take stimulants.

IM: It sounds as if you're on pins and needles a lot of the time.

BB: If you gotta do it, you got no choice. You want to make a living in this sport, that's what you gotta do.

IM: Race cars keep going faster and faster and there are more crashes, but the drivers keep doing it, right? What do you think your total drug bill is for the year?

BB: About $60,000, but it's going to be higher next year. Just this last year I had to add [blank]. Right now it's the number-one bodybuilding "supplement" in the competition ring. All these guys you see getting bigger, it's that. No question. Two years ago . . . I don't want to take nothing from [blank], really nice guy, nice family man, but physique-wise he was flat as a pancake. Now he's bigger, 20 to 30 pounds heavier. It's all [from this stuff].

[Blank] is heavy on it. Of course, we all are. I'm scared shitless.

IM: Are you guys pretty frank with each other about what you're taking?

BB: Only with friends. I mean, I get questions in the gym all the time, and I tell them I take [a popular protein powder]! Yeah, we talk.

IM: You don't feel you need to keep secrets and maintain an edge?

BB: There are no secrets. There's one guy out there—I won't mention his name—he's a top pro who helps out the other pros with their [blank] 'cause we don't know how to do it, so we go to him. He helps us out.

IM: I know the old-timers say there's no camaraderie in the sport anymore.

BB: Oh, there's some. But the only thing we talk about is—

IM: Drugs and training.

BB: We don't talk about training, because most of the guys—

IM: All train alike?

BB: Well, yeah. We don't train that hard. [Most of the guys] are half asleep when they [work out].

IM: So it's mostly just the drugs. The top guys really don't have an inkling how to train without them. Do you think most of the top 10 guys are taking pretty much the same thing, then?

BB: Yeah, they're all jabbing themselves just as much, but I think [winning] has to do with your estrogen levels and your normal testosterone levels, your receptor abilities and things like that. You know, it's a genetic thing. Some people are more susceptible to steroids. Five milligrams might hit me differently than it might hit you.

IM: I asked you this earlier, and I know you said you think that it's just all part of the game, but aren't you afraid that this will catch up with you later in life?

BB: I am. I don't think I'll be able to have children. My doctor told me my sperm count is way too low. And my thyroid [is blown out].

IM: Do you feel that the sport indirectly promotes the whole drug thing?

BB: Yeah, but then you have people saying that nobody makes us. But this is our childhood dream. This is something we want to do, and for the most part we don't have other jobs.

IM: Do you think this drug test they had at the Olympia was a step in the right direction?

BB: It was a step in the right direction for the sport and probably a step in the wrong direction for people's careers, because I know four people who [should have] tested positive. But we can beat the drug tests. Next year if they want to get diuretics, that's fine. We'll use plasmics. It's fairly simple. There's always exotic steroids. "Let's change some molecule on the 17th position, and it can't be detected." [Blank] still can't be detected.

IM: This is the most eye-opening interview I've ever had. I appreciate your opening up to me.

BB: You're welcome. It could be because I'm very low on carbohydrates.

IM: And you're pissed off.

BB: Yeah, you know the diuretic scene is very difficult. I'm back there with my IV bag and heart monitor. It's just the situation. You take a person and put him into a lab in a freak science experiment. Then you throw him on stage, and you take him off to pump blood back into him. Is that a sport?

The training is pretty much beaten to death. In fact, your magazine for the natural athletes is what I recommend. Professional bodybuilding [is about] drugs. Of course, there's abuse in every professional sport—boxing, basketball, baseball, football.

IM: How long do you think you can keep at it? I mean at this pace?

BB: Well, I've been on for . . . oh God. I'll tell you right now, if anybody's going to die next, it's going to be [blank]. He's too old to be messing with [junk] like that. His pancreas I don't think is too good.

There's a look that you get. I can see it. [Blank, a top pro] is very ill. I understand what he wants to do for the sport, and he can do some great things, but he's dying and every contest he loses is a blow to him. He's killing himself literally because he wants to make this sport better. Eventually he's either going to win the contest or he's going to die.

IM: He's really playing Russian roulette?

BB: Yeah, he was using [blank] before any of us. I prefer his look back [a few years]. He wasn't big but aesthetic—a pleasing physique. Something a kid would look at and say, Hey, I would like to look like that. Now he should be concentrating more on certain bodyparts, but instead his body is getting bigger, his stomach, his head, everything.

IM: It's a scary look. Yes, the body's getting bigger, but all the internal organs are getting large, bloated.

BB: They should have a contest for the biggest growth-hormone gut.

IM: Got anything else you want to get off your chest?

BB: Yeah, you know I have a hard time thinking because of all the things I'm on now. But they don't talk about how much drug [abuse] there is. And it's not just the steroids. We've got to use speed and stuff like that. We have to use a lot of diuretics, things that aren't too healthy, and they don't feel good. Lots of guys are using cocaine—not just because they like it, but it helps you get cut up, it helps you not eat.

With drugs there's use and abuse. But at our level, I feel we're getting exploited, you know? They pump us full of drugs . . . or we pump ourselves full of drugs to make ourselves look like freaks, and we get on stage and that's our job. But we don't get paid hardly anything. The guy who uses our pictures, the supplement companies, make all the money, and they don't give us nothing. If it wasn't for our picture, they wouldn't have nothing to promote.

IM: Yeah, and you gotta keep risking your life to try to make a few bucks winning a show.

BB: I'll tell you what: [some] of the guys, like [blank], are gay prostitutes.

IM: Think so?

BB: I know so. That's how they can afford all those drugs. That's definite. Of course [certain people in] the gay community are going to walk up and say, Hey, we'll give you so much to have sex. That's just like a straight guy walking up to Cindy Crawford and saying it. But for us it's a way to make a good $10,000 a month. It helps with our drug bill and sometimes they just give us drugs for the act.

IM: When you think about it, you guys can't make much money.

BB: There's not much money in the contracts. Especially with the drugs, the living, the food. You have to sacrifice your—

IM: Integrity?

BB: Yeah, your integrity, your pride. It's all a sacrifice. The drugs, the prostitution. These guys don't want to do that. They have to look in the mirror. They know they're sacrificing what makes them a man.

And all this crap you see about carb loading and sodium. Bunch of shit.

IM: So you don't think they actually do sodium loading? It's all just drugs?

BB: Precontest every once in a while you catch a guy in McDonald's or eating pizza. You can do that kind of thing—of course, in moderation.

IM: But you're a pretty heavy supplement user?

BB: I don't use supplements at all! No vitamins, nothing.

IM: You don't think that vitamins and minerals would help protect you somewhat from all the drugs?

BB: Yeah, but—

IM: You've got to put your money where it's going to be the most effective, right? On drugs.

BB: Right. I'd like to see a $1 million prize [for a bodybuilding contest]. That's something else that would help the sport. If there's a decent amount of money in there, it would be something people would watch.

Unfortunately, I think people want to see the freaks at this point. Really big mothers up there. It's like you said, you really can't go backward. I guess you have to let [it] self-destruct and see what happens.

IM: I don't want to see any of you guys die.

BB: We will. I guarantee you. You're going to see lots of guys dying in the next few years.

IM: I hope the drug test is a step in the right direction, and maybe they'll start judging for more aesthetic physiques. If they did backtrack to more of the Bob Paris look, I think it would help.

BB: Is that ever going to happen?

IM: How much longer do you think you're going to go on with it?

BB: Till I reach my goal. Or it beats me.

IM: Have you ever experienced any kind of depression or rage?

BB: Oh, yeah. Beaten many people—gotten out of hand. I feel bad about that.

IM: Having all that coursing through your system has to do something to you mentally.

BB: Well, besides that, you feel a lump here, and you feel scared, and you don't know what's going on.

IM: Do you get checked by a doctor regularly?

BB: I get the blood tests, and he reads it. It's foreign to me. I just ask how much longer do I have to live, what am I doing wrong?

IM: But he doesn't do any MRIS on you? It's just basically a blood test?

BB: No. He checks my thyroid, sperm count. Of course, I'm never going to be able to have children.

IM: Perhaps some of this will reverse itself once you—

BB: No, I have irreversible damage.

IM: That's really sad.

BB: I think it happened last year. When I upped everything, I shut my thyroid down. And if I go off the [blank], I'm going to get fat. I'm going to stay on the stuff permanently. If I go off, I'm going to rebound. None of these guys go off. It's just nonstop. These guys do what it takes.

Don't you see that they're exploiting us? They're selling us. They're pumping us up, putting us on stage, throwing us off, and they're collecting the money. And we're back there rolling around in death.

In the process, they will make money. Sell ourselves. Sell our souls, and we don't get much. And even if you take the drugs, it's no guarantee you're going to win. You have to have something going on there.

But [the people who run this sport] say, Keep it going, keep it going. And watch their wallets getting bigger. They don't care.

IM: But you did say looking like that helps you with women?

BB: That makes it a little worthwhile, but I never had any problem with the bitches. I got plenty before. Now I'm bigger, so I get a lot more. But you also get the bad—that includes harassment from the homos.

I want to say for the guys who want to take their physiques to a [higher level], weight training, eating right, and exercising will help you achieve your goals. What's big to you may be small compared to a pro, but like I said, Lee Labrada will look huge to a lot of guys. So you can attain your goals, get bigger, get better with the women, look good. You may not win Mr. Olympia, but you can still have something to be proud of [without the drugs].

[Competitive bodybuilding, for the most part] is all chemistry. It's chemical warfare. Andreas Munzer had something we never had. All those striations and [blank] drugs, but look what it did to him. He died by the sword. And [blank] pocketed everything Andreas ever did.

We have to deal with the rat race and the counterfeit steroids. All these guys saying, Yeah, I fell down and broke my arm. That's not true. That's the dealer breaking their arms because they didn't pay for their shipment of growth hormone.

IM: You say you go to Mexico for a lot of this stuff?

BB: Yeah, I go to Mexico. The European tour is where most of us get our drugs.

[Switches subjects again] You don't need drug testing. Just a Lee Labrada. It didn't take a ton [of drugs] to do that. Pick that, and there you go. All the other guys will have to trim down to look like that.

IM: Go for the aesthetic physique. That's one of the big steps they have to take. By the way, isn't there a drug that you can inject directly into the muscle to blow it up?

BB: Oh, yeah, [blank]. Use that for my peak on my biceps. [Blank] uses it everywhere—80 to 100 shots. Tell you right now, it hurts like hell. But it's hard to predict. It may look good five days before the show, then it lumps out and you'll get guys with the real lumpy, weird-looking biceps.

This whole sport is about being a bitch. You gotta be a bitch to pay your bills. You gotta be a bitch to win. That's what it's all about. Total exploitation. I'd like the athletes to make a little more money. All these magazines talk about how much Michael Jordan and Mike Tyson make. They don't talk about how much we make, 'cause it's disgraceful. What am I going to do? Sell pictures of myself?

IM: Do a lot of the guys sell drugs on the side?

BB: Oh, yeah. I've done that myself. Now it's a lot harder.

IM: So what else? Is there anything you can think of that you're really pissed off about?

BB: Well, I'm pissed off that we have to use this amount of drugs. I was happier with my physique last year. [They want us] in the 270-pound range.

IM: Don't you think the magazines are a little at fault too?

BB: Yeah, they are. They don't print nothing about the drug regimen. They're selling fake dreams to kids: Take this protein powder, and you're going to look like that. And it ain't true. Drugs play a predominant role, and most of the [champions'] training articles lead to over-training. You know that. And unless you're on steroids, you're going to end up unhappy and lose your dream.

IM: I guess it's a vicious cycle.

BB: The insulin's very dangerous. I'm feeling it right now. I'm getting real tired, headaches, weakness. I breathe hard. Not a good drug to take.

IM: What's the danger with the insulin? It's a hormone, so what's the big problem?

BB: You can die right there. I mean, there isn't one of us who hasn't been in shock. You really don't know.

IM: Have you ever had to go to the hospital because of it?

BB: I've been in the hospital a few times, yeah. They had to use half a bag of glucose intra-venously to keep me going. I didn't have any glucose in my liver, because I did too much insulin. My brain was starved, and I was beginning to fall asleep, go into a coma. It's the most painful feeling you'll ever feel. During that time, your mind's going nuts.

What am I getting out of all this? A cover picture? That won't pay the bills. Maybe they should start giving back to the athletes instead of taking. If they're gonna make it where we have to be bigger, we should get something out of it.

Golfers make more money than we do. I saw how much they make at these rodeos too. They collect $50,000 for riding some damn bull. They don't have to take drugs to do that.

IM: The danger's there for eight seconds, then they're out of there. You guys have danger all year long.

BB: Yeah it's dangerous.

IM: To say the least.

INDEX

References to photos are indicated by an *f* following the page number.